Artificial Ice

Artificial Ice

Hockey, Culture, and Commerce

EDITED BY
DAVID WHITSON AND
RICHARD GRUNEAU

UNIVERSITY OF TORONTO PRESS

Previously published by Broadview Press, 2006 Copyright © David Whitson and Richard Gruneau.
Originally published as A Garamond Book.

Library and Archives Canada Cataloguing in Publication

Artificial ice : hockey, culture, and commerce / edited by David Whitson and Richard Gruneau.
Includes bibliographical references and index.

ISBN 9781551930558
1. Hockey—Social aspects—Canada. 2. Hockey—Economic aspects. I. Gruneau, Richard S., 1948–
II. Whitson, David, 1945–

GV846.5.A78   2006   796.9620971   C2006-901463-9

We welcome comments and suggestions regarding any aspect of our publications—please feel free to
contact us at news@utphighereducation.com or visit our Internet site at www.utppublishing.com.

North America
5201 Dufferin Street
North York, Ontario, Canada, M3H 5T8

2250 Military Road
Tonawanda, New York, USA, 14150

ORDERS PHONE: 1-800-565-9523
ORDERS FAX: 1-800-221-9985
ORDERS E-MAIL: utpbooks@utpress.utoronto.ca

UK, Ireland, and continental Europe
NBN International
Estover Road, Plymouth, PL6 7PY, UK
ORDERS PHONE: 44 (0) 1752 202301
ORDERS FAX: 44 (0) 1752 202333
ORDERS E-MAIL: enquiries@nbninternational.com

The University of Toronto Press acknowledges the financial support for its publishing activities of the
Government of Canada through the Canada Book Fund.

CONTENTS

FOREWORD

■ ROY MacGREGOR

I have often argued—sometimes seriously, sometimes just for fun—that the entire history of modern hockey can be explained by the mere existence of Wayne Gretzky. No Gretzky, no crisis.

This is said with the greatest of respect and even affection for the man who many say was the greatest player the game has ever seen and all agree was the biggest star those outside the game may ever see. But the fact is, he made them all go crazy—and I was right there as a witness.

It was in the weeks before Christmas 1992. The National Hockey League governors were meeting, as per usual, in West Palm Beach at The Breakers hotel, where the smell of must and old money always seemed stronger even than the smell of the sea air or the freshly mown grass of the next-door fairways.

Change was in the air. The NHL had a flamboyant new chairman of the board, Bruce McNall, who had replaced the hidebound John Ziegler—"If it ain't broke, don't fix it"—and was intending to "fix" the northern game in such a way that it would soon be unrecognizable. He was right, of course, only he just didn't quite envision exactly how it would all work out.

McNall was a master dream-spinner capable of hypnotizing anyone who listened, whether they be bankers or team owners or reporters. The banks, and the courts, eventually caught up to McNall's wild fantasies, but the hockey world is still sorting out what made sense and what made none at all.

Sports, he told them, were merely "in their infancy of exploitation." He saw a future, largely propelled by pay-per-view television, in which a team might pull in "well over $100 million just for television cable rights in the playoffs." He was able to show them the effect that Gretzky had had in the Los Angeles market in the few seasons since McNall had pried the great player out of Edmonton for $15 million (U.S.) and an exchange of players that made it look like a real "trade." Gretzky, with his star quality, movie-star wife, good looks, and transcendent appeal that could get hockey on the late-night talk shows, was merely the beginning of something extraordinary for the game. Through Gretzky, hockey could expand into the Southern States and, to prove this, McNall was able to produce two new owners—Disney and Blockbuster—that would herald the game's arrival into the Big Time. The Disney "halo," it was said, would apply to every franchise, from Anaheim to Ottawa. More expansion, at a minimum $50 million (U.S.) a pop, would provide an effortless stream of money until the television revenues would take off. Spend now and pay later, was the message, and the other owners bought it so rapturously that they never said a word as McNall pocketed half the Disney fee, $25 million, as an "indemnification" fee for invading the Greater LA market, with a population roughly the size of Canada itself.

They would pay later, alright. With a lost season, lost fans, lost television opportunities, and a game that seemed, by the summer of 2005, as lost as it had ever been since the NHL began operations in 1917.

Had there never been a Wayne Gretzky there would never have been that singular player to transcend the sport, taking it from Saturday night hockey in Canada to weekday soap operas and Saturday morning cartoons in America. No Gretzky, no Disney and no Blockbuster—both now gone from the game—and no McNall spinning fables of pay-per-view millions to eager ears. In fact, had there never been a Gretzky Blip, the history of hockey might have continued on a slow-growth plane, as the story of a major/minor North American sport, almost exclusively northern, with a fanatical base in Canada and a moderate following in the United States.

Instead, you have the slow, continuous growth until the Gretzky trade in 1988, then the salary explosion, the expansion madness, the network television hopes, and, following Gretzky's retirement in 1999, the slow, then quickening, descent into financial crisis, the year-long lockout, and a desperate struggle to return to even a shadow of what it once was—or at least once thought itself to be.

It is telling that six years after retirement, Gretzky remains the game's biggest star and only transcendent personality. All that may change as the 2005–6 NHL season, the first since the lockout, reconfigures itself around an eighteen-year-old kid named Sidney Crosby, who is expected, over time, to haul the game back up to Gretzky levels. Whether this will happen or not—remember Eric Lindros? remember Alexandre Daigle?—is a moot point, but it is also a perfect point of departure for the publication of *Artificial Ice: Hockey, Culture, and Commerce*, David Whitson and Richard Gruneau's long-awaited second look at the national game in all its cloaks and complexities.

▬▬▬▬

A dozen years ago I was just starting out on what would become a full decade of covering the NHL. I had long been fascinated with the national game and its larger meaning for this country. I was particularly intrigued by what seemed an annual argument among the artistic community concerning the overwhelming amount of hockey on CBC television each spring. Seemingly appalled by a country that would force news of the real world to wait for the play world, these righteous people contended that the CBC should get out of the hockey business, lucrative as it might be, and concentrate, instead, on culture.

It had always struck me that hockey *was* culture in this wintry country. I would further argue that it is impossible to know a people until you know the game they play. To understand America, you need to know football. To understand Brazil, soccer. Rare is the country so taken with one sport as is Canada—a sport that can be said to define the country as well as anything else in that it battles the elements, in that its population can be fierce when pressed but humble when not, in that it has become, rightly or wrongly, the face of success that Canada likes best to present to the rest of the world.

When I got my hands on *Hockey Night in Canada: Sport, Identities, and Cultural Politics*, Gruneau and Whitson's 1993 examination of the national game, I discovered I wasn't alone in thinking this. I already knew that some others believed this—Ken Dryden and I had argued the point in *Home Game* a few years earlier—but this was academic support backed with methodology and research. Only it didn't read like academia—it didn't have academia's insecure and lugubrious language, impenetrable points and pointless concepts. It read like a damn good book, which is exactly what it was, and is.

What the authors did then, and what *Artificial Ice* does today, is treat the national game in much the same way as that other national game, politics, might be handled in an intense examination. This strikes me as quite appropriate, in that during the lockout year Canadians turned a vitriol and scepticism usually reserved for politicians onto hockey players and owners. It also reminded me of something Roch Carrier said to me when I was trying to write a newspaper essay explaining just why this silly child's game means so much to this country. "When I was growing up," the National Librarian and author of *The Hockey Sweater* told me, "hockey was our 'politics.'"

This book, then, is about the *other* politics of this cold country—hockey. It is far-reaching and tough and even appreciative at times. It challenges the mythologies—some of which I'm sure I share responsibility for as a sportswriter!—and it questions the dogma of a game that in Canada is also part religion. It is all covered here, from the shifts in Quebec hockey to the problems of minor hockey, the rise and recognition of women's hockey, the folly of expansion, the small-market dilemma, the labour situation, and the marketing of a game that has grown far beyond the financial reach of the original, blue-collar fan base.

There is much to agree with, much to disagree with, much to ponder, and even some to cause you to shrug and shake your head in bewilderment. As it should be in all good discussions. Best of all, it is all readable, just as *Hockey Night in Canada* was, and for this the editors are to be congratulated. There is a sense of the person writing in most of the essays, and this is most welcome.

As Hart Cantelon writes in his chapter, "It seems that the future of professional hockey is 'more up for grabs' than it has been at any time in the recent past."

This is equally true for all other forms of the national game. And exactly why *Artificial Ice* is as timely as the whistle at the start of a brand-new game.

ACKNOWLEDGEMENTS

This book has been more than two years in the making, and as editors we want to thank those colleagues, friends, family, and others without whom it might never have come to fruition.

First and foremost, a collection of articles can be only as good as its contributors make it, and we want to express our deepest thanks to all of those who have contributed—for their enthusiasm for the project, for their willingness to make what in some cases were several rounds of revisions when analysis of the business of hockey was overtaken by events, and for their patience.

Second, we want to thank each other. Many readers will know that we've worked together in the past, and our collaborations have always been collegial in the best sense of that word: both thought-provoking and enjoyable. This time, however, each of us was burdened with medical problems that required major surgery and protracted post-operative recuperation. Our health crises meant that the other partner had to pick up the baton unexpectedly at various junctures, and this was always done in a spirit of generosity and good humour. Further to this, we each want to express our profound thanks here to our surgeons: Dr. John Mullen (for Dave) and Dr. Clive Duncan (for Rick). Without their skills and expertise, neither of us would be where we are today, and this book would most likely never have been completed.

It is also appropriate, both of us believe, to publicly thank Peter Saunders, the publisher of Garamond Press, for his faith in the project and his patience. Peter encouraged us for years to follow up *Hockey Night in Canada* with another book, and then had to wait even longer while we solicited contributions and worked through the various delays.

Finally, we want to thank our respective partners, Cathie McDougall and Shelley Bentley, as well as the Gruneau family: Danielle, Charlotte, and Jesse. In addition to living through the periods of absorption in work that are part of every book project, in this instance Cathie and Shelley had to help us through times of ill health that put extra burdens and stresses on them. Without their constant companionship and support, this book would not have been possible.

Artificially created ice for skating was first developed in England between the 1840s and 1870s, and the first major arena installation occurred in Chelsea in 1876. Within a year after Chelsea's rink opened, a small experimental ice surface was laid down in New York City, and in 1879 Madison Square Garden installed the first major artificial ice surface in North America. More than three decades later, in 1911, Canada's first arena featuring artificial ice, Vancouver's Denman Arena, was built and quickly became home to the famous Vancouver Millionaires hockey team.[1] By the 1920s and early 1930s, artificial ice was a standard feature in the new downtown hockey arenas that would become the storied homes of legendary NHL hockey teams in Toronto, Montreal, Detroit, Boston, New York, and Chicago.

More broadly, artificial ice played a key role in the complex web of factors that drove the institutional development of hockey across North America. Artificial ice has allowed the game to be played regularly, and for longer periods of time, in places where winter temperatures are inconsistent; it has provided relatively consistent ice quality for games and training; it has helped to make comprehensive league schedules possible; and it has created the possibility of planning "big games," such as the Stanley Cup series, far in advance. All of these were necessary elements in the growth of hockey as both an aspect of popular culture in North America and a business. The example of the spread of artificial ice invites us to recognize how culture and commerce have been intertwined virtually from the inception of the development of hockey as we know it today.

However, there is another sense in which we can understand the phrase "artificial ice," and this is as a metaphor for larger changes in hockey, and the meanings that Canadians attach to the game. In Canada, hockey has been widely understood as connoting a kind of happy naturalism, a direct expression of our ability to survive, indeed to thrive, in an inhospitable land of ice and snow, long winters, and vast open spaces. This naturalism has been sustained in innumerable images of apple-cheeked boys on frozen ponds, and in a host of literary references to hockey's roots in the Canadian climate and landscape. The British Columbia writer Doug Beardsley exemplifies this tendency to naturalism when he writes: "Ice binds us together, shapes and defines both our style and our substance. It informs us, connects us rink by rink to ourselves."[2] In contrast, the metaphor of "artificial ice" potentially disrupts this kind of naturalism. In the past one hundred and thirty years Canadians have taken several stick, ball, and ice games of different types—shinny, shinty, bandy, and rickets, among others—and refashioned them into a distinctive national sport. Canadians moved the game of hockey indoors into arenas with artificial ice; we organized hockey, standardized it, regulated it, and put it to a variety of cultural and economic uses. In other words, hockey, like artificial ice, is not "natural" at all. It is a human social and cultural product, something that we Canadians have "made" over a period of years.

To say that hockey is something that Canadians have made, though, raises the question: made for what purpose? The answer is that at varying times in our past, Canadians have put hockey to many different purposes. Initially, most Canadians saw hockey as simple fun and recreation, an opportunity to get exercise or compete casually in pickup games of various types. For some Canadian educators, the game also became a forum for teaching boys the masculine virtues of the time: strength, toughness, quiet fortitude, fraternal loyalty. By the end of the nineteenth century, others began to view hockey as a vehicle for the rehearsal of middle-class values: the amateur code, self-discipline, respect for authority, and the virtues of fair play. At the same time, many Canadians, both consciously and unconsciously, began to derive local and regional identities from hockey, based on the supposedly representative character of sports teams in their communities. Local teams became "our" teams, and they carried the standard of civic pride and virtue into the arenas of rival teams from across town or from other communities.

It was not long, of course, before some Canadians began to use the game to make money. Promoters sought to capitalize on hockey's representative meanings by actively promoting identifications with the local team and charging admission to games. Meanwhile, good players began to try to make a living at the game, which often meant moving away from their home communities and playing for teams willing and able to offer higher wages. Although there were successful teams in small towns in many parts of Canada in the early twentieth century, the best players gravitated fairly quickly towards bigger centres of population: Montreal, Ottawa, Toronto, Winnipeg, and Vancouver. As hockey became a popular spectator entertainment, moreover, manufacturers and advertisers tried to find ways of linking their products to successful players and teams. By the mid-1920s hockey had become a thriving business in Canada, firmly centred in a growing web of enterprises that included equipment manufacturers, arena construction, the popular media, and others who traded on the game's advertising value.

After the development of a popular press in the late nineteenth century, sport in general quickly became an important source of both commercial and cultural narratives. Canadians, like their counterparts in the Americas and West European countries, wanted to read stories about the successes of local teams and the exploits of star players. Beginning with telegraphy, and with the later development of newspaper wire services in the early twentieth century, hockey soon became a key element in the making of a

Canadian national popular culture. In a young country lacking in national symbols, hockey provided a common cultural reference point for Canadians from diverse regions and backgrounds.[3] In the 1920s and 1930s, radio accelerated and consolidated this trend by providing the technical means through which unprecedented numbers of Canadians could participate in the same cultural experience at exactly the same time—a broadcast of a "live" hockey game. NHL hockey, in particular, became the primary source for this common cultural experience as fans across the country followed the progress of the league's season on the radio and in the popular press—even in rural communities that were thousands of miles from Toronto or Montreal. By the end of the 1930s radio audiences for NHL hockey had grown to two million listeners and *Hockey Night in Canada* had become a national Saturday-night ritual.[4]

Still, while the experience of hockey was widely shared across the country, the game always raised significant differences in meanings, and evaluations of the qualities of different teams and players varied widely. An important part of hockey's appeal was its ability to combine the sense of an imagined national community with dramatic symbolic commentary on some of the most important sources of difference in Canadian life. Thus, the meanings attributed to teams and players often depended on differences in ethnicity, social class, race, gender, and region. The most obvious example is the powerful identification that formed between the Montreal Canadiens and the team's francophone fans. Indeed, hockey's capacity to attract enthusiasts in Canada's diverse communities helped to define the game's truly national reach. From the 1920s through the 1960s, growing numbers of Canadian boys were playing the game in every part of Canada, supported by a vast and growing infrastructure of volunteers. Many communities also had prominent women's teams, at least until the 1950s, as well as men's teams whose players represented a variety of ethnic and religious constituencies.[5]

Nonetheless, it was hockey's attachment to a hypermasculine vision of "Canadianness" that became the core element in Canada's emerging hockey mythology. After World War I, when Canadian men's amateur teams began to travel to Europe, they proved to be virtually unbeatable. The widespread circulation of stories about Canadian successes in international competitions—on radio and in the newspapers and magazine articles—cemented the notions that hockey was Canada's game and that the passion, skill, and physicality of "our" hockey players made them the best in the world. In the 1950s these ideas and others in Canada's hockey mythology were reinforced by the advent of television. Building on the Canada-wide radio audience that had grown up around the exploits of the Toronto Maple Leafs and Montreal Canadiens, *Hockey Night in Canada* on television quickly became the Canadian Broadcasting Corporation's most popular program, drawing English-speaking audiences of as large as 3.5 million viewers, along with another 2 million French-speaking viewers, by the early 1960s.[6] The generation that grew up in the early postwar era was exposed to years of televised game commentaries and interviews, and these just added to the sediment of taken-for-granted assumptions built up by earlier generations of players, coaches, managers, sportswriters, and radio commentators. The result was a near national consensus in which the core assumptions of Canadian hockey mythology were felt viscerally and rarely questioned: *Hockey is our game; it expresses something distinctive about how we Canadians have come to terms with our unique northern environment and landscape; it is a graphic expression of "who we are"; the game's rough masculinity is a testament to the distinctive passion and strength of the Canadian character; we are better at it than anyone else in the world; and the National Hockey League is the pinnacle of the game—as well as a prominent Canadian institution.*

Interestingly, through the 1950s and early 1960s, while so many Canadians seemed to accept these mythological assumptions, the industry involved in the commercial marketing of hockey narratives was still quite small. Important hockey games were regularly covered on television and radio, and there were many "how to play" books, boy's fiction books, and books that celebrated great teams and star players. However, outside of occasional newspaper or magazine articles that raised questions about the financial side of the game, or offered occasional complaints about "American" influences on Canadian hockey, there was very little critical reflection about the game's place in Canadian society. At the time when the game seemed most organically connected to Canadian culture— when Canadians appeared to "live" the game most intensely—few people felt any need to analyse or reflect upon the role of hockey in Canada.[7] It was as if hockey's place in Canadian culture was almost too obvious to discuss or, arguably, the game was viewed as too sacred to risk profaning through critical analysis.

Myths in any culture have a complex character. On the one hand, they often distil and dramatize the deepest truths about a society and its people. That is why myth so often blurs into the realm of the sacred. On the other hand, myths are also often highly misleading, suggesting an abstract, even sacred, "truth" that has little grounding in historical reality. In this case, myths hide historical truths behind the façade of the sacred and the illusion of consensus. The myth is true because "everybody" knows it to be true as a matter of belief or common sense.[8] At the moment of its greatest strength a mythology thus insulates itself from criticism. Anyone who questions the core assertions that make up the mythological system can simply be written off as either a fool or a heretic. It is fascinating to note, then, how Canada's once-powerful hockey mythology—with its emphases on the "naturalness" of hockey's place in Canadian culture and on the pre-eminent place of the National Hockey League—had begun to show significant cracks by the mid-1960s. Those cracks appeared as a result of four coinciding events that called hockey's mythic certainties into question by provoking both a new degree of self-reflection and an unprecedented discussion of the state of the game and the strength of its Canadian "roots."

First, when the NHL bypassed Vancouver in its initial expansion in 1967, in favour of expanding into California, the league gave the lie to its long-standing claim to be a national institution more than a business. The Liberal government of the day threatened the NHL with anti-combines legislation, and Vancouver was awarded a franchise (along with Buffalo) a couple of years later.[9] However, many Canadians were hit with the realization that NHL teams were not public institutions at all. They were simply profit-maximizing businesses, and Canada's history in the game carried no weight in the calculation of business opportunities. NHL expansion thus had the effect of challenging one of the cornerstones of Canada's postwar hockey mythology.

A second set of demystifying events arose in the early 1970s with the creation of the World Hockey Association as a rival to the NHL. The WHA opened up debate across the country by challenging the NHL's hitherto unchallenged place as the best hockey league in the world. The new league broke ground by recruiting underage and European players; it opened up the game to a more offensive style; and it brought professional hockey to Canadian cities that had not seen major professional teams since the early part of the century. The WHA also had the competitive effect of raising player salaries, bringing them more into line with salaries in other North American professional sports. At about the same time professional athletes began to challenge the restrictive nature of player contracts in the courts, and players' associations in all the major league sports became more organized and militant.

Still, in the area of collective bargaining hockey lagged far behind other major league sports through the 1970s. The head of the National Hockey League Players' Association (NHLPA), Alan Eagleson, controlled the association completely and ran it less like a trade union than as a personal fiefdom. At a time when players in other sports were winning major concessions from owners, Eagleson consistently adopted conciliatory bargaining positions in his dealings with the NHL. He insisted on maintaining complete control over all aspects of the operation of the players' association, including the dispensation of player pensions.[10]

The famous 1972 Summit Series between Canadian NHL players and the Soviet national team was a third event that called key aspects of Canada's postwar mythology of hockey into question. The 1972 series was the culmination of a debate that had grown through the late 1950s and 1960s about Canada's place in international hockey. When Canadian amateur and semi-professional teams began to lose major international matches, we Canadians consoled ourselves with the belief that we were not sending our best players to those events. If Canadians sent our top NHL players to represent the nation, the argument ran, we would win easily. A few people outside the NHL believed that we did not need to send top professionals to win major international matches; what was needed, instead, was a national team development program that would select and prepare good college and junior players for international competitions. However, the NHL did everything it could to block the creation of a Canadian national team that would offer even a temporary alternative to NHL employment to good young players (notably, at the time, Bobby Orr). The NHL's opposition to the national team concept made it clear to many Canadians that the league owners put their own interests ahead of the interests of Canadian fans who wanted to be represented by the strongest possible team. Even when Eagleson did organize a team of top Canadian NHL stars to play the powerhouse Soviet national team in September 1972, NHL intervention prevented participation by any players who had defected to the WHA. Most importantly, this meant the exclusion of superstar Bobby Hull, who had left the NHL's Chicago Blackhawks for the Winnipeg Jets; and Hull's exclusion from Team Canada served to demonstrate to many Canadian hockey fans the hypocrisy of the NHL's claims to being a national institution.

Despite such debates, though, the core myth of Canadian hockey supremacy was sustained and even reinforced when Canada won the 1972 series in the final game, on Paul Henderson's last-minute goal. But once the celebrations had died down it was clear to most observers that Canada's hockey supremacy could no longer be taken for granted. While Team Canada had won the series, it had done so by an eyelash. The quality of the Soviet team had surprised NHL insiders, as well as Canadian fans, and it demonstrated that Europeans were challenging Canada's historical hockey superiority. The speed and skill of the Soviet players opened up a national discussion in Canada about the need to modernize training methods and bring pace and finesse back into Canadian hockey, at a time when toughness, intimidation, and competitive intensity had become the hallmarks of the Canadian game.

In the 1970s the debate about the relative merits of skill and speed versus the virtues of strength, toughness, and competitive intensity in hockey was layered with the stubborn prejudices of many hockey insiders who seemed unwilling to question the apparent certainties of Canada's postwar hockey mythology. For example, the wide open offensive style of many WHA teams, often stocked with European players, was frequently ridiculed as inferior and "not Canadian." European players were castigated as "chickens" or as players who simply lacked "heart." In direct contrast, the dominant NHL team in the early to mid-1970s was the Philadelphia Flyers, the legendary "Broad Street Bullies." The debate that grew up around the Flyers' self-consciously aggressive style, based so heavily on physical intimidation and fighting, was the fourth major "event" that challenged key aspects of Canada's popular hockey self-image. Suddenly questions about hockey violence, and its place in a distinctly "Canadian" style of play and in the development of young Canadian players, were finding their way into a number of high-profile commentaries, reports, and commissions.[11]

Against the background of all these events, the incidence of critical and reflexive writing on the state of hockey in Canada grew significantly through the 1970s and 1980s. In addition to specific debates around key changes, moreover, an upswing in critical writing about sport also reflected the spirit of cultural critique that had become part of the US "counterculture" in the late 1960s. This tendency was represented most prominently in the United States in Jack Scott's book *The Athletic Revolution,* along with several other books by former athletes who offered provocative criticisms of North American professional sports.[12] Jim Bouton's *Ball Four,* for instance, inflamed readers across North America with its frank account of the culture of baseball. The popular mythologies of the National Football League and college football were challenged in highly critical biographies like Dave Meggysey's *Out of Their League* and Gary Shaw's *Meat on the Hoof,* and in novels such as Peter Gent's *North Dallas Forty.*[13] In Canada this trend to critical writing about sport found its first book-length expression in 1970 in Brian Conacher's *Hockey in Canada: The Way It Is.*[14] Conacher's book departed from the usual celebrations of professional hockey, offering insider criticisms of the NHL that were unprecedented for that era. Hockey autobiographies published around the same time by players such as Derek Sanderson and Stan Mikita were less thorough than Conacher's critique, but also raised criticisms of professional hockey.[15] However, it was Bruce Kidd and John Macfarlane's *The Death of Hockey* that would capture the critical spirit of the times more than any other hockey publication.[16] Although the book found only a modest audience, it provided a provocative alternative to the usual boy's fiction, "how to play" books, and laudatory volumes about great teams or players. Kidd and Macfarlane's book can be identified, in fact, as the first sustained critical analysis not only of the NHL but also of the state of hockey in postwar Canadian culture.

There were also important developments in academic scholarship, as sport came to be viewed as a legitimate subject for scholarly research. For example, in 1974 a highly regarded US think-tank, the Brookings Institution, published a landmark academic work on the economics of the sports industry.[17] This work paralleled a striking growth in research studies and anthologies produced by sociologists, economists, and psychologists—all of which opened up new horizons for interpretive analysis of sports in Western societies. By the mid-1970s, courses in the "sociology of sport" were being offered in universities across North America, often bringing a distinctly critical approach to the subject matter and creating a growing market for textbooks and other reference works in the area. In Canada this development led to the publication of several informative studies of the economics of hockey, the "professionalization of attitudes" in minor hockey, the subculture of professional hockey, and hockey violence.[18]

With the exception of history, the humanities were slower than the social sciences to embrace sport as an area of legitimate study and research. For much of the postwar period, the humanities were heavily influenced by a critical scholarly tradition that was deeply sceptical about the role of popular amusements in Western life. Sports were especially suspect because they gave priority to the body over the mind and often seemed to promote collective irrationality, and even violence. In one version of this tradition, sports were written off as expressions of mass taste and mindless conformity, something to be contrasted to "culture," which was civilizing and educative. In other versions, spectator sports were dismissed as contemporary versions of "bread and circuses" (or, in a Marxist-influenced version, "opiates of the people"), exciting but crude spectacles that diverted popular attention away from more "important" matters such as self-development and politics.[19]

However, there were historians who insisted that sports, too, should be understood as culture, and who sought to situate the growth of sport within the broad project of Western cultural development. In many ways, this was the precisely the argument that was championed by physical educators in the twentieth century and by early supporters of the Olympic movement.[20] In the 1960s and 1970s the study of sport was also taken up by a new generation of historians who were struggling to open up their discipline to the study of social history, including the activities of everyday life and the cultures of working classes.[21] Academic journals dedicated to "sport history" sprang up, along with university programs, texts, and reference works. By the late 1970s and early 1980s, moreover, new approaches to cultural studies in the humanities were beginning to legitimize the analysis of sport as an element of popular culture. This practice began with works in Britain that examined the meanings attached to working-class cultural practices, notably football.[22] Instead of dismissing the field of popular culture as "lowbrow," scholars in the humanities began to pursue the analysis of "the popular" with unprecedented enthusiasm. The issue was no longer to pronounce upon differences between "good" culture and "bad" culture; rather, it was to examine the role of culture in maintaining or challenging relations of power, and in producing different forms of identity. In this context, sports could potentially be as fruitful an area to study as art, literature, or theatre.

In Canada, meanwhile, it was well-known literary figures who prepared the way for "taking hockey seriously," predating developments in the academy by at least a decade. Morley Callaghan, who was one of the earliest Canadian writers of any stature to pay attention to hockey, argued provocatively that hockey was Canada's "only national drama."[23] Along similar lines, in 1965 the West Coast poet Al Purdy made a compelling case for the game as a central aspect of Canadian culture. In his poem "Hockey Players" Purdy called hockey a "Canadian specific" and delved into the rink's literal and metaphorical connections to the landscape. The "Canadian specific," Purdy argued, accommodated a unique ambivalence; hockey was at once a combination of "ballet and murder."[24] At a roughly similar time, the Montreal writer Hugh Hood offered a number of finely grained discussions of hockey in Canadian community life, in addition to a book-length discussion of the Montreal Canadiens' star Jean Beliveau.[25] Other well-known authors, including Hugh MacLennan and Mordecai Richler, also contributed to a growing body of Canadian postwar writing depicting hockey as an authentic part of the complex lived experience that was Canadian life.[26] Significantly, much of this work was tinged with a romantic sense of loss, suggesting that hockey—as a traditional and organic part of Canadian culture—was threatened by commerce and Americanism.

Through the 1970s and 1980s, then, Canadian essayists on hockey gave voice to the cultural nationalism of those years, in both Quebec and English-speaking Canada. Anglo-Canadian nationalism in particular—seeking clear markers of Canadian cultural distinctiveness—seemed to embrace hockey with a sense of urgency. Not surprisingly, then, one of the major interpretive works on hockey in the early 1980s was by Peter Gzowski—an iconic nationalist figure. Gzowski believed that the "sour" period in post-war Canadian hockey—from NHL expansion in the late 1960s through the mid-1970s—had given way to better times, as the WHA and NHL merged, European players became common in the NHL, and Canadian international teams began to win again. It seemed time to celebrate hockey again, and Gzowski's initial intention to write a book chronicling the rise of the Edmonton Oilers quickly broadened into a fuller discussion of the importance of hockey in Canadian culture. Published in 1981, Gzowksi's *The Game of Our Lives* treated hockey with a reverence that parallels how English literary critic Richard Hoggart celebrates the place of soccer in English working-class life in his classic book *The Uses of Literacy*.[27] In Gzowski's romantic rendering, the "game of our lives" was an indelible part of a distinctly Canadian way of life, and the swashbuckling success of the young Edmonton Oilers (including, of course, Wayne Gretzky) was framed as marking the renewal of Canada's "ownership" of hockey, something that had been threatened in the previous decades.

Gzowski's book reflected, and in turn fed, a more widespread "discovery" of hockey in the 1980s as a distinctive and important element of Canadian culture. In 1983, for example, Ken Dryden's *The Game* re-examined Canadian hockey, and NHL hockey in particular, with a critical sensitivity unprecedented in writing on Canadian sport.[28] Rather different in tone but no less influential in its reception, Roch Carrier's children's story "The Hockey Sweater," which depicts a young French-Canadian boy's disappointment at receiving a Toronto Maple Leafs sweater as a Christmas gift, quickly became an iconic work.[29] Published in the same year as Dryden's book, Roy MacGregor's novel *The Last Season* offered darker and more multi-layered observations on hockey's place(s) in the lives of Canadians.[30] With the publication of works like these, the significance of hockey in Canadian culture was being articulated in new ways, and cultural references to hockey seemed to move from the margins to the mainstream. This was true, moreover, across a range of the popular arts: from the renewed popularity of old songs by Stompin' Tom Connors to the hockey references in the songs of the Tragically Hip; from Carrier's and MacGregor's fiction to plays by Rick Salutin and Ken Brown; from a new appreciation of hockey images in the paintings of William Kurelek to the popularity of hockey images by contemporary artists such as Ken Danby.

It would not be long, though, before other work started to appear that sought to strike a different sort of balance, recognizing hockey's place in postwar Canadian life while also drawing attention to problems, conflicts, and a changing Canada. One essay in Ken Dryden and Roy MacGregor's *Home Game*, for example, published in 1989, depicts the struggles of a small Saskatchewan farm village to raise money for a new hockey arena, and it linked this effort with the struggles to survive of rural communities across the country—communities in which arenas had once been the centre of community life.[31] In another chapter the authors describe—sympathetically but not uncritically—the demands that minor hockey makes on a Toronto family's energies and resources, in a time when most elite players no longer come from rural communities but from the sub-urbs of our major cities. Still, the "hockey problem" that arguably prompted the greatest critical commentary in the late 1980s was Wayne Gretzky's move from Edmonton to Los Angeles in the summer of 1988. Occuring within two years of the implementation of the Canada–US free-trade agreement, the sale of Gretzky conjured up many old ghosts, both about the apparent role of the United States in the corruption of hockey and about Canada selling out its natural resources to the Americans.[32] In pure business terms, many commentators and fans acknowledged that the Gretzky trade was an astute deci-sion by Edmonton owner Peter Pocklington, who sold a depreciating asset at the moment of its greatest value. But the trade's symbolic and practical implications for Canadian hockey were powerful nonetheless. At the very least, the Gretzky trade sig-nalled an abrupt end to the Edmonton Oilers dynasty and raised the prospect that no Canadian NHL team was likely to have the same kind of success in the immediate future. In the continental market, the future growth of professional hockey was clearly envi-sioned to be in the United States, and Canadian NHL teams outside of Toronto and Montreal would be hard-pressed to find the money to keep their stars at home.

A renewed spirit of critique in writing about hockey in the late 1980s and early 1990s was given additional impetus by the publication of David Cruise and Alison Griffith's provocative book *Net Worth: Exploding the Myths of Pro Hockey*.[33] This was the first book-length critical examination of the business of hockey since Kidd and Macfarlane's pioneering critique in the early 1970s. Cruise and Griffiths launched a direct assault on many of hockey's foundational myths, raising disturbing questions about the actions of storied NHL owners such as Conn Smythe and the Norris brothers, NHL presidents Clarence Campbell and John Zeigler, and NHLPA leader Alan Eagleson—all of whom in official accounts were regarded as "builders" of the game. To underscore the force of Cruise and Griffith's critique, a major controversy developed in the early 1990s around Eagleson's business dealings, leading to criminal charges, a conviction for fraud, and Eagleson's fall from any influence in the game. All of this led to intriguing questions about the tight-knit nature of the hockey subculture and the apparent unwill-ingness of the Canadian sports media to investigate Eagleson's actions. Indeed, the

Eagleson "corruption story" was first broken by an American journalist working for a small newspaper, rather than by an established Canadian sportswriter, which pointedly revealed the limitations of mainstream sports journalism in Canada.[34] Reporters who worked the hockey beat were largely captives of their insider sources, and many Canadian hockey writers had developed close friendships with Eagleson and other insiders. The result was that hockey journalism was often little more than a promotional appendage of the NHL. The Eagleson story highlighted the difficulties of doing critical or investigative work into the workings of Canadian hockey, or into the truisms of Canadian hockey mythology.

Despite this, one effect of the Eagleson affair was to encourage greater self-reflection—along with a much more critical impulse—in a new generation of Canadian sports journalists. The core aspects of Canadian hockey mythology still had their stubborn supporters in the Canadian sports media in the early 1990s; however, it seemed unlikely that there would ever again be the same kind of cheerleading that had existed in the early 1960s. If many of the taken-for-granted assumptions of Canadian hockey mythology had been effectively debated during the 1970s and 1980s, the changing cultural and economic conditions of the 1990s produced new, and arguably greater, challenges for sportswriters to analyse and comment on. For example, with the deregulation of trade and the impacts of technological innovations in communications, there could be no doubt that the entire professional sports industry in North America was entering a time of transition. In this environment, intelligent sports writers asked new questions about the future shape of professional sports, rather than rehashing old traditions and ideas. Even the core argument in Canada's postwar mythology—Canada's apparent ownership of hockey—was more in question than ever before.

In fact, the future extent of Canada's representation in NHL hockey seemed increasingly uncertain in the 1990s, which provided for considerable speculation in the sports media. Canadian NHL teams were badly hurt in the early 1990s, when the value of the Canadian dollar dropped while NHL salaries kept rising. Faced with paying rising salaries in US dollars, but having old arenas that were unable to provide the ancillary revenues (from luxury boxes, and flexible electronic advertising) that were becoming normal in US professional sports venues, several NHL teams in smaller Canadian cities threatened to leave for greener pastures unless they received greater subsidies from governments. However, Canadian sportswriting had developed to a point where these demands could be discussed with a critical acuity that would have been unusual by the standards of the 1960s. Indeed, a number of prominent Canadian sports journalists at the time—including Stephen Brunt and David Shoalts in *The Globe and Mail*, Roy MacGregor in *The Ottawa Citizen*, and Cam Cole in *The Edmonton Journal*—produced insightful work that played a significant role in elevating public understanding of the changing economics of sports. Most importantly, these columnists were reluctant to adopt uncritically the owners' line that NHL teams were public institutions that "needed" public subsidies if they were to survive. The old equation of the interests of NHL owners with the interests of the Canadian public was no longer repeated in Canada's sports pages as if it were a truism.

It was the ferment and uncertainties of the late 1980s and early 1990s that provided the intellectual context for the publication of our earlier book, *Hockey Night in Canada*. As academic researchers with lifelong interests in both sport and Canada, we were perplexed that so little sustained scholarly attention had been devoted to the place of hockey in Canadian life, despite all the claims about the game's importance. With that in mind we set out to explore in detail the complex and changing role of hockey in Canadian life. We reassessed hockey's history in this country, with attention to how differences in power between regions and between various social groups had shaped the game's development. There were many hockey-like games played in Canada in the nineteenth century, and we sought to explain how and why the game we know today was able to push aside those competing forms. We wanted to explain how "a" way of playing hockey had emerged in Canada, to become "the" way of playing the game. We also wanted to explain how the NHL was able to emerge as the dominant professional league, ahead of several other competing pro leagues, and how the NHL was able to construct its place as a "major league" sport in the public mind between the 1920s and 1940s. More broadly, we tried to show how hockey's prominent place as an icon of Canadian culture did not emerge "naturally." Rather, it was a social and cultural product, an "invented tradition."[35]

Hockey Night in Canada explored a wide range of other issues as well, including the work world of professional hockey players; the positive and negative aspects of youth hockey; debates about hockey violence; the ways in which changes in Canadian communities have influenced the game; the changing nature of fandom in a more globalized media environment; and the history and politics of international hockey. However, out of all this analysis, the aspect of our book that seemed to generate the greatest public interest at the time was our discussion of the pressures faced by cities to attract (or hold onto) major league sports franchises in North America, and particularly the competitive pressures faced by NHL owners in "small markets," many of them in Canada. We predicted that the changing economics of major league sports—including rapidly rising player salaries, the increased importance of media revenues and other ancillary revenue streams (like luxury-seating)—would make it more difficult for Canadian franchises outside the major media markets to survive, let alone prosper. We speculated on what reactions this might evoke in a Canada that was changing rapidly, evolving from a mostly rural population of British and French origins—in which English-French rivalries were of huge symbolic importance—to a mostly urban country in which a great many people (especially in our major cities) come from regions of the world where hockey, and indeed winter, don't exist.

Throughout the 1990s, events in the NHL unfolded largely along lines we had antici-pated. Salaries continued to rise, making the economics of small-market franchises ever more precarious. The Quebec Nordiques and the Winnipeg Jets each left Canada in the mid-1990s for homes in larger television markets in the United States. Team owners in other provincial Canadian cities worried publicly that they, too, might have to relocate, and individually and collectively they put pressure on Canadian governments to offer them the tax breaks and other subsidies from public funds that would allow them to compete on the proverbial "level playing field" with their US counterparts, many of whom were enjoying generous public subsidies. This pressure culminated, in 1998–99, with an investigation of the "needs" of Canada's professional sports franchises con-ducted by a Standing Committee of the House of Commons, chaired by Dennis Mills, a Liberal MP from Toronto who had owned a major junior (OHL) hockey team and was an uncritical supporter of professional sport. The Mills Committee recommended a package of public funding measures that were intended to improve the financial for-tunes of Canada's National Hockey League franchises.[36] In January 2000, Industry Minister John Manley announced that the federal government was poised to offer just this kind of assistance.

The surprise came when this announcement was greeted with an extraordinary public outcry. Some hockey fans objected to subsidizing high player salaries, and to the lack of loyalty to fans and communities that was manifest in the demands of both play-ers and owners. Others were less concerned with hockey, and simply objected to the spending of public money on sport while programs intended to address urgent social needs remained chronically underfunded. It was obvious, though, that a significant seg-ment of the Canadian public did not want to subsidize NHL hockey, *even if this meant Canada losing more of its NHL teams*. Although many Canadians still professed to care about hockey, the NHL game simply did not have the same mythological hold on Canadians that it had in the past. Put a little differently, NHL hockey was no longer regarded by most Canadians as a "priceless" part of our heritage, something to be saved at any cost.[37]

If anything this view seemed to grow even stronger during the NHL lockout in 2004–05. Not only did Canadians reach a point where they no longer saw NHL hockey as a priceless part of our heritage, but most Canadians also found that they got on just fine without NHL hockey and did not really miss it much. At least some of this lack of enthusiasm for NHL hockey stemmed from the diminishing entertainment value of the NHL "product"—a grinding, boring, defensive game, filled with obstruction, and played over such a long season that regular matches often seem meaningless. But, at a deeper level, and far more importantly, Canada today has become a very different country from the Canada of the 1960s and 1970s. We are now a much more urban and multi-cultural country, and many of our most recent migrants have come from societies in which professional sport scarcely exists. Even among multi-generation Canadians, moreover, the range of interests available to young people (including other sports, as well as artistic pursuits and new forms of electronic entertainment) has become so great that hockey at any level is now just one recreational or consumer choice among many, as opposed to the ritual of winter life that many middle-aged Canadian men recall. Indeed, an arguably significant aspect of the outcry that greeted the Manley proposal in 2000 was simply how badly Canadian politicians, most of them men who grew up in the 1950s and 1960s, had misread the public mood.

What, then, can be said about hockey's place in Canadian life today, when both the sports industry and Canada itself have changed profoundly in the last quarter-century? It is certainly true that hockey remains an object of special interest to a great many Canadians. Registrations in youth hockey have levelled off in recent years, but they remain substantial. The women's game continues to grow in popularity, and adult hockey leagues and pickup games have no shortage of participants. As far as fan interest is concerned, the gold-medal performance by Canada's men's hockey team in the 2002 Salt Lake City Olympics was watched by more than ten million Canadians, nearly one-third of the country. The Canadian women's gold-medal game was watched by another five million viewers.[38] In spring 2004, before the NHL lockout, hockey was the subject of water-cooler talk across the country when five of the six Canadian NHL teams made the playoffs and the Calgary Flames made an unexpected run to the Stanley Cup final. By the same token, in the absence of NHL hockey during the 2004–05 season, Canadians turned out to watch junior hockey and other levels of community hockey in unprecedented numbers. The 2005 Memorial Cup final, between London and Rimouski, in particular, generated the kind of national attention usually limited only to NHL playoff games.

Even more visibly, the number of books, plays, artworks, and film and television productions on various aspects of hockey in Canada has become overwhelming in the past decade. If reflective self-analysis about hockey's place in Canadian culture was minimal in the late 1950s and early 1960s, it now seems to be everywhere, from bookstores to theatres and art galleries, and even university classrooms. Still, it is difficult not to get the feeling that there are powerful elements of nostalgia in this current boom of cultural work on hockey, as if we are now more desperate to hang on to cultural markers of Canadianness, in a world in which our sovereignty may be less certain than it was in the past. Another dimension of this nostalgia may well be rooted in a collective yearning on the part of some Canadians for the less culturally diverse and less-complicated Canada that they remember from their youths.

Whatever the sources of the boom in cultural work on hockey, though, it seems ironic that our interest in analysing hockey's Canadianness may coincide with many Canadians no longer caring about hockey with the passion of previous generations.

As Ken Dryden recently observed (from his new seat on the government benches, as opposed to his former post as president of Maple Leaf Sports & Entertainment), it may be that what was once a passion for most Canadians is now simply a habit.

Of course, generalizations like these invite further questions, and it is in this spirit that we have collected the articles that make up this book. The book begins with a chapter by Jean Harvey, who focuses on the changing meanings of hockey in Quebec since organized hockey was first played in Montreal in the late nineteenth century. Harvey relates that the earliest formal hockey competition took place under the auspices of the private schools and clubs of Montreal's anglophone elite, a milieu in which French-Canadians were not welcome. However, it would not be long before good French-Canadian players were playing on teams representing Irish working-class clubs, and before French-speaking clubs were formed, notably Le Club National. What was significant about hockey's formative years in Montreal, Harvey proposes, was that the game served to dramatize the ethnic, religious, and class rivalries that characterized the city (and, indeed much of Canada) in those times. Moreover, when French players and clubs quickly developed a reputation for excellence, clubs like *le National* and later *les Canadiens* became standard-bearers for the identity and national pride of the French-Canadian people, a people who had become a subordinated community in their own land.

For almost fifty years, Harvey suggests, the Montreal Canadiens' tradition of excellence made them *porte-étendards* for French-Canadian aspirations, and gave the team a symbolic political significance that has no parallel in North American professional sports (though it does in Europe). This representative significance of the Canadiens would reach its most dramatic expression with the Richard Riot in Montreal in the spring of 1955.[39] With the Quiet Revolution of the 1960s, though, with its flowering of cultural and entrepreneurial activity in Quebec, and with the growth of the sovereignty movement that led to the election of a Parti Québécois government in 1976, the political meanings of the Canadiens would be steadily diminished. Once the Québécois people (a designation now preferred to "French-Canadians") had other vehicles for the expression of national feelings and identifications, the Canadiens would inevitably become more like a normal North American sports team, albeit one with the proudest winning tradition in their sport. *Les Canadiens* still attract a loyal and enthusiastic following today, Harvey concludes, but enthusiasm rises and falls according to the team's success, as it does with most teams, and hockey has become—especially among young people—more like a consumer choice.

This last issue—the meanings that hockey has for contemporary Canadian youth—is the central focus of the next chapter, by Brian Wilson. It is in our youth that we are likely to be more ardent sports fans than at any other stage in our lives, and thus any sport that aspires to a central place in a nation's popular culture has to connect with the nation's youth. It has to be the sport that kids play, informally, in schoolyards and parks;

it also has to be what they insist on watching on their television sets, and care enough about to discuss enthusiastically with their peers. And, although hockey once enjoyed an unchallenged position as the sport of choice of Canadian youth, in the past couple of decades young people growing up in Canada have had many more choices. As far as participation is concerned, soccer registrations now outnumber registrations in minor hockey, and basketball is played increasingly widely, both in the high schools and informally in schoolyards and parks, especially in our major cities.

In the realm of spectatorship, specialty sports channels now give Canadians access to many sports that were not readily available in Canada before, and basketball is gaining in popularity. The National Basketball Association's large number of black stars has made the league, and the game of basketball, of greater interest than hockey among many young people in Canada's non-white minority communities; and NBA stars (and NBA merchandise) have a greater drawing power than do their NHL counterparts among youths attracted by anti-authority or "cool" role models. What is most significant, though, Wilson proposes, is that the NBA has achieved considerable success in articulating its game (and star players) with other aspects of the consumer culture that attracts contemporary youth—popular music, videos, clothing—and that hockey (and the NHL) may face an increasing disadvantage in reaching youth as a result of this, even in Canada. Youth culture is now an increasingly global (and, thus, US-influenced) phenomenon, in which interests and allegiances are framed as matters of consumer choice, rather than as regional or national loyalties.

In chapter 3 Mary Louise Adams mounts another kind of challenge to the idea that hockey is something around which all Canadians happily unite. Adams, a former figure skater and coach, as well as a sociologist, reminds us that not all Canadians share the same happy memories of hockey that we've attributed to men raised in the postwar decades, and that for many girls and women the memories are much less positive: of girls being forced off outdoor rinks when the ice was taken over by boys playing hockey, of figure skaters (and women's hockey) being forced to accept inconvenient ice times at municipal arenas because boys' hockey "naturally" took priority, or of their families' lives being organized around the interests of their fathers and brothers in hockey. Adams invites readers to recognize that not every Canadian is enamoured of hockey; indeed that quite a few Canadians—many (but not all) of them women—resent the privileged place that hockey occupies in our public culture, resent the claims that hockey has made on public resources (including public spaces as well as money), and certainly don't agree that hockey is what unites us or makes us Canadian. To such claims (and the men who make them), Adams responds, "What country do these men live in?"

Adams does not speak for all Canadian women here, though, and indeed one of the things that *has* changed most visibly in the hockey landscape over the past two decades is the extraordinary growth of women's hockey. Even as registrations in boys' leagues have levelled off, girls' hockey registrations have risen steeply, albeit from a much smaller base. After a time not long ago (in the 1970s and 1980s) when girls had to take provincial minor hockey associations to court in order to establish their rights to play, today in most parts of Canada females who want to play hockey find a welcoming structure of opportunity. In chapter 4 Julie Stevens discusses and evaluates these developments, from court cases and the entrenched prejudices that they challenged, to the present, when Canada's women have won Olympic gold, cheered on by millions, and when Canadian star Hayley Wickenheiser's efforts to play professional hockey became an international media story.

Stevens, not surprisingly, applauds the legitimacy achieved by girls' and women's hockey, including the opening up of opportunities for girls to play and the increase in opportunities for the best adult women to keep developing their skills (in university hockey, for example) and to represent their country. Success at the highest level, especially, creates valuable role models for girls, allowing them to have the hockey aspirations that boys have always had. Still, for Stevens, pleasure in these successes must be qualified by the recognition that as hockey for girls and women has become integrated into the Canadian "high-performance" system—under the auspices of Hockey Canada—it appears to have lost the sense of community it once enjoyed, and now manifests some of the same abuses and attitudes that distort men's hockey.

The subculture of minor hockey, and the entrenched attitudes that have made change so difficult, is also the subject of the chapter by Mike Robidoux and Pierre Trudel. Years of research—their own, and that of other scholars—show conclusively that permitting bodychecking in boys' hockey leads to an increase in injuries. The question the authors pose is why Hockey Canada persists not only in disregarding this conclusion but also in seeking a solution other than the obvious step of eliminating bodychecking in the younger age groups.

Hockey Canada has initiated several debates on the subject, but has backed away from authorizing a ban. It has developed instructional programs to teach young players how to bodycheck more safely. It has even commissioned its own research into the subject, hoping that the results might indicate a different conclusion. The problem, say Robidoux and Trudel, is that Hockey Canada is hamstrung by contradictory expectations. On the one hand, its mission statements commit it to providing a safe and positive environment for young players who want to learn the game. Meanwhile, though, many individuals in the Canadian minor hockey system see their purpose as the production of Canadian talent. This means turning out players capable of going on to major junior hockey and, in some cases, to the NHL; and that requires players who can hit and intimidate, or at least survive intimidation. Ultimately, despite the collapse of many aspects of Canada's older hockey mythology, there remain many hockey insiders, at every level of the game, who believe that hitting and intimidation are the "Canadian way."

The final chapter in Part I takes on the issue of race and the challenges that follow from hockey's legacy of racism. Robert Pitter outlines the problems of using race as an intellectual concept, and an empirical way of categorizing people. However, as he points out, only the most colour-blind history of hockey in Canada could fail to note the difficulties experienced by non-white players—both black and Aboriginal—in getting opportunities to play the game at high levels. Black and Aboriginal players and teams were found in Canada as early as the late nineteenth century, but, consistent with the systemic racism of Canadian society in that time, they were informally barred from most official hockey organizations. Later, in the 1940s and 1950s, coloured players excelled in minor professional leagues but did not get the opportunities to play in the NHL that their minor-league achievements clearly warranted. The last couple of decades has seen the emergence of a small number of highly successful and widely respected black stars, including Grant Fuhr and Jarome Iginla. However, according to Pitter, young black and First Nations players still face racist behaviours and attitudes—from opponents, fans, and even sometimes their own coaches and teammates—on their way up through minor and junior hockey. Moreover, hockey even now is distinctly "whiter" than its main competitors—football, basketball, soccer, and baseball—a fact that may influence the sporting choices of promising non-white athletes. In any event, hockey's continuing whiteness challenges the popular myth that the game unites all Canadians.

In Part II of the book we move from discussions of the culture of Canadian hockey, and the game's changing place in Canadian culture, to examinations of the changing economics of professional sport and the particular challenges facing the NHL in its efforts to "grow the game." To begin Mark Rosentraub offers a comprehensive discussion of the structural relationships between player costs and revenues in the four major league sports, and the challenges that rapid salary rises in the last fifteen years have posed for the survival of small-market franchises as they struggle to remain competitive. Rosentraub pays particular attention to the vexatious issues of salary caps and revenue-sharing—issues at the heart of the recent negotiations between the NHL and NHLPA—and takes readers through the historical differences of the professional football, basketball, baseball, and hockey leagues.

One common issue resurfaces, at least in every negotiation that seeks to tie salary increases to revenues, and that is the matter of finding agreement on exactly what revenues are to count as deriving from the sport, and are therefore potentially to be shared with the players and perhaps with other teams. Revenues from national television, gate receipts, and even game-day concessions are obvious candidates for sharing. But what about local media revenues, income from arenas owned by separate but related companies, or income from property developments adjacent to the facility and from insignia merchandise? Serious negotiations require agreed upon ways of identifying team incomes, as distinct from the incomes of other businesses that are often part of the same corporate family, and as Rosentraub points out, negotiations are made more difficult—certainly in the case of hockey—because in the past owners have used creative accounting practices to make it appear as if their teams were making limited amounts of money, while all the while their steadily rising franchise values would suggest otherwise. Agreement on what revenues are to count, Rosentraub proposes, is therefore the necessary precursor to any meaningful agreement on salary caps or revenue-sharing.

In the next chapter, Robert Bellamy and Kelly Shultz provide a detailed look at television revenues and how the sports/television environment has been transformed by the growth of alternatives to the traditional broadcast networks. They present an overview of the early history of sports television in the United States, outlining the profitable marriage between professional sports and the major US networks. This partnership brought more money than ever before into sports: advertising revenues fuelled the spectacular growth in what the networks would pay for exclusive rights, which in turn fuelled equally spectacular growth in both franchise values and player salaries. However, the four major league sports have differed greatly in the income that they have been able to derive from television; the NFL and NBA have steadily increased their revenues, while major league baseball (MLB) and the NHL (to an even greater degree) have stalled or declined. Initial differences in popularity and presence in US markets have been built on (or eroded by) smart (or poor) business decisions about how to sell the sports to television. The most enduring problems have followed from the determination of big-city owners in baseball and hockey to sell local media rights themselves, a strategy that was good for their particular teams but reduced the values that the leagues could realize from national broadcast rights (revenue typically shared across the league)—thus widening the gaps between franchises that can generate large revenues from local media (for example, the New York Yankees, New York Rangers, Atlanta Braves, Toronto Maple Leafs) and those that can't. These revenue gaps have been further magnified by the growth of cable networks and specialty sports channels, and by the interest that media corporations have shown in owning sports "content" (owning teams whose games then become cheap programming for their television outlets). Yet this convergence of content and distribution capacity has not proven to be the bonanza that was once predicted, and in a media environment with more sports product than ever before, making money from sports television is not as easy as it once was. Bellamy and Shultz are critical of some of the strategic decisions that the NHL has taken over the years, and they query whether the league can ever aspire to more than a small niche in the US television market.

The following chapter, by Dan Mason, is also critical of the NHL's strategies for expanding hockey's footprint in the United States. Mason gives readers a historical perspective on the NHL's efforts to expand into US markets, especially in the Sunbelt states, and argues that US expansion was always intended to put the league in a position where it could land a national television contract with one of the major US networks. This contract was what would make hockey profitable in markets where the game had no roots, and where live audiences would take time—and creative marketing—to build. This was also what would, in the long run, justify franchise values that were based on marketers' optimism that hockey could be sold in the United States. However, the networks' first attempts to build hockey audiences in the United States in the late 1960s and early 1970s yielded disappointing results, and contracts with the NHL were not renewed. Franchises in cities like Oakland and Atlanta also failed after only a few years. Yet the NHL would not be deterred from its game plan of promoting hockey in what it saw as booming American markets, and the 1990s saw new franchises established in Tampa Bay and Miami, in Anaheim and the Bay Area (now San Jose), and in Atlanta (again) and Nashville, as well as relocations to Carolina, Colorado, and Phoenix.

Optimism was also spurred for a time by a television contract with the new Fox Telelvision network. However, despite some innovative (and, for hockey traditionalists, controversial) attempts to sell the game to audiences who didn't know hockey, Fox's audiences remained disappointing and the network refused to renew at the same rates. The NHL chose instead to go to the cable network ESPN, but this left hockey once again without a presence on any US broadcast network. Mason's analysis queries the NHL's television strategies and indeed the larger strategy of US expansion, raising larger questions about where the game's future lies, questions that take on added urgency in the aftermath of the 2004–05 lockout. It is telling, for example, that following the NHL's inability to resolve its labour difficulties in a timely manner, in summer 2005 ESPN decided to pull out of NHL hockey, and the league was perhaps fortunate to secure a deal with the smaller Outdoor Life Network (OLN).

At this point we turn to another aspect of the contemporary professional sports business, namely the new arenas and stadiums that have replaced the legendary venues of the 1920s and 1930s, and the role that sports and entertainment facilities play in the new downtown economy. John Hannigan, a University of Toronto sociologist who has studied the transition of many North American downtowns from economies based on industry and transportation to "new economies" based on knowledge industries and upscale consumption, writes here about the transition that Toronto underwent in the last quarter of the twentieth century, a transition symbolized in the Toronto Maple Leafs' move from Maple Leaf Gardens (built in the Depression era) to the Air Canada Centre. The Leafs' new home is typical of the current generation of sports facilities in that it has a lot of luxury boxes, which facilitate selling season tickets to corporate clients, professional sport's new fan base. The Air Canada Centre also offers other revenue opportunities that distinguish it from the old Gardens—electronic advertising, and restaurants and night clubs—as well as being designed as a suitable home for NBA basketball. It is consistent, therefore, with the needs of professional sports operators everywhere to maximize the revenue-generating potential of their franchises in every way possible (the Montreal Canadiens pursued the same agenda with their move away from the Forum). What's also significant, Hannigan suggests, is that the Air Canada Centre and SkyDome (now the Rogers Centre), the Hummingbird Centre for the Performing Arts, the Harbourfront Centre, and other high-end commercial and residential developments that have transformed downtown Toronto in the last twenty years are all part of a concerted effort to establish Toronto's reputation as a "world-class" city, involving both public and private money. This strategy is by no means unique to Toronto; indeed, we see at least parts of it in almost every major league city. However, we are left with the question of what a "world-class city" really means, and what the benefits and costs of these downtown transformations are.

The final two chapters turn to thinking about international hockey and the game's expansion outside North America, and to comparisons between developments in the business of hockey and trends in that most global of professional sports, soccer. In the first of these chapters, Hart Cantelon opens with a brief history of Canada's representation in international hockey, including the efforts of Father David Bauer to establish a Canadian national team. He also shows how Canada's national interests were always subordinated to the interests of the NHL. Cantelon then moves on to consider the increasingly global labour market for hockey players. In the 1980s and 1990s, this trend primarily meant European players—mostly from the former Soviet Union and Czechoslovakia, and from the Scandinavian countries—pursuing opportunities to play in the NHL, where they could make much higher salaries than those available in Europe. However, the NHL lockout of 2004–05 saw many European players returning to their home countries, and some Canadians playing in Europe, too, and Cantelon invites us to imagine this as the beginning of a larger trend. Canadians, as we've noted, have always believed the NHL to be the best league in the world. However, it's at least conceivable, given the proven excellence of the Swedes, Russians, and other Europeans who have played in the NHL, that European professional hockey might develop a league that would be competitive in every sense, and Cantelon speculates as to the changes that this possibility might set in motion in the hockey world.

In the book's final chapter, Julian Ammirante draws comparisons between hockey's growth as a world sport and developments in soccer/football in Europe and other continents that have made "futebol" a far more global game than hockey, or any other sport. For Ammirante, the steady progress of the commercialization of sport has led to a series of developments that can now be found in both games (and others, too), many of them phenomena highlighted in earlier chapters in this section. Ammirante discusses the increasingly global labour market for players (far more global in football than it is in hockey), and the role of European labour and human rights laws in reducing restrictions on player movement. He also discusses how the advent of pay TV in Europe has opened the door to unprecedented television revenues for Europe's major football leagues (in Italy, England, and Spain), yet also widened the gaps between the resources available to the biggest metropolitan-based clubs in these nations, and clubs based in smaller cities, and smaller countries. These discrepancies in wealth have reduced competitiveness in the major football leagues (Serie A in Italy, the Premier League in England, and la Primera Liga in Spain), and led to changes in the format of major European competitions.

The most important changes of all, in Ammirante's view, have to do with the nature of owners—the same trends towards corporate ownership that Mason and others have noted in North American professional sports—and with consequent changes in the relationships between clubs, players, and fans. Where the fans were once typically loyal supporters of clubs that were local institutions, today the corollary of owners who are mobile investors and players who move routinely in search of higher wages is fans for whom the choice of a favourite team is more often than not a *consumer* choice. This world of sports is transitory, in other words highly provisional, and very dependent upon marketing and promotion (and the resources that can be invested in these). The meanings of sporting allegiances are thus becoming very different from what they once were, and this is as true, Ammirante concludes, in Europe as it is in North America.

We return, with this observation, to the changing place of hockey in Canadian culture, and we are reminded of how culture and commerce are not, ultimately, separate fields of analysis but are inextricably intertwined. In our introduction to *Hockey Night in Canada* more than ten years ago, we suggested that hockey's mythical connections with notions of Canadianness were in need of critical analysis, rather than further romanticization, even though the critique of hockey is not a practice that meets with universal approval in Canada. Today, in our view, the events of the last ten years in the hockey business—and the global promotion of many professional sports in regions where these sports have no historic roots in popular culture—only serve to underline the need for the sorts of critiques offered here.

Notes

1 The history of artificial ice is closely intertwined with the history of refrigeration. See R. Thevenot, *History of Refrigeration Throughout the World* (Paris: International Institute of Refrigeration, 1978). Useful historical information on the development of artificial ice for skating can be found in Fred and Joan Dean's on-line book *The History of Ice Skating*, pp. 29-32 <www.iceskate-magazine.com>, and in Ernst Barends' work on the history of speed-skating ovals, 1999 <www.gironet.nl/home/cvstave/schaatsen/article/400EN.html>.

2 Doug Beardsley, *Country on Ice* (Winlaw, BC: Polestar Press, 1987), p. 185.

3 There are striking parallels here between hockey in Canada and soccer in Brazil. Like Canada, Brazil is another comparatively "new" nation with a colonial past where a sport has come to figure prominently in popular ideas of national identity. See Alex Bellos, *Futebol: Soccer, the Brazilian Way* (New York: Bloomsbury, 2003), esp. ch. 2.

4 Scott Young, *The Boys of Saturday Night: Inside Hockey Night in Canada* (Toronto: Macmillan, 1990), p. 38.

5 Since the early 1990s a growing body of work has sought to recover the rich and diverse history of hockey outside of "mainstream" accounts of the game's development. For example, on the history of women's hockey see Brian MacFarlane, *Proud Past, Bright Future: One Hundred Years of Canadian Women's Hockey* (Toronto: Stoddart, 1994) and Julie Stevens and Joanna Avery, *Too Many Men on the Ice* (Independent Publisher's Network, 1998). Pathbreaking histories of hockey in Aboriginal and African-Canadian communities can be found in Frank Cosentino, *Afros, Aboriginals and Canadian Sport in Pre-World War One Canada* (Ottawa: The Canadian Historical Association, 1998); Cecil Harris, *Breaking the Ice: The Black Experience in Canadian Hockey* (Toronto: Insomniac Press, 2003); and George Fosty and Darril Fosty, *Black Ice: The Lost History of the Coloured Hockey League of the Maritimes 1895–1925* (New York: Stryker Indigo, 2004).

6 Paul Rutherford, *When Television Was Young: Primetime Canada, 1952-1967* (Toronto: University of Toronto Press, 1990), p. 245.

7 One notable exception can be found in the strong critique of US influences in hockey found in Bill Roche, ed., *The Hockey Book* (Toronto: McClelland and Stewart, 1953).

8 This discussion draws on our earlier work in *Hockey Night in Canada: Sport Identities and Cultural Politics* (Toronto: Garamond Press, 1993), pp. 131-33.

9 The Canadian economist Colin Jones notes how NHL owner James Norris argued as late as the mid-1960s that NHL owners' involvement in hockey was more for the "love of the game" than for profit. By the same token, league commissioner Clarence Campbell testified before a government committee that the NHL was a "public institution" more than a business. See Jones, "The Economics of the National Hockey League," in Richard S. Gruneau and John Albinson, eds., *Canadian Sport: Sociological Perspectives* (Toronto: Addison-Wesley, 1976).

10 Aspects of Eagleson's prominent place in hockey, his failings, and subsequent downfall, have been discussed in several provocative works, including David Cruise and Alison Griffiths, *Net Worth: Exploding the Myths of Pro Hockey* (Toronto: Viking, 1991); Bruce Dowbiggin, *The Defence Never Rests* (New York: Harper Collins, 1993); and Russ Conway, *Game Misconduct: Alan Eagleson and the Corruption of Hockey* (Toronto: Macfarlane, Walter and Ross, 1993).

11 Examples include William R. McMurtry (commissioner), *Investigation and Inquiry into Violence in Amateur Hockey* (Ministry of Community and Social Services, Government of Ontario, 1974); and Gilles Neron and Jean-Noel Bilodeau, *Violence in Hockey* (Report submitted to Minister of Sport, Claude Charron, Government of Quebec, 1977). One of the earliest book-length critiques of hockey violence can be found in Gary Ronberg, *The Violent Game* (Englewood Cliffs, NJ: Prentice Hall, 1975).

12 Jack Scott, *The Athletic Revolution* (New York: The Free Press, 1971).

13 Jim Bouton, *Ball Four* (New York: Simon and Schuster, 1970); Dave Meggysey, *Out of Their League* (New York: Ramparts Press, 1970); Gary Shaw, *Meat on the Hoof* (New York: St. Martin's Press, 1972); Peter Gent, *North Dallas Forty* (New York: Morrow, 1973).

14 Brian Conacher, *Hockey in Canada: The Way It Is* (Toronto: Gateway Press, 1970); republished in 1971 (Toronto: Pocket Books) under the title *So You Want to be a Hockey Player?*

15 See Derek Sanderson (with Stan Fischler), *I've Got to Be Me* (Boston: Dodd, Mead, 1970); and Stan Mikita, *I Play to Win* (Toronto: Pocket Books, 1970).

16 Bruce Kidd and John Macfarlane, *The Death of Hockey* (Toronto: New Press, 1972).

17 Roger Noll, ed., *Government and the Sports Business* (Washington: The Brookings Institution, 1974).

18 Much of this research from the early 1970s can be found reprinted or summarized in Richard S. Gruneau and John G. Albinson, eds., *Canadian Sport: Sociological Perspectives* (Toronto: Addison-Wesley, 1976).

19 We summarize and discuss these two viewpoints in greater detail in Gruneau and Whitson, *Hockey Night in Canada,* pp. 11-30.

20 The most important academic source underlying this view is Johann Huizinga, *Homo Ludens* (Boston: Beacon Press, 1955, originally published in 1938). For a discussion of the role of this viewpoint in the Olympic tradition see Richard Gruneau, "When Amateurism Mattered: Class, Moral Entrepreneurship and the Winter Olympics," in Larry Gerlach, ed., *The Winter Olympics: From Chamonix to Salt Lake City* (Salt Lake: University of Utah Press, 2004).

21 There are actually two related lines of development in the 1960s and early 1970s here: one coming from within the field of physical education and the other from within the more formal discipline of academic history. In Canada, for example, the first line of development is represented in the pioneering work of Max and Nancy Howell, and, more notably, in the many doctoral dissertations on sport history produced by Max Howell's students at the University of Alberta. See Max Howell and Nancy Howell, *Sports and Games in Canadian Life* (Toronto: Macmillan, 1969). A University of Windsor sport historian, Alan Metcalfe, extended this descriptive historical tradition and pushed it in new directions by focusing on topics such as "Organized Sport and Social Stratification in Montreal, 1840–1901," in Gruneau and Albinson, eds., *Canadian Sport: Sociological Perspectives*; and "Working Class Physical Recreation in Montreal," *Working Papers in the Sociological Study of Sports and Leisure*, vol. 1 (2) (Queen's University Centre for Sport and Leisure Studies, 1978). Sport was also finding its way into more mainstream historical work in Canada, notably through the influences of Toronto's Bruce Kidd and the Carleton university historian S.F. Wise, both of whom wrote for academic and popular audiences. See Bruce Kidd, "The Continentalization of Canadian Sport: Football," *Canadian Dimension* 6(2), 1969; Kidd and Macfarlane, *Death of Hockey*; S.F. Wise and Douglas Fisher, *Canada's Sporting Heroes* (Toronto: General Publishing, 1974); and S.F. Wise, "Sport and Class Values in Old Ontario and Quebec," in W.H. Heick and R. Graham eds., *His Own Man: Essays in Honour of A.R.M. Lower* (Montreal: McGill-Queen's University Press, 1974). By the early 1970s, historical writing on sport in Canada was also influenced by new directions in labour history and cultural history in Europe, led by people such as the British historian E.P. Thompson. Notable examples of Thompson's influences can be found in Canadian writing on sport in the 1970s in Robert Malcolmson's work on *Popular Recreations in English Society, 1700–1850* (Cambridge: Cambridge University Press, 1973) and in Bryan Palmer's discussion of baseball in *A Culture in Conflict: Skilled Workers and Industrial Capitalism in Hamilton Ontario, 1860–1914* (Montreal: McGill-Queen's University Press, 1979).

22 Although he spends very little time discussing popular sporting recreations, E.P. Thompson's book *The Making of the English Working Class* (Harmondsworth: Pelican Books, 1968) is the definitive source in this British tradition. Another definitive work in this tradition, Richard Hoggart's book, *The Uses of Literacy* (London: Penguin, 1958), notes the importance of "football" in British working-class life. By the early 1970s the emerging "cultural studies" approach to sport was evident in works such as Ian Taylor, " Soccer Consciousness and

Soccer Hooliganism," in Stanley Cohen, ed., *Images of Deviance* (London: Penguin, 1971) and Charles Critcher, "Football and Cultural Values," *Working Papers in Cultural Studies*, no. 1 (University of Birmingham Centre for Contemporary Cultural Studies, 1972).

23 Callaghan's references to hockey are aptly covered in several recent edited collections; see Doug Beardsley, ed., *Our Game* (Vancouver: Polestar Books, 2000) and Michael P. Kennedy, ed., *Words on Ice: A Collection of Hockey Prose* (Toronto: Key Porter, 2003).

24 Reprinted in Al Purdy, *The Caribou Horses* (McClelland and Stewart, 1995). An assessment of Purdy's hockey poetry can be found in Rob Winger, "This Combination of Ballet and Murder: Some Thoughts on Hockey Poetry in Canada," *Arc* 53 (Winter, 2004).

25 See the references to hockey in Hugh Hood, *Around the Mountain* (Toronto: Peter Martin, 1967), and Hugh Hood, *Strength Down the Centre: The Jean Beliveau Story* (Scarborough, ON: Prentice Hall, 1970).

26 Some useful examples of MacLennan's and Richler's writing on hockey can be found collected together in Dick Wimmer, ed., *The Fastest Game: An Anthology of Hockey Writing* (Indianapolis: Masters Press, 1997).

27 Peter Gzowski, *The Game of Our Lives* (Markham, ON: Paperjacks, 1983) and Hoggart, *Uses of Literacy.*

28 Ken Dryden, *The Game* (Toronto: Macmillan, 1983).

29 Roch Carrier, *The Hockey Sweater* (Toronto: Tundra, 1985).

30 Roy MacGregor, *The Last Season* (Toronto: Macmillan, 1983).

31 Ken Dryden and Roy MacGregor, *Home Game* (Toronto: McClelland and Stewart, 1989).

32 On the social and cultural implications of the Gretzky trade, see S.J. Jackson, "The Gretzky Crisis and Canadian Identity in 1988: Rearticulating the Americanization of Culture Debate," *Sociology of Sport Journal*, 11 (1994); a broader discussion of the issue of "culture" and free trade that captures some of the critical sentiment of the time can be found in R. Davies, "Signing Away Canada's Soul: Culture, Identity and the Free Trade Agreement," *Harper's* (278) 1989.

33 Cruise and Griffiths, *Net Worth.*

34 See Conway, *Game Misconduct.*

35 Eric Hobsbawm and Terence Ranger, eds., *The Invention of Tradition* (Cambridge: Cambridge University Press, 1983).

36 *Sport in Canada: Everybody's Business* (Ottawa: Government of Canada, 1999), Report of the Sub-Committee on the Study of Sport in Canada, Standing Committee on Canadian Heritage.

37 For a fuller discussion, see D. Whitson, J. Harvey, and M. Lavoie, "The Mills Report, the Manley Subsidy Proposals, and the Business of Major-League Sport," *Canadian Public Administration* 43, 2 (2000), pp. 127-56.

38 Roy McGregor, "Cultural Power Play," *The Globe and Mail*, April 10, 2004.

39 See also Gzowski, *Game of Our Lives*, pp. 127-30.

PART ONE

Hockey in Contemporary Canadian Culture

CHAPTER ONE

Whose Sweater Is This?
The Changing Meanings of Hockey in Quebec

■ JEAN HARVEY

What is a national sport? It is a sport that crops up from the essence of a nation, that is, from its soil and its climate. Each time, playing hockey is to repeat again that men have transformed the immobile winter, the frozen land, the suspended life and that all of this they have transformed into a buoyant, vigorous and passionate sport.[1]

After entering my classroom at the University of Ottawa, I reach the podium and start up the multimedia system. I will introduce my lecture on sport and French-Canadian identities with a film, Roch Carrier's *Le chandail* (The hockey sweater). In this now classic film, based on a story set in the 1950s, a young French-Canadian boy, a fan of *les Canadiens,* gets trapped into wearing a Toronto Maple Leafs jersey while playing at his rural Quebec village rink. This situation leads him into a series of problems with the parish priest as well as with his friends, all of whom are wearing Montreal Canadiens jerseys with Maurice Richard's number nine on the back.

While the multimedia system warms up, I glance at my students. Almost all of them are French Canadians; the rest are mostly products of French immersion schools, with a few brave individuals taking on the challenge of their first class in French. Some of them wear hockey paraphernalia; and I notice a New Jersey Devils sweater and a cap of the Colorado Avalanche, among others. No Montreal Canadiens, no Ottawa Senators, no Toronto Maple Leafs? When I question my students about why they choose to wear these team colours, one says he is a fan of New Jersey goaltender Martin Brodeur; another argues that the Avalanche are a great hockey team that were once the Quebec Nordiques; a third just believes that the jersey of the Mighty Ducks looks cool. Why are none of them wearing a Canadiens sweater? Isn't it the club of French Canadians? Isn't there a francophone player on the Montreal club whom they can identify with? Patrice Brisebois or Jose Théodore perhaps? And if not Montreal, isn't Ottawa the home of the Sens?

Apparently, as this example implies, hockey has undergone a change of meaning among French-speaking Canadians; and that shift is what I propose to explore here, starting from the beginnings of the involvement of French Canadians in the sport. In particular I look at four historical transitions that shaped, and then reshaped, the meanings attached to professional hockey in Quebec over the course of the twentieth century. The important shifts in meaning, as I see them, are reflected in the transitions from J. Ambrose O'Brien to George Gillett (as owners of the Montreal Canadiens), from Aurèle Joliat to Saku Koivu (as *les Canadiens'* star players), from the Forum to the Bell Centre (as the Canadiens' home rink), and from Radio-Canada to RDS (as the team's main broadcaster). These transitions, in turn, reflect larger historical changes: changes in the business of professional hockey and its typical owners; in the participation of French Canadians in professional hockey as players and local heroes; in the social meanings and functions of the arenas where the Canadiens have played; and in the meanings and values attached to the Canadiens as a media product.

These various transitions relate to the history and the social role of Montreal's *Les Canadiens*, that emblematic club created by and owned for most of its history by English Canadians, but crafted for French Canadians. Indeed, *Le club de Hockey Canadien* would become, from very early in its history, a mirror as well as a vector of French-Canadian struggles for equality in Canada and for the recognition of their identity as a people and as a nation, within or eventually outside of Canada. I should note at the outset that the analysis offered here of the changing meanings of *Les Canadiens* should not be read as a comprehensive treatment of hockey in Quebec. I mention the Quebec Nordiques only briefly, and I do not attempt to cover community hockey at all. Moreover, in an analysis focused on changes in professional hockey, I do not discuss women's hockey, which in recent years has grown rapidly in Quebec.

Nonetheless, contrary to a current myth that has hockey emerging out of the frozen ponds of Canada's winter, in his answer to the question "What is a national sport?" Roland Barthes reminds us that the key issue is what Canadians have made of their encounters with the weather and the landscape. Canadians themselves are the source of hockey's deep-rooted meanings and myths. Drawing from Barthes's *Mythologies*, Richard Gruneau and David Whitson propose that the myth that hockey is a product of Canada's nature "creates a kind of cultural amnesia about the *social* struggles and vested interests ... that have always been part of hockey's history."[2]

Yet for Michael Robidoux:

> Hockey is more than a mythological construct; it is a legitimate expression of Canadian national history and identity. Hockey *does* speak to issues of gender, race, ethnicity, and region in this nation, albeit not in an entirely positive manner. For this reason, hockey moves beyond symbol and becomes a metaphoric representation of Canadian identity.[3]

Adopting (and adapting) Robidoux's idea, I will argue here that hockey has historically served to represent and give voice to French-Canadian identities—that is, to those who first imagined themselves as French Canadians but are now mostly Quebecers. Still, just as there is more than one Canadian identity, there are also several French-Canadian identities that we need to address when we consider the changing meanings of hockey in French Canada and, more specifically, in Quebec.

French Canadians in Hockey: 1880–1909

In the last three decades of the nineteenth century, 80 per cent of the Quebec population was still living in rural areas; however, the industrialization and urbanization of Quebec were gaining momentum.[4] Rural Quebec social life, organized around the parish, was dominated by the priest and the local elites: lawyers and notaries, landowners, and physicians. The influence of parish priests was felt well beyond their role as guardians of the parishioners' souls; it extended to all aspects of social and private life. The Quebec clergy of that time promoted a traditional way of life and a conservative view of all aspects of politics. In fact, it relentlessly boosted its ultramontane vision of society,[5] and closely monitored the daily life of the people, including their recreation. For the conservative circles of the Church, full control of French-Canadian society was the best strategy for the preservation of the French culture in Canada. If, through massive English immigration, the British authorities slowly succeeded in placing French Canadians in a minority position in Canada, the French Canadians could best survive as a people under the protection of the Church. Religion and the French language would be the two pillars of French survival on this continent.

Several factors added to the power of the Catholic Church in Quebec. First, the Canadian state gave the provinces effective authority in key social sectors—education, health care, and social services—and in several provinces, including Quebec, provision of these services was deputized to the churches. In Quebec, moreover, the English authorities saw the Catholic Church as an ally in the exercise of social control over French Canadians. After all, the highest ranks of that Church had proved their loyalty to the Crown with their condemnation of the 1837–38 uprisings. Moreover, the pyramidal structure of parishes and dioceses within the Catholic Church created an effective communications network, facilitating not only dissemination of the official Church position on any issue of importance but also a close monitoring of any cross-currents in the field.[6]

Overall, how strong was the power of the Church? This power was, to begin, mostly cultural because the English retained firm control over the economy and the state apparatus, despite the presence of some French Canadians in these sectors. Then too, as with all forms of hegemonic power, it was never complete. French Canadians did not always obey the orders of the clergy, and in liberal circles, such as the Institut Canadien, there was opposition to the Church's stranglehold on Quebec society and interest in the benefits of sports and physical education. For example, as early as 1848, Sir Étienne Taché made a speech at the Institut Canadien arguing for the importance of introducing physical education in the classical colleges, where intellectual work was everything.[7]

However, to protect its faithful from assimilation the Catholic Church used two main strategies. First, it strongly condemned all cultural products of Anglo-Canadian society, including sports and the arts. Second—and this had become a systematic enterprise by the early 1930s—it created a whole range of parallel organizations in order to curtail the contact that young French Canadians might have with the forces of assimilation. In the very different context of 1960s Ontario, "ethnocultural" church leaders would also establish their own sports (and youth) organizations, precisely in an effort to keep their youth attached to their own communities and away from the assimilative influences of "mainstream" institutions.[8]

In the meantime, though, in the early part of the twentieth century the dominant conservative forces within Quebec's clergy forcefully condemned any form of leisure and entertainment that was not under their own moral and organizational control. This approach was especially true for sports. For example, according to Donald Guay, the Church strongly condemned the participation of French Canadians in horse racing,[9] a sport that was fingered not only because it was an English institution and facilitated contact with English culture, but also because betting and public alcohol consumption, not to mention the occasional fights that broke out, were contrary to the behaviour expected of a responsible family man. Horse racing was thereby constructed as a menace to the French-Canadian family structure.

At a deeper level, conservative elements in the Catholic Church were dubious about any leisurely physical activity, including sport, lest this result in too much attention paid to the body to the detriment of the much more important soul. The body is the receptacle of the soul, but its instincts also make it vulnerable to evil influences; thus, to cultivate the body through sport (let alone worship physical beauty or prowess) was seen by the Church as socially dangerous. It was in this social context, then, and against this kind of moral opposition, that modern sports made their appearance in Montreal and other major Canadian cities in the late nineteeth century.

Still the Church's attitude didn't prevent French Canadians from getting involved in sports. For example, in the first lacrosse match between whites and First Nations people in 1844, the white team was composed of a majority of French Canadians.[10] Indeed, even as the clergy continued to exercise strong control over popular life in rural Quebec, their hold was much less secure in towns and cities, especially Montreal. Both the French-Canadian bourgeoisie and working class were attracted to sports, and quickly became involved, despite the Church's position.[11] Nonetheless, clerical opposition helps to explain why French Canadians became involved in hockey later than did the English and Irish of Montreal. Another factor was that until late in the nineteenth century, Montreal's main sports organizations and clubs were run by the English, for the English, with only a token presence by a few members of the French-Canadian bourgeoisie.

No information is available on how many French Canadians were present at the first recorded hockey game, held at the Victoria Skating Rink on March 3, 1875. We know, though, that with a few notable exceptions, French Canadians were largely absent from the world of public, "official," sport until the 1890s. According to most observers, it was in this decade that French Canadians began to get seriously involved in the game of hockey.[12]

The first two significant French-Canadian hockey clubs were those of the Collège Sainte-Marie and Mont St-Louis, two bilingual Catholic colleges.[13] The influence of the Irish was very important, according to Michel Vigneault, in introducing their French schoolmates to competitive hockey.

In 1898, the Irish built their own college (Loyola) and parted physical company with their French friends. The ties between the two would remain strong, however, and play a critical role in the French gaining entry to Montréal's game. Not only did the first French players in the senior league play for the Shamrocks (Belcourt and Ernest Pagnuelo in 1897, Théophile Viau and Louis Hurtubise in 1902), but perhaps even more indicative of the Irish support—and how crucial it was—is the fact that the Shamrocks always voted in favor of having a French-Canadian team join the senior hockey ranks while the other teams did not accept the French until 1905.[14]

The first French hockey clubs without college affiliations were le National and the Montagnard. Le National was originally created in 1894, the first year of existence of the Association Athlétique d'Amateurs le National (AAAN), a multi-sport organization that was an initiative of French-Canadian businessmen who wanted to emulate the MAAA (Montreal Amateur Athletic Association) model.[15] The organization's mission was clearly stated; it was to get French Canadians more involved in sports. However, the initiative was also patriotic; indeed, for its founding members (not unlike what Pierre de Coubertin was arguing in France, at about the same time), getting French youth involved in sport was a national duty. The goal of the AAAN was to demonstrate "that our race, in the world of sport like in other spheres of life, is not inferior to the other races."[16] Thus, one AAAN board member, Laurent-Olivier David, publicly advocated "the importance, for French-Canadian youth, to enroll in this essentially national club. The strength of the growing generation must be developed through gymnastics, athletic exercises, etc. The English play almost all sports and French-Canadians remain indifferent. They must embark in the movement."[17]

Le National sponsored many kinds of sporting activities, including a lacrosse team and a hockey team. In hockey, le National played mostly exhibition games during its first years of existence. However, the club joined the Federal Amateur Hockey League (FAHL) in 1904 and then moved to the Canadian Amateur Hockey League (CAHL) in 1905. The Montagnard Hockey Club, which had been created in 1898 by the famous snowshoe club of the same name, joined the FAHL in 1905. If there is a consensus among historians that French Canadians were, with few exceptions, excluded from the English social clubs that brought organized sports to Montreal (and, indeed, to Canada) in the late nineteenth century, and that French Canadians were not encouraged to practise games in their Church-run school system, there is also evidence that, at least in Montreal and Quebec City, they were as interested in sports as were other ethnic groups in these communities. Indeed, even though the first real French-Canadian hockey club didn't emerge before 1894, as early as 1896 a sport journalist in *La Presse* proclaimed hockey as the national sport of Canada[18] —a strong indication that hockey already meant a lot for at least some French Canadians, and that hockey could quickly become an arena for ethnic representation and rivalry.

"Representative Sport": The Club of a Nation, 1909–64

According to Donald Guay and Gilles Janson, that French Canadians became interested in hockey, and indeed in sport in general, was a function of their progressive acculturation to English culture. For them, sport was a cultural practice foreign to French-Canadian culture, which at that time largely manifested the traditions and practices of a rural society. Therefore, even to take up competitive sports, and the time commitments and social practices associated with the development of organized sport in Montreal, was itself an indicator of cultural assimilation. Here, Guay and Janson closely reflect the official position of the Catholic Church. Conversely, I share the opinion of Jean-Pierre Augustin and Christian Poirier that French Canadians' enthusiastic engagement with sports, and especially hockey, is better seen as an example of a subordinate people's appropriation of practices *from* the dominant culture than as an example of assimilation.[19] This is not exceptional in the history of sports. Arjun Appadurai treats the taking up of cricket in the Indian subcontinent in this way, and C.L.R. James develops a similar analysis of the meanings of cricket in the West Indies.[20] In the first half of the twentieth century, then, French-Canadians enthusiastically took up hockey and made it a symbol of their national identity, of their fight for survival and for the survival of their culture, on an English-speaking continent and within a country dominated by the English.

Sport has in many places played an important role in the imagination of nation,[21] and in Canada hockey became especially important in the French-Canadian imagination. The Montreal Canadiens became the *porte-étendards* of the French presence in North America, and this in turn explains why it was so important that the Canadiens were a winning club, a club that could beat the Anglos, and especially the Toronto Maple Leafs. What warrants closer examination, here, though, is the idea of "representative sport," for it is the tradition that sports teams "represent" the communities they come from that has helped to make the place of sport in modern popular culture. As Alan Ingham, Jeremy Howell, and Todd Schilperoort remark: "'Representation'—whether it is used in the Durkheimian sense of an organically produced signifying practice that binds people together as a 'we,' or in the more typical sense of [agents] acting on behalf of the community—presumes bonds of sentiment and loyalty among … the symbol, the agent, and the collectivity."[22]

At the beginning of the twentieth century in Canada, though, most sporting competition took place within cities rather than between them, and sports clubs represented the ethnic and religious communities found in most Canadian cities of that period. Metcalfe has shown how in the late nineteenth century, sports competition in Montreal was organized by private clubs that gave social form to upper- and middle-class identities, as well as to Protestant and Catholic affiliations, and to the English, Irish, and French communities that were significant in Montreal in those years.[23] This pattern, in which club teams were made up of members of the social group they "represented," and games between teams with names like Thistles or Shamrocks re-enacted the typical local rivalries of that time, was repeated across the country. Rooting for the home team, when this meant members of the local community or club, was the normal, even the "natural" response. However, as better travel links made intercity competition possible, and as professionalism—the hiring of "agents" from elsewhere to represent a community—became more and more normal, the meanings associated with "representative" sport would become more complicated.[24]

Some of these complications are apparent in the founding and subsequent history of Le Club de Hockey Canadien. On December 4, 1909, the newly formed National Hockey Association held a meeting in Montreal's Windsor Hotel. At the initiative of J. Ambrose O'Brien (who was also owner or part-owner of three other clubs in the NHA, in Renfrew, Cobalt, and Haileybury), the league agreed to establish a Montreal-based franchise to be composed exclusively of French-Canadian players: *Les Canadiens*. Why? First, in Montreal, there was the tradition in which the city's amateur teams had clear ethnic identities. Second, the newly created league wanted to attract French-Canadian fans, of whom there were many, away from its rival league (the renamed Canadian Hockey Association) of which le National was a part. Even the name of the new club was carefully chosen to assist in the project of constructing them as the team of French-speaking Montreal. In the eighteenth and nineteenth centuries, the word *Canadiens* was used to identify a very precise national group, namely descendants of the original French settlers in Canada. After the Conquest, French Canadians continued to think of themselves as the original *Canadiens*, while the conquerors and the later British settlers and other immigrants they brought to Canada were collectively referred to as "the English." Even after Confederation, people distinguished "English-Canadians" from "*les Canadiens*," and only in the twentieth century did the French start to identify themselves as French Canadians, while Anglo Canadians started to identify themselves as Canadians.[25]

However, despite O'Brien's plan to make the team the representatives of Montreal's French-speaking population (he stated publicly, for example, that he wanted to sell the club to French-Canadian owners as soon as possible, and this was achieved one year later), French-speaking Montreal did not immediately accept the Canadiens as their club. Le National was the established francophone club, and O'Brien's initiative was seen by many as simply an attempt to buy their support for the new NHA team.[26] However, after the dismantling of Le National in 1910, French Canadians came gradually to support the Canadiens. Over time, several factors would help the team become the representatives, or "national team," of French Canada. Most important, perhaps, the francophone press quickly became a strong booster of the club, giving them lots of coverage—and in ways that highlighted their representative role. Later on, French broadcasting of Canadiens' games on radio (1938) and eventually on TV (1952) not only brought "the Habs" into many Montreal-area homes, but also spread their drawing power and mystique beyond the city, attracting French-Canadian support from across Canada.

When the Canadiens moved into the Forum in 1924, the team's national status was reinforced in several ways. Concretely, the move gave the team a building accommodating around 18,000 fans and thus ensured that the Canadiens could achieve the income necessary to compete financially with any other team. The structure of professional hockey in North America underwent dramatic changes between 1925 and 1928, when owners in smaller Canadian cities—for example, in Hamilton, and in Western Canada—found that they could not compete with teams based in the big new arenas (seating 15,000 to 20,000) being built in New York, Chicago, and other US centres. This prompted the sale of the Hamilton team to Madison Square Garden promoter Tex Rickard, and the closure of the Western Hockey League and sale of its player contracts to the new teams that were being created in the United States. The owners of the Montreal and Toronto teams recognized that they too needed arenas with comparable capacity, and despite uncertain economic conditions they were able to raise money to finance construction of the Forum and Maple Leaf Gardens. These arenas kept the two Canadian cities in the same league as New York, Boston, Chicago, and Detroit, thus helping to establish hockey's place (in that era at least) as a "major league" sport in American popular culture. Over the years, as these arenas became the sites of famous games and famous goals, and the homes of teams known throughout hockey, they also became part of the collective memory of their respective cities. They became buildings of special historical significance in the eyes of every hockey fan.[27]

Probably the most important factor in the national significance of *les Canadiens*, however, was the phenomenal success of their teams in the years from 1930 to 1980. Dynasties in almost every decade made the Canadiens by far the most successful team in the history of the NHL, with twenty-four Stanley Cups. Indeed, had the structure of professional hockey not changed dramatically in later years, the Montreal Canadiens— along with teams like the New York Yankees and soccer's Manchester United or Real Madrid—might have been considered one of the emblematic franchises of world professional sport. The Canadiens' success in their glory years was built upon their virtual monopoly on good French-Canadian players. Still, despite O'Brien's initial plan to construct the Canadiens as an exclusively French-Canadian team, subsequent owners quickly adopted a policy of fielding the strongest possible lineup in order to win. Thus Canadiens teams regularly included a mixture of French and English players.[28]

However, the Habs enjoyed a linguistic advantage in scouting and signing young talent in Quebec (especially in rural Quebec), which was reinforced by NHL/CAHA rules that, prior to the 1960s, decreed that once a boy had played for a minor team affiliated with a professional club, he remained the property of that club for as long as the club was interested.

This meant that the Canadiens effectively controlled junior hockey in Quebec in those years; and not surprisingly, just as Carrier's story "*Le Chandail*" suggests, most young boys in Quebec grew up aspiring to play for *les Canadiens*. Thus, although Canadiens teams regularly included fine English-speaking players (including Dickie Moore, the Mahovlich brothers, Larry Robinson, and Ken Dryden), it was the excellence of their French stars—Aurèle Joliat, the Richard brothers, Jean Béliveau, and Guy Lafleur—that spoke most directly to national feelings. This was especially the case, moreover, when the team was beating the Anglos. Indeed, it was their rivalries with the Montreal Maroons in the 1930s and later the Toronto Maple Leafs—each rivalries in which *les Canadiens* were successful more often than not—that arguably made the Habs, for a time, symbolic representatives of French-Canadian aspirations and frustrations.

This sense of representation remained true, moreover, even though the ownership and management of the team were not always French. There were English-Canadian investors in the Canadian Arena Company, which owned the Forum for many years, and indeed substantial English-Canadian investment in Molson's Brewery. Still, from Léo Dandurand through to the end of the Molson era the club was owned by important Montreal families and businesses, which only underscores the notion that the team was a Montreal institution and helped cement French-Canadian identifications with the club.

Owners of the Canadiens

1909: J. Ambrose O'Brien

1910–21: Le Club Athlétique Canadien, also wrestling promoter in Parc Sohmer

1921–35: Léo Dandurand

1935–57: Canadian Arena Company (Molson representative on the board)

1957–72: CAC purchased by Molson

1972–78: Charles Bronfman

1978–2001: Molson

2001: George Gillett 80%, Molson 20%

During this earlier era, one event dramatized like no other before or since the nation-alist sentiments that had attached to the *Canadiens*, and to hockey, by the 1950s. This was the famous Richard Riot, which followed the suspension of Maurice "the Rocket" Richard in March 1955 for the remainder of the season, including playoffs, by the NHL's (very Anglo) commissioner, Clarence Campbell. Richard's suspension resulted from a fight on March 13, 1955, with Hal Laycoe of the Boston Bruins. Richard was rushing to the net in an attempt to score yet another goal, Roch Carrier reminds us in his bibliogra-phy of the Rocket,[29] when Laycoe lashed out with his stick and hit the Rocket's face. Noticing that his face was bleeding, Richard threw his gloves on the ice and rushed at Laycoe. A linesman tried to control Richard by twisting one of his arms behind his back. Laycoe took advantage of this and threw punches at Richard, who was unable to defend himself. For Richard, there was only one solution; he punched the linesman and then rushed again to fight with Laycoe, who refused the invitation. The next day the Boston papers, and most of English Canada's papers, were a chorus demanding a strong penalty for Richard's actions. In Montreal the French-language papers argued that the punch to the referee was accidental and that Richard was just trying to defend himself.

A suspension for the duration of the season was unprecedented in the NHL of that era, and, from the perspective of Montreal fans, Richard was both the leader of *les Canadiens* and a player whose fiery spirit, as well as his skills, made him the target of persistent ille-gal obstruction by opposing players, offences rarely penalized by NHL referees. The per-ception was that both Richard and the *Canadiens* were being victimized by a decision that deprived the team of their best player at the most crucial part of the season. Indeed, the decision was seen by many Canadiens supporters as yet another example of discrim-ination—against Richard, against the Canadiens, against Montreal, and against French Canadians—and when Campbell took his accustomed seat at the next Canadiens home game (the league office was then in Montreal), fan hostility was manifest and insults turned into projectiles. After the first period a fan threw a tear-gas bomb in Campbell's direction, and acrid smoke quickly spread around the Forum, sending fans rushing out-side.[30] As word of the protests in the arena spread, moreover, hostilities broke out in the streets. Anti-English sentiment was rampant; English-owned businesses were attacked and looted, and order was restored only through the use of riot police.

In the days that followed the riots, Maurice Richard himself spoke out against the violence in the streets, claiming that he was simply a hockey player, not a spokesman for political grievances. However, the anger unleashed by his suspension surely showed that French Canadians in the Quebec of the 1950s resented very keenly their status as a sub-ordinate group, dominated and discriminated against by a wealthy and powerful English minority. Richard may have been "only" a hockey player, but he was a genuine French-Canadian hero and a symbol of the circumstances that many French Canadians felt themselves to be in. Indeed, some observers have claimed that the level of French anger and grievance publicly demonstrated in the Richard Riots was the spark that fuelled later and more explicitly political protests against the conservative social order in Quebec, protests that would lead to the Quiet Revolution of the 1960s.[31]

Expansion in Hockey and the Modernization of Quebec: 1965–90

Over the first forty years of their history, then, *les Canadiens* forged a special place for themselves as a club that both collectively and in the persons of their individual French-Canadian heroes served as representatives or *porte-étendards* of the aspirations of the French-Canadian people. Indeed, in this *les Canadiens* acquired significance that went well beyond the North American sports norm, in which teams represent cities and sometimes regions but rarely inspire anything that connects with real political differences or the passions associated with those differences. There are some parallels in European soccer, where Celtic and Rangers have been standard-bearers for the tensions between Glasgow's Catholic and Protestant communities, or where rival teams in Rome and Madrid have had historical associations with fascist (or royalist) and working-class political organizations. Perhaps the closest parallel, though, with *les Canadiens'* history as representatives of national aspirations can be found in the history of FC Barcelona, where *Barça* represented the aspirations of the Catalan people against royalist Spain (and against Real Madrid).[32] Between 1965 and 1990 the representative significance of the Canadiens would steadily diminish, partly as a result of changes in the structure of professional hockey, but even more because of political and social changes in Quebec. Together these different changes would weaken the relationship between the club and the people of Quebec, leaving a declining number of partisans nostalgically recalling *les Canadiens* of years past.

Changes in Professional Hockey

The changes with the most direct and obvious impacts were those in the structure of professional hockey. Most important here was the ending of the minor and junior farm systems and the introduction of the annual draft of junior-age players in 1963–64. The farm system had allowed the Canadiens (and to a lesser extent the Maple Leafs) to sign the best young players in their respective provinces at a very early age, which had in turn given the two Canadian teams (and the Detroit Red Wings, who had developed an extensive farm system in Western Canada) a decided edge over their US competitors. A universal draft became even more necessary, though, once expansion was planned for 1967, because only if the new teams (and the least successful teams in subsequent seasons) were able to draft the top juniors of their day could expansion teams ever become competitive. However, this new procedure effectively ended the Quebec-based development system that had been the foundations of Montreal's success, and it ended the Canadiens' monopoly on the best Quebec players. Within a very few years, French-

Canadian players such as Gilbert Perrault and Bernie Parent, who once would have been destined to enjoy brilliant careers with the Canadiens, wound up helping new US teams (in Buffalo and Philadelphia, respectively) to succeed. And in subsequent years this same trend dispersed successive generations of potential Quebec heroes to US-based franchises (Mario Lemieux, Raymond Bourque, Luc Robitaille, Martin Brodeur, Vincent Lecavalier, and Martin St. Louis are only a few of them).

At the same time the Canadiens' management was forced to make uncertain choices between drafting the best available players, given the team's usually lower position in the draft, and selecting players who would maintain the francophone traditions of the team. Here the team's tradition of success sometimes came into conflict with its traditions as French Canada's team; and when management did pass over French players (like Robitaille) in favour of Anglos or players of European origins, some fans and columnists in the French-language media did not hesitate to criticize what was a gradual but steady dilution in the francophone makeup of the team. Some of this dilution would probably have occurred in any event with the influx of European players into the NHL in the 1980s and 1990s. However, rather than being able to integrate selected Europeans into a team that remained French Canadian at its core, when the Canadiens lost their privileged access to Quebec talent the club quickly lost much of its representative character. The team of Maurice Richard and Jean Béliveau became a team led by Mats Naslund, and then Saku Koivu.

Moreover, although there was always a place for French-Canadian stars like Lemieux and Bourque on US-based teams, French-speaking journeyman players have often found it hard to make an enduring place on these teams (or teams based in English Canada). Like their European counterparts, some have had difficulty "fitting in" to the cultural environment, both on and off the ice, and others have had to defend themselves against stereotypes (of Europeans or "French guys") that remain all too present in the NHL subculture. Robidoux suggests: "The well-defined structure that the professional hockey community provides needs to be recognized as the discriminatory environment that it is. The hockey 'identity' does not draw only on a definitively male model, it is definitely North American, Caucasian and prejudicially English-speaking."[33] Robidoux also draws attention to research by Marc Lavoie that demonstrates that given French-Canadians' history of success in hockey and given the number of French-speaking players produced in the Quebec Junior Hockey League, French-Canadian players are significantly underrepresented in the lineups of all NHL teams, and especially in Canadian teams other than the Canadiens. They are also greatly underrepresented on defence, despite superior statistics, and among third- or fourth-line players, where differences in talent are marginal and the cultural preferences of coaches may be decisive.[34]

Pertinent in this regard are the advent and demise of the Quebec Nordiques. Quebec City was home to a successful WHA team through the 1970s, and when the WHA folded

Quebec was one of four WHA teams (along with Edmonton, Winnipeg, and Hartford) that were absorbed into the NHL for the 1979–80 season. The Nordiques enjoyed modest successes on the ice, led by genuine French-Canadian stars, including Jean-Claude Tremblay, Réjean Houle, Réal Cloutier, Marc Tardif, and, later on, Michel Goulet. They had won the WHA's Avco Cup in 1977, and at their best they were good enough to compete with the Canadiens in the 1980s and 1990s. For fans based in Quebec City, this competition galvanized a long-standing rivalry between the two cities. The rivalry between the clubs was to be known as *La guerre de la 20* (a reference to the highway running between Montreal and Quebec). In the beginning, indeed, one motivation of the Quebec City businessmen who gained the WHA franchise was a gesture of vengeance against the Canadiens, the team that for years had blocked applications by Quebec for an NHL franchise in order to maintain its own stranglehold on Quebec fans and Quebec players. Once in the NHL, moreover, the Nordiques were not slow to play to nationalist sentiments in their efforts to win fans away from the Canadiens. It was no coincidence that the colours of the club were the same as those of the Quebec flag or that the fleur-de-lys was highly visible on the shoulders of the jersey. Marius Fortier, a member of the original ownership group, wrote of their nationalist aspirations:

> We would bring the proof to [the Quebec] people ... that it is possible to come out of its condition of *porteur d'eau* and to build a successful enterprise, despite the odds, the mocking remarks, the pitfalls. Our team constituted the only French speaking club in professional sport in North America.[35]

He mentions that one of the goals of the club was to provide a new avenue for francophones to play professional hockey.[36]

It is important, however not to overstate the nationalist agenda of the early Nordiques. Once the Nordiques joined the NHL, they, too, would get their young talent through the universal draft, which would dilute the French character of the team just as it had with the Canadiens. It would not be long before the team of Jean-Claude Tremblay and Réjean Houle became a team led by the Stastny brothers (from Czechoslovakia) and a long list of English players. Moreover, the Nordiques had several seasons in which a good record in the regular season was followed by early exits from the playoffs, in stark contrast with the Canadiens' proud record of being at their best when it mattered most. And although the Canadiens struggled (by their standards) during the 1980s, they won the Stanley Cup in 1986 and reached the final in 1988. There was never any point, therefore, at which the Nordiques seemed ready to assume the Habs' mantle as French-Canada's "national team," and although Quebec fans certainly regretted the team's departure for Colorado in 1995, its demise did not have the larger significance that any departure of *les Canadiens* from Montreal surely would have.

In the end the Nordiques may be remembered more for the refusal of junior superstar Eric Lindros to sign with the team. Lindros didn't want to live in the French environment of Quebec City, taking an attitude that not surprisingly offended many fans.
However, the larger issue in his refusal seems to have been his desire to play in a major
media market that afforded opportunities for endorsements and other ancillary income
that a small city like Quebec (or Edmonton) simply could not provide. The Lindros
affair thus early on raised issues of revenue potential, especially media revenues, that
would affect the Canadiens in the 1990s. Finally, it may be germane to note that *La
guerre de la 20* was also a war between the two giant Canadian beer companies, pitting
Carling-O'Keefe's Nordiques against Molson's Canadiens. The rivalry was for some
years a strong marketing tool for the two breweries, underscoring another kind of connection between professional sport and other business agendas.

The Modernization of Quebec

For now, though, I want to shift readers' attention to the changes that transformed
Quebec between 1960 and 1980, for in altering the nationalist "meanings" that attached
to *les Canadiens* these have been at least as important as the changes in hockey outlined
above. It is worth returning, for a moment, to the phenomenon of the Quiet Revolution,
introduced at the end of our discussion of the Richard Riots. Perhaps Premier Jean
Lesage's "*Maîtres chez nous*" slogan in the campaign for the 1960 Quebec provincial
election best describes the spirit behind the Quiet Revolution. The Lesage government
of the 1960s made major changes in Quebec life, increasing the role of the Quebec state
in many spheres: education, health, social services, culture, sport, and leisure. For example, in 1966 the Parent Report led to a complete overhaul of the education system, with
the state taking control of the whole system at the expense of religious authorities.
Another thrust of the Quiet Revolution would see the Quebec government intervene in
the provincial economy in unprecedented ways. The nationalization of electricity and
the creation of Hydro-Québec was perhaps the largest and most dramatic example of
this. Just as important, though, was the creation of the Caisse de dépôt et placement,
and of the Régie des rentes du Québec, new state organizations with mandates to invest
in Quebec's economic development and support Quebec-owned companies. All of
these initiatives were designed to help the Québécois become masters of their own
economy, which had been largely controlled by English-Canadian capital to that point.
They led eventually to the emergence of (so-called) Québec Inc., a small but extremely
influential provincial business elite, an elite that still works closely with the Quebec
state to keep within the province, insofar as this is possible, the economic tools to nurture development and keep the economy in Québécois hands.

More importantly, the Quiet Revolution represented a new phase in French nationalism. The former ideology of *survivance*, championed by the Quebec clergy and

supported by conservative intellectual and political elites, quickly changed into a "national" affirmation ideology promoted by liberal intellectual and political elites in Quebec. In this new ideology, French Canadians no longer saw themselves as a dominated minority, but rather as a majority within Quebec—and one confident of its capacity to run its own *affaires*. This also meant a new collective identity, centred on Quebec. French Canadians began to think of themselves as Québécois rather than as French Canadians; and one of the results of seeing themselves as a nation, within or eventually outside Canada, was the resurgence of language politics. After two centuries of relative calm on the issue of language, during which French Canadians spoke the language of the English bosses even when they were a strong majority in the province, in the early 1960s Quebecers started to assert that the language of the majority should prevail.[37] This new assertiveness was resisted by the English minority, a significant portion of whom didn't accept that they had to live a bit differently than they would if they were in Boston or Toronto (and indeed they still don't, as was apparent in the recent separation of Westmount and other West Island cities from the amalgamated City of Montreal). Nonetheless, making French the language of business and public life in Quebec has been a core element in the program of the Parti Québécois.

The PQ won election in November 1976 and moved swiftly to enact Bill 101 establishing French as Quebec's official language while preserving the rights of the English minority to educate their children in English schools. Parti Québécois policy has also promoted the separation of Quebec from Canada, inspired by yet another stage in Quebec's nationalism, leading to two referendums in which voters narrowly rejected this path. However, PQ activists continue to believe that separation is the only way, ultimately, to protect Quebec's French culture and character, and to assert Québécois control over the province's economic development.

The changes in Quebec society would slowly erode hockey's privileged place as the primary feature of French-Canadian sports culture. One aspect of the modernization of Quebec's education system in the 1960s was the introduction of compulsory physical education, from grade one up to the CEGEP, the post-secondary colleges. Moreover, physical education now had to be taught by university-trained physical educators, at least at the secondary and college levels. These professional physical educators put a new emphasis on the educative potential of sports and introduced young Quebecers (both male and female) to alternatives to the traditional team games (hockey, football, baseball). This was further reinforced by the presence and the aftermath of the 1976 Olympic Games in Montreal, which exposed Quebec youth to a whole array of new sports, thereby broadening their sporting horizons. For example, European handball has thrived in Quebec since the 1970s, and Quebec has become the primary source of players for the Canadian team. Since the 1980s, moreover, soccer has grown exponentially in Quebec; and more recently, Quebec athletes have been pioneers in establishing short-track speed skating and freestyle skiing as new Olympic sports. These new initiatives have led to the emergence of new Quebec heroes, as well as new traditions in which Quebec is seen to excel. In short, since the 1960s, Quebec youth have become involved—and excelled—in many sports other than hockey, which has contributed to hockey becoming less central to Quebec sport culture and to Quebecers' sense of themselves than was the case before the Quiet Revolution.

In an introductory essay to his play *Les Canadiens*, author Rick Salutin notes that on the evening of November 15, 1976—the night that the PQ was elected as the government of Quebec—the Canadiens were playing a home game, in the Forum, against the St. Louis Blues. However, it quickly became apparent to everyone in the arena, players and audience alike, that most of the fans were much more interested in the election results being flashed on the scoreboard than in what was transpiring on the ice. As it became obvious that Quebecers had elected their first nationalist government, moreover, a festive mood grew, and it became apparent that for most people in the audience the election victory mattered much more than the game. Salutin remarks on what a profound shift this was, "that the team was being *ignored*, by their *fans*, in the middle of a *game*, because of an *election*."[38] He proposes that the Richard Riots of March 1955 perhaps marked the high point in the public's tendency to identify the fate of *les Canadiens* and players like Richard with the cause of Quebec. Since then, Quebec had changed a great deal:

> [From] the Quiet Revolution in the early sixties, Quebecers began to express their sense of national pride and desire for self-assertion in ever more direct ways.... Movements arose demanding greater opportunity for francophones in the economy, and for French language rights. Provincial government activity expanded. Francophone cultural activity exploded.... And the more Quebec expressed its national feelings in these *many* ways, the less it had to channel so much of its feeling through its hockey team.... The Canadiens no longer bore the weight of all that national yearning.[39]

Corporate and Media Revenues: 1990s–Present

I want now to move to the 1990s and examine yet another set of changes that have transformed hockey in the last ten to fifteen years. First, an explosion in player salaries made it increasingly difficult for small-market franchises to survive. Second, teams had to do everything possible to maximize revenues and develop new sources of revenue. This led to, among other things, the replacement of older arenas with new ones capable of generating more revenue from concessions, from advertising and "naming rights," and from corporate seating (luxury boxes and "club" seats, both offering value-added services). It also led, in the NHL, where shared network revenues are much smaller than in other major-league sports (see chapter 8) to teams needing to do everything possible to maximize local media revenues, especially those from pay TV or cable and satellite television. Finally, all of these developments contributed to the emergence of a new type of owner in professional sport. Locally based owners (whether individuals or businesses) have frequently given way to investors with deeper pockets, often media or entertainment corporations, or others based outside the community (see chapters 8 and 12). Their investment is in a franchise (which can be moved or sold), or in the sport as content for their various media products; it is not in the city, which can be readily abandoned if their investment does not pan out.

The effects of each of these changes are reflected in the recent history of the Canadiens. Average NHL salaries rose from $180,000 in 1989 to more than $1 million ten years later (all figures US$).[40] In the 1980s teams in Edmonton and Calgary (or Montreal) could win Stanley Cups with total player budgets in the vicinity of $5 million. By the first decade of the new century teams that were spending less than $35 million usually found themselves losing their best players to free agency and rarely able to remain competitive for long.[41] For teams to be able to sign elite players to long-term contracts required predictable revenues in excess of this figure, and salaries rose only because teams in the major metropolitan markets and teams owned by major media corporations (teams in Colorado and Anaheim, for example) have actively pursued major free-agent signings (see chapter 7). Certainly, Montreal is not a small market for hockey purposes. The Forum was regularly filled to capacity, and the media revenues that the Canadiens received—from Radio-Canada for *La Soirée du hockey*, and from Quebec radio stations for carrying the games in Montreal and elsewhere—were better than those enjoyed by other teams in Canada (with the important exception of the Toronto Maple Leafs). However, the money the Canadiens could make from selling hockey, in the Forum and in the Quebec media market, was no longer sufficient to keep the team in the NHL's elite, and this shift was reflected in its declining performances in the 1990s. The Canadiens did win one Stanley Cup in 1993, but in most years they were not contenders, and they even missed the playoffs on several occasions (almost unheard of before). Although questionable personnel decisions may have played some part in this decline, it's also relevant that over the 1990s the Canadiens were no longer buyers of top talent in the free-agent market.

Clearly something had to be done if the fabled Canadiens were not to become just another hockey team, and team management made the decision to replace the tradition-rich but aging Forum with a new arena, one capable of generating substantial additional revenues. The Molson Centre opened in 1996, amid much fanfare, and quickly became an important cultural and business landmark in the city. There was also much optimism that its enhanced revenue potential would restore the Canadiens to their glory days. It seats more people (in excess of 21,000) than did the old Forum, and it has more corporate boxes and many more seats at premium prices. As a result the Canadiens' revenues from gate receipts rose to become among the highest in the NHL.

However, the team's overall financial picture was not entirely revived by the new building. The construction of the Molson Centre was financed entirely by private money, creating a major debt load for Molson and its partners. The Canadiens were thus placed at an ongoing financial disadvantage compared to quite a few US teams whose new arenas have been financed from public funds. The Canadiens also pay more in municipal property taxes than do other NHL teams. The owners have pushed for relief from this tax burden on several occasions, notably during the Mills Commission hearings in the late 1990s; but the city points out that the Molson Centre is a private business occupying some of the most valuable real estate in downtown Montreal, and that the city simply cannot afford to forego tax revenues on this valuable property without curtailing municipal services that matter to many citizens. Here, it is noteworthy that while many US jurisdictions have scrambled to attract (or keep) major league sports franchises, either by financing their places of business from public funds or by offering generous tax exemptions, Quebec has to its credit, resisted demands to subsidize professional sport.[42] Some cities would argue that Quebec has paid a steep price for this—in the loss of the Nordiques, and later the Expos. However, Quebec society has accomplished other social goals by spending public funds in other ways, and the province's rich sport culture encompasses much more than professional sports. Moreover, few would try to argue that Quebec City and Montreal are anything but thriving and culturally vibrant cities, despite the departures of professional sports teams.

Even more important than public subsidies to the Canadiens' long-term profitability is the value of the team as an advertising vehicle and a media property. In 2002, for instance, the Canadiens found it difficult to reach agreement with Radio-Canada to renew *La Soirée du Hockey* at a mutually acceptable fee. In May 2002 Radio-Canada announced that its broadcasting deal with the NHL would expire at the end of the 2001–2 hockey season because tentative talks with the cable-TV network Réseau des Sports (RDS) had failed.[43] In fact, in March RDS had concluded a four-year deal with the NHL, the Canadiens, and the Ottawa Senators for broadcast rights to a minimum of thirty regular games and playoff games up to the conference finals.[44] However, Radio-Canada's withdrawal provoked controversy not only among fans, but also in Canadian political arenas. French-speaking fans, inside and outside Quebec, would either have to watch *Hockey Night in Canada* (in English) or subscribe to cable or satellite television. Then Heritage Minister Sheila Copps, the minister responsible for national unity (including sports and the CBC) expressed concerns that "throughout Canada, the French-speaking public would not have any more access to Canadiens games on La Soirée du hockey."[45] After several parties appeared before the House of Commons Standing Joint Committee on Official Languages to comment on this issue, RDS and the hockey team began new negotiations with Radio-Canada, and a three-year deal was ultimately reached with RDS. The

CBC would broadcast between twenty and twenty-five matches on Saturday nights, as well as the Canadiens' post-season games.[46]

What's at stake here, both in the Canadiens' efforts to secure a deal with RDS to gain more television exposure than Radio-Canada's *La soirée du hockey* broadcasts can give them, and in Radio-Canada's unwillingness to guarantee more to the team than it can expect to recoup from advertisers, is the need of the Canadiens (like all sports teams) to maximize not only their revenues from media but also the value of the team to French-language broadcasters (whether RDS or Radio-Canada) in the selling of advertising. In the new economy of professional sports, it is the revenues that team owners have expected from television, revenues that until very recently have risen steadily, that have fuelled both the explosion in player salaries and the comparable rises in franchise values that have enabled some owners to sell at big profits even while recording operating losses.

In the case of the Canadiens, and in the early decades of televised hockey on the CBC and Radio-Canada, the team used to be one of hockey's primary media properties, and its revenues from broadcast television were among the league's best. Today, though, with broadcast revenues (and therefore shared revenues) either growing slowly (in Canada) or declining (in the United States), and local revenues from cable and satellite television becoming the most important source of income (and income disparity), the value to advertisers of the local market becomes crucial. The question is how much money can be made in the Montreal and Quebec markets through hockey-related advertising; and the unfortunate answer is that the value of the entire Quebec market to advertisers is distinctly less than that of the New York market, the Southern California market, or even the English-Canadian markets into which the "Leaf Nation" sells advertising. Therefore, the value of television ads on Habs' games, and thus the revenues that the Canadiens can realize from this source (and from rink advertising, the value of which derives from the size of the television audience) leaves them falling behind the league's wealthiest teams, even as they pull away from teams in some of the smaller media markets. This is true, moreover, even though Montreal has now recovered from two decades of economic difficulties, and the Quebec economy is booming.

Many of the same issues also lie at the heart of the recent and controversial sale of the Canadiens, in 2001, to US ski developer George Gillett—this after a long history, through most of the last half of the twentieth century, of being wholly or partly owned by Molson Breweries and the Molson family, both long-time fixtures in the Montreal business community. This type of ownership was consistent with other examples in North American professional sports (including Labatt's ownership of the Toronto Blue Jays) in which major brewers believed that their associations with popular sporting institutions would sell enough beer to offset any operating losses incurred by the teams. By the late 1990s, however, with the costs of sports ownership rising and the shareholders of what are publicly owned companies questioning the payoff on these operating

losses, both Canadian breweries placed their sports holdings on the market. The Blue
Jays were eventually sold to the Rogers communications empire, and it was likewise
assumed by many observers that the most likely purchaser of the Canadiens would be
BCE, the Montreal-based parent of Bell Canada and many other media enterprises,
including CTV, RDS, and TSN. This would have been consistent with a now-familiar pattern in US pro sports, in which team ownership by cable television networks provides
popular sports programming and helps to sell subscriptions. Sports ownership is thus
profitable for the cable companies, even if the teams themselves lose money on operations. In the NHL this model has proved lucrative in Colorado and Philadelphia,
enabling these teams to spend as much on players as those in the largest metropolitan
markets. What's interesting in Montreal is that BCE reportedly looked very carefully at
buying the Canadiens and decided instead to make a much smaller investment in
acquiring naming rights to the Molson Centre, which was renamed the Bell Centre in
2002. In the words of then CEO Jean Monty, "By associating our name with one of
Quebec's foremost venues, Bell hopes to reinforce its commitment to the cultural and
sporting life of Quebecers.... The Bell Centre's visibility will contribute significantly to
positioning the Bell brand and will enable spectators to enjoy an even more diversified
Bell experience."[47]

Behind this flowery rhetoric, though, BCE purchased an association with a popular
Quebec institution, but at a small fraction of the investment that owning the team
would have required. Why the company chose not to purchase the Canadiens has never
been made public; nor, indeed, have the reasons why Gillett, whose business interests
don't offer anything like the corporate synergies that owning the Montreal Canadiens
would have provided to the owners of TSN, went ahead. What's striking, however, and to
some people disturbing, is that a major Montreal company (indeed a major Canadian
company), one with obvious business synergies available if it bought the Canadiens,
apparently decided that the team was not an attractive investment. Indeed, although
most media stories focused on how the ownership of one of Quebec's "national" institutions was passing into the hands of an American, the deeper story, arguably, is that
Quebec's most powerful business interests—including Molson's, BCE, Power Corp., the
Caisse Desjardins, and other pillars of 'Quebec, Inc.'—all came to the conclusion that
NHL hockey in Montreal was no longer a good investment. Some would say that this is
simply a business judgment—and an astute one—on the NHL business model of recent
years; others might argue that with a salary cap established at any level below $40 mil-
lion, it may be Gillett who has been proved the more astute.

Mixed and Confused Messages

What is clear is that these important Quebec investors were not making a negative judgment on the future of Montreal. High-tech investment (in telecommunications and

biotech) has created many jobs for "symbolic analysts" in Montreal in recent years; meanwhile, major property investments (both in new projects, and in refurbishing hotels and retail properties in *Vieux Montréal*) have transformed Montreal's real estate market. Montreal is booming, in other words, and these companies are participating in the boom. Thus it may be that, not unlike Salutin's analysis of the declining *political* significance of the Canadiens in the "new" Quebec of the 1970s, today's Quebec business class simply has too many better opportunities to pursue (both within Quebec, and globally) to be concerned, in the ways in which their predecessors might have been, with keeping a symbolically important but economically marginal business in Quebec hands.

In the Montreal of the 1950s and 1960s, the Canadiens were read—and quite differently, by different groups in Quebec society—as *porte-étendards* of competing identities and national projects. By the 1980s their representative significance had been diminished, both by changes in the game and by larger changes in Quebec society. The Canadiens had become more like an ordinary hockey team, even though the team still had the ability to act as a rallying point for civic boosterism, not unlike most professional sports teams with any history of success.

Today, for Quebecers, hockey involves mixed and confused meanings, and the game is now just one sport among many leisure choices. Fewer Quebecers now play hockey, and the sport is no longer the national signifier that it once was. Many Quebecers still have a profound love for the game, and it's still true that when the Canadiens have a successful playoff run, Montreal comes alive with excitement that may be unmatched in any other hockey city. There are still those, often from the older generations, who cheer for *les Canadiens* as if they represented more than just a hockey team; but this identification now has more to do with nostalgia than anything else.

Nostalgic identifications can, of course, be both powerful and widely shared, as the 2002 furor over the demise of *La Soirée du hockey* demonstrated. However, the 1950s idea, in which *les Canadiens* stood for the common destiny of the French-Canadian people, is now clearly defunct. Quebecers have found new avenues for their national affirmation through politics and the economy. The club, meanwhile has not been seen as "French" for more than twenty years, and is perhaps now better understood as a brand name. In this, of course, it is no different than other North American sports franchises.

Notes

1 Roland Barthes, *Le sport et les hommes* (Montreal: Presses de l'Université de Montréal, 2004 [1961]), p. 55. Author's translation.

2 Richard Gruneau and David Whitson, *Hockey Night in Canada: Sport, Identities, and Cultural Politics* (Toronto: Garamond Press, 1993), p. 132.

3 Michael Robidoux, "Imagining a Canadian Identity through Sport: A Historical Interpretation of Lacrosse and Hockey," *Journal of American Folklore*, 115,456 (2002), p. 221.

4 See Michel Bellefleur, *L'évolution du loisir au Québec: essai socio-historique* (Sainte-Foy: Presses de l'Université du Québec, 1997), p. 17.

5 Doctrine that sees the Church authority as being superior to the authority of the state. That doctrine prevailed within the Catholic Church in Quebec from the 1840s to the 1950s, although being continuously challenged from within by its more liberal factions and from without by the governments of both Quebec and Ottawa.

6 See Jean Harvey, "Sport and the Québec Clergy, 1930-1960," in Jean Harvey and Hart Cantelon, eds., *Not Just a Game: Essays in Canadian Sport Sociology* (Ottawa: University of Ottawa Press, 1988), pp. 69-70.

7 See Jean Harvey, "Force physique, citoyenneté et réformisme modéré au Bas-Canada," *Bulletin d'histoire politique*, 11,2 (2003), pp. 77-86.

8 Robert F. Harney, "Homo Ludens and Ethnicity," *Bulletin of the Ontario Multicultural Society*, 7, 1 (1985), pp. 1-12.

9 Donald Guay, *Histoire des courses de chevaux au Québec* (Montreal: VLB, 1985).

10 See Alan Metcalfe, "Le sport au Canada français au 19e siècle: le cas de Montréal 1800-1914," *Society and Leisure*, 6,1 (1983), p. 109.

11 However, following Linteau, in his *Histoire de Montréal,* one can ask, given the tough times that working people in Montreal (many of whom were French Canadians) were living in during these decades, whether leisure, as we understand it now, was part of their lives. Leisure "… was essentially reserved for the elites. The main sports were snowshoeing, skating, curling, lacrosse, and swimming. Horse racing was popular, but it is a spectator sport. Participation sports were played in organized clubs where not everyone was welcomed, and where members needed to be able to pay membership fees. Snowshoeing is probably the sport that attracted the biggest number of participants, the most ancient club being the Montreal Snow Shoe Club (formerly the Tuque Bleue Snow Shoe Club) established in 1843 and counting six-hundred members in 1884.… Skating, which occurs at the Victoria Skating Rink, is performed within an elitist ambiance and has more to do with a mundane activity than sport. Starting from the 1880s and the 1890s, one can witness an increasing interest in sporting participation. In 1877, there were 85 sport clubs in Montréal touching ten different sports; in 1894 these numbers are respectively 245 and 23" (p. 119). "Sport in Montréal remains essentially organized and played by Anglophones. It remains also principally an activity of the elite, even if some democratization started to happen at the end of the Century" (p. 120).

12 Gilles Janson, *Emparons-nous du sport: les canadiens-français et le sport au XIXe siècle* (Montreal: Guérin, 1995); see also Guay, *Histoire du hockey au Québec* (Chicoutimi: Edition JCL, 1990).

13 Michel Vigneault, "French-Canadian Tradition." in *Backcheck: A Hockey Retrospective*, Library and Archives Canada <www.collectionscanada.ca/hockey/h36-2101-e.html>.

14 Vigneault, "French-Canadian Tradition."

15 Janson, *Emparons-nous du sport*, p. 128.

16 *La Presse*, May 17, 1895, p. 1, quoted by Janson, *Emparons-nous du sport*, p. 139. Author's translation.

17 *La Presse*, March 28, 1895, p. 1, quoted by Janson, *Emparons-nous du sport*, p. 139. Author's translation.

18 Donald Guay, *La conquête du sport* (Outremont: Lanctôt, 1997), p. 88.

19 Jean-Pierre Augustin and Christian Poirier, "Les territories symboliques du sport: le hockey comme élément identitaire du Québec," *Bulletin d'histoire politique*, 9,1 (2000) pp. 104-27.

20 Arjun Appadurai, *Modernity at Large: Cultural Dimensions of Globalization* (Minneapolis: University of Minnesota Press, 1996); C.L.R. James, *Beyond a Boundary* (London: Faber, 1964).

21 See Benedict Anderson's influential *Imagined Communities* (London: Verso, 1983); on sport and nation, see Richard Holt, *Sport and the British* (London: Heinemann, 1984), and *Sport and Society in Modern France* (London: Heinemann, 1980).

22 Alan Ingham, Jeremy Howell, and Todd Schilperoort, "Professional Sports and Community: A Review and Exegesis," *Exercise & Sport Science Reviews, 15* (1988), p. 437.

23 Alan Metcalfe, *Canada Learns to Play: The Emergence of Organized Sport, 1870-1914* (Toronto: McClelland and Stewart, 1987).

24 See David Whitson, "*Hockey and Canadian Identities: From Frozen Rivers to Revenue Streams,*" in D. Taras and B. Rasporich, eds., *A Passion for Identity: Canadian Studies for the 21st Century* (Toronto: Nelson, 2001), pp. 217-36.

25 In the 1960s, with the emergence of Quebec nationalism, French Canadians living in Quebec started to think of themselves as Quebecers or Québécois, while those in other provinces remained French Canadians. As a result, new francophone minority identities emerged: Franco-Ontarians, Franco-Albertans, francophones outside Quebec. Meanwhile the Acadians, since the English conquest and the subsequent deportation, always remained a strong French ethnic minority group within Canada.

26 François Black, *Habitants et glorieux: Les Canadiens de 1909 à 1960* (Laval: Mille-Iles, 1997), p. 25.

27 Gruneau and Whitson, *Hockey Night in Canada*, chs. 3, 4.

28 Moreover, since 1936–37 French Canadians have never been the majority of players on the Canadiens' rosters. See François Black, *Habitants et glorieux, les canadiens de 1909 à 1960* (Laval: Éditions Mille-Iles, 1997), p. 45.

29 Roch Carrier, *Le Rocket* (Montreal: Stanké, 2000), pp. 206-14.

30 Carrier, *Le Rocket*, p. 212.

31 Alain-G. Gagnon and M.B. Montcalm, *Québec: au-delà de la Révolution tranquille* (Montreal: VLB, 1992), p. 65.

32 See J. Burns, *Barca: A Peoples' Passion* (London: Bloomsbury, 1999).

33 Michael Robidoux, *Men at Play* (Montreal: McGill-Queen's University Press, 2001), p. 145.

34 Marc Lavoie, *Désavantage numérique* (Hull: Vents d'Ouest, 1998).

35 Marius Fortier and C. Larochelle, *Les Nordiques et le circuit maudit* (Sainte-Foy: Lotographie, 1978), pp. 67-68.

36 Fortier and Larochelle, *Les Nordiques*, p. 127.

37 Marc Levine, *La reconquête de Montréal* (Montreal: VLB, 1997), pp. 75-76; translated from *The Reconquest of Montréal* (Philadelphia: Temple University Press, 1990).

38 Rick Salutin, *Les Canadiens* (Vancouver: Talonbooks, 1977), p. 19.

39 Ibid, pp. 19-20.

40 For more details on salary rises through the 1990s, see Marc Lavoie, *Avantage numérique, l'argent, et la Ligue Nationale de Hockey* (Hull: Vents d'Ouest, 1997).

41 The appearance of the (relatively) low-budget Tampa Bay Lightning and Calgary Flames in the 2004 Stanley Cup final does not negate the general truth of this observation.

42 For a fuller discussion of these issues, see D. Whitson, J. Harvey, and M. Lavoie, "The Mills Report, the Manley Subsidy Proposals, and the Business of Major League Sport," *Canadian Public Administration*, 42, 3 (2000).

43 Reuters, "Fin de la legendaire Soiree du hockey a Radio-Canada," 2002
   <cf.sports.yahoo.com/020530/3/77am.html>.
44 Réseau des Sports. *La LNH à RDS pour 4 ans.*
   <www.rds.ca/information/fr.corp.communique.hockey.html>.
45 Canadian Press, *L'avenir de la Soirée du Hockey à la SRC est assuré pour trois saisons*
   <cf.sports.yahoo.com/020723/1/7ko6.html>. Author's translation.
46 Canadian Press, *La survie de la Soirée du hockey à la SRC sera discutée au Parlement*
   <cf.sports.yahoo.com/020531/1/77ml.html>, RadioCanada, *La Soirée du hockey à
   RadioCanada* <www.rogers.com/english/aboutrogers/historyofrogers/index.html>.
47 Bell Canada, *Molson Center to Become the Bell Center in September*
   <www.bce.ca/en/news/releases/bc/2002/02/26/6834.html>.

CHAPTER TWO

Selective Memory in a Global Culture: Reconsidering Links between Youth, Hockey, and Canadian Identity

■ BRIAN WILSON

According to many commentators, hockey, the cold outdoors, and dreams of professional hockey stardom still embody what it means to be a young male in Canada. For example, in a recent *Globe and Mail* article journalist Roy MacGregor suggests that the continued prevalence of art, literature, and theatre-based representations that link hockey with Canadian identity (and in many cases, with nostalgic visions of youth and childhood) is evidence that the national pastime still holds our collective imagination. The article quotes Roch Carrier, author of "The Hockey Sweater": "When I was growing up, hockey was our 'politics.' We knew there was somebody in Ottawa and somebody in Quebec—but the people who really mattered to us were in hockey."[1] A similarly vivid link between being a Canadian boy and playing hockey was made by Peter Gzowksi, a renowned broadcaster and author of *The Game of Our Lives*:

> When I talk about these things, I can get this picture of one big Dixon Park Rink [in Galt, Ontario, where Gzowski grew up] that extends from somewhere in the Maritimes … all the way to the Rockies…. It's as if it's one giant rink where every Canadian boy of my time is involved in the same game of hockey or shinny with the same rules, and the same sense of it, and the same sound-memories of your skates against the ice and the puck against the boards or the slide of the puck…. Two Canadian males can sit down and if they can talk about nothing else, they can almost always talk about that and have that shared memory. It's all built up in who we are or who we were.[2]

It would seem from these expositions by prominent Canadian pundits that the centrality of hockey in the lives of young Canadians, especially boys, is unquestionable, even natural. Moreover, because of these early experiences of playing hockey the desirable values and characteristics that a young Canadian would embrace and adopt (for example, being gritty, tough, hard-working, and determined) are consistent with orthodox perceptions of what it means to be a "good Canadian." Yet the idea that hockey is a profoundly positive and powerful connection point for Canadian youth (and for those remembering their youth) in a country renowned for the diversity of its inhabitants seems somehow implausible. It seems equally surprising that a singular cultural activity, even one invested with so much historical meaning, would be the basis for a transcendent youth experience in an era in which powerful and various global cultural influences are increasingly part of young Canadians' lives. Indeed, soccer, not hockey, is now the most popular participation sport among Canadian children aged five to fourteen.[3]

Based on these observations, it seems fair to suggest that links between youth, hockey, and Canadian identity are not as straightforward as some commentators claim. This point logically leads to a series of questions about the meaning of hockey in Canada and in Canadian youth cultures. Are claims of links between youth, hockey, and Canadian identity exaggerated? If so, how are they exaggerated, and why? Who benefits from the promotion of a mythical association between hockey, youth, and Canada? To what extent do these visions of "Canadian youth" include girls, or those from diverse racial and ethnic backgrounds? Do they equally represent youth in urban and rural settings? Are there broader cultural forces at work that have threatened feelings of community that were, at one time, reinforced through shared hockey-related experiences? Could cultural representations linking hockey, youth, and Canadiana be, in some ways, reactions to this threat? If hockey has become less prominent as a youth cultural activity in Canada, why is this? Can (and should) these trends be reversed? Is hockey only somewhat relevant for youth in Canada, and is it destined to stay that way?

Examining these kinds of questions will, I hope, help us to assess the broad idea that a link, natural or otherwise, exists between hockey, youth, and Canadian identity. My survey begins by considering how power relations and struggles among privileged and marginalized groups are embedded in the promotion of "mythical" understandings of sport—and in this case, nostalgic visions of youth, hockey, and Canadianness. A second and related consideration is how the positioning of hockey among other social practices in the lives of young Canadians has been altered and weakened because of global cultural forces and influences—which includes a discussion of globalization and its apparent impacts on both hockey and youth cultural activity. A further question is whether youth at the millennium are less committed to any one activity (sport-related or otherwise), and, in this way, have adopted "neo-tribal" cultural identities. Finally, what are the implications of these trends for hockey and its meaning in the lives of young Canadians?

To begin, though, I want to state clearly that I am *not* arguing in this chapter that hockey has become unpopular with "Canadian youth," nor am I attempting to deny personal and collective memories and experiences associated with hockey. Still, I believe that the overly simplistic and nostalgic view that hockey, youth, and Canada are inherently and positively linked is both flawed and problematic. Indeed, there are processes at work that are transforming both the meaning of hockey for many youth, and the prominence of hockey within youth-targeted media and cultural venues within Canada—

processes that may, in fact, be contributing to decreases in participation rates in hockey and, more broadly, to the diminished importance of hockey in the life worlds of many young Canadians.

Myth, Memory, Community, and Hockey

In his influential 1957 book *Mythologies*, French social theorist and literary critic Roland Barthes described "myths" as partial truths or fictions that emphasize certain versions of reality and exclude other versions. For Barthes, these myths help to conceal a structure of power that tends to favour certain groups and marginalize or oppress others. He argued that myths are effective in this capacity because they can make structures of power appear as "natural" and unchangeable—as though people played no role in creating and reinforcing them. For this reason, challenging myth-based ideologies that underlie certain societal institutions is not only difficult, but can also appear unreasonable and unnecessary.

For example, the Canadian sport historian Patricia Vertinsky has shown how women and girls in the late nineteenth and early twentieth centuries were excluded from participation in some sports because of the taken-for-granted (fictional) belief that female reproductive organs can be damaged by heavy exercise.[4] Mythical claims and convictions like this one can, and have, become so deep-seated that they begin to appear as "eternal truths." For this reason, ongoing and often radical forms of resistance and consciousness-raising are required in order to demythologize such "common-sense" understandings and ultimately to inspire and instigate social change. Scholarly research can play an important role in this process by evaluating the evidence standing behind these different myths, examining the functions that different myths serve, and showing who benefits from the maintenance of these belief systems.[5]

In their book *Hockey Night in Canada*, Richard Gruneau and David Whitson did just this, adopting Barthes's position as a departure point for critiquing some of the myths that surround hockey, especially those that embody the idea that hockey is a natural adaptation to the cold Canadian environment (an element that makes the sport "naturally" Canadian).[6] In describing the prominence of these myths, Gruneau and Whitson point to the array of instances in Canadian popular culture in which this link is made, and they offer the example of a Canadian Spirit Whiskey advertisement in which hockey is said to be "as much a part of Canada as the cry of the loon at dusk on a Northern Ontario Lake." The problem with these kinds of links between nature and hockey, according to the authors, is that they create:

> a kind of cultural amnesia about the social struggles and vested interests—between men and women, social classes, regions, races, and ethnic groups—that have always been part of hockey's history.... This naturalization of hockey, along with its lore,

traditions, and major organizations, has been easily manipulated by people with an interest in defending hockey's status quo.[7]

With these same concerns in mind, Margaret MacNeill conducted a study of media production practices during and coverage of the 1988 Calgary Olympic men's hockey tournament.[8] Through interviews with those responsible for media production, she uncovered some of the processes through which certain (mythological) understandings of the game were privileged over others. She found that these understandings or beliefs directly influenced decisions made about game coverage (for example, camera angles used, choices about what images to show and not to show; types of storylines highlighted; game commentary). These decisions, in turn, reinforced certain dominant beliefs about the game. Specifically, she found that the idea that hockey is an indigenous Canadian sport "for men and boys" was taken for granted by those working behind the scenes, and for this reason was both consciously and "instinctively" promoted on screen and through commentary. These findings reinforce concerns about what mass-mediated messages say about "who and what matters most to Canadians," and about who tends to be excluded (implicitly and explicitly) from these narratives.

While there is an abundance of writing that describes how ideologies that privilege some groups and marginalize others are embedded in and reinforced through everyday cultural practices and media messages, it is also important to acknowledge, as Gruneau and Whitson do in *Hockey Night in Canada*, that not all myths necessarily or exclusively serve dominant interests. This idea is pursued in a recent essay by Alan Ingham and Mary McDonald, who consider the view that organized competitive sports and sport teams (and the myths and memories associated with them) can be important foundations and reference points for community life and feelings of belonging. In exploring this idea, the authors suggest that sports and teams can act as "representation collectives" (a concept drawn from the seminal work of sociologist Emile Durkheim), meaning "signifiers of we-ness," objects that individuals share affective bonds with and, for this reason, nodes around which social solidarity can be generated and maintained.[9]

Despite their guarded optimism, Ingham and McDonald ultimately conclude their essay and investigation cynically, suggesting that the type of community inspired by contemporary major sports is, for the most part, temporary and fleeting, with connections between people being established only momentarily around major events. In fact, the authors' position resembles that of Barthes when they suggest that "community"— and the term's (often strategically nostalgic) associations with competitive sports and teams—becomes "perverse" when:

> the interests of domination are concealed in the concept, and when opposition to these interests is designated as selfish, that is, when city managers, in their role of

entrepreneurs of the public interest and speaking on behalf of the community as a whole, repress and exploit communities of locality in the interests of the dominant corporate groups. The capacity for concerted action among the rich and powerful is nowhere better exemplified than in their attempts to persuade ordinary citizens to give up some of their hard-earned dollars (in the form of taxes) to subsidize their projects.... Community, in the utopian sense, involves trust and obligation, and representational sport, especially in North America, provides no basis for such. Here franchise relocations are frequent, and the threat of relocation plays a large role in the blackmailing of urban centers with regard to stadium improvements.[10]

Anouk Bélanger's study of strategies used by Molson Breweries to market the move of the Montreal Canadiens' home rink from the historical Forum to the Molson Centre, a more profitable venue, similarly demonstrates how collective memories and sport-related signifiers of community and tradition have been used by private business to mobilize support for a franchise (the Canadiens) and an associated brand (Molson).[11]

The idea of "natural" links between hockey, Canada, and youth, then, might very well be seen as reflecting and reinforcing existing structures of power, marginalizing those who do not share this "Canadian experience." Conversely, and following the more optimistic position explored by Ingham and McDonald, the widely promoted connection between youth, hockey, and Canada may still be an important reference point for imagining a distinctive Canadian national community.

Collective Memory or Selective Memory? Reconsidering and Disrupting "Natural" Links between Youth, Hockey, and Canada

A problem that underlies many claims about "Canadian youth" and prototypical Canadian experiences—claims that underlie many visions of hockey as a representational collective—is that they are based on the dubious assumption that Canadian youth share a common experience or identity. Canadian journalist and author Irshad Manji elaborated on this critique in her discussion of another concept broadly understood to be a signifier of what it means to be Canadian—multiculturalism. In her 1997 Harold Innis Memorial Lecture at the University of Toronto, Manji referred to her childhood experience of coming to Canada in 1972 as a political refugee (along with over four thousand others), following her family's expulsion from Uganda under the violent dictatorship of Idi Amin. She pointed out that the year 1972, for media producers in Canada, appeared to signify only the classic Canada–Soviet Union hockey showdown during the Summit Series. In her speech she described the media coverage in the weeks leading up to the twenty-fifth anniversary of these coinciding moments in Canadian history, and raised concerns about network decision-making on issues around Canadian identity, hockey, and social cohesion:

A silver jubilee seems the perfect "hook" on which to hang stories. And yet, in monitoring our national media these last several weeks, I've heard nothing about the
story of Canada's East African refugees. Instead, CTV airs "September 1972," a two-
hour prime-time documentary recounting Paul Henderson's glorious goal. *The
Globe and Mail's* broadcast week trumpets along: "September 1972 marks the 25th
anniversary of 'the series that changed hockey' and 'the greatest moment in
Canadian sport.'" Greatest or not, why do we continue telling this story to the
exclusion of others? Network executives argue it's what Canadians still want.
Hockey stokes our solidarity with each other. Really? In a 1996 Environics poll, the
Canadians surveyed ranked hockey well under multiculturalism as a symbol of
national unity.[12]

In a study I was involved in that examined issues related to race, media, and the
sport experiences of youth, fifteen- to nineteen-year-old "Black" respondents in Toronto
explained in no uncertain terms how the hockey-youth-Canada relationship is not a
"natural" one. Several youth in the study—who were self-identified basketball players
and fans—indicated that they played sports and were part of sport cultures that they
were exposed to growing up in Southern Ontario.[13] For these young Canadians, hockey
was a sport that they might have played if their cultural environment had been different. Three statements from interviewed youth typify this position:

> When I grew up, my brother was playing soccer. From the time I was like four, I was
> playing soccer, until I was like fourteen. Then I started watching basketball, I started
> playing basketball. So what am I going to do, stand there, you know? I like to do the
> sport. I'll bet if all our friends were playing hockey, I'd probably be playing.

> If I was living out in Winnipeg, or out in Moose Jaw or something like that, I'm sure
> I'd be slapping sticks with the rest of those people, man.

> You're likely to play the sports your friends play. Whatever you're brought up playing,
> you're going to play that. In the West Indies, my parents were brought up to play
> cricket.... So, if he's my friend [referring to another respondent] and we grow up play-
> ing basketball, we're going to play that sport. It doesn't really matter where you're
> from, what colour you are. It doesn't matter. It's like your roots, wherever you grow up.

The last comment is especially pertinent because it highlights the diverse backgrounds, traditions, and cultural preferences of young people in Canada. It seems to
point to the idea that the "Canadian memory" of being young and playing or watching
hockey is more selective than collective. Alan Bairner extends this position in his book

Sport, Nationalism and Globalization, where he argues that blindness to diversity is common in statements about national identity, in Canada and elsewhere:

> Despite Toronto being recognized as the world's most ethnically diverse city, at one level Canada is still constructed as a white nation and sport has not been entirely successful in contradicting that view.... It is relatively easy for some people in multicultural societies to regard the success in certain sports, such as boxing, of members of ethnic minority groups as evidence that these are not appropriate pastimes for the hegemonic white population. Thus, those who achieve recognition in such pursuits are marginalized to the extent that their authentic citizenship—their belonging to the nation—is symbolically withheld.[14]

"Natural" associations between youth, hockey, and Canada are similarly precarious when gender issues are taken into account. As Gruneau and Whitson point out, the exclusion and mistreatment of females in and around "Canada's game" has been integrally related to the historical development of hockey as male preserve.[15] Canadian journalist Laura Robinson, a prolific writer on this topic, has detailed the ways in which females have been and are marginalized in their attempts to participate in "the Canadian game." For example, she describes how for girls interested in the hockey, ice time in local arenas is extremely difficult to come by, a point that led a Vancouver family to file a lawsuit against municipally run community centres (which was eventually settled out of court) because centre administrators were giving "an inordinate proportion of facilities and services to male hockey players."[16] (See also chapter 3.)

Robinson's work on the experiences of and problems associated with young males in minor hockey also brings into question mythical views about the relationship between youth, hockey, and Canadianness.[17] The sport's links with violence towards women, drug and alcohol abuse, and child molestation are among the concerns raised by those who critique depictions of hockey that are overly favourable. In sum, it seems more than fair to suggest that these findings of serious social problems associated with youth hockey are grounds for questioning the nostalgic, innocent, and unwaveringly positive portrayals of the game in the lives of young Canadians. Of course, there are also broader forces that are changing the sport of hockey and the popular imagery associated with the game and altering the way in which researchers understand youth leisure interests and youth (sub)cultural formations.

Youth Culture, Sport, and the Positioning of Hockey in an Increasingly Global Context

In recent years, concerns have been raised by those in the Canadian hockey world about increasing dropout rates from and decreased participation in minor and youth hockey for males. In a twelve-part series entitled "Game in Crisis" that ran in *The Globe and Mail* in 1998, reporter William Houston outlined a number of problems that have contributed to this trend in youth hockey. These included an overemphasis on winning among parents and coaches (which was linked with youth dropout), and bad publicity derived from well-known cases of emotional and physical abuse of youth and children in hockey—publicity that was apparently leading some parents to channel their children into other sports. In the final segment of the series, Houston drew on interviews with various experts around the game (especially Murray Costello, president of the Canadian Hockey Association at the time) to construct a set of potential solutions to the crisis. Recommendations included: enforcing zero tolerance for coaches who abuse children; reducing elitism in minor and junior hockey by postponing the "tier-system," which groups children by ability-level, to twelve years of age (instead of bringing it in at eight years, which was the system at the time); taking fighting and stick work out of the amateur game; and reducing the cost of hockey so that the game can be played by both the affluent and those with less money. Houston concludes his article optimistically, stating that key hockey people, like Costello, feel that "hockey can find its way back" if the focus of the game returns to "the child rather than the ego of a parent or coach."[18]

These sorts of analyses powerfully demonstrate how trends within minor hockey in Canada are not only having an important impact on the willingness of young Canadian males to participate in or continue to participate in hockey, but also setting up barriers to developing high-performing (national team and NHL) Canadian hockey players. It is also notable and commendable that Houston refers to the financial barriers that serve to exclude some youth from minor hockey. In a general way, then, it makes sense that the successful implementation of his recommendations would enhance the image of the sport and improve the hockey experience for children and youth—although the extent to which these changes would have any impact on the significance of the sport in the increasingly multifaceted and diverse cultural lives of young people is unclear.

Obscuring and Distorting "Canadian Hockey": Thinking Through the Impacts of Globalizing Forces

Even in its early formations, Canadian hockey commentators expressed concerns about the influences of the United States on "Canada's game."[19] In the past twenty years, though, these concerns have understandably been amplified as the relationship between (US) corporate interests, mass media, and the evolution of the NHL has become increasingly intertwined. Toby Miller and his colleagues describe the pervasiveness of these developments:

> Virtually every aspect of hockey—the form and content of games, the broadcasting style, personnel, franchise selections, and TV contracts—has been marketed to American audiences, advertisers and sponsors. For example, although the number of

NHL teams has more than quadrupled since 1967, only six of the 30 clubs are now located in Canada.... Additionally, some traditional "hotbeds" of hockey in relatively small Canadian cities have been overlooked or disbanded, with franchises granted or shifted to sunbelt cities that have no "natural" affinity with hockey, but possess the right demographics for U.S. owners, advertisers, sponsors, and TV networks (for example, Anaheim, Atlanta, Dallas, Phoenix, Miami, Tampa Bay, Raleigh, Nashville, and San Jose).... To many Canadian ears, teams with "showbiz" names like the Anaheim Mighty Ducks and the San Jose Sharks do not have quite the same resonance as the "culturally authentic" appellations such as the Canadiens or Maple Leafs.[20]

These authors' analysis is based, in part, on arguments made by Whitson and Gruneau, who have shown how major league sport has become increasingly integrated with other brands, products, and corporate interests through cross-marketing.[21] The Anaheim Mighty Ducks is a classic example of a cross-marketed sport franchise—an NHL franchise owned by a major corporation (Disney), named after a fictional team from a Disney movie, and purchased in hopes of promoting a variety of Disney-related products and services (including the theme parks located around Anaheim).

These processes and related others are central to discussions about and research on globalization and Americanization. Work on these topics in the social science literature tends to focus on the impacts of global cultural forces, especially the widespread dissemination of transnational corporate brands and interests, on aspects of local cultures.[22] In this context, debates exist about the extent to which the processes and forces that appear to originate in the United States have an effect on Canada and other countries, and the ways in which Americanizing influences are resisted and altered in local contexts. Joseph Maguire's argument that the spread of transnational cultures creates a situation in which there are "diminishing contrasts between cultures, but increasing varieties of cultures" is a commonly referred to position that accounts for the complex relationship between local cultures and global forces.[23]

While remaining sensitive to this more nuanced understanding of the interactions between global forces and local cultures offered by Maguire and others, we should not understate the potency and persuasiveness of American culture and its impact in Canada. There is an abundance of evidence showing that American culture and media have an immense influence on Canadian cultural practices, although this influence varies from audience to audience. James Winter and Irvin Goldman, in an essay on mass media and Canadian identity, reviewed a series of studies that described the high levels of knowledge that various Canadian audiences have of American (compared to Canadian) culture (such as celebrities, history, and politics).[24] In a study on Canadian youth audience interpretations of US-based athletic apparel advertising, Robert Sparks and I argue that studies like those cited by Winter and Goldman, while not "proving" media effects, certainly support the view that the US media are a powerful cultural conditioner for Canadian audiences, youth or otherwise.[25]

The sale of Wayne Gretzky from the Edmonton Oilers to the Los Angeles Kings in 1988 is a dramatic reference point for researchers studying these kinds of Americanizing forces as they relate to sport. Sociologist Steve Jackson detailed Canadian media coverage of and commentary around Canada's "loss" of Gretzky, finding that Gretzky's personal fate appeared to signify the "inevitable impact that Americanization would have on Canada."[26] The potency of the trade was seemingly amplified because of its timing, which coincided with political and popular debates around the *Canada–United States Free Trade Agreement*, which ultimately took effect on January 1, 1989. The Gretzky sale was especially pertinent in this context because it underscored the importance of sport celebrity-athletes in marketing the NHL to US audiences, and the role that these same athletes had come to play in the mass promotion of corporate sponsors and their brands. Following the Oilers-Kings exchange, Nike began to incorporate the more marketable, Los Angeles–based Gretzky into its ongoing campaign of hip and youth-oriented advertisements, which included multi-sport superstar Bo Jackson and, of course, Michael Jordan, the pre-eminent global sport icon at the time.

It would seem that the NHL, Gretzky, and hockey would receive a boost from these developments not just in the United States but also in Canada. Although the traditional associations between Canadianness and hockey would be distorted or lost in this "new look" production of hockey and its celebrity representative, at least the game would seem to have an increased appeal for some youth in Canada. Indeed, the irony of this time period is that the sale and movement of Gretzky to the United States possibly increased the game's popularity among many Canadian youth (at least in the short term) who might have otherwise been disinterested.

In the United States, though (and as described in chapter 9, on media transnationalism, Canadian identity, and hockey) the NHL did not become as popular as its promoters would have hoped.[27] Ratings on Fox fell over the years the network was contracted to broadcast the NHL (a five-year contract beginning in 1994–95), and the agreement was not renewed. ABC-ESPN subsequently attempted to revitalize interest in televised NHL games, with a five-year deal signed in 1999 worth $600 million (US). More recently the failure of these networks to successfully market the game (evident from a continued decline in ratings) led the NHL to again shift networks. However, the broadcast deal signed with NBC prior to the 2004 lockout merely confirmed the league's status as a secondary sport behind NBA basketball, Major League baseball, and NFL football in the United States. The deal positioned the NHL on the same level (of perceived popularity and profitability) as the Arena Football League and televised soccer. Houston described the situation in a *Globe and Mail* article at the time:

Gary Bettman, the National Hockey League commissioner, put a brave face on the league's new television agreement, but the absence of a conventional rights fee, or any money up front at all, didn't leave much room for celebration.... The best it could do was a deal with NBC in which both sides share advertising revenue. After NBC's production and distribution costs are covered, plus the cost of pre-empting prime time shows during the Stanley Cup final, the league will make some money—if there's any left over.... The good news for the NHL is that it will continue to receive air time on a main US broadcast network.... But the NBC-NHL deal is probably bad news for Canadian networks and hockey fans. Because of its partnership with the league, NBC is likely to get as many Saturday afternoon match-ups as it wants, particularly during the playoffs. This will mean fewer Saturday night games on CBC.[28]

These trends raise further questions about why hockey has been less successful in the United States and what this means for hockey fans in Canada. Houston argues that one of the reasons for the league's failure below the border has been the recent retirement or diminished ability of superstars such as Wayne Gretzky, Mark Messier, and Mario Lemieux. He also suggests that the style of play that has become the norm in the NHL has prevented replacement superstars from emerging. Houston contrasts NHL hockey, which "has allowed obstruction and defensive tactics to shut down its best offensive players," with the NBA, a league that has been far more effective in marketing the game and its celebrities "by allowing the stars to excel on the court."[29]

Sociologists who study the marketing practices used to promote athletes such as Michael Jordan and Tiger Woods to global superstardom would no doubt agree with, but extend, Houston's view. Carrington and his co-authors, for example, emphasize the role of Nike, McDonald's, and Gatorade, along with the NBA, in distributing Jordan's image "through the world's major cities, deindustrialized urban wastelands, excessively affluent fortresses, or even rural hinterlands."[30] The success of the league and its celebrities, while being somewhat attributable to the NBA game itself, is arguably due more to the corporate strategies underlying and driving the league and those associated with it. An example of this strategy is embedded in James Lull's description of the immense cultural power that Jordan and the various companies associated with him have acquired—power that makes Jordan (and his sponsors) marketable across gender, race, and class lines, and certainly to young people across the Canada-US border. Lull explains the meticulous construction of Jordan's image:

Every detail is managed to perfection—from the slow motion, high flying slam dunks on TV to the broad, disarming smile staring at us from the Wheaties box. His bigger than life persona is part of an inviting pool of contemporary symbolic resources used to fashion cultural power.... The cultural agents range from inner-city black boys whose lifestyle is glorified by the commercial media to suburban white girls who high-five and call each other "homegirls."[31]

The importance of Nike's presence in the promotion of Tiger Woods and, by association, the Professional Golf Association (PGA), are similarly notable, as Cheryl Cole and David Andrews outline:

> Upon turning professional, Woods officially signed with IMG. He also signed a $49 million five-year sponsorship deal with Nike, which expected that Woods' racial difference *and* prodigious talent would "revolutionize" the public's relation to golf.... The success of America's latest revolution, orchestrated around Woods' body and style, would be measured in terms of the diversification and expansion of the market for golf-related products and services both within the United States and abroad.[32]

Some might argue that despite the message sent by the NBC deal, and in the face of US-based changes in the game, hockey fans in Canada are not influenced by the low popularity of the sport in the United States, that the continued high ratings on CBC are evidence that the game is still alive and well with Canadians at least.[33] However, given the powerful evidence showing how globally promoted cultural forms (including celebrities and sport-related products) clearly have an impact on local cultures, Canadians, especially young Canadians, would not seem to be immune to these (non-hockey-related) influences. That is to say, if corporations and networks in the United States are not aggressively promoting hockey in the United States *or Canada*, they are most likely instead marketing sports and celebrities that will compete with Canadian-based media productions of hockey for viewership and interest.

Merrill Melnick and Stephen Jackson's study, "Globalization American-Style and Reference Idol Selection: The Importance of Athlete Celebrity Others among New Zealand Youth," would seem to reinforce this thesis. Their survey of 510 New Zealand youth (average age=14.5 years) showed a variety of intriguing patterns supporting the idea that "youth are heavily influenced by global media in general and American popular culture in particular."[34] They found that US celebrities were extremely popular with New Zealand youth (and influenced the "emotions, feelings, ideas, beliefs, values, self-appraisals, and behaviors" of a group of these youth), a finding attributable to the large amount and often spectacular nature of US programming they are exposed to. These findings are in many respects consistent with results reported in the study that Sparks and I conducted, in which NBA players (and the athletic apparel commercials they were featured in) were shown to influence not only young males' consumer habits, but also their styles and peer cultural behaviours. Melnick and Jackson's conclusion that "the 'reach' of popular American media should come as no surprise to those who study the influence of American popular culture on worldwide commodity-sign consumption" is consistent with the argument made here—that Americanization influences how Canadian youth understand hockey.[35]

Youth Culture at the Millennium: Neo-Tribes, Global Media, and the Diminishing Relevance of Hockey in Canada

Just as the media environment that young people inhabit has evolved over time, the types of choices that youth make about their involvement in peer cultural groups and leisure activities have also changed. Researchers Andy Bennett and Ben Malbon argue that participation in leisure activities and groups (such as involvement in groups defined by a particular taste in music or interest in sport) has become increasingly "neo-tribal" for young people—meaning that youth are now more culturally transient, moving easily between activities, interests, and peer groups, showing little loyalty to any group or activity in particular.[36] As Malbon puts it, "Unity of identity, and in particular an identification with a sub-cultural grouping, appear to be less significant than ever before."[37] This does not mean that social class, race, ethnicity, gender, and geographic location—traditional markers helpful in explaining and describing youth identity groups and cultural interests and preferences—are no longer relevant for those attempting to describe the leisure activity patterns of youth (such as access to expensive sports that, like hockey, require financial resources). It does suggest, though, that youth who are exposed to a greater number and variety of cultural options (such as sports and music from around the world) and array of influences (for example, global celebrities such as David Beckham) will tend to construct identities that are more hybrid and individual. Although Bennett and Malbon's position should not be overstated—many youth still remain committed to a few activities and maintain somewhat stable memberships in peer (sub)cultural groups—the authors do identify an important trend that will remain relevant as generations of young people negotiate cultural identities in an increasingly cosmopolitan, mass-mediated world. Recent research shows that Canadian youth are spending less time playing any sports (not just hockey) as other activities come to take on more importance in their lives—which is evidence of this trend.[38]

These developments are in some respects akin to what theorists of globalization have called "deterritorialization," a term used to describe how citizens are decreasingly committed to the cultural practices associated with the countries they reside in. The term is important here because it speaks not only to the increasingly neo-tribal tendencies of youth consumers, but also to the threat that global influences pose for local cultures—especially the resultant disruption of historical (and seemingly "natural") associations between particular places and particular cultural practices. In fact, this threat commonly inspires attempts to re-establish local identities and traditions. John Tomlinson, in his book *Globalization and Culture*, describes the process:

[Globalization] promotes much more physical mobility than before, but the key to its cultural impact is in the transformation of localities themselves…. This is in many ways a troubling phenomenon, involving the simultaneous penetration of local worlds by distant forces, and the dislodging of everyday meanings from their "anchors" in the local environment. Embodiment and the forces of material circumstance keep most of us, most of the time, situated, but in places that are changing around us and gradually, subtly, losing their power to define the terms of our existence. This is undoubtedly an uneven and often contradictory business, felt more forcibly in some places than others, and sometimes met by countervailing tendencies to re-establish the power of locality. Nevertheless deterritorialization is, I believe, the major cultural impact of global connectivity.[39]

One could argue that this phenomenon is taking place in Canada among those in denial about the changing cultural landscape and its inevitable impact on the meaning of hockey.

If the related movements towards deterritorialization and neo-tribalism are considered together, it would certainly seem that the meaning of hockey as a cultural form and social practice within Canada has changed, and that the importance of the sport has been diminished for many young people. Moreover, it would also seem that altering the image of the game in order to improve its perception among youth can be, at best, only marginally successful. That is to say, while changes in hockey over time and social problems associated with the game might have resulted in decreased participation rates and declining levels of enthusiasm about the sport, broader forces are at work that are having an impact on all aspects of culture (not just sports) and their meanings. For this reason, the claim that hockey, youth, and Canada are linked will appear increasingly exaggerated and simplistic as time goes on.

Conclusion

Hockey, while not nearly as central to what it means to be Canadian as some claim, remains an extremely popular sport and continues to inspire feelings of pride and a sense of community among many people living in this country. Television ratings on *Hockey Night in Canada* on the CBC have remained high over the past decade, and it is unlikely that Canadian fan interest will drop off substantially in the future, despite the cancellation of the 2004–5 NHL season. Furthermore, public displays of extreme support for Canadian teams during major championships are almost guaranteed. The game also remains an important part of community life in many pockets of the country, especially in towns and small cities that are not as influenced by major league professional sport. As Gruneau and Whitson noted in 1993:

While senior hockey has since withered away in most parts of Canada, junior hockey still thrives—and still matters—in places like Kamloops, Medicine Hat, and Swift

Current in the West, or Peterborough, Belleville, and Kitchener in Ontario. Moreover, senior hockey continues to hang on in parts of Saskatchewan and Atlantic Canada that remain isolated from urban entertainment.[40]

Of course, and as the same authors acknowledge, rural communities are becoming increasingly connected to global forces and technologies. They are also, in many cases, struggling economically as local (often resource-based) industries begin to fail—a development that sometimes means that local recreation and hockey facilities are not properly maintained. Still, there are clear examples of towns that actively unite and resist these impacts through innovative efforts to revitalize or rethink industry and through the recognition that sport-related services can help to maintain a sense of collective identity within the community, a crucial component for community survival.[41] It seems, however, as though this resistance will become increasingly futile as movements towards urbanization and globalization continue to evolve.

The diminished significance of hockey in the lives of young Canadians, though, should not be viewed as necessarily "good or bad." Hockey is a sport rife with tensions and problems that do not represent everything that is good about Canada, contrary to some depictions of the game. Social problems related to gender and race that underlie the sport, and the widespread concerns about abuse and violence in the youth game, are examples of these tensions. With the diminished importance of the sport (on both the professional and local levels), perhaps young people who have negative experiences with the game will feel enabled to "tell their stories"—a point that Laura Robinson alludes to in her work on the Canadian Hockey League and her discussion of problems associated with treating minor hockey players as "young gods." In turn, through thoughtful intervention, the experiences of youth in and around the (less significant, but still potentially valuable) sport will be improved, and positive memories of a game less burdened with contradiction will be produced.

Notes

1 Roy MacGregor, "Cultural Power Play," *The Globe and Mail*, April 10, 2004, pp. R1, R7.

2 Quoted in Martin Laba and Richard Gruneau, *Hockey: The Canadian Game*, Part 3, *Myths and Markets* (Vancouver, BC: School of Communication, Simon Fraser University and The Knowledge Network, 1989).

3 Frances Kremarick, "A Family Affair: Children's Participation in Sports," in Statistics Canada, *Canadian Social Trends*, catalogue no. 11-008, Ottawa, Autumn 2000, pp. 20-24.

4 Patricia Vertinsky, *The Eternally Wounded Woman: Women, Doctors, and Exercise in the Late Nineteenth Century* (Manchester, UK: Manchester University Press, 1990).

5 See Jim McKay, *No Pain, No Gain? Sport and Australian Culture* (Toronto: Prentice Hall, 1991).

6 Richard Gruneau and David Whitson, *Hockey Night in Canada: Sport, Identities, and Cultural Politics* (Toronto: Garamond Press, 1993).

7 Ibid., p. 132.

8 Margaret MacNeill, "Networks: Producing Olympic Ice Hockey for a National Television Audience," *Sociology of Sport Journal*, 13,2 (1996), pp. 103-24.

9 Alan Ingham and Mary McDonald, "Sport and Community/Communitas," in R. Wilcox, D. Andrews, R. Pitter, and R. Irwin, eds., *Sporting Dystopias: The Making and Meaning of Urban Sport and Cultures* (Albany, NY: State University of New York Press, 2003), p. 17. See also Emile Durkheim, *Elementary Forms of Religious Life* (New York: Free Press, 1965).

10 Ingham and McDonald, "Sport and Community/Communities," pp. 24, 28. See also C. Euchner, *Playing the Field: Why Sports Teams Move and Cities Fight to Keep Them* (Baltimore: The Johns Hopkins University Press, 1993); A. Ingham, J. Howell, and T. Schilperoort, "Professional Sport and Community: A Review and Exegesis," *Exercise and Sport Sciences Reviews*, 15 (1987), pp. 427-65; K. Schimmel, A. Ingham, and J. Howell, "Professional Sport Teams and the American City: Urban Politics and Franchise Relocation," in A. Ingham and J. Loy, eds., *Sport and Social Development* (Ottawa: Avante-Guarde Communication, 1993), pp. 211-44.

11 A. Bélanger, "Sport Venues and the Spectacularization of Urban Spaces in North America: The Case of the Molson Centre in Montreal," *International Review for the Sociology of Sport*, 35,3 (2000), pp. 378-97. See also J. Nauright and P. White, "Nostalgia, Community and Nation: Professional Hockey and Football in Canada," *Avante*, 2 (1996), pp. 24-41.

12 Irshad Manji, *Canada: Why Innis Can Save Us (But McLuhan Can't!)*, The Harold Innis Research Foundation Fourth Annual Memorial Lecture, Innis College, University of Toronto, Nov. 6, 1997 <www.utoronto.ca/hirf/irshad.htm>.

13 Brian Wilson, "Audience Reactions to the Portrayal of Blacks in Athletic Apparel Commercials," Master's thesis, University of British Columbia, Vancouver, 1995. The respondents in the study self-identified as "Black," "African-American," "Trinidad and Tobago," and "Trinidadian/Canadian/Black" when asked about race-related identities. See also Brian Wilson and Robert Sparks, "'It's Gotta Be the Shoes': Youth, Race, and Sneaker Commercials," *Sociology of Sport Journal*, 13,4 (1996), pp. 398-427; Brian Wilson and Robert Sparks, "Impacts of Black Athlete Media Portrayals on Canadian Youth," *Canadian Journal of Communication*, 24,4 (1999), pp. 589-627; Brian Wilson and Robert Sparks, "Michael Jordan Sneaker Commercials, and Canadian Youth Cultures," in David Andrews, ed., *Michael Jordan Inc.: Corporate Sport, Media Culture, and Late Modern America* (Albany: State University of New York Press, 2001), pp. 217-55.

14 Alan Bairner, *Sport, Nationalism, and Globalization: European and North American Perspectives* (Albany, NY: SUNY Press, 2001), p. 131.

15 Gruneau and Whitson, *Hockey Night in Canada*.

16 Laura Robinson, "Games Boys Play: The Office Antics of the Men Who Run Women's Hockey," in P. Donnelly, ed., *Taking Sport Seriously: Social Issues in Canadian Sport* (Toronto: Thompson Educational Publishing, 2000), p. 82. It is also notable that the classic "Canadian memory" of ponds and hockey is most often framed as a "memory for men" (although watching *Hockey Night in Canada* and local hockey games is understood as a more inclusive activity).

17 Laura Robinson, *Crossing the Line: Violence and Sexual Assault in Canada's National Sport* (Toronto: McClelland and Stewart, 1998).

18 William Houston, "The Solution: Canada's Amateur Governing Body Needs to Stop the Win-at-All-Cost Attitude That Is Driving away Young Players in Droves," *The Globe and Mail*, April 17, 1998.

19 Bruce Kidd, "How Do We Find Our Voices in the "New World Order"? A Commentary on Americanization," *Sociology of Sport Journal*, 8,2 (1991), pp. 178-84.

20 Toby Miller, Geoffrey Lawrence, Jim McKay, and David Rowe, *Globalization and Sport* (Thousand Oaks, CA: Sage, 2001), p. 75. See also Daniel Mason, "Get That Puck Outta Here: Media Transnationalism and Canadian Identity," *Journal of Sport and Social Issues*, 26,2 (2002), pp. 140-67. Mason's study of Fox television's use of the FoxTrax puck in the broadcasts of hockey, a puck technologically designed so that its movements could be highlighted for television viewers who might have trouble following the puck, similarly describes the processes through which US networks threatened the authenticity of the game (and its coverage) and its associations with a traditional form of Canadian identity.

21 David Whitson and Richard Gruneau, "The (Real) Integrated Circus: Political Economy, Popular Culture and Major League Sport," in Wallace Clement, ed., *Understanding Canada: Building on the New Political Economy* (Montreal: McGill-Queen's University Press, 1997), pp. 359-85.

22 See Ben Carrington, David Andrews, Steven Jackson, and Zbigniew Mazur, "The Global Jordanscape," in D. Andrews, ed., *Michael Jordan Inc.: Corporate Sport, Media Culture, and Late Modern America* (Albany: State University of New York Press, 2001), pp. 177-216; Steven Jackson, and David Andrews, "Between and Beyond the Global and the Local," *International Review for the Sociology of Sport*, 34,1 (1999), pp. 31-42.

23 Joseph Maguire, "Sport, Identity Politics, and Globalization: Diminishing Contrasts and Increasing Varieties," *Sociology of Sport Journal*, 11 (1994), pp. 398-427.

24 J. Winter and I. Goldman, "Mass Media and Canadian Identity," in B. Singer, ed., *Communication in Canadian Society* (Scarborough, ON: Nelson Canada, 1995), pp. 201-20.

25 Wilson and Sparks, "Michael Jordan, Sneaker Commercials, and Canadian Youth Cultures," pp. 230-31.

26 Steven Jackson, "Gretzky Nation: Canada, Crisis and Americanization," in David Andrews and Steven Jackson, eds., *Sport Stars: The Cultural Politics of Sporting Celebrity* (New York: Routledge, 2001), p. 172.

27 Mason, "Get That Puck Outta Here."

28 William Houston, "Decline in Ratings Forces the NHL into Cozy NBC Deal," *GlobeandMail.com*, May 19, 2004 <www.globeandmail.com/servlet/story/RTGAM.20040519.wtruth20/BNStory/Sports>.

29 William Houston, "CBC Celebrates Playoff Ratings amid Decline in U.S.," *The Globe and Mail*, June 9, 2004, pp. 53, 59.

30 Carrington et al., "Global Jordanscape," p. 181.

31 James Lull, *Media, Communication, Culture: A Global Approach* (New York: Columbia University Press, 1995), p. 78.

32 Cheryl Cole and David Andrews, "America's New Son: Tiger Woods and America's Multiculturalism," in David Andrews and Steven Jackson, eds., *Sport Stars: The Cultural Politics of Sporting Celebrity* (New York: Routledge, 2001), pp. 70-86. Nike has continued to make efforts to attain market share in hockey, purchasing long-time equipment producer Bauer. However, the economic upside in the hockey industry is limited, according to Chris Zimmerman, CEO of Nike Bauer hockey, a point that would at least partially account for the more modest efforts of the company to promote the game and its stars on as large a scale as Jordan and Woods. Reasons cited for this limited upside include: interest in the game (and its equipment) in the United States is largely regionally based (in the Northeast, in major urban

markets, and in the northern Midwest); equipment is costly, thus limiting the number of potential consumers; and ice hockey's growth is structurally limited because of the dependence on the number of ice rinks—a concern for Nike representatives at a time when few new facilities are being built. See Robin Moody, "Bauer Nike CEO Again Focused on Market Share," *The Business Journal* (Portland), July 14, 2003 <portland.bizjournals.com/portland/stories/2003/07/14/story5.html>.

33 This was especially during the hockey playoffs of 2004, which included a run to the Stanley Cup finals by the Calgary Flames.

34 Merrill Melnick and Stephen Jackson, "Globalization American-Style and Reference Idol Selection: The Importance of Athlete Celebrity Others among New Zealand Youth," *International Review for the Sociology of Sport*, 37,3-4 (2002), p. 429.

35 Ibid., p. 442.

36 Andy Bennett, "Subcultures or Neo-Tribes? Rethinking the Relationship between Youth, Style and Musical Taste," *Sociology*, 33,3 (1999), pp. 599-617; Ben Malbon, "Clubbing: Consumption, Identity and the Spatial Practices of Every-Night Life," in Tracey Skelton and Gill Valentine, eds., *Cool Places: Geographies of Youth Cultures* (New York: Routledge, 1998), pp. 266-86.

37 Malbon, "Clubbing," p. 278.

38 See Sport Canada, *Sport Participation in Canada: 1998 Report* (Ottawa, 2000); Sport Canada, *Fact Sheet: Reconnecting Government with Youth Survey 2003*, Canadian Heritage, Ottawa, 2004 <www.pch.gc.ca/progs/sc/info-fact/youth_e.cfm>.

39 John Tomlinson, *Globalization and Culture* (Chicago: University of Chicago Press, 1999), pp. 29-30. See also Arjun Appadurai, "Sovereignty without Territoriality," in P. Yaeger, ed., *The Geography of Identity* (Ann Arbor: University of Michigan Press, 1996), pp. 40-58.

40 Gruneau and Whitson, *Hockey Night in Canada*, p. 206.

41 Ibid. See also Philip Hansen and Alicia Muszynski, "Crisis in Rural Life and Crisis in Thinking: Directions for Critical Research," *Canadian Review of Sociology and Anthropology*, 27,1 (1990), pp. 1-22

The Game of Whose Lives? Gender, Race, and Entitlement in Canada's "National" Game

■ MARY LOUISE ADAMS

This chapter is about hockey, gender, race, and Canadian nationalism. There is no deep abiding love of the game beneath this critique, no nostalgia for a pre-expansion NHL, for cleaner styles of play, for the sport's better days. If it has had better days in my lifetime, I've never noticed. Like many women my age (mid-forties) or older, my experiences with hockey are minimal. I can recall watching just one complete tele-vised game: the men's gold medal match at the 2002 Salt Lake City Olympics. I know that in grade seven we got to go to the school gym for the final of the 1972 series, but I don't remember actually watching it. A few times I have made an effort to watch at least some of the women's Olympic or World Championship finals, hoping, in part, to see the Canadian women win, but also simply to see non-girlie women being feted on TV. One winter, the first at my current teaching job, I played half a dozen pickup games with some of my new colleagues and a handful of grad students in an effort to be collegial. I've also joined the department's hockey pool three times during the regular season and once during the playoffs. I've won money twice. Needless to say, if hockey ceased to exist tomorrow, my life would not really change.

What, then, to make of *The Globe and Mail*'s Spring 2004 publication of not just one but four editorials on hockey, on consecutive days: "How to Save Canada's Game"?[1] What to make of claims that "Hockey is the national id," as poet Richard Harrison has written, or that "Hockey *is* life in Canada,"[2] as author Roch Carrier has put it? Do these men live in the same country as I do?

If hockey is life in Canada, then life in Canada remains decidedly masculine and white. Despite increasing numbers of female players, hockey still makes a major contri-bution to discourses of Canadian national identity that privilege native-born, white men. In its roles as national symbol and everyday pastime, hockey produces a very ordinary but pernicious sense of male entitlement: to space, to status, to national belonging. Hockey is part of the obfuscating construction of the so-called "ordinary Canadian," a creature whose evocation in popular political commentary helps to homogenize discourses about an increasingly heterogeneous population.

In any number of banal ways, hockey—at all levels—perpetuates the notion that certain kinds of men count for more in the fabric of national life than do other kinds of men or women. In this sense it's not just the troubled National Hockey League game but pond hockey too that's a problem. We need to keep assessing the implications of the thing that is hockey in Canada. At the very least, we need to attend to hockey's persistence as a central signifier of Canadianness, despite decades of tremendous social change since that equation was first forged.

Canada's Game?

In popular media discourses it goes without saying that hockey is *the* Canadian sport. For confirmation we need only look to the men's gold medal victory over the Americans at the Salt Lake City Olympic Games in 2002. More than ten million viewers watched the game on CBC television (12.6 million viewers at the end), making it the most-watched television program in Canadian history.[3] Newspaper coverage on the day after (February 25, 2002) was spectacularly over the top. The *National Post*, for instance, published a full-page colour photo on page one, under the headline "Gold!" (which appeared in gold type). Four more full pages and a lead editorial followed in the front section, which closed with a full-page Canadian flag poster, paid for by Chevrolet. The paper had more pages on the game in a special Olympics section. *The Toronto Star* ran three pages of coverage in its front section, six-plus pages in the sports section, two and a half pages in the "Greater Toronto" section, and a full-page colour poster of the victorious team in a special Olympic review section. "O Canada!" sang the paper's front page, the exclamation mark formed with a dangling gold medal. By comparison, *The Globe and Mail* seemed restrained: the full front page (but not a full-page photo); three additional pages in the front section, including Chevrolet's full-page Canadian flag; and seven pages in a special Olympic section, including a full-colour poster of the men's team in the centrefold. Articles in the *Star*, *The Globe and Mail*, and the *National Post* made clear the importance of the win to the nation, many of them conflating team and country: "Canada's Moment of Truth"; "Reclaiming 'Our Game'"; "In Our Hearts We Know It's Our Game"; "All of Canada Is Cheering"; "Proud to Be Canadian." An article in *The Globe and Mail* quoted a fan from Vancouver who claimed there was "no finer moment for Canadians everywhere."[4]

The men's hockey victory in Salt Lake City made clear the place of hockey in popular versions of Canadian nationalism. The victory also made clear the centrality of gender to national mythmaking. Four days before the nation came to a standstill (as the *National Post* put it) for the men's final, members of the Canadian women's hockey team had won their own gold medal match, also against the Americans. Although the women's victory was certainly seen to be sweet, it was celebrated in much the same way as victories in speed skating or skiing. It was not portrayed, as the men's victory would be, as confirmation of the "hockeyness" of this country or as a boost to national morale.

While the women's win added to Canada's gold medal tally, the men's victory propped up the national psyche.

Coverage of the two wins was staggering in its lopsidedness. Even the day after the women's final (February 22, 2002), the men's team and the men's game were still able to garner more coverage than the women's. In *The Globe and Mail*, the women were afforded a large photo (about one-third of the page) on the first page of the special Olympic section. Stories about the team took up about two-thirds of the centrefold on pages six and seven. Men's hockey took up the rest of pages six and seven and all of pages two and three. In *The Toronto Star*, the women's team was featured in a quarter-page photo on the first page of the special Olympic section. A story on their final game received half a column on the first page and less than a third of a page on page four. A column by sports journalist Randy Starkman also appeared on page four. Photos and articles about men's hockey, in contrast, took up all of pages two and three, portions of pages four and five, and half of page seven. The women were covered in two stories, the Canadian men in five, other men in three.

In a special commemorative edition of *Maclean's* magazine that appeared after the Games, men's hockey was similarly privileged. The article on hockey devoted twenty paragraphs to the men's team and two to the women's.[5] A separate article was devoted to covering the spectators of the men's game. The issue featured Mario Lemieux, of the men's hockey team, on the front cover and Danielle Goyette, of the women's hockey team, on the back. A "Winners' Gallery" photo of the men's team took up two pages. A "Winners' Gallery" photo of the women's team: half a page. Readers were also told that the men's victory (no mention of the women) "deserves to be considered among the defining moments in Canada's collective experience, right there with pivotal elections and Expo 67."[6]

It certainly doesn't take any special training in gender analysis to make sense of this pattern. There can be no mistaking which of these teams is understood to be more important. Is there anything women could do in this country to merit the kind of coverage that the men's team received? To merit half the coverage? To merit a full front page? Obviously, winning at hockey won't do it. In my recollection the only event involving women that sustained multi-page coverage over several days was the murder of fourteen women students at the École Polytechnique in Montreal in 1989. And even in that instance, it was only the local paper, the Montreal *Gazette*, that devoted the entire front page and several additional pages in the front section to the tragedy.[7]

Typically, research and writing on gender and hockey focus on women's access to and negotiation with the game or, more commonly, on how hockey contributes to idealized notions of manliness.[8] At elite competitive levels, men's hockey—the hockey that really counts—promotes a hard, aggressive masculinity. We see this masculinity reinforced in the celebration of fighting, in the idolization of players willing to give and take the biggest hits, and in the longevity of Don Cherry's vitriolic "Coach's Corner" on CBC television. Some social critics worry that a game as violent and aggressive as men's professional hockey figures so prominently in the sense that many Canadians have of their national identity. While I share these concerns, the argument I want to make about gender and hockey in Canada is not a response to violence in the sport. Were elite men's hockey to become a kinder, gentler game tomorrow, my argument would remain unchanged. The point I want to make is independent of the facts of hockey, per se; indeed, to varying degrees it would apply, I suspect, to most "national" sports. Simply put, so-called national sports afford men—in general, and certain men in particular—an opportunity to represent the nation in a way not open to women. Sport helps to construct the different versions of citizenship available to men and women. Would national teams generate such frenzied patriotism if national teams had no men? Could we ever imagine a game played primarily by women as this country's (or any other's) national game, as central to its national identity?

Benedict Anderson says that nations are distinguished from one another by the stories they tell about themselves.[9] The homogenization of difference and other processes of exclusion are key to this national story-making and to the formation of national identities. In the drive to construct a cohesive representation of the "imagined community," not all stories are equal. As feminists ask: whose stories count as "our" stories, and who gets to tell them?[10] After the Salt Lake City Olympics, Canadians might well ask, whose stories channel enough authority to bring the nation to a standstill? National stories communicate to citizens preferred ways of being, preferred histories, and these tend to reflect the most powerful economic and social groups. And while national stories do change over time, their taken-for-grantedness can make them appear very solid. As Philip Corrigan writes, "In confirming our sense of what and how we are, [the taken for granted] allows us to forget how we might be different."[11]

In contemporary discourses on hockey, the possibility of being different lies close to the surface yet rarely breaks through—the response to the women's gold medal in Salt Lake City being just one example of a lost opportunity to develop notions of hockey that make sense independently of ideas about gender. While I was working on this chapter, *The Globe and Mail* published a special section called "Stanley Cup Showdown" to mark the first game of the 2004 Stanley Cup finals between the Calgary Flames and the Tampa Bay Lightning. It was the first time in more than ten years that a Canadian-based team had made it to the finals. A full-colour close-up of Calgary Flames captain Jarome Iginla filled the section's front page alongside the headline: "Canada's Captain, Canada's Team."

On its own, the publication of a special section suggests the exaggerated importance of hockey to popular national discourses although, in this case, these discourses had the potential to stretch. Jarome Iginla is the first black team captain in NHL history, and he is being touted as "Canada's Captain"? While there is irony here—in what other realm of society, besides sport, could a black man be touted as "Canada's Captain"?—there also exists the possibility of shifting hockey's limited racial narratives and, by association, maybe shifting notions of Canadianness a little bit too. Turn the page and the feature on Iginla seems promising: "Iginla Seen as New Face of the NHL."[12] New face, indeed: in 2002–03 only fourteen of the more than six hundred athletes on NHL rosters were black. The all-time list of black men playing in the NHL includes only thirty-eight names, beginning in 1958 with Willie O'Ree.[13]

In this context, *Globe and Mail* readers might be forgiven for expecting an article on changing demographics in the league or on the distance that hockey needs to travel to reflect the national community from which it draws—and which the game is supposed to symbolize. Instead the article talks simply about Iginla's personal characteristics, about how kind he is, and how he would make a good successor to Wayne Gretzky as hockey's ambassador. The only mention of race appears in a sidebar in Iginla's own words: "When I was growing up, I was aware I was a black hockey player. I was the only black hockey player on my team. As far as trying to make it to the NHL, I know what other black players meant to me in terms of following my dream."

In an article about Iginla's scoring statistics or his hockey skills, the elision of race from the main story would be less of an issue. But in a story proposing Iginla as hockey's next figurehead—published in a country in which 1) hockey is seen by many to symbolize the nation, 2) hockey is played primarily by whites, and 3) racism continues to shape the daily experiences of people of colour, the neglect of race seems naively hopeful, reflecting the beliefs that race doesn't matter in sport's meritocracy, that race is not an important Canadian issue (see also chapter 6).

In a sport dominated by white men, Iginla's race is significant not just in terms of the numbers of black players, but in terms of the sport's contribution to the construction of whiteness in this country. The national community imagined through stories about hockey is a racialized community. Narratives about hockey as the "glue that holds us together," as the childhood pastime that "we" all share, as our "national religion," help keep whiteness central to dominant notions of Canadian identities. These are narratives that evoke small-town and rural Canada—Canada at its whitest. These stories link hockey with the Canadian landscape and the Canadian past, both realms in which people of colour, though present, have been marginalized. As Ruth Frankenberg has written, whiteness is a structural advantage and a standpoint from which white people see the world. More important to this discussion, it is also a "set of cultural practices that are usually unmarked and unnamed."[14] In Canada, hockey is one of those practices.

If Hockey Is a Metaphor, What Does It Mean?

In both popular and political discourses hockey symbols and hockey metaphors have become trite clichés, an easy shorthand for a shared national identity. In commercials for hardware stores and beer, for cola and donuts, hockey serves to mark an unambiguous Canadianness. When country/pop superstar Shania Twain hosted the 2003 Juno Awards (for the Canadian music industry), she wore costumes representing each of the Canadian NHL teams. For instance, in one segment, Twain wore a strapless blue gown emblazoned with the Vancouver Canucks logo; in another she wore a cropped and sequined Canadiens jersey with low-rise, flared pants—not the glamorous garb we've come to expect of award-show hosts. In this case, glamour was beside the point: hockey symbols helped to constitute the Juno Awards (notorious for being ignored by television audiences) as a celebration of Canadian culture and community. Hockey references infused the show (and the host) with an identifiable Canadianness that the musicians being celebrated—Twain herself, Avril Lavigne, Diana Krall, none of whom differ substantially from their American counterparts—could not. In 2004 the Juno's hockey theme continued. The festivities opened in Edmonton with a charity hockey match between a team of former NHL players and a team of Canadian musicians led by Jim Cuddy of the band Blue Rodeo.

Politicians have long known the value of demonstrating a knowledge and love of hockey, perhaps the next best thing to simply wrapping themselves in the flag. That is why we so often witness politicians of all stripes donning the jerseys of local teams as the politicians try to connect their political identities symbolically to the imagined regional and local communities of players, volunteers, and fans. Still, while the comfortable association between hockey and Canadianness might be the glue that binds us together, that glue positions various groups of Canadians differently in relation to dominant discourses about who "we" really are. The use of hockey references as a cultural shorthand for Canadianness helps to perpetuate a national identity rooted in masculine experience. Indeed, the most simple hockey reference can help bring a virile sheen to almost any situation. For instance: an article about "Cocktails for Canada Day" appears in *Toro*, "Canada's magazine for men." It lists the ingredients for a drink called the Canadian, then the instructions for mixing: "Shake vigorously with cracked ice and strain into a chilled cocktail glass. He shoots, he scores!" The article on the very next page of the magazine looks at the types of smoked fish a host might consider serving in lieu of salmon. We learn the following about rainbow trout: "In the fall, as salmon are busy spawning, the rainbow trout gets fat feeding on the salmon's eggs. It just goes to show, you've got to keep your head up when you're crossing the blue line."[15] A few hockey references, and there is no risk that discussions of cocktails and hors d'oeuvres will sound gay. For years, media profiles of male figure skaters have relied on similar techniques: detail the skater's hockey-playing background, use hockey language to describe his tricks. Here's a description of Brian Orser getting ready to jump: "He sweeps up-ice like Bobby Orr on a rush.... Just over the blue line, where a winger would start to cut for the net, Orser turns and glides backwards."[16] Hockey metaphors and hockey analogies are ways through which Canadians can talk to each other about men and masculinity. It bears noting that hockey references evoke femininity only by throwing that category into question, which would be no great concern, and could actually be a useful discursive intervention, except that we are talking about a sport that is supposed to represent the nation, not just the male half of it.

The Gender of Ice Time

I've been talking about hockey as a pervasive aspect of discourses about Canadianness. It's important, though, not to forget that these discourses have material attachments in the actual practices of hockey and shinny. I live in Kingston, Ontario, an "amalgamated city" with a population of slightly over one hundred thousand people. Here, more than 50 per cent of all municipally scheduled ice time goes to minor hockey.[17] This doesn't include old-timer hockey, school hockey, regular pickup games, or the five hours rented by an adult women's recreational league. In terms of organized youth sports in 2002–03, boys' minor hockey got 278 hours (there would have been a few girls on these teams), girls' minor hockey got 53 hours per week, ringette got 12, and other skating organizations (speed, figure, synchro) got 60. There are no policies in place to assess gender or other forms of equity in terms of the allocation of recreational services in our community. The priority for ice allocation is to "partner groups" that are non-profit recreational groups dedicated "exclusively to minor [youth] sports." Ice is allocated to non-partner groups, such as old-timers hockey leagues or the new women's recreational league, on a historical basis. So, if a group has a particular ice time one year, they are offered the same time the next year, and so on through the years. To members of a men's old-timers league who have been playing every Thursday night for years, the policy makes perfect sense. To a group of women trying to set up a regular pickup game, it can put access to one of Canada's most scarce resources—artificial ice—out of reach. A report published in January 1994, on the first phase of an innovative women's recreation program in the (pre-amalgamation) City of Toronto, identified the practice of allocating time in sports facilities on a "historic" basis as one aspect of the systemic discrimination that hampers women's participation in organized recreation. The report notes that although a centre might be filled to capacity, if it offers just one or two activity choices for participants of just one age or gender group, then it "does not truly reflect the recreational needs of the total community."[18]

Although the numbers of girls and women playing hockey are increasing rapidly (an increase of 534 per cent between 1990 and 2000), they are still vastly outnumbered by boys and men. In the 2002–03 season, the Canadian Hockey Association registered 476,975 male players and 61,177 female players.[19] This imbalance establishes the feel of the average rink, which is obvious the minute you walk in the door. Almost nothing smells as manly as a small-town Canadian rink. The smells, the frozen spit on the rubber matting, the decades-old hockey photos—all these suggest to girls and women (including those who play hockey, but especially those who don't) that their presence in the local arena is an afterthought. This condition would be much less of an issue if the local arena was not the only public building in many small communities.

Bruce Kidd's oft-cited remark that arenas are men's cultural centres doesn't hold true just for the Air Canada and Bell Centres. This is everyday life in community rinks across the country. And what concerns me is that we are not just talking about men's cultural centres, but boys' cultural centres, which seems to me—for the early sense of entitlement it instills—to be worse. Despite their non-hockey users, rinks are clearly designed and most often used for hockey. Is there an indoor rink in this country that does not fit the standardized dimensions of either the NHL or Olympic game? How many rinks don't have boards, or glass, or netting, or red and blue lines on the ice? Rinks could look different. Indeed, the first artificial ice rinks did look different.[20] Built for the British upper classes, they were fantastic buildings with huge ice surfaces, big windows, and natural light. Designed not for hockey but for the newly developed pastime of ice-dancing, they were built in a range of shapes. It wasn't until hockey dictated the shape of multi-use rinks in Canada and the United States (see Introduction) that figure skaters had to waltz themselves around the overly tight spaces of the hockey zones.

Of course Canadian towns and cities are also full of outdoor rinks in parks. From anecdotal evidence and personal experience we know what happens on these rinks: they are colonized by people with pucks and sticks, among whom girls and women are the exception and not the rule. An admittedly brief stint of observational research on downtown Kingston outdoor rinks one winter suggested that when there is more than one rink, non-hockey-related skating can take place, although sometimes the "extra" ice surface is used as a warm-up space for the next game of shinny. Then again, the games of shinny witnessed were played almost exclusively by boys or men. Researcher Anne Warner wrote in her field notes: "Sometimes there is a 13-16 year old girl playing with a few guys, but never in the big hockey game."[21] While many women and girls would simply like to skate on these rinks, some would also like a chance to play shinny. But, as officials from the city of Toronto found in community consultations, "Often women and girls who make the effort to participate are subjected to rude, aggressive or dominant behaviour by men or boys who have for too long considered the physical activity and sport facilities their domain."[22] Not surprisingly, then, some women eventually give up and others never try to play in the first place.

Anyone who has spent any time around rinks in this country could offer a range of similar examples of gendered practices around hockey. In a discursive context in which hockey is already given pride of place, where the hockey that really counts is undeniably men's hockey, everyday rink practices reinforce and represent a sense of male entitlement—even among young boys who are among the primary users of these facilities. Will more women getting out on the ice change this? I don't think so, not until women's hockey actually counts, until women can make claims not just on the material aspects of the game but on all its symbolic attachments too.

Shinny: "The Game That Belongs to All of Us?"

Most discussions of sport and national identity tend to focus on issues related to national teams, Olympic medals, international competition. I certainly can't say whether this is the case in other countries, but in Canada, "Our Game" means more than this. Not only is it supposed to make us smugly proud of our place—our superiority—in the world, it is supposed to run through our veins. Hockey is, we are often told, part of who "we" are. Shinny is supposed to be the source of that connection.[23]

While professional hockey is frequently criticized as being an unsuitable symbol of Canadian identity, shinny holds a privileged place in narratives of Canadianness, lauded as the "true" Canadian game, as the "pure part to hockey."[24] Shinny is the game of pickup hockey. Its most idealized version happens on frozen lakes, rivers, and ponds. It is also played as a pickup game on urban rinks or, using a ball rather than a puck, as "road hockey" or "street hockey." These are supposed to be the versions of the game that suit all of "us." Reporting on the 2003 World Pond Hockey Championships held in New Brunswick, Shawna Richer writes:

> On Mother Nature's rinks, teams of four men were posed to play out the most Canadian of reveries.… Arguably the most inherent part of our national landscape, pond hockey is the opportunity to play the game at its purest, most creative form. Shinny is where the professionals began, where children have the best fun, where grown men feel like boys.… This is Canada in a box, right here.[25]

As one of the players at the tournament said, "Having teams of four makes perfect sense … you can get four guys in a room, four guys in a car. All you need are sticks and skates." Here is sport's homo-social and ethnic and racial bonding at its best. The romanticization of shinny is to expansive, pluralist notions of Canadian identity as family values discourse is to debates around sexual orientation. As Gruneau and Whitson note:

> Hockey has a capacity to induce the recollection of familiar experiences and to subtly connect this recollection to a seemingly less complicated image of Canadian society. In a time of uncertainty, and in a Canada increasingly characterized by difference, this comfortable familiarity and ability to convey an older sense of Canadian identity have an engaging and enduring appeal. They help to sustain our ability to imagine a national community.[26]

Gruneau and Whitson go on to say that "this older sense of Canadian identity is rooted in an image of a common culture that has often papered over some of the most deeply rooted inequalities and conflicts in the society." While they are speaking of hockey in general, the point they make is especially important in terms of shinny, which is the hockey closest to home, the hockey of childhood. It's not the hockey of team tryouts, pre-dawn practices, multiple concussions, or expensive registration fees. It's a kind of hockey that has indeed allowed many people to enjoy physical and social pleasure, and thus it is not surprising that some Canadians would want to imagine a Canada that reflects the values and experiences that they find in the game. The problem with this, of course, is that the culture of shinny is largely a male culture. Among women my age and older, few have had any experience with shinny at all. Like pickup basketball, shinny has codes and accepted practices that we don't know. Many women are so removed from this "Canadian tradition" that the notion of wanting to learn these codes would never enter their heads.

In typical narratives about shinny (short stories, movies, television ads), women figure primarily as mothers who make game-ending calls ("Johnny … time for supper!"), wrenching their sons away from the game and the company of other males. A recent Coke ad offered an alternative female role. A little girl follows a group of teenagers (mostly boys, but one or two girls) to a pond. The big kids get to work clearing the ice. The little girl looks dejected. When the big kids take a break, one of the boys goes over and offers the sad girl a Coke. They talk. She smiles. We are relieved, thinking she is going to get to play. In the next scene the teenagers stand in two lines, facing each other, their sticks resting on the ice. The little girl stands at the top of the formation. The camera zooms in on her face. There's a pause, and then she starts to sing "Oh Canada" in a sweet little girl's voice. Standing in for the flag, the girl symbolizes the game that the bigger kids play. Could a little boy do the same? And when the anthem is over? Does the singer sit on the sidelines and watch?

During broadcasts of the 1998 Nagano Winter Olympic Games, Labatt's Breweries launched an enormously successful hockey ad as one of a series called "Out of the Blue," designed to promote Blue, the company's most popular beer label. It is less sentimental and less explicit than the Coke ad in its manipulation of national feeling, but more typical in how it represents women's relationship to shinny. The ad opens with shots of people in winter coats on a busy urban sidewalk. It's a grey cold day; we can see their breath. A young white man in his twenties, wearing a wool and leather athletic jacket (red and white, reminiscent of the recent Canadian national team uniforms made by Roots), walks towards us carrying a big hockey bag and a hockey stick. He's kicking a crumpled up pop can as he walks. After a few kicks, he starts to handle the can with his stick. Another hockey-stick-carrying white man, in his thirties or forties, crosses paths with the can and hits it onto the street. A third white man, who is in his fifties (see—this game appeals to all ages!), runs from across the street and intercepts the can with his briefcase. Looking surprised but pleased with themselves, the three men start to play "ball hockey" in what appears to be the middle of Toronto's Bay Street, centre of the country's financial power (see—even powerful guys love to play!). Other men join in, creating goal posts out of gym bags and bike racks. Men in their shirt sleeves run from office buildings, hockey sticks in hand. People on the sidewalk stop to watch and cheer. Window washers look down from their perches. A hard-hatted city worker looks up from a manhole. Office workers fill the windows above the street. The crowd—inside and outside—does "the wave." The music in the background—Gary Glitter's 1972 song, "Rock and Roll, Part Two," otherwise known as the "Hey!" song—is festive, happy, insistent, and the play on the street is intense until the standard game-breaking call of "Car." Only this time, in this place, the call is "Streetcar," and the crowd and players disperse to the sound of its bell. A voice-over says, "Almost anything can happen out of the blue." In the final scene, two young men, one South Asian, one white, are having an animated conversation in a bar, while a young white woman looks on.

The ad represents shinny as it is played every winter day on rinks and streets all across Canada: the players are white and male. The only woman to capture the attention of the camera is an older woman who seems to be disapproving of or confused by the game. People of colour appear in the ad simply as a way of marking diversity in the crowd. Even in the final scene, the white woman and white man are centred in the frame, while the South Asian man is off to the side and barely on the screen. Of course, there are places in this country where people of colour and women and girls do play shinny. But these don't figure in any substantial way in the nostalgic fantasy of shinny that the ad is meant to convey, a game so ingrained in the Canadian psyche that no words are necessary, that strangers (the imagined community) are in complete synch with each other, that even those not playing are able to share in the vibes of the game. This is what Gruneau and Whitson mean by "a less complicated image of Canadian society," "a comfortable familiarity." For something truly "Out of the Blue" we would need to see an ad with women of any race or men of colour as the main characters. Or what about a pickup game among a group of gay men? Or, better yet, what about representing shinny as it has been experienced by many Canadian girls and women: a game of exclusion that takes up too much ice time and leaves them sidelined in what is supposed to be one of the most fundamental expressions of a shared Canadian culture?

So central is shinny to the project of national mythmaking that a state-approved representation of it appears on our money. The back of a recently issued five-dollar bill shows a group of children playing shinny on a frozen pond, a row of snow-covered evergreens in the background, a rosy glow from behind the trees, suggesting either the setting sun (and therefore a long day of play) or a rosy past. The bill also shows an adult teaching a child to skate and an Asian girl on a toboggan, but these scenes are dwarfed by the hockey vignette and they aren't bathed in a nostalgic pink. The theme is winter, as evidenced by two large snowflakes anchoring the set of images, and hockey takes the place of pride. A quote, in both French and English, from Carrier's "The Hockey Sweater," probably the best-known of any Canadian short story, underlines the theme: "The winters of my childhood were long, long seasons. We lived in three places—the school, the church and the skating rink—but our real life was on the skating rink." On this particular skating rink, we see four children: two of indistinguishable sex or race in the distance, a white girl skating away from us (so we can clearly see her long hair) in the middle, and in the foreground a smiling white child who could be either a girl or a boy, although in this context, with nothing to clearly identify the child as a female, he will be read as a boy. Skating towards us, the boy takes up half the image.

Nostalgia is a powerful means of keeping us from imagining how Canada might be different; it is part of the process of marginalizing women and people of colour, of limiting the stories we can tell about ourselves. At this particular historical moment, nostalgia for shinny is not about the complicated fabric of an evolving urban society. Rather, as Gamal Abdel-Shehid has written, it is a process invested with "timelessness, history-lessness, and, by extension, racelessness."[27] Nostalgia for shinny is part of what Eva Mackey would call the constitution of a Canadian-Canadian identity, that is, an unhyphenated Canadian identity. Canadian-Canadians are "ordinary Canadians," a term used politically to maintain definitions of national citizenship that are free of reference to "culture, race, sexual preference and gender." Shinny fits well into attempts to articulate an overarching, enduring Canadian culture that persists in the face of immigration and changing social relations of race, ethnicity, gender, and sexuality. Canadian-Canadian identity and culture are, by contrast, "unmarked, non-ethnic, and usually white." Mackey writes, "If Canada is the 'very house of difference,' it contains a family with a distinct household head."[28] And, we might add, if he doesn't play shinny now, at one time he certainly did.

Canada looks quite different today than it did in the late nineteenth century, when hockey was originally promoted as our national sport.[29] Yet, despite tremendous social change, hockey remains central to popular notions of Canadianness. What this means, simply, is that those groups that were once served by the privileging of hockey—certain groups of white men—remain dominant in this country. Our so-called national symbols help to keep them that way by contributing to a national culture that reflects and promotes their interests and that continues to place their image at the centre of a shared national identity. While narratives about hockey might not represent the diversity of Canadians, they do represent important aspects of the organization of power in this country, as Michael Robidoux suggests in an article about early links between hockey and Canadian nationalism.[30] Narratives about hockey tell us about a lot more than idyllic childhoods and wintry landscapes. Anticipating cultural changes that will shift relations of power in Canada, Gruneau and Whitson speculated, in 1993, that the automatic association of hockey and Canadianness would be far less significant in coming years.[31] A decade later we can keep hoping, but we aren't there yet.

Notes

1　"How to save Canada's game (1)" *The Globe and Mail*, April 10, 2004, p. A20; "How to Save Canada's Game (2)," April 12, 2004, p. A12; "How to Save Canada's Game (3)," April 13, 2004, p. A18; "How to Save Canada's Game (4)," April 14, 2004, p. A14.

2　Both cited in Roy MacGregor, "Cultural Power Play," *The Globe and Mail*, April 10, 2004, p. R1.

3　James Deacon, "How Sweet It Is!" *Maclean's*, March 11, 2002, p. 21.

4　"Flags Wave as Nation Celebrates," *The Globe and Mail*, Feb. 25, 2002, p. A5.

5　*Maclean's*, March 11, 2002, pp. 16-23.

6　Ibid., p. 19.

7　"Campus Massacre," *The Gazette* (Montreal), Dec. 7, 1989, p. A1. *The Gazette* published three stories on p. 1, followed by their continuations on p. A2, five further stories, diagrams, and maps on p. A3, and six stories on p. A4. *The Toronto Star* addressed the massacre in two of four stories on the front page and in three further stories that took up most of p. A3. In *The Globe and Mail*, one of six stories on the front page addressed the massacre. The continuation of this article and one further article appeared on p. A5. *The Vancouver Sun* printed one large story on p. 1 (one of three articles) and followed that with a further six articles on pp. A18, A19.

8　On women's access to and negotiation with the game, see, for instance: E. Etue and M. Williams, *On the Edge: Women Making Hockey History* (Toronto: Second Story Press, 1996); Nancy Theberge, *Higher Goals: Women's Ice Hockey and the Politics of Gender* (Albany: State University of New York Press, 2000). On hockey and manliness, see, for instance, Richard Gruneau and David Whitson, *Hockey Night in Canada: Sport, Identities, and Cultural Politics* (Toronto: Garamond Press, 1993); Laura Robinson, *Crossing the Line: Violence and Sexual Assault in Canada's National Sport* (Toronto: McClelland and Stewart, 1998).

9　Benedict Anderson, *Imagined Communities: Reflections on the Origin and Spread of Nationalism* (New York: Verso, 1983).

10　Sita Ranchod-Nilsson and Mary Ann Tétreault, eds., *Women, States and Nationalism: At Home in the Nation?* (London: Routledge, 2000).

11　Philip Corrigan, "Doing Mythologies," *Border/lines* (Fall 1984), p. 20.

12　Eric Duhatschek, "Iginla Seen as New Face of the NHL," *The Globe and Mail*, May 25, 2004, p. C3.

13　Cecil Harris, *Breaking the Ice: The Black Experience in Professional Hockey* (Toronto: Insomniac Press, 2003), p. 14.

14　Ruth Frankenberg, *White Women, Race Matters: The Social Construction of Whiteness* (Minneapolis: University of Minnesota Press, 1993), p. 1.

15　Mark Kingwell, "Cocktails for Canada Day," *Toro* (Summer 2004), p. 55; Shaughnessy Bishop-Stall, "So Long, Salmon," *Toro* (Summer 2004), p. 57

16　Richard Wright, "Blade Spinner," *Saturday Night* (July 1987).

17　Interview (conducted by Michele Donnelly) with Dave Flindall, Facility Bookings, Department of Community Services, City of Kingston, May 2, 2003.

18　City of Toronto, Department of Parks and Recreation, Women in Action, Phase One—Awareness, *Final Report*, January 1994. pp. 11, 14.

19 Statistics supplied by Hockey Canada, June 1, 2004.

20 See Mary Louise Adams, "Freezing Social Relations: Artificial Ice and the Social History of Skating," in Patricia Vertinsky and John Bales, eds., *Sites of Sport: Space, Place, Experience* (London: Routledge, 2004), pp. 57-72.

21 Visits were made to four city parks in Kingston in February 2004; observations conducted by Anne Warner.

22 City of Toronto, Department of Parks and Recreation, *Final Report*, p. 10.

23 David Battistella, "We Need a National Shinny Day," *The Globe and Mail*, Jan. 31, 2003, p. A13.

24 Ibid.

25 Shawna Richer, "Village's Simple Treasure Savoured at Night," *The Globe and Mail*, Feb. 1, 2003, p. S3.

26 Gruneau and Whitson, *Hockey Night in Canada*, p. 7.

27 Gamal Abdel-Shehid, "Writing Hockey through Race: Rethinking Black Hockey in Canada," in Rinaldo Walcott, ed., *Rude: Contemporary Black Canadian Cultural Criticism* (Toronto: Insomniac Press, 2000), p. 82.

28 Eva Mackey, *The House of Difference: Cultural Politics and National Identity in Canada* (Toronto: University of Toronto Press, 2002), p. 12.

29 See Michael Robidoux, "Imagining a Canadian Identity through Sport: A Historical Interpretation of Lacrosse and Hockey," *Journal of American Folklore*, 115,456 (Spring 2002), pp. 209-25.

30 Ibid., p. 218.

31 Gruneau and Whitson, *Hockey Night in Canada*, p. 270.

CHAPTER FOUR

Women's Hockey in Canada: After the "Gold Rush"

■ JULIE STEVENS

Team Canada's gold medal in women's hockey at the 2002 Winter Olympic Games was the culmination of a decade of expansion for women's hockey in Canada. The Olympic victory would not have been possible without a dramatic growth in the competitive opportunities available to Canadian women players, especially at the adult and elite levels. These include intervarsity leagues in both Canada and the United States, the emergence of a senior women's club system (including the National Women's Hockey League), and Canadian national women's programs, encompassing both the senior and under-22 national teams. Although such developments offer many reasons for women to celebrate—new opportunities for female players, and more public attention to the women's game—they have also brought changes that some players and organizers in women's hockey view as losses. Certainly, while "progress" has been made in women's hockey in recent years, it has had its costs.

Creating Opportunities for Women in Hockey: The Use of the Courts

Women have played hockey in Canada since the end of the nineteenth century. Despite considerable opposition, along with periods of decline, there has been an overall increase in women's participation in hockey throughout the twentieth century. As part of a more general upswing in women's sports, the number of female hockey players, teams, and leagues has increased significantly over the past thirty years. The 1970s was a time of rapid growth in the women's movement in North America, and this was a catalyst for the passage of much gender equity legislation. Sports were not the most important issue on the equity agenda, but in the United States an important step was taken with the passage of Title IX of the Educational Amendments Act. Title IX was significant because it required publicly funded educational institutions to give equal funding support to men's and women's sports.

In Canada the women's movement was also successful in influencing public opinion and politicians to support the passage of the Canadian Charter of Rights and Freedoms and of provincial human rights legislation. In sport, it was the provincial legislation that enabled female hockey players to mount legal challenges to the barriers raised by the male-dominated Canadian hockey establishment. Until the 1970s, minor hockey officials in Canada had resisted girls playing hockey, typically citing the "traditions" of the game. The first public controversy in Canada involving women and hockey occurred in 1955, when an eight-year-old girl named Abigail Hoffman cut her hair and registered for a team in the Toronto Hockey League. Abigail called herself "Ab" and no one checked the gender on the birth certificate. She matched her teammates and opponents stride for stride, and was named to the league all-star team. When rumours about a girl playing prompted an investigation, it was discovered that "Ab" was Abigail. Although she was allowed to finish the season with her team, pressures from players, coaches, and league officials prompted Hoffman to join a girls' team the following season. She later quit hockey, joined a track club, and became a Canadian Olympian in athletics.[1]

In her book *The Girl in the Game*, Ann Hall comments, "By the late 1970s, sport-related complaints of sex-discrimination began to come to the attention of provincial human rights commissions," and "A majority of cases involved girls wishing to play on all-male sports teams, usually at the all-star level."[2] During this time period, three notable court cases involved girls seeking to play hockey on boy's teams. In each of these cases, the minor hockey association sought to prevent a girl from registering through legal claims that Canadian Amateur Hockey Association regulations limited membership to males.[3] In two of the cases the judges came to a broad interpretation of the CAHA's public mandate and ordered the minor hockey associations to allow girls to register. In the third case an Ontario Court of Appeal decision ruled that the minor hockey association was a private, not public, entity and did not have to allow girls to register. Despite these mixed rulings, in 1984 the CAHA passed a policy that allowed girls twelve years of age and under to play on boys' teams, but only in areas where girls' teams did not exist. Later Ontario became the only province with specific legislation designed to segregate sports on the basis of gender, when Section 19 (2) was adopted into the Human Rights Code in 1982.[4] This had the effect of prohibiting women from filing discrimination charges if male amateur sports clubs refused them a tryout.

This Ontario legislation would be contested in 1986 when Justine Blainey, a player in the Metropolitan Toronto Hockey League, challenged the league's ban on girls. Surprisingly, the Ontario Hockey Association (OHA), the governing body for boys' hockey, and the Ontario Women's Hockey Association (OWHA), the governing body for girls' hockey, both supported the ban, albeit for different reasons. The OHA argued that it was a private organization and should be able to set its membership rules as it liked. The OWHA arguments emphasized different issues, most importantly that girls playing on boys' teams would inhibit the development of girls' teams and leagues. Blainey, with support from the Canadian Association for the Advancement of Women in Sport (CAAWS) and the Women's Legal Education and Action Fund (LEAF), argued that the Canadian Charter of Rights and Freedoms entitled her to access to the best competitive and coaching opportunities available to boys, and that these developmental opportunities were not available in girls' hockey at that time. Blainey ultimately won her case, and went on to participate briefly in the women's national team program.

More recent legal battles have been less concerned with the rights of women to play on male hockey teams and more focused upon equal access for men and women to publicly funded sports facilities. Unequal ice time affects the quality of a female hockey program in a variety of ways, including the hours available for games and practices and the length of travel time. Unsatisfactory ice times undermine the sport's appeal to girls, and also to their parents, who pay significant registration fees for their daughters and want convenient ice time in return. Several legal and policy challenges have targeted municipal governments that manage public ice facilities, but, according to Elizabeth Etue and Megan Williams, female hockey advocates have not fared well in getting city councils to increase the proportion of ice time allotted to girls' and women's teams, despite overwhelming evidence of unequal access.[5] Even when municipal governments have revised their facility-use policies, too often this has had little effect because there have been no repercussions for those who fail to comply.[6] Advocates for women's hockey recognize that networking and educational efforts to encourage city councils to change policies are necessary in achieving changes. However, many advocates also believe firmly that "female hockey players must insist on equitable ice time by using one of the most effective means employed so far: human rights complaints."[7]

The progression of legal and policy battles outlined here follows a general pattern of challenges to inequality for women in sport in general during the past three decades. According to Hall, many of the cases regarding sex discrimination in sport did not revolve around "whether a girl should be allowed to play on a boys' sports team, but whether an amateur sports organization ... fell within the definition of public services and facilities in provincial human rights legislation."[8] In many instances, the case for public status, and therefore the legal requirement to adhere to human rights legislation, were based upon whether a sport association received public funding and used publicly funded facilities.

Feminist critics of sport have tended to view any successful ruling in sex discrimination cases as a human rights victory. Hall notes that the Blainey case was especially important because "it helped focus debate around an issue that split the women's sport community: sex-separated versus sex-segregated sports and organizations."[9] However, there is mixed opinion about the consequences of human rights victories within the women's hockey community. Etue and Williams agree that the "controversy sparked by the Blainey case set off a larger debate about the female game."[10] For some, such rulings enabled girls to play the game, and opened up opportunities for talented female players to get the coaching and the competition that would help them develop their talents. However, other women's hockey leaders, notably those within the OWHA, believed that the

Blainey ruling would undermine the women's game by creating an exodus of players away from girls' teams and leagues. These arguments are grounded in different ideas about what is best for girls, and they lead to different models for female hockey. Hall refers to these opposing positions as the "integrationist" and "separate-but-equal" approaches.[11]

An understanding of why such fundamental differences emerged between the OWHA and its sister organization CAAWS requires a recognition of the political environment in which the Blainey case evolved. The OWHA's effort to preserve the women's game as a separate system held merit; but it came under tremendous criticism from feminist sport advocates for promoting a position that they believed undermined the larger quest for equality for women. Specifically, Etue and Williams suggest that by stressing women's hockey as being primarily fun, friendly, and recreational, the OWHA position reinforced widely held views that the "real" sport is masculine. By implication, then, women's hockey was inferior. Helen Lenskyj calls this the "female deficit" model of sports, in which traditional male sports values are idealized and the quality and serious-ness of women's sports are disparaged.[12] By contrast, advocates who wanted to protect the integrity of the women's game did so in the belief that "separateness" would protect women's hockey from many of the problems and excesses of mainstream male-domi-nated hockey. They also believed that separateness would help to keep administrative control of the game in the hands of female sports administrators and coaches.

In the court battles involving women and girls in hockey, then, individuals, women's sports organizations, and advocacy groups did not always seek the same outcomes. In many cases the player's goal was simply to play on a team that offered better opportuni-ties to her as an individual. Sports organizations and advocacy groups, meanwhile, tended to view legal battles as a means to preserve or challenge underlying gender dif-ferences within the hockey system and in Canadian society at large. More recent court battles related to ice facility access have most often been spearheaded by an individual, such as a player or a parent, and have rarely involved an organizational movement. In addition, Canada has seen a veritable explosion of girls' and women's teams and the status of the women's game has risen dramatically, due in large part to the successes of the Canadian women's national team and the resulting media coverage. As a result, debates about the values and models of governance that are best for the development of women's and girls' hockey no longer have a high public profile.

The Changing Organizational Structure of Women's Hockey in Canada

The earliest organizations to sponsor women's hockey developed independently of, or were only loosely affiliated with, the organized structures of hockey for boys and men in Canada. In the 1920s and 1930s, women's hockey was organized by several provincial associations and by the Dominion Women's Hockey Association, which was a member of the Women's Amateur Athletic Federation. The decade of the 1920s, in particular, was a time of remarkable advances for women in Canadian sport, and the issue of women's control—captured in the popular slogan "Girls' sport run by Girls"—was pivotal to the identity of these women's organizations.[13] Women's hockey flourished in many school- and community-based leagues, and some commercially sponsored leagues, too, and it achieved unprecedented levels of visibility and press coverage. By the 1930s women's hockey in Canada included regional competitions and a national championship, run by independent governing associations at the provincial and national levels.

However, the immediate postwar decades would not be a favourable time for women's sports. The social momentum of the 1930s, which had seen advancement by women in politics and the workplace, as well as sport, was lost in the retrenchment of the 1940s and 1950s. Etue and Williams propose that the "Ozzie and Harriet" social attitudes of this time period were products of a conservative backlash against the independence that many women had achieved during the war years.[14] In this context, moreover, with large numbers of women returning to the home to raise families in the postwar suburbs, new suburban sports facilities and the sports and recreation organizations that ran them became focused on meeting the needs of boys. Television also played a key role in representing the postwar culture of sport as an inherently masculine world. The "major league" commercial sports soon became a staple of weekend television, sponsored by advertisers who targeted male wage-earners. In the 1930s radio had helped men's hockey stake its claim to being the national game. The first television broadcast of *Hockey Night in Canada* on CBC simply reinforced the already dominant view that the national game was a game for men. Against the background of these developments, female hockey declined significantly during the 1940s and 1950s. Most local women's leagues died, leading to the demise of the women's national hockey championship.

Then, in the increasingly open cultural atmosphere of the late 1960s and 1970s, women's hockey began to make a comeback. The legal challenges to the human rights code helped to put women's hockey back into the public eye and open up opportunities for girls to play. Since the 1980s the evidence clearly shows that female hockey has been on the rise. For example, in 1988 there were only 7,321 registered female players in Canada; by 2003 the number had climbed to 61,177.[15] New programs and events were developed with the purpose of enhancing the developmental opportunities available to girls at the community level. Many provinces expanded their provincial championships to include several divisions for girls and women, and provincial Winter Games programs added girls' hockey competitions. Regional competitions for women and girls, such as the Western Shield and Atlantic Challenge Cup, and national initiatives such as Hockey Canada's Program of Excellence, which includes the under-17 regional, under-18 national, and National Junior teams, now connect competitive provincial forums with national development programs. University women's hockey became important in creating another elite level of competitive opportunities for adult women players.

Canadian Interuniversity Sport (CIS) staged the first women's national varsity hockey championship in 1998. From 1998 until 2003, eleven different institutions competed at the CIS championships. The 2003–4 women's hockey university season included twenty-eight teams from across the country—a notable increase in teams given that in the early 1990s the Ontario Women's Intercollegiate Athletic Association (OWIAA) nearly cancelled hockey due to a low number of teams. Women's hockey also expanded significantly within the national Collegiate Athletic Association (NCAA) in the United States. While a collegiate championship was staged in 1998 by the American Women's College Hockey Alliance, a partner organization between USA Hockey and intercollegiate hockey programs, the NCAA staged its first Division I championship in 2001 and first Division II championship in 2002. A total of seventy-two teams, including thirty in Division I, two in Division II, and forty in Division III, competed in the 2003–04 NCAA season.

The 1990s can also be characterized as the age of women's international hockey. The decade began with the first Women's World Ice Hockey Championship in 1990 and ended with the inclusion of women's hockey in the 1998 Winter Olympics. In preparation for the 1990 world championships, the CAHA began the women's national team program in 1989. Additional international events were added, including the Three Nations Cup (later the Four Nations Cup), the Pacific Rim Challenge, and various international exhibitions. The world championship moved from a biannual to an annual event, and the Olympics became a permanent fixture on the international schedule. Consequently, the current state of the game offers a greater number of hockey opportunities for girls and women compared to any time in the past.

Still, despite this atmosphere of expansion and competitive success, women's sports in Canada have been steadily integrated into national governing bodies—like Hockey Canada—that oversee the development of both male and female athletes. The first example of a merger between women's and men's associations dates back to 1954, when the Women's Amateur Athletic Federation (WAAF) was incorporated into the Amateur [men's] Athletic Association of Canada.[16] However, most of the mergers have occurred much more recently. The Canadian Women's Intercollegiate Athletic Union joined the Canadian [men's] Interuniversity Athletic Union in 1978. The Canadian Women's Field Hockey Association and Canadian Field Hockey Association [men] amalgamated in 1991 to form Field Hockey Canada, and men's and women's curling merged in 1990 to form the Canadian Curling Association. In part, these changes have come about as a result of funding regulations by Sport Canada that have required the amalgamation of separate men's and women's federations, in the belief that this would lead to more efficient and effective "high performance" programming. The era of girls' sports run by girls is thus long gone.

Paralleling these changes in sports governing bodies, the political approach of women's sport advocacy organizations like the Canadian Association for the Advancement of Women in Sport (CAAWS) has shifted to working within the sport system to improve opportunities for women and girls, rather than challenging it from the outside. Hall suggests that a change in government funding to CAAWS—funding that used to come from the Secretary of State Women's Program now comes from the Sport Canada Women's Program—led the association to shift from a feminist advocacy group to a mainstream sport organization.[17] The outcome has been more modest, reform-oriented strategies for change, rather than challenging the dominant assumptions or operating practices of the Canadian sport system. Organizations such as CAAWS now lobby politicians and sport leaders to improve opportunities for women and girls, but they no longer push for legislation that would change Canadian sport in any fundamental ways. The idea of a separate but equal women's sport system no longer garners enough support to be on the public agenda.

The Limits and Possibilities of Contemporary Canadian Women's Hockey

On the surface it seems clear that women's hockey has benefited a great deal from its newfound popularity. But do the advances in women's hockey during the last fifteen years actually represent progress? To answer this question we need to extend our thinking beyond the growing numbers of players and programs, and the international success of Canadian women's teams. Instead, we need to question the ideals and values upon which the apparent recent successes of women's hockey are founded.

The rapid escalation in the public profile of female hockey, mainly due to the media's focus upon the international game, has created a profound growth in women's programming.[18] While recreation programs have expanded, a majority of resources are focused upon the elite and competitive tiers of the game, so that female hockey now mirrors the competitive pyramid that exists in male hockey.[19] In addition, the participation life cycle of girls' and women's hockey now follows the same pattern that occurs in boys' and men's hockey. As girls enter the game, there is high participation from ages eight to fourteen years; then competitive and elite hockey opportunities are emphasized from fifteen to twenty years of age. National and junior national teams and university, college, and competitive women's club competition dominate from twenty to thirty years. Finally, after thirty years of age, women's recreational hockey becomes popular again. In other words, a female player may enter minor hockey and play until her mid-teens, when recreational opportunities tend to decline, and then remain out of the sport until her thirties or forties, at which time she may return to the game as an adult recreational player.

Prior to the 1990s the female game was characterized by a "development ethic" in which the focus was on participation and learning, as opposed to a "performance ethic" that focuses on winning.[20] In many leagues youth teams were flatlined to balance skill across teams. Although a national championship was held in the 1980s, the event symbolized a gathering of teams rather than a battle between them. The expansion of female hockey at the competitive elite levels has led to greater social acceptance of women and girls in the game. Many parents now have new expectations that both their daughters and sons will have the same opportunities. However, it is most often women and girls from middle-class families who make their way up to the elite levels in hockey. Extra coaching, equipment, skating camps, and private hockey schools are often the difference between being a good recreational player and an elite competitor, and these opportunities are not within the reach of many Canadian families. Consequently, the growing acceptance of women's hockey, and improved opportunities for girls and women to succeed in hockey, arguably have less to do with gender than with social class. The explosion of interest in women's hockey, and the growth of opportunities for girls and women in hockey, seems mostly a middle-class phenomenon.

While parental support for daughters playing hockey signals an important change from the past, and is a very happy experience for many girls, the downside is that some parents have become very ambitious. Parents of players on elite teams are often concerned with one key question: "How can my daughter make the national team?" The competitive attitude among parents whose daughters are involved in hockey mirrors the types of behaviour witnessed among some parents of boys playing hockey. The only difference is that for girls and their parents, the goal is the national team and the Olympics, and perhaps college scholarships, as opposed to the allure of a professional career in the National Hockey League.

It is difficult to know whether a different type of women's hockey system might change or soften this competitive attitude by returning to an emphasis on playing the game for its own sake. The established competitiveness reflects dominant views of the nature of sport, and the role of sport in individuals' lives. Women's hockey is now a game administered by the larger Hockey Canada network, which is a pyramid of competitive opportunities aimed at reaching elite level competition. In principle, female hockey may be different, but with the growth of international competition it is now situated within a sports system in which parents of female hockey players have similar ambitions to parents of male hockey players, or parents of girls who compete in elite swimming and gymnastics. Substantial changes in public values and in the leadership of women's hockey would be needed to modify this high-performance emphasis.

The issue of changing values can be related to the transition that women's hockey has experienced since the early 1990s. Before that time, hockey for women and girls had more of a "community" atmosphere. Participation was the focus, and beginners were welcomed—the woman who had always wanted to play, or the girl who finally found a team where she was accepted. In order to allow players of diverse ages and skill levels to play together, women's hockey embraced a "no intentional bodychecking rule." However, since 1990 the promotion of "high performance," particularly by the national and provincial hockey programs, has eroded that ethos and supplanted it with a more competitive model. Now the most skilled players are selected for talent development in Canada's high-performance programs, and the rest are left to fend for themselves. Development for the sake of participation is seen as a distraction from the ultimate performance ethic.

Susan Birrell and Diana Richter found that women who played in a feminist softball league in the United States in the 1980s believed that most organized sport was "rigid, hierarchical, conservative, elitist and alienating." They were determined to "keep the dominant values represented in institutionalized sport from reasserting themselves in other levels of recreational play," specifically, in their own league. They believed that "when outcome is privileged over the process of play, those whose skill levels are less developed are often disenfranchised from sport."[21] However, the Canadian female hockey system has now enthusiastically embraced many of the values associated with organized sport that Birrell and Richter's subjects criticize here. This has not only changed the nature of recreational female hockey, but, in some cases, the resources available to recreational or non-competitive hockey have also been cut back to better support the high-performance program. In the year leading up to the 1998 Olympics, $500,000 was spent on the women's national teams, whereas only $25,000 was allocated to the CHA's women's/girls' program designed to increase participation. The priority here is all too clear.

Birrell and Richter's account of a participatory ethos within women's softball, like the discussion earlier of a similar ethos in Canadian women's hockey, illustrates how what were small subcultures—even countercultural activities—in the 1980s have become integrated into the mainstream sport culture and changed as a result. As women's competition has expanded at the elite levels, up to and including the Olympic Games, key values that once guided the subculture of women's hockey have been left behind. Some of the reason for this shift simply comes down to the lure of resources and recognition. In women's hockey, accepting funding from Sport Canada has meant embracing a high-performance ethic. To get funding, women's hockey must conform to the ethos of the Canadian sport system and be accountable for spending the money "effectively." What Sport Canada wants is world championship titles and Olympic gold medals.

Performance pressures are now visible in many areas of programming in women's hockey. For instance, the under-22 program—initially designed to help develop strong junior players throughout the country—has experienced a talent drain similar to the one that has existed in junior men's hockey for some time. From 1998 until 2001, about 25 per cent of the national under-22 team included Canadians playing on NCAA (US university) or US high-school teams. That figure increased to 55 per cent in 2001–02. The lure of the NCAA has increased, moreover, even though each province in Canada established elite provincial team programs once female hockey was included in the Canada Games, and despite expansion of a competitive under-18 club system throughout the country.

All of this points to a talent drain of young Canadian players away from local, regional, and national development programs to the United States. In addition, the NCAA has begun to attract elite Canadian coaches. Of the women involved in the national team coaching pool, three of them—Shannon Miller, the 1998 Olympic team head coach, Melody Davidson, the 2006 Olympic team head coach, and Margot Page, the 2003 under-22 national team head coach—are among the ten women who coach in the NCAA Division I. The opportunity to compete and work in the US college system is beneficial for individual players and coaches who want to enhance their hockey experience. However, the Canadian development system as a whole may be disadvantaged when, for example, players are not released from their college teams to participate in national or provincial camps and competitions. In addition, the absence of the most talented young players inhibits the natural process of modelling that occurs from the talented to the less talented players. Having role models in local and regional programs helps to improve the overall quality of the Canadian talent pool.

The irony is, though, that despite the ongoing professionalization of women's hockey, many people still devalue the game as an inferior version of men's hockey. For example, instances when a woman has competed on a professional or semi-professional men's hockey team have garnered considerable media and public attention, but they have also attracted disparaging comments and putdowns of women's abilities. Specific examples include Manon Rhéaume, who played in an NHL pre-season game, as well as East Coast Hockey League and Quebec Major Junior League games; Hayley Wickenheiser, who played for the Kirkkonummi Salamat in the Finnish Second Division men's professional league; and Kim St. Pierre, who tried out for the McGill University men's team in the Canadian Interuniversity Sport league.

Among these examples, the Hayley Wickenheiser story raises a crucial set of questions about the relationships between men's and women's hockey. Wickenheiser is widely recognized as a dominant player within the international women's game. However, her reputation becomes far more complex within the scope of her involvement in men's professional hockey. Wickenheiser did not believe that she could develop to the fullest in female hockey, so she sought to compete in the men's game. She saw no viable opportunities for her to do this in Canada, and she was denied access to men's teams in Italy. She finally landed a contract with a men's professional team in Finland, where she played in 2003. The Canadian media coverage of Wickenheiser's career increased significantly after she left women's elite hockey and joined the team in

Finland. The exposure she received extended far beyond any attention she had received while playing women's semi-pro hockey in North America (in the National Women's Hockey League) or while on the Canadian women's national team.

Nancy Theberge has considered the issues raised when elite women try out for elite, professional men's hockey teams, and she argues that what is at issue is that women's sport has a constant struggle for credibility, and the "inferiorization of women's athletic achievements [is] at the centre of this struggle."[22] In her analysis of Manon Rhéaume's hockey career, Theberge suggests that there is a downside to women seeking to play on men's hockey teams. Specifically, she argues that when "men's hockey is positioned as superior and women who play with men come to represent the heights of female achievement ... it may be argued that the dominant interpretation is a powerful—but troubling—re-confirmation of masculine hegemony in sport."[23]

Of course, the "dominant interpretation" is not the only one that is available. For example, Hayley Wickenheiser is a strong symbolic figure for many girls—she provides a role model for many young players, and her career proves that girls can play at very high levels. For many girls and women who believe that their sport is ignored, or who have felt that "doors of opportunity" have been closed to them, Wickenheiser's opportunity to play in Finland represents a triumph. And this reading is held even though Wickenheiser's experience in Finland did not satisfy her in the end and she returned to be with her family and to rejoin the Canadian women's national team. What is important to many is that she went, and she lasted.

Still, it is clear from public discussion of Wickenheiser's experience in Finland that there is little agreement on the "real" Hayley Wickenheiser story. One way to read her experience is simply to argue that she is the best female hockey player in the world and that her career shows how the calibre of female players is potentially very high; comparable indeed to lower-level male professional players. However, another reading, and the reading often consistent with the "dominant interpretation" of the status of women's hockey, depicts Wickenheiser almost as a kind of comic sideshow. Her playing experience in Finland demonstrates to some that even a top female player can't "stack up" against Second Division European male players. In this view, her "only" reaching the lower branches of professional male hockey ends up as a discourse of "failure" that supports arguments for the superiority of men's hockey. In this discourse, women's hockey is not something to be valued on its own terms; rather it is locked into an inevitably invidious contrast with male hockey at the highest levels. By contrast, proponents of an older "separate but equal" model for the development of women's hockey simply don't care to make the comparison with the men's game. They insist that the game be evaluated and supported on its own merits, as an independent and separate sporting entity.

However, although values and legitimacy are important issues, governance and control are arguably the most crucial issues at stake in the debate between integrated or "separate but equal" hockey systems. Contemporary liberal feminists seek female equality with men by extending to women those rights and privileges being afforded to men, while other feminists (radical feminists, or feminists who celebrate what makes women different) often argue for separate institutions and activities.[24] In sports these two views have led to different strategies. Some women try to make a fuller place for themselves in the existing sport system, while others try to establish separate sport institutions, run by women and based on a different set of values. In her discussion of women's sport in Canada, Hall comments that the liberal reformers have sought "to provide girls and women with the same opportunities and resources as boys and men, and to remove the barriers and constraints to their participation." In contrast, she notes, other feminists have advocated "an unequivocal women-centred perspective, which recognized and celebrated differences among women and at the same time seriously questioned male dominated and male-defined sport."[25] The liberal feminist view, which supports an integrated sport model, would applaud the addition of elite hockey opportunities for women and girls, because its adherents believe that girls should have the same competitive opportunities as boys. It would also accept the governance of the female game within the established male hockey network as an appropriate step towards the benefits of integration. However, this type of change clearly moves hockey closer to the model of other sports, in which national associations provide programs for both sexes and are required by Sport Canada to demonstrate an effective development program for girls and women.

Commenting critically on this approach, Birrell and Richter argue that the boom in women's sport has simply accommodated more women into a system of male sport.[26] From this perspective, the accommodation that has occurred in women's hockey is disconcerting. Indeed, the female hockey community has clearly experienced two significant shifts in its foundational characteristics.[27] First, the community is no longer controlled from within. The power of female governance forums, such as the national Female Council, within Hockey Canada, has not been very strong. Notably, the expansion of the women's high-performance program within Hockey Canada has resulted in a shift in decision-making authority from the Female Council to the Women's International Policy Committee. This change essentially reflects a move from a separate but equal to an integrationist governance structure, and it is an approach mirrored by provincial and local hockey associations across the country. With this approach women have arguably won broader acceptance, and a grudging respect for women's hockey, but the cost has been the loss of effective control over the organization of the women's game. Today the separate but equal model sought by the OWHA remains an isolated campaign within the Canadian hockey system.

At the same time female hockey organizations have been increasingly bureaucratized and assimilated into an integrated amateur sport system that has undergone a high degree of professionalization. The sources of this professionalization are complex, but they appear to spring in part from the institutional pressures placed upon sport by the federal government.[28] By the very nature of its separateness, female hockey had long maintained independent, grassroots volunteer-based management structures.[29] Then, with the incorporation of women's hockey into the Hockey Canada structure, which began in 1982 with the reinstatement of the national championship and became further entrenched over the 1990s with the addition of international events, changed things significantly. The values and participatory focus of the female game were challenged by a new emphasis on results, and on the development of professionalized programs designed to fit with the new emphasis on high performance.

As the diverse and informal community of women's hockey began to evolve into a rational talent-production system, player involvement became increasingly viewed in light of its value in the high-performance sport machine. Alternative sport models, including but not limited to women's sports organizations, have increasingly been perceived as disorganized, inefficient, and unproductive. Here Lenskyj's "female deficit" perspective in performance has been extended into the organizational sphere.[30] Sport structures not embracing the traditional male competitive values and attitudes in sport are seen as inferior. In this way the transformation of the female game and the evolution beyond older participation-based values are seen as an institutional necessity.

Nancy Theberge and Susan Birrell believe that the increasing involvement of girls and women in sport in recent years is cause for optimism, but that other aspects, such as women's power and influence in educational and amateur sport, are less encouraging. They identify examples of alternative women's sport models—the Association for Intercollegiate Athletics for Women, and the Women's Olympic Games—but they still believe that there is a "persistence of ideological struggle over the values and meanings of women's sport."[31] Without a governing association that exclusively serves the development of women's and girls' hockey, resistance or reorientation of the women's hockey model is unlikely. Unfortunately, previous discussions about women's hockey as a site of struggle do not really offer a specific alternative women's hockey model. Kristin Bell-Altenstad and Susan Vail note this uncertainty in future direction, remarking: "Feminists are not unified in answering the question: how can equality ultimately be achieved?"[32]

Values, Direction, and Control

In *Hockey Night in Canada*, Gruneau and Whitson argue, "The debates around hockey for girls and women have simply been one small indicator of a much broader set of re-evaluations and struggles in recent years over the nature, direction, and control of hockey in this country."[33] While they recognize that old hockey traditions die hard (and have their die-hard defenders), Gruneau and Whitson suggest that there is room for optimism that women's hockey offers opportunities to resist the old ways of doing things.

Unfortunately, I do not believe that any significant struggle now exists over the values and future direction of the women's game; nor is it clear how women might exercise a greater degree of control over the development of women's hockey under current circumstances. Despite the growth of female hockey in the country, there are few, if any, examples of resistance to the male hockey network by leaders in the female hockey community. Even the OWHA, the only women's hockey governing body in the country, has increasingly adopted the values inherent in a professionalized (male) elite performance model, rather than continuing the effort to cultivate an alternative, more self-consciously egalitarian and participation-based sport model.

Of course, the broad philosophical debate over whether to emphasize high performance or to emphasize broad-based participation is by no means new. But it is a debate that supporters of women's sports might well be urged to reconsider.

Notes

1 This case is discussed in greater detail in J. Avery and J. Stevens, *Too Many Men on the Ice: Women's Hockey in North America* (Victoria, BC: Polestar Books, 1997).

2 Ann Hall, *The Girl and the Game* (Peterborough, ON: Broadview Press, 2002), p. 163.

3 The Canadian Amateur Hockey Association (CAHA) was created in 1914, and Hockey Canada was created in 1969. In 1994 the CAHA merged with Hockey Canada to form the Canadian Hockey Association. In 2003 the Association changed its name to Hockey Canada in order to simplify its title.

4 See Avery and Stevens, *Too Many Men on the Ice.*

5 E. Etue and M. Williams, *On the Edge: Women Making Hockey History* (Toronto: Second Story Press, 1996).

6 M. Williams, "Women's Hockey: Heating up the Equity Debate," *Canadian Woman Studies*, 15,4 (1995), p. 78.

7 Etue and Williams, *On the Edge*, p. 190.

8 Hall, *Girl and the Game*, p. 177.

9 Ibid., p. 181.

10 Etue and Williams, *On the Edge*, p. 163.

11 Hall, *Girl and the Game.*

12 Helen Lenskyj, *Women, Sport and Physical Activity: Selected Research Themes* (Ottawa: Ministry of Supply and Services Canada, 1994).

13 See the discussion of women's sports organizations in the 1920s and 1930s in Bruce Kidd, *The Struggle for Canadian Sport* (Toronto: University of Toronto Press, 1996).

14 Etue and Williams, *On the Edge.*

15 Registration report, *Hockey Canada*, Calgary, 2003.

16 Hall, *Girl and the Game.*

17 Ibid.

18 Julie Stevens, "The Declining Sense of Community in Canadian Women's Hockey," *Women in Sport and Physical Activity Journal*, 9,2 (2000), pp. 123-40.

19 Avery and Stevens, *Too Many Men on the Ice.*

20 Stevens, "Declining Sense of Community in Canadian Women's Hockey."

21 S. Birrell and D. Richter, "Is a Diamond Forever? Feminist Transformations of Sport," in S. Birrell and C. Cole, eds., *Women, Sport and Culture* (Champaign, IL: Human Kinetics Press, 1994), pp. 234, 235.

22 Nancy Theberge, "Playing with the Boys: Manon Rhéaume, Women's Hockey and the Struggle for Legitimacy," *Canadian Woman Studies*, 15,1 (1995), p. 40.

23 Ibid., p. 41.

24 P. Elliot and N. Mandell, "Feminist Theories," in N. Mandell, ed., *Feminist Issues: Race, Class and Sexuality* (Scarborough, ON: Prentice Hall, 1998), p. 5.

25 Hall, *Girl and the Game*, p. 174.

26 Birrell and Richter, "Is a Diamond Forever?"

27 Etue and Williams, *On the Edge*.

28 Donald Macintosh and David Whitson, *The Game Planners: Transforming Canada's Sport System* (Montreal: McGill-Queen's University Press, 1990).

29 Stevens, "Declining Sense of Community in Canadian Women's Hockey."

30 Lenskyj, *Women, Sport and Physical Activity*.

31 Nancy Theberge and Susan Birrell, "Structural Constraints Facing Women in Sport," in D.M. Costa and E. Guthrie, eds., *Women and Sport: Interdisciplinary Perspectives* (Champaign, IL: Human Kinetics, 1994).

32 K. Bell-Altenstad and S. Vail, "Developing Public Policy for Women in Sport: A Discourse Analysis," *Canadian Woman Studies,* 15,4 (1995), p. 109.

33 R. Gruneau and D. Whitson, *Hockey Night in Canada: Sport, Identities, and Cultural Politics* (Toronto: Garamond Press, 1993), pp. 172-73.

CHAPTER FIVE

Hockey Canada and the Bodychecking Debate in Minor Hockey

■ MICHAEL ROBIDOUX AND PIERRE TRUDEL

The issue of violence in Canadian ice hockey is nothing new. There have been reports of "overt brutality evident in open fighting on the ice and in mob scenes involving fans and players" almost from the outset of the modern game.[1] Today the game's potential for violence continues to be on display at various levels, from youth hockey to the professional leagues. But the incidents that typically get the greatest public attention are those that occur in the NHL. The most prominent recent incident occurred in the winter of 2004 when the Vancouver Canucks' superstar Todd Bertuzzi sucker-punched Colorado Avalanche forward Steve Moore behind the head and drove Moore's head down into the ice, breaking his neck in the process. Lawrence Scanlan, who wrote the book *Grace under Fire*, a historical examination of violence in hockey,[2] responded to the incident by writing in a *Globe and Mail* "Commentary": "How did hockey come to this place? How did the game come to be this way? Truth is, now more, now less, it has *always* been this way. And maybe, just maybe, that's why we like it. Maybe we like a little blood with our beer and our popcorn and our 'He shoots! He scores!'"[3]

While incidents such as the Bertuzzi case get the publicity, violent behaviours have also been documented in local minor hockey associations across Canada. These problems of aggression and violence in Canadian minor hockey have been identified and discussed in scholarly research and in federal and provincial government reports for more than thirty years. Despite the many recommendations in these studies, and reports about how to reduce aggression and violence in minor hockey, research suggests that very little has changed since the 1970s.[4] By contrast, attitudes to violence in Canadian society at large have changed notably since the end of World War II. Corporeal punishment is no longer acceptable in schools; the police and courts have cracked down on domestic violence; and many schools and communities have instituted "zero-tolerance" policies to violence. Remarkably, hockey appears to have remained relatively insulated from this broader shift in values. What are the ongoing sources of excessive violence and aggression in youth hockey? What is Canada's main governing body, Hockey Canada (formerly the Canadian Hockey Association [CHA]), doing to rectify this situation?

Before delving into these questions we need first to clarify the meaning of the words "aggression" and "violence," and consider how these concepts relate to hockey. In his book *Violence and Sport*, Michael Smith explains that aggression "is usually regarded as the more generic concept. More often than not, aggression is defined as any behaviour designed to injure another person, psychologically or physically. Malicious gossip is a form of aggression; so is a punch in the nose."[5] Violence for Smith is a component of aggression because it "refers to the physical side of aggression, hence the term 'violent aggression.' Violence is behaviour intended to injure another person physically." Taking up Smith's violence typology, Ann Hall, Trevor Slack, Gary Smith, and David Whitson have adapted it to ice hockey (see Table 5.1).[6]

Table 5.1
A Hockey Violence Typology

Relatively Legitimate

Brutal Body Contact	**Borderline Violence**
Conforms to the official rules of hockey, more or less accepted. Hard bodychecks are the best example.	Violates the official rules of hockey and the law of the land, but widely accepted. An obvious example is hockey fights between equally willing and capable opponents.

Relatively Illegitimate

Quasi-Criminal Violence	**Criminal Violence**
Violates the official rules of hockey, the law of the land, and to a significant degree informal player norms; more or less not accepted. Hockey examples include fights between mismatched opponents, cross-checking a player from behind, hard bodychecks into the goal post, or hard bodychecks in the open ice aimed at or below knee-level.	Violates the official rules of hockey, the law of the land, and players' informal norms; not accepted. Hockey examples include deliberate attempts to injure, such as stick-swinging, butt-ending, spearing, and kicking; also, invading the stands to settle a score with a fan, or physically abusing an official.

This typology is significant because it not only identifies aspects of violence in hockey, but also categorizes their acceptance in the sport. Thus, while quasi-criminal and criminal violence are far from the norm in hockey, other forms of violence, such as excessive bodychecking, are widely viewed as "legitimate" and actively encouraged. Hockey's formal rules allow for the use of violent play within specified limits to attain a tactical advantage. In a game in which players literally fight for the puck, aggressiveness and violence are part of any player's learned repertoire of hockey skills. Still, within the informal culture of hockey, aggressiveness and violence outside the official rules of the game are also often viewed as legitimate tactics by many players, coaches, and fans. Illegal tactics such as punching, slashing, charging, cross-checking, verbal threats, and outright fist-fighting are widely understood to be "necessary" in certain situations to retaliate against perceived threats; to intimidate and frustrate opponents and throw them off their game; and to strategically negate the dangers posed by "skill" players. The problem is that the lines between the "official" and "unofficial" rules governing aggression and violence in hockey are so easily and so often blurred. Hockey's official rules are meant to set limits on the strategic uses of aggression and violence, but interpretations of the legitimate and illegitimate uses of violence vary considerably.

The case of bodychecking provides a good example of the difficulty of assessing the lines between the seemingly legitimate use of violence and its illegitimate uses. Bodychecking involves the regulated use of physical force to gain an advantage within the formal rules of hockey. But it is also often used excessively as a tactic to intimidate opponents; it can be deployed with a deliberate intent to injure another team's star player; it is routinely linked to aggressive penalties; and it clearly leads to an increase in injuries. In other words, bodychecking in hockey can easily slide from being a legitimate tactical skill to an act of deliberate aggression and violence (for example, body-contact not immediately relevant to the flow of play, but designed to intimidate, or aggressive checking meant to cause an injury).

The ease of this transition has made bodychecking one of the most contentious issues in hockey played at younger ages—and it is an issue evident in the position taken by Hockey Canada on the question of excessive aggression and violence in youth hockey, and in particular of when to introduce bodychecking in minor hockey. Until recently bodychecking did not start until the peewee division.[7] Then, in May 2002, Hockey Canada announced that for the 2002 season hockey associations across the country could introduce bodychecking a division lower, with nine- and ten-year-olds.[8] The decision led to considerable media coverage and public outcry, and it paved the way for subsequent flip-flops in Hockey Canada's position.

The Origins and Mission of Hockey Canada

Hockey Canada's history begins early in the twentieth century. The precursor to Hockey Canada, the Canadian Amateur Hockey Association (CAHA), was founded in 1914 to supervise all amateur hockey in Canada. The CAHA was created to regulate hockey in the interests of promoting sportsmanship, fair play, and the technical development of the game. In the early years of the century, amateur sports organizations such as the CAHA took the control of violence seriously as an important part of their mandate. The promotion of amateur sport was rooted in emerging middle-class concerns for controlled emotion, and the marriage of physical and moral development. The goal was to provide children and young adults with positive sporting experiences, *not* to be a training ground for professional players.

Richard Gruneau and David Whitson note how the CAHA gradually began to change in the forty years after its inception in 1914. The organization began to act less like an alternative to professional hockey and more like a feeder system for the pros. By 1947, "The CAHA had become little more than a junior partner of the NHL; it couldn't even determine the eligibility of its own members or change its own playing rules without NHL approval."[9] Still, as a matter of policy the CAHA clung to much of the earlier rhetoric about the organization's broad developmental role in the provision of sport for children and youth. As late as 1975 a CAHA report was stating that "the CAHA objective" was to "encourage positive skill learning in the context of a better understanding of what the game of hockey is all about."[10] The same report states: "When interests such as developing a boy for professional hockey begin encroaching on these fundamental ideas of minor hockey, then a serious second look must be taken at that program."[11]

In 1969, in response to Canada's poor showings in international hockey, a second national administrative structure, Hockey Canada, was put into place to improve Canada's national hockey program. In 1994 the two organizations—the CAHA and Hockey Canada—were fused together to become the Canadian Hockey Association, but were to uphold the foundational principles of the older Canadian Amateur Hockey Association. These principles, as stated by the CHA, were to ensure "the advancement of amateur hockey for all individuals through progressive leadership by ensuring meaningful opportunities and enjoyable experiences in a safe sportsmanlike environment."[12] The latest development has been the recent name change from the Canadian Hockey Association back to Hockey Canada. A press release of May 2003 announced that the CHA would change its name to Hockey Canada for practical reasons; the name is supposedly easier to use, it is more readily adaptable to bilingualism, and has no acronym.[13] However, this change is so recent that much of the documentation on Hockey Canada continues to be listed under the old CHA banner. The point is, despite these name changes, there have not been any major alterations to the mission initially established under the Canadian Amateur Hockey Association. The "Minor

Hockey Development Guide" available on Hockey Canada's website offers the guiding philosophy of the organization: "Hockey Canada believes every player should have the chance to participate in the great game of hockey.... The goal of Hockey Canada is not to put players in the NHL, but rather to ensure a meaningful, enjoyable experience."[14] The same document also states: "Winning and losing should not be a priority for young players. Players should learn to compete in practice, and want to get better, but it needs to be put in the proper context by MHA's [Minor Hockey Associations] coaches and parents."[15] Statements such as these are deliberate expressions that run counter to elitist or hypercompetitive sport philosophies. So, apparently, by its own admission Hockey Canada should not be mistaken for a developmental system focused only on high-performance or professional sport leagues. Hockey Canada continues to claim a broader public mandate.

Research on Violence in Canadian Minor Hockey

Anyone who has spent much time in community arenas across the country can see first-hand that the mission stated by the governing bodies (CAHA, CHA, and Hockey Canada) of minor hockey often seems more like mere rhetoric than reality. The safe and positive developmental environment promoted by the regulators of minor hockey is often subsumed by a highly competitive, unsafe, and, sometimes, violent culture that has caused concern for many parents, coaches, players, researchers, and physicians. To address these concerns federal and provincial governments have funded a great deal of research focused on the prevalence of violence and the rates of injuries experienced in Canadian youth hockey.[16] Research materials in government reports have variously come from hearings, surveys, and/or interviews with coaches, players, parents, officials, and league representatives. But, too often, government reports on youth hockey violence have been superficial and are based solely on the perceptions that different groups in hockey—parents, coaches, players, and organizers—have of one another. The result is a blaming game of sorts, in which one group points the finger at another group, labelling them as the source of the problems that each group is encountering.

The litany of solutions offered in such reports is depressingly familiar. Problems of violence and safety can be rectified: if better training for coaches is provided; if coaches avoid a winning at all costs approach; if codes of conduct for parents are designed; if more effective training can be put in place for referees to allow them to better reinforce the rules; and if more people are better informed about the negative influences of professional hockey and the media on kids. However, the many government studies on youth hockey violence rarely address the actual impetus for violence, or the presence of differing conceptions about what violence is. Instead it has been the academic community that has undertaken the task of exploring and documenting violence and injuries in hockey and that, in limited cases, has made an impact on minor hockey in Canada.

Among the first scholarly contributions are the works of Edmund W. Vaz[17] and Michael D. Smith.[18] Based on his ethnographic study of youth hockey in the Toronto region in the early 1970s, Vaz was quick to take the Canadian Amateur Hockey Association to task by pointing out the difference between CAHA ideology and CAHA practice. He stated:

> Despite the ideology of the Minor Hockey League (with its emphasis on sportsman-ship and fair play, good citizenship, loyalty and the development of 'moral character') it is no longer possible to conceal the fact that youngsters who play organized hockey are engaged in worklike activity, and it is a myth to believe that their sole motivation is the pursuit of pleasure.[19]

In a later article, "Institutionalized Rule Violation and Control in Organized Minor League Hockey," Vaz outlined three key factors for the presence of violence in youth hockey: "(a) institutionalized rule violation and the use of physical force are institution-alized behavior; (b) such behavior is structurally inevitable; and (c) the kind and amount of rule violation and violence that occur result largely from an informal control system operating."[20]

Smith has also been critical of the pervasive violence in youth hockey. In his "Reference other" theory, Smith identifies the various supporting factors for youth hockey violence:

> Quantitative and qualitative data on hockey violence, in particular, indicate that play-ers perceive a pervasive climate of violence approval, though this varies greatly by 'ref-erence other' and by age and competitive level. In the eyes of hockey parents, coaches and others, violence both expresses strong character and helps win hockey games, the former at all levels of competition, the latter increasingly as performers move upward through the system.[21]

Smith argues that these reward systems are very much tied into mass media representa-tions of sport and its tendency to glorify violence. He goes so far as to say that "media presentations of professional hockey provide observers with blueprints for violent behavior in their own games."[22]

These trends, identified nearly thirty years ago, remain surprisingly consistent with recent research on minor league hockey in Canada. At the conclusion of their ethno-graphic study of moral values in youth ice hockey, Dany Bernard and Pierre Trudel conclude: "If we compare minor hockey 25 years ago [referring to the works of Smith and Vaz] and minor hockey today, we have to admit that few improvements have been made.... The sub-culture prevailing in minor hockey doesn't contribute to the development of the whole person."[23] Attitudes towards violence and aggression remain remarkably similar in that they are justified when conducive to competitive edge. A series of studies conducted with teams from atom to bantam (nine to fifteen years old) indicates that while coaches do not directly encourage violent actions from players, and even censure players who receive too many useless penalties, coaches will occasionally congratulate players for a penalized action executed to save a goal.[24] Similarly, coaches will accept verbal intimidation between players especially when it causes the opponent to lose concentration and/or take some form of retaliatory penalty. Central to this notion of sanctioned violence is the role of bodychecking. Coaches exhort players to carry it out with greater intensity; yet seldom is bodychecking taught properly during practices or games. Perhaps even more disconcerting, players often know what a fair bodycheck is but attest to using the hit for other purposes; for example, for intimidation or to retaliate for a check received, legal or not.

The impact of bodychecking and the ensuing violence can reach dangerous levels due simply to physics. For example, researchers have demonstrated significant differences in the force of impact between players in the same age range because of disparities in height and weight. Within the same leagues G. Régnier and his co-researchers[25] documented a 31.5-centimetre height difference and 37.2-kilogram difference between peewee players (twelve to thirteen years old), while Bernard and others[26] found a 41-centimetre height difference and 47.7 kilogram weight difference within the bantam-aged players (fourteen to fifteen years old). It should come as no surprise, then, that legitimatized body contact, compounded with enormous size discrepancies, creates a physically precarious environment for many young players. While it is difficult to make accurate assessments of minor injuries resulting from bodychecking—because coaches are often unaware of players' scrapes and bruises, and players are not contacted after each game—studies show that there is on average at least one minor injury per game per team, and major injuries (sprains, fractures, concussions, dislocations) vary greatly between teams and leagues, ranging from one major injury per six games to one per twenty-two games.[27] Data from these studies also suggest that bodychecking leagues were found to have a twelve times greater rate of fractures than were leagues without bodychecking. The research on the impact of bodychecking (given or received) in youth hockey is clear: bodychecking is responsible for about 45 per cent of the minor injuries and 70 per cent of the major injuries in youth hockey. Contrary to beliefs that playing hockey without bodychecking would result in more incidents of dangerous stick violations and roughness, the data suggest otherwise: at the peewee level, there were 3.3 less penalties (9.1 vs 12.4) per game in the league where bodychecking was not allowed, and there were also fewer roughing, high-sticking, slashing, and elbowing penalties.

A number of minor hockey initiatives have been implemented in response to government reports and academic studies that have identified the numerous problems plaguing Canadian minor hockey. One such initiative has been to put in place training courses for all parties involved in the minor hockey system. In this regard Hockey Canada has been actively providing courses for coaches, players, mangers, referees, trainers, and parents—although the effectiveness of these courses is not known because few of them have ever been assessed. One of the few training initiatives that did undergo an assessment was an intervention strategy by Trudel and his colleagues to help coaches teach players to use bodychecks correctly.[28] Coaches were asked to participate in training sessions at the start of the season, and the program provided teaching materials (written documents and videos). However, a later assessment of this intervention strategy showed no significant differences in the frequency of legal bodychecks per game, the type and frequency of penalties, and the number of injuries.

The authors underlined the difficulties that they faced in making their assessment because they were forced to rely on the good intentions of the coaches, who were not obliged to use the proposed strategy. In the Trudel study, a majority of the coaches carried out the proposed tasks, but some admitted that they did not entirely follow the intervention strategy, citing such reasons as lack of time and excessive player turnover. Coaches are not always willing to comply with requests to include new material in their coaching methods. For example, another study reported that "22 of 34 minor league coaches refused to participate in a video about concussion prevention because they thought that watching the video would make their players less aggressive and successful as a team."[29] In referring to an intervention project conducted by USA Hockey to measure the effectiveness of an introductory bodychecking video created to help decrease injuries in bantam and high-school hockey, another team of researchers noted that they did not receive sufficient coaching compliance to conduct the study adequately.[30]

Bodychecking at the Atom Level,
and the Position of Hockey Canada

The research evidence is clear: despite well-intentioned initiatives tried over the years, the problems of violence and accompanying injury rates in Canadian minor hockey remain high. Moreover, many of these initiatives do not directly target the primary source of injury, which is bodychecking. Studies conducted in the United States have come to the same conclusion regarding the role of bodychecking in youth hockey.[31] Thus, the only plausible options would be to eliminate bodychecking altogether or to impose minimum age requirements—the second of which is the stance taken by major medical associations, such as the Canadian Academy of Sports Medicine and the American Academy of Pediatrics.[32] Both of these associations argue that injuries in hockey can be reduced by limiting bodychecking for players fifteen years of age and younger. A Canadian Medical Association article recommends that bodychecking not be introduced until players reach the age of seventeen to eighteen, because most physical growth is not complete until that point.[33]

Not satisfied with what scholarly researchers and physicians were providing, Hockey Canada commissioned a study by W.J. Montelpare to dispute previous research findings that documented significantly higher injury rates in youth bodychecking hockey.[34] Montelpare's study of atom-aged players initially reported no significant increase in injuries, but these conclusions were later revised when the CBC television documentary *Disclosure*[35] exposed errors in the data. A recalculation of Montelpare's data revealed that the injury rate was actually four times higher in hockey with bodychecking when compared to non-contact hockey.

Hockey Canada's first reaction to this criticism was to defend Montelpare's study. Hockey Canada stated publicly that the CBC was incorrect in its findings and that Montelpare's initial conclusions were valid after all. It claimed to have sought the advice of two independent researchers who substantiated Montelpare's findings. A spokesperson for Hockey Canada explained that they "reworked the numbers and there's no statistical difference [between injuries in hockey without bodychecking and hockey with bodychecking]" and that "they had independent researchers look at it and analyze the numbers. They came up with the same conclusion."[36] Not satisfied with this response, William Houston of *The Globe and Mail* went directly to the "independent researchers" to hear what it was they exactly said. According to Houston, the first researcher verified that the CBC was correct and that "there was a four-fold increase in injuries between the non-bodychecking and bodychecking." The second researcher similarly denied substantiating Montelpare's results to Hockey Canada. On the contrary, Houston noted, this "independent researcher" had "fought against lowering the age of bodychecking for years."[37]

The CBC's rebuttal to the Montelpare study created so much publicity that Hockey Canada was pressured into revising its position on bodychecking as early as the atom level. The organization proposed to return to the old policy of introducing bodychecking at the peewee level. Still, Hockey Canada decided to allow certain minor hockey associations to continue to experiment with bodychecking in what it referred to as "controlled research environments."[38]

Once again this decision is not without critics. The issue of liability in these "controlled environments" is the first concern here, considering the amount of research already indicating the increased risk of injury that young children face in playing contact hockey.[39] The second concern is that more research on the results of bodychecking in youth hockey seems unwarranted at this point. More than thirty years of research already exist on the topic, which even the main branch of Hockey Canada (Ontario Hockey Federation) responsible for commissioning the Montelpare study acknowledges.[40]

Promoters of early bodychecking in youth hockey have responded to such conclusions by arguing that the problem does not lie in the existence of bodychecking itself, but rather in the poor execution of bodychecking and in how young players have not learned how to protect themselves. For that reason, they argue, youth need to learn how to hit and receive hits from one another, and they need to do this sooner rather than later in minor hockey. Eliminating bodychecking at early ages in youth hockey, the argument runs, simply has the effect of ensuring high rates of injury when bodychecking is introduced at the older ages. The solution is to introduce bodychecking as soon as possible, but in a controlled manner with an emphasis on proper technique for giving and taking hits.

Hockey Canada argues that it plans to ensure a fun and safe environment for youth, while maintaining the *integrity* of the Canadian game. In a public statement in spring 2003 it stated:

> It is Hockey Canada's policy that checking skills are critical to the game of hockey and when performed properly can create quality scoring opportunities or help a team regain control of the puck. Just like skating, puck control, passing and shooting there are key progressions to the skill of checking. When taught correctly, checking skills greatly enhance a player's enjoyment of the great game of hockey.[41]

To support this move the organization implemented a new education initiative to teach kids the proper techniques of hitting to "become effective and complete players." The four-step progression program (positioning and angling, stick checks, body-contact, and bodychecking) is supposed to reduce the risk of injury from bodychecking because, once the program is completed, children will know how to give and receive hits properly.

While efforts to teach youth the proper techniques of bodychecking may appear to supply a solution to injuries in youth hockey, these initiatives do not take into consideration several important factors. One consideration is not so much the actual technique of bodychecking but its particular uses and consequences. Bodychecking in Canadian hockey has always been more than merely a defensive tactic to remove an opponent from the puck, as the definition provided by Hockey Canada suggests. It has also been a means of deliberately intimidating opponents, of punishing opponents, as well as a means of inspiring a team to play better.[42] For example, K. Colburn Jr. in his participant observation research of hockey teams in Ontario and Indianapolis quotes one player as follows: "I use violence in my work as a defenseman. Not cheap stuff, but good, solid bodychecks. This makes others keep their heads up. They become intimidated. That makes them throw away the puck that much faster."[43] This player clearly places an emphasis on playing within the rules, but in general the strategic deployment of violence to win a tactical advantage can easily lead to notable escalations in violent play through repeated acts of intimidation and retribution. Thus the level of violence associated with bodychecking can quickly move beyond official rules and beyond what many parents and fans believe is an acceptable level of tolerance.

Still, for many Canadians the tolerance of violence associated with bodychecking is high. After recording about fifty peewee contact games in Alberta, one research effort observed that the hits occurring on the ice were consistently met with cheers from parents, often to the chagrin of other parents who were, as one coach phrased it, not used to "seeing their little Johnny getting hit."[44] On several occasions, the researchers noted, "the bigger the hit, the bigger the cheer," a tendency that reinforces for children and parents not only what constitutes desirable playing behaviours but also the rewards that follow these behaviours.

A focus group interview the following year in Ottawa pursued these attitudes further, asking parents to comment on video images of bodychecking incidents that were recorded over a two-year period in Alberta and Ottawa. Despite the severity of many of the hits, many parents acknowledged the pragmatics of a punishing style of hockey. One exchange went as follows:

> Robidoux: If you think about it in terms of this particular play, if the person was hurt or somehow intimidated, is that then effective in terms of playing hockey?
> Dad 1: Well, the bottom line is, it is effective. But is it right?
> Dad 2: It's very effective. Absolutely effective but I don't think it has any place in the game personally.
> Dad 3: You've got a definite advantage; you're going to intimidate your opponent.
> Dad 2: As a matter of fact, some coaches will tell their players to go out and do this in the first minute to set the tone.[45]

Another factor that potentially limits the effectiveness of Hockey Canada's four-step progression program to teach "safe" and "controlled" bodychecking is that even if the values of aggression and violence could somehow be made to disappear in minor hockey, the tremendous growing spurts of youth between the ages of nine and fifteen—most notably between thirteen and fifteen—create serious size disparities, which in turn completely undermine any idea of a safe bodychecking system. The well-trained 170-pound child simply becomes more effective at delivering a punishing hit to a 100-pound child who may be trained to receive a hit, but not to receive the impact of the well-executed collision.[46] The idea of lowering the age of bodychecking to nine-year-old players in competitive leagues prior to growth spurt patterns is also not a solution. First, size would become a key determinant in the player selection processes of those competitive leagues, unfairly discriminating against smaller youth whose growing spurts come later in life. Second, those kids who do catch up to others in size later down the road would not have been safely introduced into contact hockey—and they would now be playing with children already trained in giving and receiving hits. William Montelpare, David Scott, and Mike Pelino's conclusion of their studies on the relative age effect is illuminating:

> Players at a young age must be permitted time to mature and develop as hockey play-ers. Coaches must be patient in the development of individual skills and ensure that all players receive an equal opportunity for skill development.... It may be that hockey, by means of its physical nature and its age division system, creates extra competitive stress for young athletes. The young hockey player who feels that he or she is at a physical disadvantage may lack confidence. This may increase competitive stress, resulting in poor performance, and reduced fun.... As a final note, hockey coaches and administrators must be wary of "cutting" players. It is possible that a perception of a player's poor skill might actually be an indication of a player's lack of readiness to learn the required skills. Thus, if a child is late to mature he or she may not demon-strate the expected skills of a specific age group.[47]

But, perhaps more importantly, research indicates:

> The incidence rates of concussion and other hockey-related injuries increase with increasing age, when more bodychecking is expected, and with higher levels of play, which suggests a dose-response effect. Learning to bodycheck when young does not reduce a player's rate of injury as he or she ages, and it prolongs the risk exposure.[48]

Yet another factor relates to an important incongruence found in a paragraph of Hockey Canada's pamphlet "Teaching Checking—A Progressive Approach": "A common misconception is that the skill of checking begins at a certain age or category of play. In fact, checking is a 4-step progression that begins the first time a young player steps on the ice. Body checking is the fourth and final step of a four step teaching pro-gression."[49] By allowing bodychecking at the atom level (nine to ten years of age) for competitive leagues, Hockey Canada decides that the skill of checking begins at a cer-tain age or category of play. Even more, the progression approach is not respected because players are allowed to bodycheck at a time when even the basic skills of skating and shooting have not been completely mastered. In the province of Quebec, atom players are still part of the initiation sector.[50] From our perspective a more accurate application of the four-step progression would have been to concentrate on the first step (positioning and angling) at the atom level, stick-checks at the peewee level, body-contact at the bantam level, and bodychecking at the midget level.

At this point, then, the solution to problems of excessive violence and injury in minor hockey should be obvious, and that is to remove bodychecking from prepubescent players. The most basic issues of violence and safety in youth hockey can only be addressed through the elimination of bodychecking for young players and its carefully controlled introduction among high-school-age players.

Attempting to Explain the Pro-Bodychecking Position

Given the existing research, and the mounting criticisms from parents and other critics, why has Hockey Canada been so insistent on the necessity of bodychecking in minor hockey? Presumably Hockey Canada reflects the position of an equally broad or broader constituency of hockey fans and parents who have a high tolerance for the existence of aggression and violence in hockey—a level of tolerance that often seems at odds with the zero-tolerance position on violence so widely promoted elsewhere in communities across the country. We suggest that this high level of tolerance for violence within Hockey Canada, and throughout the pro-bodychecking lobby, arguably has roots in four different, but not necessarily unrelated, areas of influence.

The Identity Crisis Facing Hockey Canada

The perceived mission and role of Hockey Canada are riddled with ambivalence because of the organization's roots in an older morally based educational philosophy matched with a commitment to develop professional-calibre elite players. As a result, Hockey Canada still claims rhetorically to promote and to ensure positive and reaffirming sport experiences; yet it somehow has to reconcile this with an elite player development focus. In other words the organization tries to be all things to all constituencies in hockey. The potential for conflict and contradiction is obvious.

One such conflict comes, for instance, when Hockey Canada finds itself in the position of being responsible for hockey's international competitive "successes" and "failures." A success is measured by how Canadians fare in an international hockey tournament and "our" ability to maintain (re-establish?) ourselves as the dominant hockey power in the world. In this context, all other measures of success, such as personal enjoyment, participation rates, and public health, become of far lesser value. When Canada fares well within an international framework, Hockey Canada's system of development receives praise. When Canadians do not fare well (and as international parity is more and more apparent, this is happening more often), they can blame Hockey Canada. For instance, following Canada's 3-2 loss to the Russians in 2000, *The Toronto Sun* offered a typical commentary:

> Predictably, Canada's lack of skill compared to the European teams came to the forefront. Since the country finished fourth at the 1998 Olympics, the lack-of-skill issue

has been debated more times than Mel Lastman has stuck his foot in his mouth....
Likewise, the Canadian Hockey Association admits a need to soldier on and reshape
the minor system, trying to find a better way.[51]

Thus the debate rages on, and when representatives from Hockey Canada make comments such as vowing to reshape the system, it is apparent where they sit in this debate.

The difficulty here is that Hockey Canada's apparent responsibility for securing
global hockey supremacy seems inconsistent with the recreational and educational philosophy on display in its official mission statement. More importantly, because the vast
majority of players in Hockey Canada's minor hockey system will never be professional
players or international elite players, many parents believe that the organization has a
responsibility to the majority rather than to the elite minority. In one of our studies on
minor hockey in Canada, we asked parents if they were aware of Hockey Canada's "official" development philosophy and mandate, and did not find a single parent who knew
it. In the Ottawa focus group meeting, the parents were asked if they knew what
Hockey Canada's actual mission statement is. All said no, with one father replying, "I
don't, but I'll bet you it has nothing to do with [body] contact." After we briefly went
over the mission statement and paraphrased its mandate, the same father said, "It
sounds like a perfect mission statement if they'd follow it."[52]

Internal Pressures

It is clear that Hockey Canada's commitment to reduce ice hockey violence is limited.
Rather than engaging in serious dialogue between all invested partners—parents, participants, coaches, officials, researchers—the organization is offering little more than
instructional information on checking—its new four-step program. By contrast, the
Ontario Hockey Federation (OHF), the largest of the thirteen branches of Hockey
Canada, is very active in the debate. The OHF has furthered pilot studies on bodychecking, and it has disseminated "official" information about the subject on its website.[53] In a
recent installment on bodychecking, it attempted to quell public concern regarding the
introduction of body contact among nine- and ten-year-olds, and to defend its efforts
to continue to study the effects of bodychecking on this age group. The OHF writes:

> For every "expert" who presents a very convincing or compelling argument, another
> takes a different view with similar vigor and conviction. What we want to ask is for
> every parent to continue to do his or her part and we will continue to work vigilantly
> to try and do our job as effectively as possible. And doing our job, in part, is trying to
> continue our work, our pilot study, so that when we have truly done our research over
> a period of years, we will have not just opinions—as strong-willed and powerful and
> convincing as those opinions on all sides of this issue understandably are—but we

will have real data, accurate statistics. Statistics and data that are not just meaningless numbers, but actual meaningful information that will be the basis for real analysis and decision-making.[54]

The OHF's position has a familiar ring. It mimics the tobacco industry's long-standing denial of causal connections between smoking and cancer—and the industry's cries for additional research—in the face of a well-established body of evidence that has simply offered conclusions different from what the Federation wanted to hear. In a similar vein, the OHF disqualifies thirty years of research, official statements by both the Canadian and American Medical associations, and many of their "own" experts (most notably Montelpare) who maintain that bodychecking significantly increases the risk of injury.

If the organizations responsible for making decisions on the subject are setting themselves up as authorities on research and on what constitutes legitimate findings— as opposed to independent researchers and/or medical institutions—it is likely that bodychecking will remain for pre-adolescent players in youth hockey. In response, Bernard and Trudel argue:

> In order to bring requisite changes, we will have to offer completely new hockey structures and conceive new ways of developing coaches. Based on our results, we can advance that what hockey is doing doesn't meet the moral expectations of our society. Therefore, we have to be conscious that any strategy to change ice hockey subculture will face high resistance.[55]

The Influence of Professional Hockey

During a May 23, 2003, airing of *Hockey Night in Canada's* "Coaches Corner," a telling exchange occurred between Ron MacLean and Don Cherry. The subject was the CHA's decision to raise the age for bodychecking in youth hockey to peewee rather than atom, which had been the practice in some associations over the 2002–03 hockey season. Not surprisingly, Cherry argued in favour of implementing bodychecking at an earlier age. He dismissed any research that would argue otherwise because this research was conducted by "scientists" and not hockey players or former coaches. MacLean abandoned his adversarial role and jumped in to support Cherry by providing an equally illuminating rationale for his argument. He stated that one merely needs to look at the "Quebec system," which introduces bodychecking later than most other hockey associations (in bantam, or thirteen- to fourteen-year-olds), and to consider how many "NHL superstars" Quebec had produced recently.

The temptation would be to counter this with Marc Lavoie's statistical study of Quebec-born professional hockey players and their overall out-performance of

English-Canadian NHL players, but that would only miss the point again by imposing a professional hockey framework as the standard upon which to evaluate the Canadian minor hockey system.[56] Hockey Canada is not primarily meant to be a developmental system for the National Hockey League but rather an overarching organization that matches player development with a mandate to ensure positive and safe playing experiences for Canadians. The vast majority of evidence suggests that bodychecking at the atom, peewee, and bantam ages promotes excessive violence and compromises safety. The argument that we need these things to develop professional and elite-level international hockey players—a suspect argument in itself—simply elevates one of the goals of Hockey Canada: to a position where it effaces the "official" mission of Hockey Canada, to provide safe and positive playing experiences for the nation's youth.

Hockey, Canadian Nationalism, and Masculinity

Why are youth hockey organizations such as Hockey Canada and the Ontario Hockey Federation going to such lengths to disprove what even their own "experts" are telling them, and continuing to put kids unnecessarily at risk? The recent name change of the national umbrella organization that administers minor league hockey—going from the Canadian Hockey Association to Hockey Canada—provides insight into this question. The name Hockey Canada communicates the idea that the country and hockey are one. The implication is that the state of one depends on the other, which is to say to tamper with hockey would be to tamper with the nation. Thus, for some people, any call to change the manner in which the game is played at any level is interpreted as not only an attack on the game but also an attack on Canada.

From his pulpit on "Coaches Corner," Don Cherry epitomizes the view that criticism of any of the tenets of faith in hockey's subculture is "un-Canadian." When such criticisms involve bodychecking the negative reaction typically intensifies because many people have construed the physical component of the game as the essence of Canadian hockey. Since the game's modern origins, Canadians have taken pride and celebrated qualities of toughness, aggression, and stoicism, the fodder for establishing a uniquely Canadian sport heritage.[57] Some of the earliest games were riddled with violence and were severely criticized in conservative newspaper reports. In 1875 *The Daily British Whig* described one of the first games ever played: "Shins and heads were battered, benches smashed and the lady spectators fled in confusion."[58] *The Montreal Witness*, reporting on the same game, explained: "Owing to some boys skating about during play an unfortunate disagreement arose: one little boy was struck across the head, and the man who did so was afterwards called to account, a regular fight taking place in which a bench was broken and other damages caused."[59]

The very excessiveness of the game of hockey was what made it distinctive and subsequently embraced by Canadian sport enthusiasts. These qualities were grounded in the emergent construct of masculinity in colonial Canada and had tremendous symbolic value in attempting to articulate a Canadian identity in the face of British imperialism and American encroachment. It has not merely been the game but the physically aggressive and reckless manner in which it was played that connoted an ideal of the Canadian sports*man*, necessarily distinct from other sport-nation identities. As one of us wrote elsewhere, in discussing this relationship between hockey, Canadian nationalism, and masculinity:

> Hockey displayed men who were perceived to be stoic, courageous, and physically dominant: precisely the same images of masculinity valued in First Nations culture, and later by early Canadian settlers. These historically pertinent attitudes attracted Canadians to hockey as the game provided Canadian males with an identifiable image outside of a British Framework. Moreover, through hockey competitions, Canadians could exude superiority over Americans.[60]

In international contexts throughout history, excessively physical components have often been disparaged, yet Canadians have romanticized this condition as simply being a reflection of the rugged realities of existence in northern North America. Canadian hockey has been styled around these virtues, and Canadian players have been moulded by these traditions. As international parity is gradually achieved, these virtues are repeated as the last remaining thread of a Canadian advantage. In the 2004 World Cup, for instance, Canada narrowly escaped defeat in the semi-finals by a determined Czech team and then squeaked by the Finns to win the tournament championship. In almost typical fashion, however, it was not Team Canada's superior play that was cited as the source of victory, but instead the intangible qualities that only Canadian players bring to the ice. *Toronto Sun* reporter Al Strachan captures this best when he writes:

> Shane Doan, the stereotypical Canadian hockey player, put Canada in front 34 seconds into the third period.... After that, it was just a matter of who wanted the World Cup championship more.... At a time like that, when a hockey championship is on the line and it's just a matter of playing your heart out, Canadian heritage is such that there is no real question of what will happen next. Losing is not an option.... They sacrificed their bodies for the cause. They threw themselves in front of pucks and at the Finns. And now, they are world champions, Olympic champions and World Cup champions.[61]

The issue here, then, is twofold: removing bodychecking would be to put the Canadian game at risk; similarly, de-emphasizing toughness, aggression, and physical intimidation would be to take the Canada out of hockey. Hockey's traditionalists, including many of the people in Hockey Canada, seem intent on maintaining these defining features of Canadian hockey, and their passion is to maintain Canada's place as the premier hockey nation in the world. The consequence, however, is that this passion sometimes has the effect of creating a developmental emphasis that runs contrary to what may be in the best interests of the majority of young players involved in minor hockey across the country. In the end, led by the traditionalists and their quasi-religious sense of the rightness of their position, Hockey Canada is largely unable to play a major role in "Leading, Developing, and Promoting Positive Hockey Experiences" in this nation.

A Mandate and a Mission

Ice hockey has been and still is part of a Canadian culture that has no shortage of differing viewpoints. Therefore it should not be a surprise to see the issue of bodychecking raising many passionate debates. On one side are those who argue fiercely that bodychecking is a necessary component of Canadian hockey, and that removing it at the youth level would be to meddle with one of Canada's sacred institutions. There are also those who believe that introducing bodychecking at the earliest stages of the game would better prepare players to deal with body-contact as the children get older and are more capable of delivering bone-crushing checks, thus reducing injuries. Another point of view comes from those aware of how Major Junior and professional scouts typically reward big, bruising players (such as Scott Stevens and Todd Bertuzzi). By discouraging this style of play at an early age, the argument runs, it may disadvantage certain athletes who are physically suited to this style of play.

On the other side of the debate are those who think first and foremost of children's safety and of creating positive environments for children's sport. They argue that introducing bodychecking at an early age places children unnecessarily at risk. In addition, the argument runs, the promotion of bodychecking at early ages is too often accompanied by an emphasis on hyperaggressive violent play, complete with excessive emotion in the stands, which creates a profoundly negative atmosphere in many games. Related to this is the issue of outright discrimination, whereby the introduction of bodychecking and the celebration of related aggressive play prevent children and parents not wanting to be put at risk from participating in hockey.

In our view, while both of these positions can be strongly argued, it is the critics of bodychecking and aggressive play in youth hockey, ironically, who have the mandate and mission statement of Hockey Canada on their side—to provide a safe and fun environment for all kids to enjoy the great game of hockey. Perhaps, if Hockey Canada has lost faith in this mission statement, it is time to give someone else the job of developing a youth hockey system designed to emphasize enjoyment, skill development, and socially positive values.

Notes

1 Richard Gruneau and David Whitson, *Hockey Night in Canada: Sport, Identities, and Cultural Politics* (Toronto: Garamond Press, 1993), pp. 75-76.

2 Lawrence Scanlan, *Grace under Fire: The State of Our Sweet and Savage Game* (Toronto: Penguin Canada, 2003).

3 Lawrence Scanlan, "We Like Our Hockey with a Little Blood," *The Globe and Mail*, March 11, 2004, p. A19.

4 See Dany Bernard and Pierre Trudel, "The Values of Coaches and Players about Rule Infractions, Violence, and Ethics," in D.J. Pearsall and A.B. Ashare, eds., *Safety in Ice Hockey: Fourth Volume* (Philadelphia: American Society for Testing and Materials, 2004).

5 Michael Smith, *Violence and Sport* (Toronto: Butterworth, 1983), p. 2.

6 Ann Hall, Trevor Slack, Garry Smith, and David Whitson, *Sport in Canadian Society* (Toronto: McCelland & Stewart, 1991), p. 215.

7 As of 2002 the peewee division became made up of eleven- and twelve-year-olds. Age classifications have changed over the years, however. Peewee was at one point the division for twelve- and thirteen-year-olds.

8 Hockey Canada, "CHA'S AGM Concludes in Toronto, ON," May 28, 2002 <www.hockeycanada.ca/e/news/2002/nr046.html>.

9 Gruneau and Whitson, *Hockey Night in Canada*, p. 104.

10 Pat Doherty, *Guide for Minor Hockey Administration* (Vanier, ON: Canadian Amateur Hockey Association, 1975), p. 3.

11 Ibid., p. 7.

12 Canadian Hockey Association, *Fair Play Means Safety for All: A Parent's and Guardian's Guide to Understanding Abuse and Harassment* (Ottawa: Canadian Hockey Association, 2001), p. 2.

13 Hockey Canada, press release, May 20, 2003 <www.hockeycanada.ca/e/news/2003/nr056.html>.

14 C. McNabb, *Minor Hockey Development Guide: Development Philosophy*, p. 2 <www.hockeycanada.ca/e/develop/players/downloads/mhadev.pdf>.

15 Ibid., p. 8.

16 See G. Meagher, *Minor Age Hockey in Canada: A Blueprint for the 70's and Beyond* (Ottawa: Department of National Health and Welfare, 1971); W.R. McMurtry, *Investigation and Inquiry into Violence in Amateur Hockey* (Toronto: Ontario Government Bookstore, 1974); R. Gross, *Saskatchewan Hockey Task Force: Final Report* (Regina: Department of Culture and Youth, 1974); V. Toner, *New Brunswick Hockey Study Report: Report and Recommendations* (Fredericton: Ministry of Youth, 1976); G. Néron, *Rapport Final du Comité d'Étude sur la Violence au Hockey Amateur au Québec* (Quebec: Gouvernement du Québec, Haut commissariat à la jeunesse, aux loisirs et aux sports, 1977); J.J. Urie and L.E. Regan, *Interim and Final Reports on Minor Amateur Hockey in Canada* (Ottawa: Government of Canada, 1979); B. McPherson and L. Davidson, *Minor Hockey in Ontario: Toward a Positive Learning Environment in the 1980s* (Toronto: Ontario Government Bookstore, 1980); and B. Pascall and S. White, *A Report on Eliminating Violence in Hockey in British Columbia* (Victoria: Ministry of Small Business, Tourism and Culture, 2000).

17 See Edmund W. Vaz, "What Price Victory?" *International Review of Sport Sociology*, 9, 2 (1974); Vaz, "Institutionalized Rule Violation in Professional Hockey: Perspectives and Control Systems," *Canadian Association for Health, Physical Education and Recreation*

Journal, 43 (1977); Vaz, "Institutionalized Rule Violation and Control in Organized Minor League Hockey," *Canadian Journal of Applied Sport Science*, 4,1 (1979); Vaz, *The Professionalism of Young Hockey Players* (Lincoln: University of Nebraska Press, 1982).

18 See Michael, D. Smith, "Significant Others' Influence on the Assaultive Behavior of Young Hockey Players," *International Review of Sport Sociology*, 9, 3-4 (1974); Smith, "The Legitimation of Violence: Hockey Players' Perceptions of their Reference Groups' Sanctions for Assault," *Canadian Review of Sociology and Anthropology*, 12 (1975); Smith, "Social Learning of Violence in Minor Hockey," in F.L. Smoll and R.E. Smith, eds., *Psychological Perspectives in Youth Sports* (Washington: Hemisphere, 1978); and Smith, "Towards an Explanation of Hockey Violence: A Reference Other Approach," *Canadian Journal of Sociology*, 4 (1979).

19 Vaz, "What Price Victory?"   p. 34.

20 Vaz, "Institutional Rule Violation," p. 83.

21 Smith, *Violence and Sport*, p. 107.

22 Smith, "Social Learning of Violence," p. 105.

23 Bernard and Trudel, "Values of Coaches and Players," p. 163.

24 See J. Côté et al., "Observation of Coach Behaviors during Different Game Score Differentials," in C.R. Castaldi, P.J. Bishop, and E. Hoerner, eds., *Safety in Ice Hockey: Second Volume* (Philadelphia: American Society for Testing and Materials, 1993); W. Gilbert et al., "Development and Application of an Instrument to Analyse Pedagogical Content Interventions of Ice Hockey Coaches," *Sociology of Sport On-line*, 2,2 (1999); P. Seaborn, P. Trudel, and W. Gilbert, "Instructional Content Provided to Female Ice Hockey Players during Games," *Applied Research in Coaching and Athletics Annual*, 13 (1998); P. Trudel, J. Côté, and D. Bernard, "Systematic Observation of Youth Ice Hockey Coaches during Games," *Journal of Sport Behavior*, 19,1 (1996); P. Trudel, J-P. Dionne, and D. Bernard, "Étude Qualitative de la Violence au Hockey: Perceptions d'Entraîneurs et de Joueurs," *Canadian Journal of Sport Sciences*, 17,4 (1992); P. Trudel et al., "Analyse des Comportements de l'Entraîneur par Rapport à la Violence au Hockey," *Canadian Journal of Sport Sciences*, 16,2 (1991); S. Wilcox and P. Trudel, "Constructing the Coaching Principles and Beliefs of a Youth Ice Hockey Coach," *Avante*, 4,3 (1998).

25 G. Régnier et al., "Effects of Bodychecking in the Pee-Wee (12 and 13 Years Old) Division in the Province of Quebec," in C.R. Castaldi and E. Hoerner, eds., *Safety in Ice Hockey* (Philadelphia: American Society for Testing and Materials, 1989).

26 D. Bernard et al., "The Incidence, Types, and Circumstances of Injuries to Ice Hockey Players at the Bantam Level (14 to 15 Years Old)," in Castaldi, Bishop, and Hoerner, eds., *Safety in Ice Hockey: Second Volume.*

27 See Bernard et al., "Incidence, Types, and Circumstances"; Régnier et al., "Effects of Bodychecking"; and R. Boileau et al., *Rapport d'Étude sur la Mise en Échec au Hockey Pee-Wee* (Québec: Rapport remis à la Régie de la Sécurité dans les Sports du Québec, 1986).

28 See P. Trudel et al., "Stratégie pour Rendre le Hockey Mineur plus Sécuritaire et moins Violent, Partie 1: Fondements Théoriques et Méthodologiques, " *Revue des Sciences et Techniques des Activités Physiques et Sportives*, 27 (1992); P. Trudel et al., "Stratégie pour Rendre le Hockey Mineur plus Sécuritaire et moins Violent, Partie 2: Implantation et Évaluation d'un Modèle de Formation pour les Entraîneurs," *Revue des Sciences et Techniques*

des Activités Physiques et Sportives, 28 (1992); P. Trudel et al., "Effects of an Intervention Strategy on Penalties, Bodychecking and Injuries in Ice Hockey," in A.B. Ashare, ed., *Safety in Ice Hockey: Third Volume* (Philadelphia: American Society for Testing and Materials, 2000).

29 A. Marchie and D. Cusimano, "Bodychecking and Concussions in Ice Hockey: Should Our Youth Pay the Price?" *Canadian Medical Association Journal*, 169,2 (2003), p. 126.

30 A.M. Smith et al., "A Psychosocial Perspective of Aggression in Ice Hockey," in Ashare, ed., *Safety in Ice Hockey: Third Volume.*

31 J.D. Brust et al., "Children's Ice Hockey Injuries," *American Journal of Diseases of Children*, 146 (1992); S.G. Gerberich et al., "An Epidemiological Study of High School Ice Hockey Injuries," *Child's Nervous System*, 3 (1987); A.M. Smith et al., "Predictors of Injury in Ice Hockey Players: A Multivariate, Multidisciplinary Approach," *The American Journal of Sports Medicine*, 25,4 (1997); W.O. Roberts, J. D. Brust, and B. Leonard, "Youth Ice Hockey Tournament Injuries: Rates and Patterns Compared to Season Play," *Medicine & Science in Sports & Exercise*, 31,1 (1999); G.W. Sutherland, "Participant in a Round Table on Hockey: Optimizing Performance and Safety," *The Physician and Sport Medicine*, 11,12 (1983).

32 Canadian Academy of Sports Medicine, "Position Statement: Violence in Ice Hockey," 1988 <www.casm-acms.org/PositionStatements/HockeyViolEng.pdf>; American Academy of Pediatrics, "Safety in Youth Ice Hockey: The Effects of Body Checking," *Pediatrics*, 105,3 (2000) <aappolicy.aappublications.org/cgi/content/full/pediatrics>.

33 Marchie and Cusimano, "Bodychecking and Concussions."

34 W.J. Montelpare, *Measuring the Effects of Initiating Bodychecking at the Atom Age Level: Final Report to the Ontario Hockey Federation and the Canadian Amateur Hockey Association*, June 2001.

35 "Ka-boom: How Young Is Too Young When It Comes to Hitting in Hockey?" *Disclosure*, Producer Harvey Cashore, editor Gary Akenhead, CBC, Jan. 14, 2003.

36 William Houston, "CHA Has Bungled over Bodychecking," *The Globe and Mail*, Jan. 22, 2003, p. S1.

37 Ibid.

38 Hockey Canada, "CHA Board of Directors Carries Motions on Checking in Minor Hockey; Focus Placed On Four Step Teaching Progression and Research Framework," May 19, 2003 <www.canadianhockey.ca/e/news/2003/nr054.html>.

39 Marchie and Cusimano, "Bodychecking and Concussions."

40 Ontario Hockey Federation, 2003, "Bodychecking Concerns Us All" <www.ohf.on.ca/News%20FILES/2003/ohf_comments.htm>.

41 Hockey Canada, "Background on Checking" <www.hockeycanada.ca/e/develop/checking/check_back.html>.

42 See Bernard and Trudel, "Values of Coaches and Players"; Trudel, Dionne, and Bernard, "Étude Qualitative"; Smith, "Towards an Explanation of Hockey Violence"; Vaz, *Professionalization.*

43 K. Colburn Jr., "Deviance and Legitimacy in Ice-Hockey: A Microstructural Theory of Violence," *The Sociological Quarterly*, 27,1 (1986): 64.

44 M.A. Robidoux and J. Bocksnick, "Playing beyond the Glass: Parental Aggression in Minor Hockey in Canada," in Linda K. Fuller, ed., *Sexual Sports Rhetoric* (Binghamton: Haworth Press, forthcoming).

45 M.A. Robidoux, "Focus Group Interview with Minor Hockey League Parents," Ottawa, July 2003.

46 As observed in Robidoux and Bocksnick, "Playing beyond the Glass."

47 W.J. Montelpare, D. Scott, and M. Pelino, "Tracking the Relative Age Effect across Minor Amateur and Professional Ice Hockey Leagues," in Ashare, ed., *Safety in Ice Hockey: Third Volume*, p. 258.

48 Marchie and Cusimano, "Bodychecking and Concussions," p. 125.

49 Hockey Canada, "Checking Resource Guide: Teaching Checking—A Progressive Approach," Gloucester: Canadian Hockey Association, 2000, p. 4 <www.hockeycanada.ca/e/develop/checking/downloads/intro_chk.pdf>.

50 Hockey Québec, *Cahier de Réglementation et d'Encadrement du Secteur Initiation: Pré-novice, Novice, Atome* (Montreal: Produit par Hockey Québec, 2003).

51 Tim Wharnsby, "Another Golden Goose Egg," *The Toronto Sun*, Jan. 4, 2000 <http://www.slam.ca/2000WJHC/jan4_ano.html>.

52 Robidoux, "Focus Group Interview."

53 Ontario Hockey Federation, "Body Checking" <www.ohf.on.ca/Bodychecking/body_checking.htm>.

54 Ontario Hockey Federation, "Body Checking Concerns Us All" <www.ohf.on.ca/News%20FILES/2003/ohf_comments.htm>

55 Bernard and Trudel, "Values of Coaches and Players," p. 163.

56 Marc Lavoie, *Désavantage Numérique: Les Francophones dans la LNH* (Hull: Vents d'Ouest, 1998).

57 Michael Robidoux, "Imagining a Canadian Identity through Sport: A Historical Interpretation of Lacrosse and Hockey," *Journal of American Folklore*, 115,456 (2002).

58 J.W. Fitsell, *Hockey's Captains, Colonels, and Kings* (Erin, ON: The Boston Mills Press, 1987), p. 36.

59 Ibid.

60 Robidoux, "Imaging a Canadian Identity through Sport," pp. 220-21.

61 Al Strachan, "We Are the Best: Losing Not an Option for Canada," *The Toronto Sun*, Sept. 15, 2004.

CHAPTER SIX

Racialization and Hockey in Canada: From Personal Troubles to a Canadian Challenge

■ ROBERT PITTER

The asking of sociological questions is motivated, it is said, by an interest in looking beyond "the commonly accepted, or officially defined, descriptions and explanations of human actions."[1] Sociology can also lead us to understand that the *personal troubles* that individuals experience are often products of social structures: enduring structures of power and relative powerlessness that mean that relations between rich and poor or men and women, for example, tend to unfold in familiar and predictable ways.[2] The American sociologist C. Wright Mills once wrote that the ability to distinguish between the "personal troubles of milieux" and the "public issues of social structure" is an essential tool of the sociological imagination.[3] Mills also stressed that the quest to understand personal biographies can lead to sociological inquiries that can in turn help us to identify the structural issues and barriers that are often at the root of personal troubles. Here I intend to take up that approach by exploring a number of biographies of visible minority hockey players, and through the prism of their experiences consider the barriers encountered by black and Aboriginal players in Canadian hockey—and the significance of racialized identities to the very idea of being Canadian.

Like many Canadians I love hockey. It has, for me, a magical quality that has added excitement to my life in many different ways. Hockey is also a significant social institution in Canada, a frequently discussed component of Canadian culture and identity, a popular pastime that arguably touches every Canadian's life indirectly if not directly. In fact, there was a time in Canada's not-too-distant past when hockey in its various forms (ice, ball/road, roller) was an activity that was shared—for better or worse—by almost every young boy growing up in Canada. The year 2003 marked the twentieth anniversary of the publication of Ken Dryden's highly praised book *The Game*.[4] For me, Dryden's account of ball hockey captures dreams and fantasies experienced by many boys who grew up with the sport. The language Dryden used to describe the behaviours, the equipment, and even the fantasy NHL games recalls my own experiences and, I think, those of many other boys. In his account of his boyhood participation in hockey, Dryden observes that he was attracted to it because it enabled him to experience—however fleetingly—a certain sense of self-mastery and power, and not because he saw it as a path to a career:

> The backyard was not a training ground. In all the time I spent there, I don't remember ever thinking I would be an NHL goalie, or even hoping I could be one. In backyard games, I dreamed *I was* Sawchuk or Hall, Mahovlich or Howe; I never dreamed I would be like them. There seemed no connection between the backyard and Maple Leaf Gardens.[5]

Many social theorists have pointed out that the meanings individuals attach to institutions such as sports, and the roles and possibilities they see for themselves in these institutions, can vary with demographic characteristics such as gender, class, race, and ethnicity.[6] And comparing his own boyhood experiences with those of some of his Montreal Canadiens teammates, Dryden illustrates how the limits and possibilities they saw for themselves in hockey did vary. For example, when describing Rejean Houle's memories of his childhood aspirations, Dryden relates that where some of Houle's boyhood teammates had dreamed of playing in the NHL, Houle did not. When asked by Dryden to explain, Houle confides "You see, working-class people have no confidence.... It just takes a while to get some.... I never dream of something I cannot be."[7] Houle reveals to Dryden how his understanding of his own social-class position influenced what hockey meant to him, and how high he could aspire to go. Later, when Houle reached high school, the meaning he attached to hockey shifted and he began to imagine the possibility of playing in the NHL even though it was several years before he thought of this prospect as being realistic.

Like Houle, I also grew up in a working-class milieu, but my experiences and the meanings I attached to hockey were somewhat different. The parents of the boys I played with did make links between our games in the apartment-building parking lot and those at Maple Leaf Gardens. From time to time I thought how nice it might be to become a professional hockey player, even though none of the players in the NHL were black like me. I played organized ice hockey for only two years, but my love of playing the game has endured. Not only this; it has also always contributed to my personal sense of being a Canadian. Today I still play ball hockey whenever I get the chance. As far as I can recall, I never thought that the colour of my skin had anything to do with my not fully pursuing my passion for hockey and competing nationally and internationally, as I later did in track and field. I thought that the biggest thing that kept me from reaching the higher levels of hockey was money, and as an undergraduate student I used my experiences to argue that my class circumstances had been the most significant barrier. In the case of other blacks, I concluded that it also would have been economics more than anything else that kept them from playing hockey at the highest levels.

Something else I learned growing up in Canada, though, was that talking about racism is not the Canadian thing to do. As Joseph Mensah comments, and I fully agree, "Many Canadians are reluctant to admit that racial oppression and inferiorization persist in this country. As Canadians, we have the tendency not only to ignore our racist past, but also to dismiss any contemporary racial incidents as nothing but aberrations in an essentially peaceful, tolerant, charitable, and egalitarian nation."[8] Citing research by Jeffery Rietz and Raymond Breton, Mensah emphasizes their conclusion: "Despite the historical differences between race relations in Canada and race relations in the United States, Canadians and Americans are roughly similar in their attitudes and behaviours toward racial minorities."[9] However, while sport researchers in the United States have devoted a significant amount of attention to studying the intersections between race and sport, and the significance of race in every aspect of American life, Canadian scholars have until recently been all but silent. Indeed, despite the increasing heterogeneity of Canada's population and the ever increasing proportion of visible minorities in Canada and in Canadian sport, research has focused on other historically subjugated groups: females, the working class, and francophones. Scholars have looked at the barriers these groups have faced, and they have used the results of that research to advocate structural changes that could help women or francophones, for example, to overcome these barriers. However, comparatively little attention has been given to the relative absence of visible minorities in Canada's sporting history, and the impact of race on their progress in Canadian sporting institutions. Certainly, visible minorities have faced sharp challenges in hockey, challenges that I believe are related to the difficulties that blacks and Aboriginals face in being fully accepted as Canadians.

As Mary Louise Adams notes elsewhere in this book, hockey has been part of a very masculine version of Canadian identity, and the perspective presented here is certainly a male one. However, although I make no claim to speak for everyone, I will raise a series of questions about the relationships between hockey and "Canadianness." I will also explore hockey's role in promoting, instilling, or discouraging a sense of Canadian identity in Canadian people of colour.

Race, Ethnicity, and Race Relations in Canada: Myth and Reality

Race is a social construct, the meaning of which has shifted through history and across different societies. It involves arbitrarily classifying people into categories based on physical differences, most notably skin colour, by claiming that predictable links exist between skin colour and mental, social, and physical capacities.

Over the course of the past fifty years or so, reputable scientists representing a wide array of the physical and social sciences repeatedly provided evidence that ultimately led the United Nations Educational, Scientific and Cultural Organization (UNESCO) to conclude, "There is little or no correlation between the physical characteristics of groups of people and their social behaviour."[10]

Based on this and other evidence, most sociologists have acknowledged that "physical and genetic attributes such as skin colour and the frequency of distribution of blood type commonly used for racial categorizations are arbitrary and have no scientific basis." Indeed, some have called for an end to the use of "race" as a concept inasmuch as its continued use "contradicts the general recognition that no real race exists, helps reify the concept of race as though it were something concrete or real with ontological dimensions, and ultimately reproduces inaccurate and simplistic views about different groups of people."[11] However, other social scientists advocate the continued use of the concept on the grounds that regardless of whether or not race exists materially, it exists as a social construct and an ascribed identity, and one that continues to have social connotations and consequences. As Mensah puts it, many people still believe in the reality of race, and behave in accordance with their beliefs. In many instances, moreover, the consequence of that behaviour has been a creed of racial hatred that asserts the "superiority of one human group over another, based on real or perceived genetically transmitted differences."[12] Put differently, racialization—a belief in the reality of "race," and involving a readiness to classify people in terms of racial stereotypes—frequently leads to racism.

Sociologists have observed that racism can take many forms, including systemic or institutional racism (when racialization is embedded in the policies and practices of institutions) and individual racism (when racist behaviours or remarks by individuals do not reflect official policies, and may even go against them). In sport, for instance, systemic racism has been expressed in laws and sport policies that once excluded blacks and Aboriginals from interracial competition.[13] Systemic racism is also manifest in the more recent practice of "stacking," in which black players often do not get a fair chance at positions that are seen to be key to the success of a team, positions such as quarterback in football and pitcher in baseball.[14] Individual racism, of course, can be found in sport in many forms: racist remarks made by one player to an opponent, racial taunting by fans, and racial tensions that have divided some teams.

David Andrews's "The Fact(s) of Michael Jordan's Blackness" presents a contemporary example of another more subtle kind of racism in action. Andrews argues that mass media portrayals of black NBA basketball player Michael Jordan moved from representing him as racialized "other" to representations of him as colourless. Early images of Jordan coincided with popular stereotypes of the black athlete "as sports hero, mythologically endowed with a naturally muscular physique and an essential capacity for strength, grace and machine-like perfection."[15] Later in his career, Jordan was identified as embodying personal drive, responsibility, integrity, and achievement in ways suggesting that anyone—black or white, poor or rich—could realize the American dream of success if they worked hard enough. This portrayal ignored Jordan's middle-class roots and the advantages that this gave him over working-class or poor blacks. The portrayal also glossed over the reality that 24 per cent of American blacks live in poverty compared with only 8 per cent of whites,[16] and that for young men in these circumstances the chances of success are very poor regardless of their athletic ability or drive.

Discussions and investigations of racism and race relations are often complicated by the concept and theories of ethnicity, partly because the concepts of race and ethnicity often overlap. Peter Li notes that the most often mentioned attributes of ethnicity are ancestry, culture, religion, language, and *race*.[17] Not all scholars include race when defining ethnicity. Leo Driedger, for example, lists six attributes of "ethnic identification" without mentioning race: "identification with an ecological territory, an ethnic culture, ethnic institutions, historical symbols, an ideology, and charismatic leadership."[18] Those scholars who do include race in their definitions of ethnicity risk oversimplifying several important issues. First, it is simply incorrect to suggest that what it means to be black, Asian, or otherwise racialized is the same as an ethnic identity like Irish Canadian or Ukrainian Canadian. Second, such theories also imply that all members of a non-white racial group must have the same ethnic identity. Michael Omi and Howard Winant note, "With rare exceptions ethnicity theory isn't interested in ethnicity among blacks.... Similar problems can be discerned in the treatment of other racially based categories: Native Americans, Latin Americans, and Asian Americans."[19] Consequently, to discuss and investigate intersections between race, sport, and identity, we need to recognize that race and ethnicity, although frequently combined, are actually distinct, and have differing degrees of significance as far as national identity and institutionalized inequality are concerned.

Simply put, ethnic relations tend to be more flexible than race relations.[20] Because ethnic categories are based on shared cultural traits and/or heritage rather than socially selected physical characteristics, it is much easier in Canada for white immigrants (for example, of Ukrainian or Croatian origins) to "assimilate" than it is for black or Chinese migrants—or, indeed, their children. Members of a racial group cannot change the physical characteristic of skin colour that places them in a group. Consequently, racially defined groups encounter a greater variety of prejudices and conflicts than do groups that are only seen as being ethnically different. Furthermore, people belonging to groups that are considered to be both ethnically and racially different are treated worst of all. Arguably, they can be described as having the largest degree of difference to overcome if they want to conform to popular notions of Canadian identity and be fully accepted as members of Canadian society. Even though they may share the language, territorial identification, and even the historic symbols of the charter group, they still stand out as "others,"[21] existing in what Rinaldo Walcott refers to as the "in-between."

> For black Canadians, living the in-between is conditioned by their inside/outside status in the nation state; whether "indigenous black" or otherwise, in-between-ness

in Canada is conditioned by a plethora of national narratives, from the idea of "two founding peoples," to multicultural policies, to immigration policies, to provincial and municipal policing practices, and so on. The impossibility of imagining blackness as *Canadian* is continually evident.[22]

Hockey and Canadianness

Many writers and others have claimed that hockey is a central feature of Canadian identity: one of the few institutions or practices in Canadian life that "brings us all together." Consider how Roch Carrier describes hockey in his introduction to *Backcheck: A Hockey Retrospective*, the National Library of Canada's Internet homage to hockey in Canada:

> Hockey is Canada's game. But as everyone knows ... hockey is also the history of Canadians. The game reflects the reality of Canada in its evolution, ambitions, character, tensions and partnerships.... [At this site] not only will you find yourself back at the rink, but you will also find yourself back in time, exploring all of Canada.[23]

However, if we go a little further into this website, to seek out the vision of Canada that *Backcheck* presents, we find a Canada that apparently does not include Aboriginals or other people of colour. They are neither mentioned nor pictured. Do these people not play hockey? Or are they not truly Canadian?

The Canada presented on the *Backcheck* website is "purely" and exclusively white. Under the theme of hockey firsts (on the "Great Hockey Stories" page), the site has links to eighty-one archived newspaper articles and photos.[24] The firsts documented by these items include the first known photo of women playing hockey, and the first female major junior hockey player and first female NHL player, Manon Rhéaume. Yet there is no mention of hockey firsts concerning people of colour, such as the first known photographs of Aboriginals or blacks playing hockey. There is no photo or story about the first Asian, the first Aboriginal, or first black to play in the NHL (Larry Kwong, Freddie Sasakamoose, and Willie O'Ree, respectively). Likewise we learn that francophone Jacques Plante was the first goalie to wear a mask, but not that black leagues in Nova Scotia were the first to allow goalies to fall on the puck. Ironically, it is only on the children's version of the website that Aboriginals are mentioned briefly.[25] The larger story of hockey in Canada is told as if Aboriginal Canadians, black Canadians, and Asian Canadians were simply not here. It would seem, then, that this general inattention to the achievements of people of colour in hockey is an indication of racial bias.

In contrast, *Backcheck* very properly draws attention to the accomplishments of francophones and women, two groups of people who have historically had to fight their own battles against discrimination and cultural dominance. The sport we know as hockey was originally organized and promoted by anglophones who patterned its organization after that of British sports. Their approach to hockey advocated the ideals of sportsmanship and open competition, even as it took for granted the class, ethnic, gender, and racial divisions of that time (and thus reproduced them).[26] Eventually, of course, the domination of English Canadians over French Canadians, in hockey at least, was challenged by the success of a French-Canadian team, and the hockey achievements of the Montreal Canadiens have been widely heralded as contributing to a sense of collective pride among French-speaking Canadians. Moreover, this common interest and rivalry between English- and French-speaking Canadians "brought the 'two solitudes' into the same kind of regular and passionate engagement with one another."[27] Later on the children of immigrants from Eastern and Southern Europe, men with names such as Bucyk, Sawchuk, Mahovlich, and Esposito, came to symbolize the acceptance of these (white and European) "'new' Canadians into a different and more inclusive Canadian culture."[28] People of colour, though, were still kept on the sidelines. Thus, hockey does not seem to have bridged the gap between whites and non-whites in Canada in the same way that it has done for whites of many different backgrounds.

Non-White Canadian Hockey Experiences: A Tale of Two "Races"

Few scholarly investigations of race in Canadian sport have been carried out, and there are even fewer that address race and hockey. Fortunately, though, a few personal biographies of Aboriginals and blacks do exist, and they can be used to raise questions about hockey's resistance to including these groups of Canadians.

The Experiences of Aboriginals

Although the culture of Aboriginal peoples has included various sports, including hockey and hockey-like games, for a long time, discriminatory rules and other forms of institutionalized racism have long hindered the ability of First Nations people to participate in hockey alongside other Canadians. Many Aboriginal peoples across North America "played a version of field hockey that involved some type of 'puck' or ball, and curved wooden sticks."[29] Likewise, Mi'kmaq historian "Old Joe" Cope wrote, "Long before the pale faces strayed to this country, the Micmacs were playing two ball games, a field game and an ice game."[30] The sticks that these men had been using became the stick of choice for white players of the ice games of hurly and hockey as early as 1870.

However, early definitions of an amateur code and other practices in Canada served to limit the participation of "Indians" in sporting activities, essentially barring them from many sports, including hockey.[31] Over time these restrictions were lifted, but the racism that they were based on has taken much longer to disappear; indeed, it continues to colour the experiences of Aboriginal hockey players who aspire to reach the highest levels.

In the thought-provoking documentary *They Call Me Chief*, the reasons for the relative absence of Aboriginal peoples from the world of professional hockey are examined through the story of Fred Sasakamoose, who in 1953–54 became the first Aboriginal person to play in the NHL.[32] Reflecting on his experiences in professional hockey, Sasakamoose recalled, "To be a native is difficult in this world, [but] I reached my goal—the NHL." His experiences are also examined in Brenda Zeman's *To Run with Longboat*, which emphasizes the cultural differences that Sasakamoose encountered, challenges he could not completely overcome. The stories that Sasakamoose and his close friends told Zeman clearly indicate that life off the reserve required many adjustments to conditions ranging from unfamiliar technologies to the autocratic environment of professional hockey. Most difficult of all was the unfamiliar isolation from family and community. Sasakamoose played only eleven games in the NHL, and reflecting on his hockey experiences, he lamented, "A lot of times I sit down and ask myself what went wrong with my hockey life.... Maybe there were just some things I could not adjust to."[33]

They Call Me Chief also examines the stories of other Native players who made it to the NHL. George Armstrong, former Toronto Maple Leaf captain, and Jim Neilson, former New York Ranger—both products of "mixed marriages" and men who did not grow up in Aboriginal culture—were each frequently subjected to racial stereotyping, to patronizing remarks and attitudes, and to racist behaviours that made their progress to the NHL more difficult. From the times of Sasakamoose in the 1950s until the present, indeed, Aboriginal players depict a Canadian hockey subculture in which racist behaviours are endemic, ranging from routine use of the nickname "Chief" to pointedly demeaning and hostile treatment.

The film also suggests that institutional racism plays a significant role in the relative lack of Aboriginal players in the NHL. Ted Nolan, for example, argues, "The way the whole system is set up, even some of our native kids going into AAA programs, they do not [just] have to be as good—they have to be better in order to make teams. And people will say, 'Well, that's not really the case, Ted. That's bull.'"[34] Don Chesney, a non-Native coach and head scout for the Lebret Eagles in Saskatchewan, supports Nolan's claim. He recalls several instances in which outstanding Native players were ignored by other coaches who had a chance to recruit them first, perhaps because "they weren't willing to give a Native kid a chance."

In the face of all such obstacles, Native people themselves have been developing unique programs to give their young players a better chance of succeeding in hockey. As one community leader put it, "The goal is to give these young people a jumping off point, if you will, into life. A lot of these kids I do not think are NHL calibre, [but] some of them certainly are college calibre. It gives them an opportunity to be looked at by scouts."

They Call Me Chief also describes examples of Aboriginal initiatives to develop their own hockey programs, not only to increase the prospects of their most talented youth but also to strengthen their communities. Manitoba Junior Hockey League's OCN Blizzard, owned and operated by the Opaskwayak Cree Nation (OCN), has arguably had an impact that goes beyond providing opportunities for Native players.[35] According to the film, the team has changed the entire atmosphere of the Northern resource town of The Pas in which it plays. The Pas and the neighbouring OCN reserve have long been divided by racism, with tensions further sharpened in the 1970s by the murder of Helen Betty Osborne, a young Cree woman, and the many years it took for the RCMP to lay charges in her death. In recent years, though, the hockey team has made a tentative bridge between the two communities. Gordon Hooper, mayor of The Pas, remarks, "When you look at the fans, you're gonna see a mosaic of people from all different walks of life—different cultures—and they all have ... a number of things in common.... They are all cheering for the OCN Blizzard." In this perhaps optimistic reading, hockey has brought members of a divided community together to share a common interest and identity, and leaders on both sides assert that this experience has contributed to improved relationships outside the rink. Could hockey do this for the entire country?

The story of The Pas offers some promise; and perhaps a larger Aboriginal presence at all levels of hockey will move Canadians closer to a more inclusive national identity. At the same time, though, the racism documented in *They Call Me Chief* offers sobering evidence that a great deal remains to be done. The film shows all too clearly that thinking in racialized terms remains an ingrained habit in the minds of many Canadian individuals, and in organized hockey in particular.

The Experiences of Blacks

Accounts of the experiences of blacks in hockey in Canada raise some of the same concerns about the realities of racism in Canada, and in hockey in particular. However, these experiences are grounded in a different social history. Blacks have not been in Canada as long as Aboriginal peoples have been. Still, we have been here for several hundred years—even though many other Canadians appear not to know this and think of all blacks as recent immigrants. The problem of understanding the challenges of being black in Canada and the challenges many blacks face in developing a sense of Canadian identity is complicated by the varied histories of blacks in Canada. Cecil Foster suggests that they can be divided into three main groups: (1) blacks who have lived in Canada and elsewhere in North America for several generations, (2) African immigrants, and (3) Caribbean immigrants.[36] And, of course, even within these groupings there are marked ethnic differences (for example, between Jamaicans, Barbadians, and Haitians). Nonetheless, Foster argues, "A community is defined by how outsiders see it," and many white Canadians have tended to treat all blacks as one group, in recent years by ascribing the very visible culture of Caribbean blacks to all blacks, particularly in major cities such as Toronto.

Frank Cosentino's history of Canadian sport suggests that the situation for blacks in Canada in the nineteenth century was even worse than it was for Aboriginals.[37] The enslavement of blacks was a not uncommon practice, and other scholars note that the importation of black slaves to Canada from the late seventeenth to the early nineteenth century helped to define blacks as inferiors in Canadian society.[38] Blacks were placed on the lowest rung of Canada's racial hierarchy, and as they became increasingly active in sporting activities, they faced mounting efforts by whites to segregate sporting participation (as, of course, was routine in those times in the United States). By the early twentieth century in various places around Canada, several sports bodies—in baseball, boxing, hockey, and football—had enacted rules barring interracial competition between blacks and whites.

These severe restrictions did not discourage blacks from taking up hockey, Canada's favourite winter sport. As early as 1895, blacks in the Maritimes were observed playing hockey in public rinks. In the next few decades, because segregation prevented them from playing on or against white teams, Maritime blacks formed their own teams and played amongst themselves, in what was known as the coloured league.[39] Six teams came from Nova Scotia towns and one from Prince Edward Island. Teams adopted names that reflected their home communities, their respect for the monarchy, and perhaps also, I would add, their desire to be recognized fully as true Canadians: Africville Seasides, Hammond's Plains Mossbacks, Amherst Royals, and Dartmouth Jubilees. According to Garth Vaughan, the games played between blacks drew larger crowds than did many of those played by whites, and rink owners took advantage of what they felt was a financial opportunity, promoting black games in the newspapers. The popularity of black hockey games among white spectators was not, however, an indication that whites accepted blacks as equals. Racialized abuse in the stands and racist reporting in the papers were each common. By 1914, moreover, public interest had waned, and in 1928 the last coloured hockey championship was played. Nonetheless, as Vaughan notes, blacks had their own style of playing hockey, which influenced how hockey was played among whites—including the practice of allowing goaltenders to fall to the ice to stop the puck.[40]

It seems reasonable to speculate that these early Canadian black players developed a taste for hockey from their experiences of living in Canada, and from a desire to participate in Canadian culture. Like other Canadians from coast to coast, Canadian blacks have been exposed over the years to the same media celebration of hockey in newspapers, radio, and later television. We have learned that hockey is highly valued in Canadian society, and that in many circles an interest in hockey is considered a quintessential expression of Canadianness. Thus, just like many of our white counterparts, many black boys have taken up hockey with great enthusiasm, and some have had dreams of playing in the NHL. Yet, as is the case for Canada's Aboriginal peoples, little was written about the experiences of Canadian blacks in our "national game" until the very recent appearance of a number of blacks in the NHL drew new attention to the topic. This new interest demonstrates that blacks have indeed been playing hockey in Canada for many years, and that when they have been permitted, some blacks have been capable of playing at the highest levels.

Progress in hockey has always come at a price, though. Cecil Harris's *Breaking the Ice* provides interesting profiles of black Canadian hockey players, and all the players covered in Harris's book experienced racism within the Canadian hockey system. Moreover, the passage of time has not eliminated racism. Harris reports: "Each black player, I found, has had to wage a personal battle for acceptance and respect. Some eventually receive it while others never do. Facing abuse that is verbal, physical, or psychological because of their colour has been an unfortunate reality for almost all of them."[41]

A few years after Fred Sasakamoose became the first Aboriginal player to play in the NHL, Willie O'Ree became the first black player to do so, with the Boston Bruins in 1958. According to Harris, O'Ree "was called nigger so often on the ice that he thought it was his name."[42] Not much had changed since the time almost twenty years earlier when Herb Carnegie of Toronto, his brother Ossie, and Manny McIntyre became the first recorded blacks to play professional hockey in Canada, in what was then the Quebec Provincial League (QPL). Despite being named the most valuable player three years in a row (1944–47)[43] in this well-respected league, where he played alongside future hockey legend Jean Béliveau, Carnegie was never signed to play in the NHL, and he maintains that racism kept him out. He was offered a chance to sign with the New York Rangers in 1948, but found the terms unacceptable. The final offer made to him promised a salary little different from what he was already earning in the QPL, but required that he play in the minors first. As Harris suggests, Carnegie could have swallowed his pride and taken the Rangers' offer; but perhaps he saw this as a form of discrimination, something he could not accept. Maybe Red Storey, a Hockey Hall of Fame referee who once played against Carnegie, captured the situation best:

> There's a reason why Herb Carnegie did not play in the NHL. It's very simple: he's black. Don't say we don't have any rednecks in Canada.... With Herbie being black, [we] wouldn't be able to put him in the same hotels with the rest of the team and have him eat at the same restaurants and there could be problems if he [was taken] to the States to play against the NHL teams there. The NHL games weren't sold out then, and the owners might have been worried about losing the fans they already had.[44]

Canadian blacks have continued to play hockey over the years that have passed since Carnegie and later O'Ree faced these challenges. Information in Harris's book and other sources indicates that the roughly thirty-three blacks who grew up in Canada and eventually made it to the NHL come from a variety of different ethnic backgrounds.[45] I was

able to find enough information about the family background of nineteen of these players to see how they compare to the three main groups of Canadian blacks identified
above. Five players—Donald Brashear, Grant Fuhr, Tony McKegney, Ray Neufeld, and
Reggie Savage—had been adopted by white families and do not readily fit into any of the
three groups. Nine players were children of Caribbean immigrants, with one or both
parents having come from one of the islands: Barbados (Anson Carter, Jamal Mayers,
Kevin Weekes, and Peter Worrell); Haiti (Jean-Luc Grand-Pierre, Georges Laraque, and
Claude Vilgrain); and Jamaica (Graeme Townshend and Jason Doig). One player,
Calgary Flames star Jarome Iginla, has one parent from Africa (Nigeria), although Iginla
was raised primarily by his white mother. The remaining four players can be considered
to be indigenous to Canada because their parents were not themselves immigrants to
Canada: Darren Lowe, Mike Marson, Willie O'Ree, and Bill Riley.

According to Statistics Canada, until the 1990s more than 70 per cent of black
immigrants to Canada came from the Caribbean and Central or South America,[46] so it
is not surprising that only one black player has an African immigrant parent. However,
given that the majority of Caribbean immigrants to Canada are now from Jamaica,[47] it
is interesting that only two of the ten black NHL players with immigrant backgrounds
come from that island.

Many of the Internet sites and newspaper stories that I read while researching this
chapter raise the question of why there haven't been more black hockey players in the
NHL. Few hockey institutions, certainly not the NHL, are willing to admit that racism is
an issue in hockey, and even some of the black players themselves seem reluctant to discuss it. However, in an interview on CBC's *The Inside Track*, documentary filmmaker
Errol Williams challenged the NHL claim that there were not more black players with
enough talent to get to the NHL. He argued that the truth is that many black players quit
hockey before they reach the highest levels of the game because, as they rise through
the ranks, the degree of racism they encounter grows.[48] As recently as March 2003, John
Vanbiesbrouck, a former NHL goalie and a coach in the Major Junior Ontario Hockey
League, resigned in disgrace after repeatedly calling his team's black captain a nigger
during a meeting with two other players.

Certainly, the so-called absence of racism in the NHL has not kept the league from
developing policies to discourage it. As well as issuing fines and suspensions to players
found guilty of uttering racial slurs, the NHL has required each of its teams to attend a
racial diversity seminar. The OHL has taken similar actions by posting a harassment and
abuse policy statement in the dressing rooms of all its teams.

Personal Troubles and Public Issues

The stories I have shared about Aboriginal and black Canadians show that both groups
have a long history in Canada, and a long history in playing organized hockey. However,

I want to suggest that the mere fact that these stories are only now being widely told is itself evidence of the systemic racism that has been part of the fabric of Canadian sport for a long time. The history of non-whites in Canadian sport, like the history of Canadian blacks in general, has been, to coin a phrase inspired by Mensah, blacked out. Ignoring the accomplishments of non-whites in hockey, as well as the obstacles they have had to struggle against, has served to distort our collective consciousness. It does so by constructing a history of hockey, and indeed of Canada, that has overstated the contributions of some while rendering those of others invisible. Telling the stories of Aboriginals and blacks now, conversely, acknowledges that they are an integral part of our history.

It is also interesting that there is even less information available about other non-white groups in histories of Canadian sport. Statistics Canada's 2001 census reports that the Chinese are the largest visible minority in Canada; South Asians are the third largest if we include Aboriginals as a visible minority (although I have done so for this chapter, Statistics Canada does not classify Aboriginals as a visible minority). There seems to be some expectation that blacks, given their so-called high profile in other professional sports in the United States, should also be visible in hockey—an expectation that some might argue itself has racist overtones. Nonetheless, there have been a few Asian Canadians playing hockey since Chinese-Canadian Larry Kwong played one game in a New York Rangers jersey in 1948. These include Paul Kariya (part Japanese descent), Jamie Storr (part Japanese descent), Manny Malhotra (part Indian descent), and others.[49] Their stories also need attention, as does the larger story of why there are so few Asian Canadians in hockey.

Many black and Aboriginal hockey players alike have noted in interviews that the costs of playing hockey were perhaps more of an obstacle when they were children than was racism. Thus, while I have emphasized the role of racism in this paper, I want to restate the point I made at the beginning of the chapter: that social class is also relevant. It costs significantly more to play organized hockey than it does to play other popular sports such as soccer and basketball. Thus, one would expect fewer players from poor backgrounds to be able to play organized hockey. However, for many non-white Canadians, being non-white also translates into being poorer than other Canadians. In 1996 all visible minority groups except for the Japanese had average incomes lower than the Canadian average.[50] In 2000 about 42 per cent of Aboriginal people living in Census Metropolitan Areas had low incomes, more than double the national average.[51]

Is this because of systemic racism in Canada? To make such a claim credible, one would have to control for other factors such as age, education, and place of residence that might also account for differences between groups. However, using 1981 Canadian census data, Peter Li controlled for such variables for certain groups and concluded that of those groups that were visible minorities (recall that Statistics Canada did not count Aboriginals as a visible minority), blacks and Chinese faced widespread discrimination because of their skin colour.[52] More recent data suggest that this situation has not changed for blacks: "Lower employment rates and [lower] employment income and higher unemployment rates for Blacks may be related to discrimination or unfair treatment."[53] Thus, those who argue that the cost of hockey is a larger obstacle to aspiring young players than the racism within hockey must *also* acknowledge that racism in Canadian society continues to contribute to the poor economic position of many black and Aboriginal families.

There is no doubt that hockey's place in Canadian society, and indeed the world, has changed dramatically in the last hundred years. Canadians no longer dominate professional hockey as they once did in the past, and Canadian boys no longer play organized hockey in the same numbers they once did. Nonetheless, hockey continues to be a significant element of mainstream Canadian culture. A 2003 poll conducted by the Environics Research Group reported that 40 per cent of 1,340 Canadians surveyed indicated that they believed hockey was important to Canadian identity.[54] Interestingly, while 40 per cent of European immigrants to Canada shared this belief, a significantly larger proportion—60 per cent—of non-European immigrants did as well. Many of these non-Europeans are people of colour, yet we know very little about how their participation in hockey and their observation of hockey around them have shaped their ideas about what becoming "Canadian" means. Beyond those barriers revealed in the actual experiences of Aboriginals and blacks, what other barriers have the white majority raised against entry into hockey and into Canadian society at large, for people of colour who want to be accepted as fully Canadian? Speaking about racism being part of the game in a radio documentary interview, Carol Tator of York University noted:

> Racism is never acceptable.... It communicates a very bad and destructive message to children of colour: That in order to succeed, you have to deny that racism exists and the pain of what it does to you, the humiliation, the frustration. That in order to be Canadian, that in order to be part of Canada, you have to accept harassment.[55]

Here I have deliberately presented a male hockey perspective that emphasizes the pursuit of hockey as a career, based on the stories of Canadian men of colour. In recent years Canadian women have taken up hockey in ever increasing numbers. The extent to which this movement has embraced Canadian women of colour remains unknown. Research about this would be welcome, and could serve to improve our understanding of race, hockey, and Canadian identity.

Furthermore, many Canadians pursue hockey not as a road to a career but instead as a recreational experience that brings them together with others in their communities, sometimes as players and other times as volunteers and fans. It seems to me that in the backyard rinks, neighbourhood streets, and other places where hockey is played and enjoyed informally, people are more easily able to come together to share an experience that is for the most part self-affirming. Research on recreational hockey and hockey fans would most likely provide another kind of insight into the role that hockey plays in national identity formation.

However, as people become more involved in organized hockey and young players move into hockey's economic arena, people of colour do not seem to be *Canadian enough* to be spared racial slurs, stereotyping, or other barriers to their involvement and progress. These are not just personal troubles that these individuals must overcome (or not) on their own. They are, rather, public issues that Canadian society at large needs to address if Canada is to be the equitable and inclusive society that we claim it to be.

Notes

The author gratefully appreciates Andriel C. Stoeckel's editorial support and acknowledges Audrey Susin's research assistance.

1 Richard S. Gruneau, "Sport as an Area of Sociological Study: An Introduction to Major Themes and Perspectives," in Richard S. Gruneau and John Albinson, eds., *Canadian Sport: Sociological Perspectives* (Don Mills, ON: Addisson Wesley, 1976), p. 9.

2 Ibid., pp. 9-10.

3 C. Wright Mills, *The Sociological Imagination* (New York: Oxford University Press, 1980).

4 Ken Dryden, *The Game* (Toronto: Macmillan Canada, 1983).

5 Dryden, *The Game*, pp. 54-55.

6 For examples, see Anthony Giddens, *Central Problems in Social Theory: Action, Structure and Contradiction in Social Analysis* (London: Macmillan Press, 1979); Giddens, *Modernity and Self-Identity: Self and Society in the Late Modern Age* (Stanford, CA: Stanford University Press, 1991); Pierre Bourdieu, "Sport and Social Class," *Social Science Information* 17, 6 (1978), pp. 819-40; and Bourdieu, "Programme for a Sociology of Sport," *In Other Words: Essays Towards a Reflexive Sociology*, trans. Matthew Adamson (Stanford, CA: Stanford University Press, 1990).

7 Dryden, *The Game*, p. 68.

8 Joseph Mensah, *Black Canadians: History, Experiences, Social Conditions* (Halifax: Fernwood, 2002), p. 1.

9 Jeffery Reitz and Raymond Breton, "Prejudice and Discrimination in Canada and the United States: A Comparison," in Vic Satzewich, ed., *Racism and Social Inequality in Canada* (Toronto: Thompson Educational, 1998), p. 65, quoted in Mensah, *Black Canadians*, p. 2.

10 Mensah, *Black Canadians*, p. 12.

11 Ibid., p. 13.

12 Ibid., p. 14.

13 See Bruce Kidd, "The Elite Athlete," in Jean Harvey and Hart Cantelon, eds., *Not Just a Game: Essays in Canadian Sport Sociology* (Ottawa: University of Ottawa Press, 1988), pp. 288-89; and Frank Cosentino, *Afros, Aboriginals and Amateur Sport in Pre-World War I Canada* (Ottawa: The Canadian Historical Association, 1998).

14 Wilbert M. Leonard II and John Phillips, "The Cause and Effect Rule for Percentaging Tables: An Overdue Statistical Correction for 'Stacking' Studies," *Sociology of Sport Journal*, 14 (1997), pp. 283-89; B. Margolis and J. A. Piliavin, "'Stacking' in Major League Baseball: A Multivariate Analysis," *Sociology of Sport Journal*, 16 (1999), pp. 16-35; Jay J. Coakley, *Sports in Society: Issues and Controversies*, 8th ed. (Boston: McGraw-Hill, 2004), p. 315.

15 David L. Andrews, "The Fact(s) of Michael Jordan's Blackness: Excavating a Floating Racial Signifier," *Sociology of Sport Journal*, 13 (1996), p. 134.

16 Bernadette D. Proctor and Joseph Dalaker, *Poverty in the United States: 2002* (Washington, DC: Government Printing Office, 2003), p. 5.

17 Peter S. Li, *Ethnic Inequality in a Class Society* (Toronto: Wall & Thompson, 1988), p. 22; emphasis added.

18 Leo Driedger, ed., *The Canadian Ethnic Mosaic: A Quest for Identity* (Toronto: McClelland and Stewart, 1978), quoted in Li, *Ethnic Inequality*, p. 22.

19 Michael Omi and Howard Winant, *Racial Formation in the United States: From the 1960s to the 1980s* (New York: Routledge, 1986), pp. 23-24.

20 Leo Driedger and Shiva Halli, "Racial Integration: Theoretical Options," in Leo Driedger and Shiva Halli, eds., *Race and Racism: Canada's Challenge* (Montreal: McGill-Queen's University Press, 2000), pp. 69-70.

21 See Li, *Ethnic Inequality*; and Mensah, *Black Canadians*.

22 Rinaldo Walcott, *Black Like Who?* (Toronto: Insomniac Press, 1997), pp. 41-42; emphasis added.

23 Roch Carrier, "Introduction," in *Backcheck: A Hockey Retrospective*, Library and Archives Canada <www.collectionscanada.ca/hockey/index-e.html>.

24 Library and Archives Canada, "Hockey Firsts," *Backcheck: A Hockey Retrospective* <www.collectionscanada.ca/hockey>.

25 Library and Archives Canada, "Early Days of Hockey," *Backcheck: Hockey for Kids* <www.collectionscanada.ca/hockey/ kids>.

26 Richard Gruneau and David Whitson, *Hockey Night in Canada: Sport, Identities, and Cultural Politics* (Toronto: Garamond Press, 1993), p. 40.

27 Ibid., p. 304.

28 David Whitson, "Hockey and Canadian Identities: From Frozen Rivers to Revenue Streams," in David Taras and Beverly Rasporich, eds., *A Passion for Identity: Introduction to Canadian Studies*, 3rd ed. (Toronto: Nelson, 1997), p. 304.

29 "History of Native Hockey," Nativehockey.com: Promoting Indigenous Hockey in North America <www.nativehockey.com/history.html>.

30 Garth Vaughan, "Nova Scotia Mi'kmaq Story Tellers," *Birthplace of Ice Hockey* <www.birthplaceofhockey.com/hockeyists/mikmaq/mikmaq-stories.html>.

31 Cosentino, *Afros, Aboriginals and Amateur Sport*.

32 Don Marks and Gary Zubeck, *They Call Me Chief: Warriors on Ice*, VHS, directed by Don Marks (Winnipeg: Lake Releasing, 2001).

33 Brenda Zeman, *To Run with Longboat: Twelve Stories of Indian Athletes in Canada* (Edmonton: GMS2 Ventures, 1988), p. 60.

34 This and the following three quotations are all from Marks and Zubeck, *They Call Me Chief*.

35 On the OCN Blizzard, see also Bill Boyd, *All Roads Lead to Hockey* (Toronto: Key Porter, 2004), ch. 2, "Hockey on the Rez."

36 Cecil Foster, *A Place Called Heaven: The Meaning of Being Black in Canada* (Toronto: Harper Collins, 1996), p. 21; see also Mensah, *Black Canadians*, pp. 57-128.

37 Cosentino, *Afros, Aboriginals and Amateur Sport*.

38 See Bolaria and Li, *Racial Oppression*; and Mensah, *Black Canadians*.

39 See George Fosty and Darril Fosty, *Black Ice: The Lost History of the Colored Hockey League of the Maritimes, 1895–1925* (New York: Stryker Indigo, 2004) for an in-depth account of this league.

40 Garth Vaughan, "Racism, Respect Define History of Black Hockey in Nova Scotia," *Annapolis Valley Regional*, Oct. 23, 2001, p. 11.

41 Cecil Harris, *Breaking the Ice: The Black Experience in Professional Hockey* (Toronto: Insomniac Press, 2003), p. 14.

42 Harris, *Breaking the Ice*, p. 148.

43 Ari Cohen, Evan Beloff, Max Wallace, and Daniel Cross, *Too Colourful for the League*, VHS, directed by Daniel Cross and Mila Augn-Thwin (Montreal: Diversus, 2000).

44 Ibid., p. 49.

45 Harris, *Breaking the Ice*, was the primary source for information about the family backgrounds of black NHL players, but a variety of Internet sources were used to either confirm Harris's information or gather additional information about those players. The following Internet sources provided some information about black players not mentioned in Harris's book: Paul Friesen (*Winnipeg Sun*), "Right out of the Blue," *Slam! Sports* <www.juniorhockeyradio.com/Slam040421/col_friesen-sun.html>; Hockey Draft Central, "1979 NHL Draft Pick: Dirk Graham" <www.hockeydraftcentral.com/1979/79089.html>; and Robert Fachet, "Capitals Give Former First-Rounder Savage His First Go-Round in NHL," *Washington Post*, Feb. 5, 1991.

46 Anne Milan and Kelly Tran, "Blacks in Canada: A Long History," *Canadian Social Trends*, Spring 2004, p. 5.

47 Mensah, *Black Canadians*, pp. 94-96.

48 Errol Williams, interviewed by CBC Evening News (Toronto), "Black Ice: Part I," on *The Right Track*, CBC Radio One, April 6, 1997, Real Audio file <www.cbc.ca/insidetrack/media/1997apr06.ram>.

49 Tom Hawthorn, "One Minute to Make Hockey History," *The Globe and Mail*, Dec. 26, 2001; National Hockey League Players' Association, "NHL Player Search: Paul Tetsuhiko Kariya," *Legends of Hockey* <www.legendsofhockey.net:8080>; Jannelle So, "Keeping It Cool," *Audrey Magazine*, April 2004 <www.audreymagazine.com/april2004/features>; Nachiket Dave and Chetan Dave, "Manny Malhotra's Icy Dreams," *Little India* <206.20.14.67/achal/archive/Jun99/manny.htm>.

50 Mensah, *Black Canadians*, p. 149.

51 Andrew Heisz and Logan McLeod, *Low-Income in Census Metropolitan Areas, 1980-2000* (Ottawa: Statistics Canada, 2004), p. 6.

52 Li, *Ethnic Inequality*, p. 127.

53 Milan and Tan, "Blacks in Canada," p. 7.

54 Chris Baker and Jack Jedwab, "Patriotism and Canadian Identity," a poll conducted by Environics Research Group/Focus Canada for The Association for Canadian Studies <www.acs-aec.ca/Polls/Poll40.pdf>.

55 Carol Tator, interviewed by CBC Evening News (Toronto), "Black Ice: Part II," *on The Right Track*, April 13, 1997, Real Audio file <www.cbc.ca/insidetrack/media/1997>.

PART TWO

The Political Economy of Hockey

Playing with the Big Boys: Smaller Markets, Competitive Balance, and the Hope for a Championship Team

■ MARK ROSENTRAUB

Despite the Florida Marlins' improbable 2003 World Series championship, two other events defined that year's Major League Baseball playoffs. First there was the errant fan who interfered with a foul ball and brought forth yet another collapse by the Chicago Cubs. Second, not to be outdone, baseball's other lovable losers, the Boston Red Sox, engineered another defeat at the hands of the Yankees. Had manager Grady Little chosen to remove a tiring Pedro Martinez, the Red Sox might have ended the "curse of the Bambino" and eight decades of frustration—instead of finally doing that a year later.

For decades the Red Sox and Cubs had defied one of sport's axiomatic principles. What attracts people to sports is the uncertainty of outcomes and the hope that their team can compete for a championship. For the Cubs and Red Sox (at least until 2004) losing had become all too predictable; but their fans remained loyal and attendance did not suffer. More commonly, though, if winning or losing becomes predictable and certain teams never have a chance of securing a championship, fan interest, attendance, and media ratings decline.[1] Lower attendance and media ratings translate into lower profit levels for team owners and lower salaries for professional athletes. Hence, fans, owners, and players would all seem to have a vested interest in achieving a level of balance with regard to the chance to win.

As sports lore would have it, only the Cubs actually violate this principle; the Red Sox had fielded fine teams across several decades, only to lose repeatedly to their "evil empire," the New York Yankees. The Cubs, conversely, have produced decades of poor play—interrupted now and then by seasons of excellence—but remain beloved by Chicago's north-side faithful.

Normally, then, in the absence of winning or at least fielding a competitive team, attendance, interest, and revenues for sports teams tend to decline.[2] For a team to be competitive, moreover, it must either generate sufficient revenues to attract and retain quality players, or have owners who are able and willing to lose money in sports in the quest to produce a winner. To minimize their financial risks and to ensure themselves of adequate if not robust revenue, team owners typically try to secure the largest possible market area, and they jealously guard against infringement on their potential sources of income (witness the efforts of Baltimore Orioles' owner Peter Angelos to dissuade MLB from moving the Montreal Expos franchise to nearby Washington). Owners in smaller regions or markets with lower concentrations of wealth routinely push for revenue-sharing programs, and are also the strongest supporters of salary caps, whether on the amount that can be paid to any single athlete or on the total costs of players' salaries and benefits. Such mechanisms seek to offset the inherent advantages of teams in larger markets by providing access to more robust income streams. Revenue transfers from large- to small-market franchises and the proportion of total revenues allotted to player salaries have become crucial labour-management issues, and indeed crucial structural issues, for each of North America's four major sports leagues.

Complicating the issue have been the interests of players who, having battled for decades for the right to sell their services to the highest bidder, are suspicious of any system that restricts what owners can spend on salaries. These suspicions are rooted in past actions by owners, including evidence of collusion in Major League Baseball that led to the courts awarding $280 million (all figures US) in damages to the players.[3] For this reason, any mechanisms designed to reduce the amount of money that an owner has to spend for players receive careful and jaundiced reviews from the various players' unions. The 2004–05 lockout and ensuing deadlock between the National Hockey League and its players was but the latest struggle between owners and players, and among owners serving markets of different sizes and wealth.

Major League Baseball has endured several work stoppages, including the cancellation of a World Series, at times when owners could agree neither with each other nor with the players' union on a system to share revenues, cap salaries, and strive towards competitive balance. A semblance of peace was achieved in the late 1990s, and it is certainly arguable whether or not competitive balance has been achieved. The National Basketball Association lost part of a season in an attempt to achieve a plan for revenue-sharing that owners and players could accept. Still, while the NBA now has a labour-management accord that includes a substantial revenue-sharing program, there is concern that another lockout could take place in the near future. The NHL's lockout in 2004–05 was further complicated by the challenges facing teams based in two different countries, with the result that dollar-exchange rates and different tax policies produce differential effects on players.

The National Football League has achieved the most comprehensive formula for revenue-sharing of any of the four major leagues, as well as an enviable record of competitive balance and acceptable compensation plans for players. But this has not been achieved without discord over what revenues are to be included in the calculations on which both salaries and revenue-sharing are based. Thus in 2004 the leader of the NFL players' association voiced concerns about the league's exclusion of luxury-seating and in-stadium advertising from these calculations of local revenues, raising the possibility that an auto-matic extension of the existing collective bargaining agreement might not occur.

The issues of large-market versus small-market competitiveness, revenue-sharing, and salary caps, then, have a tangled relationship. One part of this struggle involves the conflicting and complementary interests of fans, owners, and players—the field of interests within which any plans to promote competitiveness, balance revenue-genera-tion capabilities, and protect the rights of players to earn appropriate salaries must be crafted. Another element is the economic and business theory that might be used to help sports leagues come up with plans for competitiveness, revenue-sharing, and appropriate compensation for players. As we shall see, the labour-management agree-ments that exist today in North American professional sports have had quite different results—although models for league competitiveness and revenue-sharing do exist, and they could ensure that member teams have reasonable chances of providing their fans with championships, or at least competitive teams.

Revenue-Sharing and League Competitiveness:
Conflicts between Individual and Collective Interests

During difficult labour and management negotiations it has probably occurred to a team owner or two that maybe what should be done is to limit franchises to the very largest markets and forget the problems of cities such as Indianapolis (NBA), Jacksonville (NFL), Milwaukee (MLB), or Ottawa (NHL). After all, the larger market areas of Boston, Chicago, Dallas/Fort Worth, Detroit, Houston, Los Angeles, New York, and Toronto host the largest concentrations of wealth in North America. The most lucrative marketing arrangements for owners and players are also found in these areas. Why not limit teams to the ten largest market areas, broadcast games to the rest of North America, and permanently set aside questions related to revenue-sharing and competi-tive balance? Disneyland and Disneyworld are in just two markets, and the Grand Canyon is in one region. Why do sports leagues have to serve so many markets and then deal with the revenue and competitiveness issues that are created when teams serve markets of different sizes and with very different concentrations of wealth? As Yankee owner George Steinbrenner is reported to have once said, no one ever put a gun to anyone's head and forced them to buy a sports team. Therefore, if someone did buy a team they should stop whining and market their team.

Why, then, should a league ever expand and place a team in a market that is smaller than the average size of the markets served by existing teams? It does this, first, because theoretically it makes sense to create a team in a new market if its presence increases total league revenues without infringing upon the market area or reducing the revenues of any existing team. This was easy in early expansions to California and the South, but more complicated when the proposed new franchise is less than eighty miles from an existing one—as was the case for a new baseball franchise in Washington or for the NHL franchise that Hamilton, Ontario, repeatedly sought in the 1980s (a Hamilton-based team would have overlapped with the "territories" of Toronto and Buffalo). Whether or not total league revenues will increase is a calculation that must consider the potential revenues added by an additional team in an underserved market (for example, could the Toronto area support two NHL teams?) as well as the allocation of a share of future league revenues to the new team. Expansion is a good business decision if the league revenues increase as a result of a new team's presence, after subtracting the new team's share of pooled revenues from such things as the broadcast of games and the sale of merchandise. If that calculation is negative—if the team's share of pooled revenues is greater than the increment produced for league revenues—expansion is bad for business.

It is possible that league revenues could increase while revenues for an individual owner decrease when a new team is added. Most leagues, however, will strive to avoid such a conflict, in order to ensure that a majority of owners do not act against the interests of other individual owners. However, examples abound where one owner believed an infringement would or did occur, and this has, on occasion brought forth compensation strategies. Expansion strategies have frequently followed demographic changes and, as a result, new teams tend to be established in the faster-growing areas in the Southern and Western United States and the Western sections of Canada.

An additional team also increases the number of competitors for existing teams, and given sufficient playing talent, the presence of one more competitive team creates both uncertainty and variety. That expanded level of competitiveness and variety is intended to generate more fan interest in existing franchises and engender new geographic rivalries that increase the revenues available to existing teams. For example, the relatively new Ottawa Senators had, by the early years of this new century, arguably developed mutually profitable rivalries with both the Montreal Canadiens and the Toronto Maple Leafs.

Expansion by a league into a previously underserved market (or a market without any team) also minimizes the possibility of other investors entering the same market and using it as an anchor for a competitive league. Expansion is thus designed to eliminate the threat of competition from other investors who could create an alternative league. This was why the old National Hockey Association (from its base in Montreal and Ottawa) sought to place teams in Toronto in 1912.[4] In baseball, conversely, the failure to include potentially viable markets led to the creation of the American League, a short-lived competitor for the National League. In the 1950s, MLB (by then a combination of the National and American Leagues) pre-empted the threat of a new Continental League when the Dodgers and Giants moved to California. In football, the NFL's decision not to expand more aggressively in the early 1960s led to the formation of a successful American Football League. Like its baseball counterpart, of course, the AFL eventually merged with the older league, re-creating the monopoly situation of one "major league" in each sport. Leagues exist in part to protect their members' market areas, and they seek to ensure that competitor leagues will not develop by working to eliminate any possibility of a "pool" of potentially profitable markets in which other investors could launch a new set of franchises.[5]

In addition, each of North America's four professional sports leagues with teams in the United States enjoys a certain level of judicial and legislative protection from market forces. To avoid the possibility of successful anti-trust actions or consumer protection lawsuits, the leagues have to be able to demonstrate that they are not deliberately excluding any viable major league market in order to protect the profits and revenues of existing franchises, and that they are not minimizing competition.[6] Expansion also pre-empts criticism from elected officials who represent areas without teams, and helps ensure that government has no interest in removing market protections from major league sports.[7] Further, existing owners may enjoy a political benefit from the existence of at least one market that could host a franchise but hasn't got a team. The presence of a potential alternative home for a team means that a city government will probably be more flexible in meeting an owner's demands for a new stadium (or improvements in an existing one), or demands for more favourable lease arrangements, in order to avoid the possible loss of the team.

These benefits are offset by associated risks. The number of wins possible in a league is fixed—the maximum number of wins equals the number of games played—and each win for one team means a loss for the opponent.[8] Thus, when a new team is added to a league, existing owners typically expect to improve their win-loss record at the expense of the new franchise. If an expansion team in a small market is successful, though, as the Edmonton Oilers were in the 1980s and the Florida Panthers (and baseball's Florida Marlins) were briefly in the late 1990s, existing owners face the potential for reduced income if their win/loss record deteriorates. Moreover, since established teams must also share joint revenues (from national television, for example, or licensed merchandising) with their new partners, this often means less income from these sources, at least temporarily. The hope, of course, and certainly the strategic assumption behind the NHL's 1990s expansion decisions, is that the league's growing "footprint"—and the sport's growing national popularity—will translate into greater total revenues from these sources, and hence larger shares for everyone (see also chapter 9). However, the addition of new teams also means that on the issue of sharing future revenues, larger-market team owners are likely to face more voices that will oppose their financial interests.

The estimated value of these risks is usually established by the price that the owner of the new team is charged for the franchise. Recent franchise fees have risen as high as $700 million paid for the NFL franchise in Houston (the Texans), though NHL franchise fees have remained much lower—$80 million for the last four franchises granted in 1997: Nashville, Atlanta, Columbus, and Minnesota.[9] In most cases the vast majority of income from franchise fees is distributed in equal shares among existing team owners. However, exorbitant entrance costs, while protecting existing owners against lost future income, carry a risk that the new owners will not be able to afford to pay the salaries needed to attract quality players. This challenge occurs especially if the new team is in a small market (such as Columbus), or in leagues (the NHL, or MLB) in which revenue-sharing is ineffective in achieving competitiveness. The result might be that the new owners will become proponents for greater revenue-sharing, or will field non-competitive teams that raise still other challenges.

Recently MLB has had to deal with these issues with regard to two franchises. First, when the Montreal Expos' ownership became dysfunctional and the team unprofitable, MLB had to take over the team, pay its bills, and embark on a multi-year process to find a new home and owner for the team. The team moved to Washington, D.C., in 2005, with an auction held to determine who would own and operate the team in its new location. To maximize the fee charged, MLB secured a lucrative ballpark development deal including a lease that minimized the costs for the new owner. Second, the ownership of the expansion Arizona Diamondbacks followed a business plan to create a winning team in a very short period of time through a series of deferred contracts to older star players. The Diamondbacks did win the World Series in only their fourth season of play, but they could not earn sufficient revenues to meet the contract obligations incurred. Within two years of winning the World Series the team had released or traded several players with robust contracts in order to reduce its payroll, and new investors had to be recruited to provide operating cash. In 2004 the Diamondbacks had the worst record in MLB, and with declining attendance levels concern about their long-term future grew. The revenues that can be generated by professional baseball in the Phoenix market may not be sufficient to attract and keep the players necessary to be competitive. These two examples point to systemic problems faced by small-market franchises in the MLB business model.

These different pressures and behaviours reflect a set of conflicting principles that help to define the revenue-sharing/expansion conundrum for leagues and individual owners. The self-interest of leagues is to maximize total revenue and protect the markets of each team. This is achieved by (1) increasing competitiveness to maximize uncertainty and fans' interest, and (2) expanding into new markets to achieve marginal gains in total revenue while inhibiting the emergence of competing leagues and challenges to a league's protections from free-market forces. For individual team owners, conversely, given that attendance and individual profitability are tied to winning percentages and overall expenditures on players and coaches, the goal is to minimize revenue-sharing and competitiveness to the point that their team consistently wins games and, possibly, championships.[10]

The tensions between the interests of large- and small-market teams and between the interests of individual owners and the league are sharpened by the interests of the players (as represented by their unions) in negotiations about plans for expansion, franchise location, and revenue-sharing. Moreover, just as there is conflict between the interests of large- and small-market owners, so too is there conflict between the interests of different groups of players. For the league's best players, their ability to maximize their salaries depends upon their right to move from team to team and attract multiple bids from several team owners. Thus expanding rights to free agency—when players are eligible to move, and what compensation (if any) must be paid to their old teams—has been of central concern to all of the unions that represent professional athletes. However, for less established or journeyman players, when owners commit too much to attract "stars," the revenue remaining for other players may well be decreased, leading to lower salaries for lesser players as well as large variances in the salary structure of a team. For that reason, some players might find their salaries improved by a system that capped the money that any one player could earn, while guaranteeing that a certain portion of total revenue would be paid out in salaries. The NBA has tried to achieve a plan that adheres to that principle; but there has been conflict over defining the gross revenues to be included in the total revenue pool available to pay players. Faced with a seemingly endless set of debates over accounting principles, some labour leaders have concluded that the best strategy is simply to let a market for players' services dictate what every player earns.

For both owners and players an inherent conflict exists between what individuals would seek in a system designed to maximize the wealth of "winners," and what a league or union would seek in a system designed to protect the interests of all its members. This conflict stems from the joint-production element of sports, an element that makes it unlike any other business. The owners of the Dallas Cowboys and New York Yankees know they will maximize revenues if they deliver winning teams; yet both owners also know that exciting games will only happen on a consistent basis when there is a good number of competitive teams in the league. If only a few top teams won all their games, fans would become bored and revenues would probably decline. Hence, owners must balance their own interests in revenue maximization with the need to have what they deem is an adequate cadre of competitive teams. For players there is a similar balance that must be achieved. Each individual wants to maximize his salary; however, he must do that while also ensuring that the teams can pay for the other quality players needed to compete for championships. As Alex Rodriguez learned, earning $25 million per year means little if his team is destined to always finish last because it cannot afford other high-quality players.[11]

Then too, the positions taken by players' unions sometimes align with the interests of high-revenue teams. With access to larger and wealthier fan bases, teams in the largest markets are typically less concerned with player costs. Normally, the Yankees (or the Rangers), the Maple Leafs, and the Red Wings would prefer to let players earn more rather than face the prospect of a season being cancelled. Thus, on the question of free agency, large-market teams have interests more aligned with those of the star players than with the owners of, say, the Ottawa Senators or Pittsburgh Penguins. Conversely, and not surprisingly, these same big-city teams resist revenue-sharing formulas that would require them to "subsidize" their small-market partners.

Finally, too, the interests of fans come into play in all of this. In their role as consumers, fans express their satisfaction with competitiveness through their purchase of tickets, luxury-seating, and souvenirs, and through their interest in watching or listening to the broadcast of games. If a league falters in its ability to sustain fan interest, revenues inevitably decline. Moreover, it is also possible for a situation to develop in which league-wide revenues appear high because of the success of a number of larger-market teams (in New York, Detroit, and Toronto, for example), while the interest of fans in one or more smaller markets dwindles as their teams become non-competitive. For example, Pittsburgh and Milwaukee made large investments in new baseball stadiums to help their teams survive; yet years after the Pirates and the Brewers were playing in state-of-the art facilities, neither has been able to produce a competitive team. Owners of both franchises call for more patience and perhaps more revenue-sharing, but the investment of public money by taxpayers has not been properly acknowledged. Indeed, discussions among major league owners, or between leagues and player unions, rarely include anything more than rhetorical acknowledgement that teams and players might "owe" some loyalty to their fans in return for commitments of public money. An issue for all leagues, then, is how best to protect fans, and whether or not a simply market solution—do not buy tickets to losing teams—actually protects fans' interests.

Theory into Practice

With these points and issues in mind, it is now time to take the theory into practice, and to examine the structures that the different major leagues have developed to share revenues, enhance competitiveness, and protect the interests of owners and players (all four major leagues have collective bargaining agreements between the players and the league). In particular I focus on the three leagues that have successfully implemented plans that afford a level of labour-management stability, and consider the outcomes in terms of competitiveness and attendance levels.

Major League Baseball

MLB has established a revenue-sharing program based on a "luxury tax" paid when a team's payroll exceeds a specified level, with no limit on what a team owner can pay an individual player. The tax threshold in 2003 was $117 million, rising to $128 million in 2005 and $136.5 in 2006, the final year of the existing collective-bargaining agreement. Expenditures above these levels were taxed at 17.5 per cent in 2003. In later years, if a club exceeded the threshold for the first time, the tax rate would be 22.5 per cent. Second-time offenders in any of the contract years would pay a tax of 30 per cent; third- and fourth-time offenders (and the offence must be in consecutive years) would pay a 40 per cent tax. The NHL Players' Association proposed an MLB-style luxury tax program as one way of resolving the 2004–05 lockout, but, as critics commented, the tax thresholds would have been too high, and the tax rates too low, to act as an effective deterrent to the big-spending teams.

In a hypothetical luxury tax program, if the salary tax threshold is $120.5 million and a team has a payroll of $150 million, the team would be exceeding the threshold by $29.5 million. This would mean that a team would pay a tax of $6.64 million (at a tax rate of 22.5 per cent) to the league's revenue-sharing pool. From an individual owner's perspective, then, the marginal revenue growth needed to break even on the expenditure of an "extra" $29.5 million in players' salaries would have to be $36.1 million. Smaller-market teams hope that this higher marginal cost deters offers to free agent players, and thereby helps to keep salary levels from escalating.

However, the luxury tax (or payroll tax), although it is the most controversial of baseball's competitiveness and revenue-sharing initiatives, is not all that significant in helping lower-revenue clubs—because the sums redistributed through this mechanism are not large enough to make a difference to them. The most important revenue-sharing element of the collective bargaining agreement involves each club's local revenues, or defined gross revenues, less receipts from the central fund administered by MLB to share income. Defined gross revenues are the heart of the matter, and, according to baseball's "Basic Agreement," refer to:

> The aggregate operating revenues from baseball operations received, or to be received on an accrual basis as reported by each Club on an annual basis in the Club's Financial Information Questionnaire. Baseball Operations shall mean all activities of a Club that generate revenue, except those wholly unrelated to the business of Major League Baseball. Baseball operations shall include (by way of example, but not by way of limitation): (a) an activity that could be conducted by a non-club entity which is conducted by a Club because its affiliation or connection with Major League Baseball increases the activity's appeal; and (b) an activity from which revenue or value is expected as a result of the decision to forego what otherwise would be Defined Gross Revenue.[12]

From the defined gross revenues, clubs can then subtract actual stadium expenses, and 34 per cent of the "net local revenue" is placed in the revenue-sharing pool, which is then equally divided among all the clubs.

How well has the program worked? While there has been greater competitiveness in teams contending for playoff berths, the results from 2003 and 2004 appear to be a bit disappointing. High-revenue teams from the largest markets dominated in 2003 and again in 2004, and while there was some reshuffling within the group of teams with winning records, a truly competitive balance has yet to be achieved. It is possible that there will be greater returns in the future as small-market teams develop and retain the players necessary to be successful; but this has not yet happened. Two smaller-market teams, the St. Louis Cardinals and Minnesota Twins, performed well in the 2003 and 2004 seasons. On a per capita basis, though, the Cardinals sell more baseball tickets than does any other team in MLB, and their historic market presence provides them with an extraordinary revenue position. The Twins play in one of baseball's weakest divisions and were eliminated in the first round of the playoffs in both 2003 and 2004. In the American League in both 2003 and 2004, the largest-revenue teams, the New York Yankees and the Boston Red Sox, played for the championship. In 2003 a small-revenue team, the Florida Marlins, won the World Series; but financial pressures made it impossible for them to retain some of the key players on their championship team, and some other players did not perform as well in 2004 as they did in 2003. As a result the Marlins did not quality for the playoffs in 2004, repeating a cycle that confronts many teams with small-revenue bases. They can succeed for a season, maybe two; but then core players can secure larger contracts from teams with large-revenue bases and they leave. Hockey fans will know that the Edmonton Oilers lost most of the key players from the championship teams of the 1980s, including Wayne Gretzky to Los Angeles and Mark Messier to New York. (See Table 7.1.)

National Football League

There are three components to the revenue-sharing and competitiveness programs of the NFL that have made for success and good outcomes for fans, owners, and players. First, the revenue shared is sufficient to permit every team to have the means to attract and retain stars. Second, there is a cap on the total salary that each team can pay to its players, and while owners with greater access to revenue can offer deferred bonuses and payments to sign a star player, those expenditures must be counted towards a team cap in later years. This can make the franchise less competitive during the years that it must live within the cap. Third, the players are assured that a definite proportion of pooled league revenues will be spent on their salaries and benefits.

For 2004 each team could spend up to $80.58 million. As of July 15, 2004, in terms of salary commitments and cap room remaining, Table 7.2 describes where each team stood. Injuries and late summer signings (including the Browns signing their first draft choice) changed these figures before the season began. What is apparent, nonetheless, is that unlike baseball, where high-revenue teams often spend 100 per cent to 150 per cent more than lower-revenue teams, the span between the lowest and highest salary commitments was only 15.7 per cent. This would alter somewhat after all first-round draft picks had agreed to their contracts, further reducing the spread. The disparities in

Table 7.1

MLB Team-Winning Percentages by Market Size: 2003 and 2004

Team	Market Size	Teams In Market	2003	2004
New York Yankees	21,199,865	2	.623	.623
Los Angeles Dodgers	16,373,645	2	.574.	525
Anaheim Angels	16,373,645	2	.568	.475
Chicago Cubs	9,157,540	2	.549	.543
Chicago White Sox	9,157,540	2	.512	.531
Baltimore Orioles	7,608,070	1	.481	.438
San Francisco Giants	7,039,362	2	.562	.621
Oakland Athletics	7,039.362	2	.562	.593
Boston Red Sox	7,007,713	1	.605	.586
Philadelphia Phillies	6,188,463	1	.531	.531
Detroit Tigers	6,074,631	1	.444	.265
Texas Rangers	5,221,801	1	.547	.438
Houston Astros	4,669,571	1	.568	.537
Atlanta Braves	4,112,198	1	.593	.623
Arizona Diamondbacks	4,095,622	1	.315	.519
Florida Marlins	3,876,380	1	.512	.562
Seattle Mariners	3,554,760	1	.389	.574
Cleveland Indians	3,352,765	1	.494	.420
Colorado Rockies	3,239,907	1	.420	.457
Tampa Bay Devil Rays	2,985,956	1	.435	.389
Minnesota Twins	2,968,806	1	.568	.566
San Diego Padres	2,813,833	1	.537*	.395
St. Louis Cardinals	2,603,607	1	.648	.525
Pittsburgh Pirates	2,358,695	1	.447	.493
Cincinnati Reds	1,979,202	1	.469	.426
Kansas City Royals	1,776,062	1	.358	.512
Milwaukee Brewers	1,689,572	1	.416	.420

salaries even before the final salary data are available, however, are notably smaller than in MLB. When all draft picks are signed and final salaries for the year tabulated, the variance in spending between teams in the NFL is substantially lower and the discrepancies that are normal in MLB (on the order of more than $100 million) simply cannot exist in the NFL.

It is possible for a team to exceed the cap in any year, and that is where differentials in local income earned by each team can have an impact on salary levels. How can that occur? A team could, for example, give a player it desires a substantial signing bonus or "up-front money." For example, a team could sign a player to a four-year contract and provide him with a $10 million signing bonus, which would be attractive to the player because he would receive more money in the early years of the contract. For the purposes of the NFL's salary cap, the team could divide the $10 million across the life of the contract. This would mean that in the first year only $2.5 million would be counted against the cap; but the balance must be counted in each successive year whether or not the player can still perform.

The second component of the NFL's competitiveness program involves broadcast revenues. Each franchise receives an equal share of the league's national media contracts, so that the share for the small- and large-market teams is identical.

Third, NFL teams draft each year in reverse order of their winning percentages, giving less successful teams first choice among new athletes that can improve the team's performance. Scheduling of games is also arranged so that teams that are successful in one year play a larger proportion of teams with winning records in the next season.

The NFL's revenue-sharing program has produced the most balanced set of championships, with teams from small markets winning (Green Bay, St. Louis) or at least playing (Charlotte) in the Super Bowl. Large-market teams have also won (New York, New England, and Dallas) the Super Bowl. However, the NFL's enduring popularity is the best indicator that this system has produced unmatched levels of fan support while reducing the effects of market size or team wealth as factors in on-field success.

National Basketball Association

The revenue-sharing and salary cap program implemented by the NBA is the most complex of all the major sports leagues, and based on media reports it is the one favoured by a majority of NHL owners. While in the period of negotiation the NHL players favoured a model similar to that of Major League Baseball, NHL management wanted a hard cap on the total amount of money that can be spent on player salaries by any team, and penalties for both players and owners when the cap is surpassed. In addition, the NHL leadership was also apparently attracted to a ceiling on the maximum salary that can be paid to any one player, and a separate salary schedule for rookies.

Table 7.2

Salary Cap Room in the NFL: 2004

Team	Salaries	Cap Room Position
Cleveland Browns	$69,182,000	$11,400,000
New Orleans Saints	$69,582,000	$11,000,000
Philadelphia Eagles	$70,282,000	$10,300,000
Dallas Cowboys	$71,382,000	$9,200,000
Arizona Cardinals	$73,052,000	$7,530,000
Minnesota Vikings	$73,282,000	$7,300,000
Detroit Lions	$73,382,000	$7,200,000
Jacksonville Jaguars	$73,582,000	$7,000,000
Kansas City Chiefs	$73,912,000	$6,670,000
Miami Dolphins	$74,282,000	$6,300,000
Cincinnati Bengals	$74,982,000	$5,600,000
Buffalo Bills	$75,082,000	$5,500,000
San Diego Chargers	$75,082,000	$5,500,000
New York Giants	$75,682,000	$4,900,000
Seattle Seahawks	$75,782,000	$4,800,000
Washington Redskins	$75,782,000	$4,800,000
Indianapolis Colts	$76,132,000	$4,450,000
Chicago Bears	$76,582,000	$4,000,000
New York Jets	$76,582,000	$4,000,000
St. Louis Rams	$76,832,000	$3,750,000
Atlanta Falcons	$77,282,000	$3,300,000
Houston Texans	$77,282,000	$3,300,000
Baltimore Ravens	$77,482,000	$3,100,000
Tampa Bay Buccaneers	$77,812,000	$2,770,000
Pittsburgh Steelers	$77,882,000	$2,700,000
San Francisco 49ers	$78,082,000	$2,500,000
Green Bay Packers	$78,182,000	$2,400,000
Denver Broncos	$78,832,000	$1,750,000
New England Patriots	$78,922,000	$1,660,000
Carolina Panthers	$79,482,000	$1,100,000
Oakland Raiders	$79,698,000	$884,000
Tennessee Titans	$80,059,000	$523,000

D.T. Rosenbaum describes the NBA system:

> If … salaries and benefits exceed 55 percent of basketball-related income (bri was
> defined in the collective bargaining agreement) then players are assessed an escrow
> tax of up to 10 percent of their salaries and benefits in order to bring the players'
> share of bri back down to 55 percent. If after assessing the maximum 10 percent
> escrow tax, the players' share of bri still exceeds 55 percent, then high-spending clubs
> are assessed a dollar-for-dollar luxury tax for every dollar of spending over the luxury
> tax threshold. This … threshold is … a team salary level that when multiplied by the
> number of teams and added to total player benefits is equal to 61.1 percent of bri (55
> percent [the salary cap] divided by 0.9).[13]

In the first year of this complex formula the players returned $131 million to the rev-
enue-sharing pool; in the following year their payment was $174 million, but spending
on salaries was so high that the teams had to contribute $173 million to reduce the
index back to the required 55 per cent. This meant a total of $347 million was then
redistributed according to a complicated formula designed to penalize higher-spending
teams. The goal of the formula was to ensure that higher-spending teams did not
receive as much as franchises that spent less, thereby creating an additional disincentive
to spending beyond the agreed levels. The intent was that if the teams paying the taxes
received fewer dollars, their effective tax rates would be higher than the 100 per cent
tax, and indeed Rosenbaum's conclusion was that the redistribution formula created tax
rates as high as 400 per cent for teams that exceeded the cap.[14] The goal of this plan,
which also includes ceilings on the amounts that can be paid to individual players (and
to rookies), was to contain spending by larger-market teams while guaranteeing that
players will collectively receive a contractually agreed proportion of the revenues
earned by the league.

Did this plan have a positive outcome on competitiveness in the NBA, in that teams
from smaller markets could achieve the levels of success more commonly associated
with teams in larger market areas? For the 2003–04 season two large-market teams
played for the championship, with the Detroit Pistons (6.1 million market population)
besting the Los Angeles Lakers (a 16.4 million-person market containing two teams).
The Pistons, however, advanced to the NBA finals after beating the Indiana Pacers (with
2.1 million in their extended market area), while the Lakers' road to the finals involved
defeating the San Antonio Spurs (2.8 million people in the San Antonio/Austin combined market areas). In 2002–03, San Antonio won the NBA championship, defeating the
large-market New Jersey Nets. However, from 1997 through 2000, one small-market
team (Utah twice, then Indiana) made the finals each year. Thus, while too few seasons
have been completed to determine the effects of the new formula, at first glance there is

little evidence that there has been a substantial change in levels of competitiveness in the league, at least as defined by participation in the NBA finals (see Table 7.3).

Table 7.3
NBA Finals' Participants and Market Sizes

(Market sizes in millions; numbers in parentheses refer to NBA teams in the area.)

Season	Finals Winner	Market Size	Finals-Loser	Market Size
1997-98	Chicago	9.2	Utah	1.3
1998-99	Chicago	9.2	Utah	1.3
1999-2000	Los Angeles	16.4 (2)	Indiana	2.1
2000-01	Los Angeles	16.4 (2)	Philadelphia	2.7
2001-02	Los Angeles	16.4 (2)	New Jersey	21.2 (2)
2002-03	San Antonio	2.9	New Jersey	21.2 (2)
2003-04	Detroit	6.1	Los Angeles	16.4 (2)

National Hockey League

In September 2004 NHL play was suspended, and the 2004–05 season was later cancelled when owners and players could not agree to cap salaries or share revenues between large-market and small-market franchises in the name of achieving a better competitive balance. The NHL did already have a modest revenue-sharing plan designed to help Canadian franchises deal with the lower value of the Canadian dollar, but the sums redistributed by this plan were very small, and the plan did not provide assistance to franchises based in US centres such as Pittsburgh, Buffalo, or Carolina.

The 2004 deadlock came with the expiry of the league's collective agreement with the NHL Players' Association, and it centred around two core issues. First, how much money are NHL teams losing (or making)? The NHL has claimed that more than half of its member teams are losing serious amounts of money; the players rejected these figures. According to the NHLPA, the official figures omit important sources of revenue: from local media, from merchandising, and from arenas constituted as separate businesses precisely for this purpose. Second, can the NHL's collective revenues be divided in a way that allows players to take a "fair" share of the total revenues from professional hockey (including the money made from "ancillary" sources) and that allows small-market teams to make money *and* be competitive on the ice?

On the first issue, the NHLPA quite simply did not believe that hockey revenues were as low as the league and its member teams were saying they were, and the owners had not given players' representatives open access to their books. In 2004 the NHL invited

Arthur Levitt, a respected US financial analyst and securities regulator, to examine the financial state of professional hockey, and Levitt produced a report that showed member teams collectively losing over $240 million in the previous season. Levitt also claimed that 75 per cent of NHL revenues were absorbed by player salaries and benefits, and that without significant changes the current NHL "business model" was destined to collapse.

The NHLPA flatly rejected Levitt's findings, and its position was later supported by the respected business magazine *Forbes*, whose annual review of the hockey industry painted many NHL teams as losing much less money (collectively, $96 million) than Levitt and the owners had claimed. The players maintained that the NHL and its member teams routinely omitted from their financial statements revenues and profits made by enterprises associated with hockey teams: an arena owned by a separate but related company, for example, or television stations owned by the same media corporations that own the teams. The players also argued that player salaries had been bid up by owners who are supposedly astute businessmen, people who would not offer salaries that would drive them into bankruptcy, as the league claimed. Regardless of the "truth," though, the challenge facing both sides was to agree on a transparent method of calculating gross hockey-related revenues, as done by MLB, the NFL, and the NBA.

Put another way, agreement on "defined gross revenue" is essential before any agreement can be reached on the other issues, and this requires a brief look at some of the ways in which team owners can make money that does not appear on the team's books. In one kind of example, suppose a team owner is a brewery (like Molson's or Labatt's) and uses games and game broadcasts to advertise its products. Since the same interests own both the team and the brewery, advertising rates can be set artificially low (that is, below market rates) so that revenues to the team are less than they might be, while the brewery gets advertising exposure at a fraction of its true value. Another version of the same dynamic occurs when sports teams are owned by the media companies that broadcast their games. The revenues that teams receive for local television coverage (on MSG Sports Network, for example, for the New York Rangers, or on Rogers Sportsnet in the case of the Toronto Blue Jays) are set artificially low, while the parent company makes lots of money on sports-related advertising. Clearly, if players' salaries are then set as a proportion of a total that omits such revenues, the athletes lose out.

Another accounting practice whereby hockey-related revenues may not appear on team books occurs when an owner operates the arena in which a team plays as a separate company. Some arena revenues, then—often those from concessions or parking or even luxury-seating—may not appear as hockey revenues; and the team's balance sheet may be further hurt if the team is charged a larger than appropriate share of arena operating expenses, while other events staged at the arena generate more profit for the arena holding company. This was alleged to have happened under the previous ownership of the Ottawa Senators. However, the important general issue is that such account-

ing practices are widespread in professional sports. The interlocking nature of the companies created to market teams is at the heart of disputes over what revenues should be
designated "defined gross revenues," and what should be the players' rightful share of
that income.

This returns us to the issue of how hockey revenues might be divided so that owners
and players could each (collectively) do well, and so that small-market teams can be
competitive. During the lockout the owners continued to maintain that only with a
hard salary cap, set at a level that small-market teams can afford ($31 million per team,
in the NHL's initial bargaining position), can small-market teams (like the Edmonton
Oilers) survive and competitiveness on the ice be assured.[15] The large-market owners
also refused to share their local media revenues (the most significant media revenues,
in hockey) with the other teams.

The NHLPA argued that in the absence of more systematic revenue-sharing than the
NHL has ever contemplated, this is simply a formula whereby the large-market teams
(Rangers, Flyers, Leafs, Stars) would make huge profits, in which players would get no
opportunity to share. However, the players' central proposal—to deter "runaway" salary
growth with a luxury tax modelled on that of Major League Baseball—set the tax
thresholds sufficiently high and the tax *rates* sufficiently low (only 20 per cent on the
first $5 million) that neutral observers agreed that the measure would not deter the rich
clubs from offering salaries that the smaller clubs could not match. Nor would it have
created a significant "pool" of funds to be redistributed among small-market teams. The
players' January 2005 offer, then, while it made important concessions—including a 24
per cent salary rollback, limits on rookie salaries, and significant changes to the arbitration system—left competitiveness as an issue for the owners to resolve. It also did not
concede that NHL revenues had stalled—and at a level well below that of the other
major league sports—let alone that salaries needed to be brought into some relationship
with revenues if the league was to survive.

In summer 2005 the NHL owners and players ended their season-killing dispute, and
the settlement has to be scored as a complete win for the owners, a potential win for
smaller-market cities, and a loss for players. This is not to suggest that players will be
impoverished, but the salary escalation that took place under the last collective agreement will be curtailed. The owners wanted and received cost certainty, establishing a
limit to a team's payroll set for 2005–06 season at $39 million. The players received pro-
tection only in that each team must spend at least $21.5 million each year. However, this
range of expenditures for players by each team includes all salaries, signing bonuses,
and performance bonuses, forming one of professional sport's firmest caps on what
players can earn. It was also agreed that salaries cannot exceed 54 per cent of league-
wide revenues. In addition, for those players with existing contracts, their salaries were
reduced by 24 per cent. Losing one season was well worth these gains for ownership,

and the owners demonstrated that they could handle the loss of a season better than could players.

The players did receive improved pension benefits and enhanced free-agency possibilities; however, their ability to negotiate an improved contract from another team will be limited by the hard salary cap. In addition, no one player can earn 20 per cent of the cap for a given team, a measure that may have a mild positive effect on the salaries paid to non-star players. Moreover, the range of salaries that any team can spend, from $21.5 million to $39 million, enables owners to compensate a star in the $6- to $7-million range, without this requiring that the salaries of other players be adjusted downwards in order to keep total spending within the cap. However, teams can buy players out of long-term contracts at two-thirds of the previously negotiated price, raising the prospect (already realized in some cases) that players can only continue their careers by accepting significantly less money elsewhere.

While many players can still expect to earn several hundred thousand dollars and probably in excess of $1 million if they have won a position on a roster, the salad days of the 1990s are gone. This is a victory for smaller markets, in that teams (like Edmonton and Pittsburgh) that were unable to compete for free agents should now be able to afford stars. Given that the salary cap applies to all teams alike, they should also be able to ice competitive teams. The larger and wealthier markets still have greater profit potential, to be sure; but a committed owner should be able to put a competitive team on the ice in all of the NHL's existing markets. Thus, while owners will still seek to maximize profits (and thus hopes of lower ticket prices are just that, hopes), the new deal does level the playing field—or the ice surface—for teams in the smaller markets of North America.

Conflicts of Interest

Professional sport is unlike any other business in that it requires joint production for success. What this means is that whereas General Motors can sell more cars if Ford or Toyota are weakened or go out of business, the Detroit Red Wings need the Maple Leafs and other teams to be competitive if they are to sustain fan interest and sell tickets. Fans will not pay substantial sums for exhibitions of athletic prowess when the outcome is not in doubt, or doesn't matter. Without games with a certain amount of suspense, professional sports as a business fails. Consequently, every owner has an interest in the competitiveness of other teams, even while they still want to win themselves. Thus, if large-market owners do not share their revenues with franchises in regions with lower populations, the small-market operations lose games too predictably and everyone's revenues decline.

Added to this unique conflict of interests is the more common conflict between management and labour as to what shares of revenues generated should belong to the workers (the players) and to owner-investors. In any negotiation between players and owners, these issues are at the heart of every discord, and of every ultimate agreement. Unfortunately, the issues have a spider-like quality to them, with linkages to other issues that make them difficult to isolate, let alone resolve. By 2000 each of the four major sports leagues had suffered through cancelled games or seasons, including the loss of a World Series for MLB, the loss of a whole season for NHL hockey, and shortened seasons for the others.

A number of remaining issues, then, must be resolved if a satisfactory level of competitive balance is to be created and sustained in professional sports. First, owners have to recognize their shared interest in maintaining fan enthusiasm across the league and throughout the season, and commit to sharing sufficient revenues amongst themselves to achieve this outcome. However, the teams that generate large media revenues (the Colorado Avalanche, and Toronto Maple Leafs, for example) have shown little willingness to share revenues systematically with other owners. Team owners don't trust each other not to use revenue-sharing money to simply enhance their own profits; conversely, owners receiving money have a responsibility to invest dollars received from revenue-sharing into players who will improve their teams.

Second, owners and players have to agree on what revenue streams will count as "hockey-related" income, now that most sports franchises are really parts of integrated media and entertainment businesses owned by one corporation or group. The value of the New York Yankees is related to their YES television media holdings, and many hockey teams are anchor tenants in multi-purpose arenas that host more than one hundred other profit-making events each year. Sports owners commonly use teams to enhance the value of other holdings, and players believe that they should share in the wealth created in these other companies. Thus, negotiations between players and owners over the designation of sports-related income, and the proportion of that value that should be dedicated to players' benefits, will always be contentious. Moreover, the two sides must now work to overcome a legacy of deep mistrust. One group of sports owners (in MLB) was recently found, for example, to have engaged in collusion to suppress salaries. There is thus legitimate concern among NHL players that owners have systematically deflected income and profits from hockey teams to other businesses they control. Without agreement between players and owners on "defined gross revenues" *and* on transparent accounting rules, an enduring labour peace in sports is highly unlikely.

These challenges, and the current state of affairs in each of the four major sports leagues, suggest that owners will continue to compete with each other and with players. Efforts to expand and enforce revenue-sharing will be resisted by large-market owners, while owners in smaller markets will continue to seek greater revenue-sharing, as well as controls on salaries. Until the various sides recognize that their destinies are, in some very important ways, shared, the logic of competing interests points to continuing labour disruptions. Indeed, just as the NHL lost all of the 2004–05 season, a potential for lost games looms for the NBA. The NFL players' association wants the pool of defined revenues increased, and income disparities between teams restrained. MLB has a new agreement in place that significantly increases revenue-sharing; but its luxury tax remains relatively toothless, and spending by a handful of perennial contenders dwarfs what most clubs can afford. Thus prospects for smooth relations in US professional sports are at best unsettled, and it would be prudent to expect stormy times in the sports business for the next several seasons.

Notes

1 S. Rosen and A. Sanderson, "Labour Markets in Professional Sports," *The Economic Journal*, 111,469 (February 2001).

2 G.W. Scully, *The Market Structure of Sports* (Chicago: University of Chicago Press, 1995).

3 Andrew Zimbalist, *Baseball and Billions* (New York: Basic Books, 1992).

4 See Richard Gruneau and David Whitson, *Hockey Night in Canada: Sport, Identities, and Cultural Politics* (Toronto: Garamond Press, 1993), p. 89; also Bruce Kidd and John Macfarlane, *The Death of Hockey* (Toronto: New Press, 1972), p. 108

5 Mark S. Rosentraub, "Private Control of a Civic Asset: The Winners and Losers from North America's Experience with Four Cartels for Professional Team Sports," in T. Slack, ed., *The Commercialisation of Sport* (London: Frank Cass & Co., 2004).

6 T.A. Piraino Jr., "The Anti-Trust Rationale for the Expansion of Professional Sports Leagues," *The Ohio State Law Journal*, 57, 5 (1996), pp. 1677-729.

7 Mark S. Rosentraub, *Major League Losers: The Real Costs of Sports and Who's Paying for It* (New York: Basic Books, 1999).

8 D.T. Rosenbaum, "The Brave New World of the NBA Luxury Tax," unpublished paper, Department of Economics, University of North Carolina at Greensboro, 2004.

9 Nashville began play in 1998, Atlanta in 1999, and Columbus and Minnesota in 2000.

10 See Scully, *Market Structure of Sports*.

11 Robert Sandy, Peter Sloane, and Mark Rosentraub, *The Economics of Sports: An International Perspective* (New York and London: Palgrave Press/Macmillan, 2004).

12 Major League Baseball, *Basic Agreement* (New York: Major League Baseball, 2003).

13 Rosenbaum, "Brave New World of the NBA Luxury Tax," p. 5.

14 Ibid.

15 Oilers' owner Cal Nichols warned in January 2005 that without the "cost certainty" that a salary cap would provide, the Oilers would seek to sell the franchise.

CHAPTER EIGHT

Hockey Night in the United States? The NHL, Major League Sports, and the Evolving Television/Media Marketplace

■ ROBERT BELLAMY AND KELLY SHULTZ

Times appear to be "looking up" for the National Hockey League. The impasse between the NHL and the National Hockey League Players' Association (NHLPA) that wiped out the entire 2004–05 season has been settled. The owners achieved much of the "cost certainty" they wanted, while players lost some of the benefits of the "market system" that had been developed in the previous fifteen years.[1] Still, despite the first optimistic news about the league in several years, the NHL remains in a precarious position within the United States.

There has been a strong perception for many years that the NHL is one of the major professional sports in the United States (or one of four major league team sports). Thus, Ted Leonsis, majority owner of the NHL's Washington Capitals, says, "I think that the NHL right now is one of the five major sports. It goes football, baseball, NASCAR, basketball, and the NHL."[2] In the United States the designation of "major league" status typically indicates that a league or association is the best there is in its sport. It attracts the world's best players; it has a large and loyal fan base; it has a presence in the largest metropolitan areas, and is considered by fans and media both in the United States and abroad to offer the best competition in the world in its sport.

In most ways the NHL meets these criteria. It attracts the best hockey players in the world by paying far higher salaries than professional leagues pay in other countries, and it exercises effective control over the global hockey labour market (see chapters 11 and 12). It is widely acknowledged to be the world's premier hockey competition, with a devoted fan base in Canada and parts of the United States and Europe. Within the United States, NHL teams enjoy near constant sellouts in the major metropolitan markets of New York, Philadelphia, Detroit, and Denver—and strong regional television ratings in several other major markets: Dallas–Fort Worth, New England, and Minnesota. However, pockets of enthusiasm do not make a sport a focus of national interest, and the NHL's problem is that hockey has not kept pace in this respect with its major league competitors, despite much effort over the last three decades to elevate the game to a more prominent place in US sports culture. Today golf, college football, and basketball, and even some minor sports, draw larger US television audiences than does the NHL.[3]

Indeed, by almost any measure of exposure or revenue, the NHL lags behind its competitors in the North American professional sports industry. NHL hockey gets little national exposure on US television; indeed, national (US) ratings on both broadcast and cable are much lower than they are for the other "Big Five" sports identified by Washington owner Leonsis. When compared with the number of NHL viewers in much less populated Canada, or to NBA audiences in the United States, the figures are striking. As Leonsis puts it, "Game one of the Stanley Cup finals between Tampa and Calgary, in the United States ... 1 million people watched that game. In Canada, 3 million people watched the game.... A typical NBA game [has] 2.5 to 3 million people watch during the playoffs."[4] The consequences of these differences in audience levels are both predictable and ominous. No "major" sport has ever suffered a larger decline in national television revenue than the NHL did in its new contracts with NBC and ESPN, signed in 2004.

The NBC contract is a "make good"/shared-risk contract with no upfront rights fees and with the network and league sharing revenues and expenses.[5] That NBC has a similar deal with the Arena Football League (AFL) is a telling indicator of the decline in the NHL's status as seen by the US networks. In contrast, a previous contract with ABC, now expired, guaranteed $600 million over five years; ABC chose not to renew that arrangement. The NHL did renew its contract for national cable telecasts with Disney Corporation's ESPN; but regular-season games were relegated to ESPN2, and the number of games to be shown has been radically reduced. National cable games have now dropped steadily: from 128 in 1999–2000 to 70 games in 2003–04 and then down to only 40 games scheduled in the cancelled 2004–05 season.[6] When ESPN found that it could generate more revenue with other programming in the 2004–05 period, it declined to renew its deal with the league. The NHL consequently entered into a new national cable contract with OLN (previously the Outdoor Life Network), a network with much less reach than the multiple ESPN networks.[7]

Where did all the optimism of the 1990s go? Why has the gap between the NHL and the other major professional sports in the United States actually gotten larger in the last decade? Why is the league in such a precarious position? A large part of the answer to these questions rests in the evolving dimensions of the television sports market. The problem is that the NHL remains a marginal television product in the United States, despite successive expansions to new US markets and extensive marketing and media efforts. Although the league has a core of devoted viewers, its audiences have enjoyed limited growth at best. While there are some NHL markets with a large base of loyal fans and high local television ratings, national audiences have been stagnant or even declining, which means that hockey struggles to earn television revenue, and it is now not possible to be a major league sport in the United States without national television coverage.

National telecasts are not only a primary source of revenue in themselves, but also the foundation of "circuits of promotion" that are essential to a league's status and to the value of other revenue streams (merchandising, venue advertising, corporate entertaining) that are now integral to the economics of major league sports.[8]

Sports and Television: A Marriage of Mutual Interests?

Many commentators over the years have pointed to a symbiotic relationship between professional sports and the popular media, a relationship in which each has contributed to the success of the other.[9] The US television industry has seen the value of live sports programming rise dramatically since the early 1960s, when it became evident that televising sports events could attract huge audiences. Not only this, but sports delivered to advertisers a highly coveted demographic group: younger males, who were difficult to reach with other kinds of programming. NFL football offered the most successful model for sports television: a carefully controlled number of nationally broadcast games was watched by huge national audiences, and NFL broadcasts on Sunday afternoons and Monday evenings quickly became something of an American institution. Although other sports, notably baseball, did not fare quite as well, especially in the regular season, for almost three decades it seemed that sports programming could be sold to advertisers for ever increasing prices.

In this context networks competed to invest in "new" sports, while sports leagues (and other sports like golf) vied to position themselves as potentially lucrative sports "properties." The growth of cable television in the 1980s, as well as the demonstrable success of all-sports cable networks (like ESPN in the United States and TSN in Canada) only intensified the search—by broadcast and cable networks alike—for successful sports programming, creating revenue opportunities for many different sports, including hockey. Through much of the 1990s, growth in television revenues continued, and sports entities (teams and leagues) signed long-term agreements with players, apparently assuming that growth would continue indefinitely.[10]

Sport in general succeeded as television programming because, first of all sporting events are typically presented live, with the attendant element of "real time" suspense. Yet, in contrast with other live events, or indeed sports events like the Masters tournament in golf, or the Olympics, a "season" of major league sport constitutes a kind of serial, made up of connected and regularly scheduled dramas, not unlike other entertainment series. This continuing presence helps to draw fans—especially uncommitted fans—into the cumulative suspense of playoff races, and the successes and failures of individual characters. There are also minimal barriers of language and literacy for sports viewers. As the major television providers became part of global media/entertainment firms in the 1990s, the importance of programming that could be sold internationally increased (even though most of those plans have yet to come to fruition). Even within the US market, sports were considered to have good potential for audience growth because most games are relatively easy to understand, and thus accessible to new viewers. Together, these factors have made sports cost-effective, especially when compared to forms of scripted programming (such as situation comedy or drama) in which seasons must be produced from scratch yet the final results may not succeed with foreign audiences. This is why, despite the constant dance between sports leagues and television networks about rights fees, until very recently fees have steadily increased.

A different kind of attraction (for networks and advertisers alike) follows from the development of RCDs (remote control devices). The rcd made it easy to navigate the multi-channel universe by *zapping* from one channel to another. More ominously for advertisers and the television industry, it also made it easy to *zip* through programs recorded on the video cassette recorder (VCR), another technology that became ubiquitous as of the 1980s.[11] Yet sports had a long-standing practice of integrating advertising and promotion with program content, an integration that had all but disappeared from most other programming by the 1970s. Thus, sports telecasts came to be regarded as excellent forums for relatively "zap-proof" advertising and promotion. New forms of actual (for example, in hockey, under/on the ice) and virtual (electronically inserted) advertising were developed, and when these techniques were combined with the in-game advertising opportunities that sports telecasts have always offered, sports properties only gained in appeal for the television and advertising industries that were becoming increasingly concerned with the zapping of advertising by an RCD-wielding audience.

Hockey's Troubles on US Television

By the late 1980s and early 1990s, then, sports rights were highly valued by the US television industry, and not coincidently this time period corresponded with new initiatives on the part of the NHL to increase its presence in the United States. Key aspects of the NHL strategy included expansion and the relocation of franchises to new US markets in the South and West; the awarding of franchises to major names in the media and entertainment industries, corporations like Blockbuster, Disney, and AOL; and the creation of a commissioner with authority similar to that of the other major leagues. By the time Gary Bettman was hired from the NBA in 1993, the rhetoric emanating from the league office and indeed from the television industry itself was that hockey had finally arrived as a fully fledged member of the Big Four of US team sports. But the anticipated growth in television revenues did not materialize for the NHL. On the contrary, the contracts signed in 2004 with NBC and ESPN meant that the league was destined to earn substantially lower revenues from US television than it had received in the previous five years from ABC.

What went wrong, then? Why has hockey fared so poorly in the United States? A number of factors came into play, including 1) cultural barriers, 2) the aesthetics of hockey as a television sport, and 3) the league's failure to grasp the changing nature of the television industry.

Cultural Barriers

There is little tradition of ice hockey in large parts of the United States, for obvious reasons of climate. Outside of a few pockets of enthusiasm in the North and North-East, children don't grow up playing the game in schools or playgrounds; nor, in most parts of the United States, do they grow up watching the game in their own communities. This cultural barrier is seen as an important factor in the NHL's difficulties in building a national "footprint" in the United States, and the placing of NHL teams in new US markets is a fundamental part of building the traditions that are crucial to the success of any cultural institution.

A small number of teams—Boston and Detroit are examples—have long traditions, with many family generations following their ups and downs; but the majority of NHL franchises has existed for thirty or fewer years. As owner Leonsis says, even with a thirty-year history the Washington Capitals are "just into our second generation of families that grew up watching the Caps."[12] The teams created or relocated in the 1990s will need to wait even longer for traditions of rooting for the home team to really catch on. Pragmatically, the placing of teams in such markets as Tampa Bay, Phoenix, and Raleigh makes sense as a reflection of population shifts in the United States. Such franchises can also help to achieve greater US media coverage of hockey, both in the cities where the teams are based, and in the regional media markets. The league has actively tried to encourage interest in these larger regional markets by using regional team names (Carolina, Florida, Colorado)—by, for example, promoting the idea that the Hurricanes are not just Raleigh's team, but "belong" to all of North and South Carolina. Still, although the Colorado Avalanche team appears to have developed a regional fan base, a pattern of relatively low attendance in Raleigh or Sunrise, Florida (the Fort Lauderdale suburb that is home to the Florida Panthers) demonstrates that this strategy is not always successful.

The NHL also tries to build interest in these newer Sunbelt cities by strategically awarding special events to them (such as all-star games, or the annual junior draft); but only those who already follow hockey pay much attention on these occasions. The reason, according to Andy Roundtree, former CFO of the Mighty Ducks of Anaheim, is simply that people have not grown up with hockey in places like Fort Lauderdale or Anaheim. "This [Orange County] is not a hockey haven.... Kids are not born or raised in a hockey environment, and we are competing with that."[13] This, of course, is the same point made by Canadian fans who have questioned the Sunbelt strategy from its outset. Roundtree, though, is among many people actively involved in building hockey in the United States who argue that success will follow from getting children playing the game. And indeed, by almost any measure there has been a large increase in the number of ice rinks and related facilities around the United States, even in the warmer areas of the country.

However, the idea that children who play a sport will become the adult spectators of tomorrow fails the test of empirical evidence. At least since the 1960s, the same argument has been made for soccer: that is, that as more kids play, the game will gain in popularity and become a widely popular spectator sport, as it is in most of the world. Obviously this has not happened, even though soccer has advantages that should make its diffusion in the United States more likely than that of hockey. Soccer is an outdoor sport; it does not require huge outlays of money for equipment or playing facilities; it has strong appeal to the largest minority population in the country (Hispanics); it is played by both boys and girls; and it is played virtually everywhere in the country. Yet, despite at least forty years of children's soccer, there is little evidence that the game is any more popular as either a spectator or a television sport than it was decades ago. The "US soccer dream" should stand as a cautionary tale for hockey advocates in the United States.

Likewise, the 1990s explosion in the number of minor league hockey teams represents another kind of attempt to piggyback on rising interest in the sport, while building a new generation of hockey fans in some decidedly non-hockey states. However, as affirmative as it may be for hockey aficionados to hear that there are teams like the Rio Grande Valley Killer Bees, the Huntsville Channel Cats, or the Jacksonville Lizard Kings, the near constant shuffling of franchises and indeed the failure of several minor leagues reveal limits to this strategy.

Finally, issues of nationality, race, and ethnicity also help explain why the NHL has had a difficult time solidifying its position in US sport. The number of Americans playing in the NHL is now significantly larger than it was in the past, mostly due to all the youth (and college) hockey programs that now exist in the country. However, there are still too many "foreign" players for many US residents to take the game to heart. This point reflects the relatively insular attitude of many US citizens, as well as the wide variety of other sports that feature predominantly American competitors. Whether an NHL hockey player is French Canadian or Russian or Swedish, if he sounds "foreign" he becomes a difficult sell as an American hero. In addition, few people of colour play NHL hockey, and as the Caucasian population of the United States declines as a percentage of the total population, the lack of racial and ethnic diversity in the NHL may continue to work against hockey's acceptance amongst the American public. The number of African-American stars in the NBA and the NFL, and of Hispanic stars in baseball, offers striking contrasts to hockey's whiteness (see chapters 3 and 6).

Aesthetics: Is Hockey "Good TV"?

The unfamiliarity of many Americans with watching hockey has also posed challenges for US networks promoting it as a television sport. Although promotional slogans have variously called hockey the "fastest," the "coolest," even the "most exciting game on earth," speed doesn't necessarily make hockey an ideal television sport when the target audience mostly comprises people who don't know the game. Indeed, since as far back as the 1960s and 1970s, when CBS and then NBC dropped national hockey coverage, the argument has been heard that hockey makes for poor television because the action is so fast, and the puck so small and difficult to see. In order to address the problem of the puck, in particular, the NHL and successive US television providers have tried a number of innovations (or "gimmicks," as traditionalists have called them) ranging from the animated "Peter Puck" character that explained the nuances of the game to NBC audiences in the 1970s, to Fox's "flaming" puck in the 1990s, an idea that elicited vitriolic objections from many Canadian fans.[14]

The speed of hockey is perhaps a more intractable issue, because standard-definition television technology is not able to follow the action to the degree that some television people believe is acceptable to viewers who are not familiar with the game. Again, this is not a complaint heard in Canada, where the CBC has been successfully televising hockey for over fifty years. Some professionals believe that the growth of high-definition television (HDTV), combined with the ever growing size of television monitors, will finally overcome the problems that some US viewers reportedly have with the speed of the game. For example, Comcast spokesperson Chris Helein proposes that "HDTV's wider picture ratio (16:9) as opposed to analog's 3:3 will ... make it easier for viewers to see and follow the action."[15] Nonetheless, we have to be sceptical that any technological innovation will have the impact that the NHL expects from HDTV. For one thing, all other sports (and, for that matter, all other programming) will also reap visual benefits from HDTV, which means that hockey won't necessarily gain any ground in the television competition.

NHL's Failure to Come to Terms with US Television

By far the most important obstacles to hockey's success as a television sport in America, though, follow from the NHL's failures over the years to recognize the economic potential of television, and to manage its television product in a way that maximizes its value to television networks and advertisers. The National Hockey League, like Major League Baseball, is a pre-television sports organization in a way that the other major professional leagues are not. Both hockey and baseball had thrived for decades with a limited number of teams located in the biggest metropolitan centres of the United States (and, in the case of hockey, Canada). In the four US cities with historic NHL teams (Boston, Chicago, Detroit, New York), hockey was second only to baseball as a major league sport, and in winter it was the only major pro sport. Baseball and hockey thus got the major share of metropolitan media coverage, which in turn contributed to the box-office success of these teams, helping to establish them as "traditions" in the biggest cities (to return to the point made by Leonsis). Indeed it was the coverage that the NHL got in the metropolitan media that helped to establish hockey's major league status in the United States. Contrast this with pro football, a sport considered second class (to the college game) in the United States until the 1950s and the rise of television. Similarly, pro basketball was not even an organized sport in the United States until the late 1940s, and it continued to have teams in minor league markets, such as Fort Wayne and Syracuse, into the late 1950s and early 1960s.

As television became increasingly ubiquitous in the United States, reaching nearly 90 per cent of US households by 1960, pro football and basketball adroitly adapted to the opportunities presented by the new medium. They were quick to place franchises in new markets, and, most importantly, they lobbied successfully for exemption from US anti-trust laws. The effect of this was to permit leagues to negotiate for shared national television and radio contracts.[16] Although the Sports Broadcasting Act applied to all pro sports leagues, it was the NFL, the American Football League (which a later anti-trust exemption would allow to be absorbed into the NFL), and the NBA that grasped the value of selling exclusive rights to nationally broadcast games. Major League Baseball did move into new markets and began national "Game of the Week" telecasts. However, the belief of many baseball owners that they were autonomous entities rather than partners led to big-city teams jealously guarding their rights to sell their own games, and the resulting glut of baseball kept MLB from developing television revenues to the degree that it might otherwise have done.[17]

The NHL's relationship to US television, not surprisingly, is the most problematic of all the major professional leagues. Limited to six teams for the first twenty or so years of the medium, dominated by conservative ownership, and led from the 1940s to the 1970s by the same league president (Clarence Campbell), the NHL adopted television only reluctantly, concentrating its efforts on Canadian television (*Hockey Night in Canada*).[18] In retrospect this approach clearly seems to be a shortsighted strategy; but it made sense for a time, given the historical roots of the game.

The NHL's first US national television contract came in 1966, several years after the other major sports had made similar arrangements. Successive expansions to twelve teams in 1967, fourteen in 1970, sixteen in 1972, and eighteen in 1974 were all attempts to expand the US footprint of the sport (see chapter 9) and enhance its status as a major league. A rival league (the World Hockey Association) also spurred expansion, just as rival leagues had provoked expansions by the NFL and NBA. However, a competitive labour market pushed player salaries to levels that couldn't be sustained by box-office revenues alone. Unfortunately for the NHL, though, while national television contracts had vastly increased the incomes of the NFL and NBA (and their visibility in US popular culture), the NHL's national telecasts, first on CBS and then NBC, attracted poor ratings. In addition, for every successful new franchise that, like Philadelphia, increased the image of the NHL as a major league, there were weakly financed franchises (for example, in Oakland and Kansas City) that folded, hurting the league's image as well as its finances.

The absorption in 1979 of four WHA franchises (Edmonton, Hartford, Quebec City, and Winnipeg), along with the relocation of Atlanta to Calgary in 1980 and Denver to New Jersey in 1982, represented setbacks for the NHL's hopes of enhancing its attractiveness to US television networks. Hartford was a marginal US television market, while New Jersey shared its market with three other NHL teams. The four Canadian cities were of no value whatever to US television providers. Thus, one of the results of this retrenchment to Canada (which was celebrated by some Canadian fans) was the end of the league's national US television contract with NBC. Nonetheless, from 1982 to 1991 the league was stable, with no franchise movement and reasonable financial health for most teams. The financial well-being was based on box-office revenues, local television and radio money, and the emergence of stars such as Wayne Gretzky and Mario Lemieux. The elusive goal of becoming big-time in the United States had not been discarded, however; it was simply in abeyance.

The NHL might have learned several lessons from these events. First, the league was late in making its move to television in the United States. The NHL's stature there as late as the early 1950s was such that it most likely could have gained national US coverage, at least for the Stanley Cup playoffs. The NFL and NBA were each still struggling for acceptance, both nationally and in the important metropolitan markets where the NHL had a traditional presence. MLB was a poorly managed collection of fiefdoms that fought rather than embraced the new medium. A limited US expansion in the late 1950s or early 1960s would have given the NHL an opportunity to become entrenched in the United States as a winter television fixture (when viewing levels are at their peak), just as it was in Canada by that time. Although prime-time games may not have attracted enough viewers to satisfy the national broadcast networks, the Stanley Cup playoffs probably would have, and weekend afternoon games would surely have been a draw. After all, US audiences were enthralled by boxing and even such faux-sports as professional wrestling and roller derby during this period. With no national competition from MLB or the NFL during most of its season, with the NBA still struggling and even collegiate basketball available only locally or regionally, the NHL arguably missed a major opportunity, just when sports were becoming an integral part of weekend network schedules.

The NHL would make more mistakes in the 1980s and 1990s. The most significant of these would follow from the apparent attractions offered by regional cable networks as an alternative to national broadcast television. By the late 1980s Regional Sports Networks (RSNs) began to develop on cable (pay) television, as regulations that had once protected US broadcasters from cable competition were modified or repealed. RSNs depend on having local sports coverage, which increased demand for local and regional television rights in all sports. In addition, the success of ESPN on a national level created yet more demand for major league sports and led to the formation of such entities as SportsChannel America (SCA), the Prime Network, and Fox Sports Net, whose business it became to provide sports programming to RSNs around the nation. It was in this context, and hoping to regain the national coverage it had lost in the 1970s, that the NHL entered into a contract with SCA in 1988.[19]

Although the revenues generated by SCA were modest compared to what the other major leagues were getting from the broadcast networks, having the league on US television did provide some money to the league as well as to teams in strong regional markets. More significantly, though, it encouraged the belief, promoted by expansion-minded US owners such as Bruce McNall as well as by Bettman, that with strategically placed franchises across the US South and with proper marketing and promotion, the time was ripe to break the perception that hockey was a foreign, or at best a regional, sport in the United States. In this strategic vision, the NHL would establish itself as a major league sport in every important part of the United States, and it would secure the levels of television coverage—and thereby revenues—being enjoyed by other major leagues (notably the NBA, where Bettman had previously worked). From 1991 to 2000, then, nine new franchises were added (with the exception of Ottawa and Minnesota, all in US Sunbelt markets), while three existing teams—Quebec, Winnipeg, and Hartford, all refugees from the WHA—were relocated to fast-growing US markets (Denver, Phoenix, Raleigh).

There is little doubt that in some respects the NHL met its goal in becoming a big-time US sport in the 1990s. Television rights fees grew for a time, merchandise sales grew exponentially, and the league attracted national US sponsors (including Bud Lite, Dodge, and Kellogg's).[20] New arenas were built, complete with corporate names and luxury boxes. The Internet made round-the-clock and around-the-globe publicity and promotion a reality, and the minor leagues expanded. All of this was consistent with sports trends of the 1990s. However, as now seems increasingly evident, the US hockey boom of the 1990s, while not as illusory as the boom of the 1970s, was not as successful as the NHL's owners, management, and fans had hoped for; and by 2005 a source of guaranteed revenue from national US broadcast television had been eliminated. The league's national cable presence had been scaled back by tens of millions of homes, and, if the claims of management during the labour dispute can be believed, the league was at a financial crossroads, with radical structural change a distinct possibility.

Limits to Growth?

A fundamental question that needs to be raised here is whether or not the NHL has reached its "natural" limits as a major US sport. There are, as we've seen, both "natural" and cultural barriers to the popularity of ice hockey in the United States that no amount of marketing acumen is likely to entirely overcome: in particular, the climate and weather of the Southern United States and the "foreign" origins of the game. However, the league brought certain problems on itself—problems that must be considered in any adequate evaluation of why the NHL still struggles to permanently establish itself as a big-time US professional sport.

First, the NHL, like MLB, continues to be plagued by serious intra-league revenue disparity. When most of a team's television revenues are generated in its local market, there are huge disparities in the income generated by, for example, the New York Rangers and the Pittsburgh Penguins. Due in part to the lower value of the Canadian dollar, moreover, there are even greater disparities between large-market US teams (Ranger, Flyers) and small-market Canadian ones (Calgary, Ottawa). This issue was addressed to a small degree in the 1990s by a payment to the small-market Canadian teams that was designed to compensate for the dollar discrepancy. However, as in Major League Baseball, there are haves and have-nots in the NHL. Although there will always be aberrations in team performance due to good management and team chemistry (illustrated by the Tampa Bay–Calgary Stanley Cup finals of 2004), there is no mistaking that small-market teams face profound financial challenges. While the 2004 Cup final was widely applauded as "proving" that small-city teams could compete, the reality is that the poor US television ratings for that series will have an influence on future revenue prospects.

Many of the problems associated with revenue disparity could be solved by a more equitable sharing of revenues between teams, as happens in the NFL. This could be achieved in part through a split of box-office and arena revenues, under the theory that without two teams there is no product to sell. Local and regional television and radio revenues could also be more equally distributed, whether fifty-fifty or by some formula that gives small-market teams a larger share than at present while also recognizing the higher team values and ostensibly higher operational costs of the large-market franchises. To date, though, too many of the large-market owners, like their counterparts in MLB, reject revenue-sharing as "socialistic" or rewarding poor management. The salary cap in the new labour agreement will probably ameliorate some of this gap, but it is unlikely to make the issue of the "haves" and the "have-nots" disappear.

Second, the league had long been reluctant to change the rules of the game to make it more high-scoring and, therefore, more visually appealing to US audiences. There are two issues here, the first of which is simply that high scoring is characteristic of the most popular US television sports, and low scoring is often cited as a factor contributing to soccer's failure to catch on in the United States. This is a position that purists in both soccer and hockey reject, even though viewer surveys suggest that ratings for the NBA and NFL are closely correlated to levels of scoring. Perhaps the more fundamental debate here, though, concerns the merits of rule changes that encourage more scoring through a crackdown on physical obstruction. This debate regularly resurfaces after US fans have been treated to Olympic hockey, where, as Fox's Stan Savran argues:

> The brand of hockey they played in [the Olympics] was fantastic ... wide open, no
> tackling, actual skating and passing.... Then [the fans] turn on the television [for NHL
> games] and what do they see? Guys ... dragging each other down, neutral zone trap,
> tackling, stick between the legs, tripping, and nothing's called and they say, "Wait a
> minute! This isn't what I saw during the Olympics!"[21]

The problem is that NHL traditionalists remain committed to a more physical style of
hockey that encourages hitting and defensive obstruction. This reflects an attachment,
especially among Canadian fans, to the physical traditions of the game; it also reflects a
belief among many managers and other hockey insiders that it is only systems of defensive obstruction (like the neutral-zone trap) that allow weaker teams (typically expansion teams) to keep games competitive. The league did adopt new rules for the 2004–05
season "to reduce the scope of defensive 'tools' a team may effectively employ," but it has
so far been reluctant to adopt more "radical" rule changes.[22]

Third, the NHL has not actively developed its international presence, even though the
opportunities for the NHL in Europe are arguably greater than are those for the other
US–based major leagues (which are faced with promoting "foreign" sports). The sport of
ice hockey has a long and successful history in Russia, Scandinavia, and Central Europe;
but while an increasing number of players from those countries now play in the NHL,
there have been no major attempts to introduce the NHL more directly into those nations
(see chapters 11 and 12). Even participation in international tournaments and the
Olympics has not been exploited to the degree that it could have been. The NHL might
have created some sort of co-venture with European counterparts—such as soccer's
highly successful Champion's League, or an "NHL Europe." Alternately, it might have con-
vinced major European club teams to join forces with the NHL, with some limited form
of interlocking schedule. Such moves in the direction of internationalizing the game may
not have helped the league in the United States, because it would have made the NHL
even more "foreign." However, the NHL would have gained substantial international
media attention, and, more importantly, the media and marketing revenues that could
have flowed from the exploding privatized media markets of Europe in the 1990s might
have gone a long way to solving some of the NHL's financial problems.

Finally, though, we must return to the NHL's continuing failures to understand the
evolving television/media market in the United States. The most recent failure, and the
one with potentially the most lasting impact, has been that instead of building and
maintaining a relationship with one national and regional television provider (most
likely Fox), the NHL has bounced from Fox to Disney/ABC and on to NBC and the OLN in
the last ten years. Of course, except for the latest deal, the league was seeking to increase
its immediate revenues. This is a justifiable business posture in most situations, and one
obviously followed by the other major US professional sports leagues. However, in

order to build brand credibility, a consistent media partner is essential. The Fox deal was a good one for the NHL for many reasons, including the excellent match between Fox's and the league's male demographic target.

This was reflected in the branding of the very aggressive and new (at the time) Fox Sports brand as having a distinct "attitude," an attitude highly suited to how the NHL was trying to promote itself. In addition, Fox put considerable time and ingenuity into trying to make NHL hockey a more television-friendly sport: with its flaming puck, its Fox Box scoring and time insert (copied by all other sports providers), and its profiles. A smaller rights fee in exchange for some form of revenue-sharing or more integrated marketing elements (NHL stars in Fox programs, Fox stars in the NHL broadcast booth) would have been an astute strategic move for the NHL. Fox, with its aggressive program to build up its Sports division—with the NFL and NHL and later MLB and NASCAR—clearly was a much better match for the NHL than one of the old-line networks that are today having difficulties defining a brand image for themselves.

The NHL's subsequent (and now ended) agreement with ABC/ESPN, in contrast, even though it was with a corporation that owned an NHL franchise (Disney), had the effect of putting NHL hockey on a broadcast network that, by the late 1990s, was suffering severe audience loss. In this context the NHL was hardly a major priority for the network, and even ESPN hardly made promoting the NHL a priority, as resources were diverted to the other major sports and to the development of its own original branded programming. Perhaps the new partnerships with NBC and Outdoor Life Network will eventually help the NHL recoup some of its lost television revenue, or even lead to new and lucrative sources of income. The OLN deal does look promising despite the lack of national penetration. Owned by the largest US cable company (Comcast), OLN will use the NHL as its most prominent and most heavily promoted programming. Comcast will also be importing the NHL-TV channel from Canada, a move that will assist in the promotion of the sport. Certainly, the NHL has nowhere to go but up after the lost 2004–05 season.[23] However, the NHL's best chance of becoming a major US television presence may have come and gone.

The Evolving Television/Media Market

The NHL, then, has failed to secure its place in big-time US sports for myriad reasons crossing the boundaries of everything from cultural prejudices to self-inflicted problems. During two major time periods (the 1970s and the 1990s), the NHL undertook strategic growth initiatives involving expansion, relocation, national television coverage, and, particularly in the 1990s, new marketing partnerships. If the past is prologue, the problems of the last few years may be followed in the next decade by yet another attempt to secure hockey a place in the top echelon of US sports. The difficulty with this scenario is the presumption that the media business will remain relatively static.

This is unlikely to be the case, as the very definition of what constitutes a mass medium or mass audience is being substantially altered.

The age of television as *the* mass medium is rapidly coming to an end. Just as motion pictures, magazines, and radio became highly specialized in their audience appeal, the television audience is now being diverted not so much to another medium (despite the increasing ubiquity of the Internet) but to a television medium itself that is becoming more crowded, more specialized, and more user-controlled. A level of inter-activity with television is now an established habit for increasing millions of viewers. A combination of satellite and cable transmission, RCDs, DVD player/recorders, and DVRs (digital video recorders, such as TiVo and Replay TV), as well as the merger of once disparate media forms via digitalization, makes the television universe of today a much different place than it was thirty, twenty, or even ten years ago. The merger of the television receiver and the Internet continues to be a likely prospect, making vast amounts of specialized content available to those who can pay.

While relatively heterogeneous mass audiences still have value to any number of advertisers, producing that audience has become increasingly problematic. Only live events that are highly promoted, such as the Academy Awards or Super Bowl, have the power to reach a mass audience on a repeated and predictable basis. What is replacing the mass television audience watching the same event is a mass television audience using the television in many different ways. This change in the very nature of the medium/audience relationship certainly does not mean that the ownership, distribution, or content of programming is particularly diverse. While a group of new television industry entrants was successful in the 1970s and 1980s, most of the channels appearing on satellite or cable or available via DVD or pay-per-view are produced by an oligopoly made up of a relatively small number of global media/entertainment industry powers.[24]

Any program supplier, including sports leagues, faces a challenge in gaining the attention of viewers/users in such a cluttered environment. Is it any wonder, in these circumstances, that most "new" consumer products today are brand extensions? Fortunately for the NHL, it already has a brand image despite the best efforts of the owners to destroy it. The league is already in the television mix for millions of Americans. However, the idea that it can grow relative to the other major US television or spectator sports is highly problematic. There is simply less room for any sport or program to prosper in the new television environment.

Despite their positive attributes as television programming, sports are not immune to changes in the television industry. The advent of "reality" programs is a case in point. Such programs, while typically heavily edited, have the "suspense" and even "real time" elements of live programming. They also allow for the integration of advertising and promotional messages, thereby neutralizing some of the advantages of sports as programming. In addition, reality and other "non-scripted" programs are inexpensive to produce compared to rights-fee based sports, and they have generated substantially higher prime-time ratings on a consistent basis. Even popular scripted programs are increasingly the site of advertising messages.[25]

Also consider that "extreme sports," in some cases directly controlled by media entities and in all cases highly promoted by the media, and NASCAR (with its stress on individual "heroics") are among the fastest-growing sports in the United States. Only the National Football League, of the traditional Big Four, has been able to thrive in this new environment. The reasons for this are many and include such structural factors as the limited number of games (increasing the perceived value of each specific game), a season coinciding with an increase in television viewing levels, a playing field almost perfect for television transmission (in standard or HDTV), and gambling. However, the NFL owners must be given credit for being the pioneers in the equal sharing of league revenues, scheduling decisions designed to lead to competitive seasons, and almost pitch-perfect exploitation of the television industry's need to maintain credibility with the financial and advertising communities by keeping the NFL on screen no matter the cost.[26]

Even the NFL would have difficulty building such a relationship with the major television providers in the United States if it had not taken action forty years ago. Even the NBA, despite its enormous success as a US and (to an appreciable degree) global sport, has had a difficult time in a more diffused environment in attracting the attention and ratings that it once gathered. MLB shares with the NHL many of the same media and marketing problems, with one key difference. Baseball's cachet as the "national pastime" gives it a place in the US psyche and economy out of proportion to its actual success as a national television product.

Prospects and Potentials

The NHL has established itself as a major league sport in most of the markets in which it has franchises. To become a truly national major league sport, though, the league has long needed to "connect the dots" so that individuals in non-franchise towns follow the league's results. However, although there are many television stations and newspapers in smaller US cities (such as Albuquerque, for example, or Wheeling) that give regular coverage to the NFL, the NBA, and Major League Baseball, the same media outlets often devote much more attention to high-school athletics, college sports, and outdoor activities than they do to the NHL. And when the league does get coverage in such media, the subject is often about on-ice violence, labour/management disputes, or poor television ratings.

The NHL at this time should not be concerned about improving its position within the US national Big Four. Rather, the league should work to maintain its present position by emphasizing its strengths. This includes a stress on the regional nature of the game, as a pro-active strategy rather than as a fallback position. For example, the league should attempt to get its national television carriers to regionalize all regular-season and most playoff coverage. Teams should be encouraged to establish their own RSNs in markets where an alliance with a MLB team makes a year-round service feasible. This could generate substantial new revenues that now go to other RSNs. HDTV and interactive television and Internet applications should be made available as "value-added" features as soon as possible. These could generate new revenue from the existing "hard-core" fan base if they are offered along with, but not in place of, conventional television coverage.

The NHL can never and will never be in the United States what it is and what it means in Canada. Attempts to make hockey a major sport in the United States have worked only marginally well at best. The conclusion has to be that going "big time" has, on balance, been more a curse than a blessing for the league. However, professional ice hockey has inherent strengths in terms of (regional) fan and media appeal, and it has the potential to thrive in a niche model. Although the diffusion of the media industry makes it more and more difficult for something new to break through the "clutter," if the new teams and the league can survive their current problems, we may eventually see second and third generations of families who truly are Florida, Carolina, or Phoenix fans. In an increasingly diffused and specialized media market, this may well be enough to be big time.

Table 8.1
NHL US National Television Ratings Since 1999

Regular Season	ABC	ESPN	ESPN2
1999–2000	1.3	0.62	0.29
2000–01	1.1	0.59	0.25
2001–02	1.4	0.49	0.23
2002–03	1.1	0.46	0.23
2003–04	1.1	0.47	0.24

Stanley Cup Finals	ABC	ESPN
1999–2000	3.7	2.0
2000–01	3.3	1.7
2001–02	3.7	2.8
2002–03	2.9	1.2
2003–04	2.6	1.2

1.0 Ratings Point equals 1% of all US Television Households (TVHH).

Sources: Andy Bernstein, "ESPN Expects Deal with NHL Soon, NHL on TV," *Street & Smith's Sports Business Journal*, May 17, 2004 <sportsbusinessjournal.com>; Ice Time: Stanley Cup Finals Ratings, *Street & Smith's Sports Business Journal*, June 14, 2004 <sportsbusinessjournal.com>; *Street & Smith's SportsBusiness Journal: By the Numbers 2004*, Dec. 29, 2003, p. 89.

Notes

1 The woes of the NHL have been well reported in the popular media. See, for example, Thomas Heath, "Report Shows NHL in Financial Trouble," *Washington Post*, Feb.13, 2004, p. D1.

2 Ted Leonsis, majority owner of the Washington Capitals, personal communication, May 24, 2004.

3 Jon A. Dolezar, "Televised Hockey Still Struggling to Get Beyond Die-hard Fans," June 11, 2003, SI.com <sportsillustrated.cnn.com/inside_game/jon_dolezar/news/2003/06/10/hockey_ontv>.

4 Leonsis, personal communication.

5 Jamie Fitzpatrick, "NHL Cuts New Broadcast Deals with NBC and ESPN," *Pro Ice Hockey*, May 21, 2004 <proicehockey.about.com/od/nhlnotebook/a/new_us_tv_deals_>. See also Rudy Martzke, "NHL as Bringing NBC into the Rink," *USA Today*, May 20, 2004, p. C3.

6 Fitzpatrick, "NHL Cuts New Broadcast Deals."

7 "OLN and NHL Partner in Multifaceted National Media Agreement," Aug.18, 2005 <www.olntv.com/nw/article>.

8 See David Whitson, "Circuits of Promotion: Media, Marketing, and the Globalization of Sport," in Lawrence Wenner, ed., *MediaSport* (London: Routledge, 1998), pp. 55-72.

9 See Robert McChesney, "Media Made Sport: A History of Sports Coverage in the United States," in Lawrence Wenner, ed., *Media, Sports, and Society* (Newbury Park, CA: Sage, 1989); on Canada, see Richard Gruneau and David Whitson, *Hockey Night in Canada: Sport, Identities, and Cultural Politics* (Toronto: Garamond Press, 1993).

10 Robert V. Bellamy, Jr., "Sports Media: A Modern Institution," in J. Bryant and A. Raney, eds., *The Handbook of Sports and Media* (Mahwah, NJ: Erlbaum, 2005); also Robert V. Bellamy Jr., "The Evolving Television Sports Marketplace," in L. Wenner, ed., *MediaSport* (London: Routledge, 1998).

11 Robert V. Bellamy, Jr. and James R. Walker, *Television and Remote Control: Grazing on a Vast Wasteland* (New York: Guilford, 1996). As of mid-2004, DVD and PVR recorders were rapidly replacing VCRs as the in-home preference for recording of television content and the avoidance of spot advertising.

12 Leonsis, personal communication.

13 Andy Roundtree, Former Chief Financial Officer, Mighty Ducks of Anaheim and Anaheim Angels, telephone communication, May 24, 2004.

14 Daniel Mason, "Get That Puck Outta Here: Media Trans-nationalism and Canadian Identity," *Journal of Sport and Social Issues*, 26, 2 (2002), pp. 140-67.

15 Chris Helein, Comcast, e-mail communication, June 3, 2004.

16 *Sports Broadcasting Act*, 1961, 15 United States Congress, Section 1291.

17 Robert V. Bellamy, Jr., "Impact of the Television Marketplace on the Structure of Major League Baseball," *Journal of Broadcasting & Electronic Media*, 32 (1988), pp. 73-87.

18 See Gruneau and Whitson, *Hockey Night in Canada*, for a fuller development of this issue.

19 Robert V. Bellamy, Jr., "Regional Sports Networks: Prime Network and Sports Channel America," in Robert G. Picard, ed., *The Cable Networks Handbook* (Riverside, CA: Carpelan, 1993), pp. 163-74.

20 2003–04 NHL Corporate Marketing Partners, *Street & Smith's Sports Business Journal: By the Numbers 2004*, Dec. 29, 2003, p. 23.

21 Stan Savran, anchor host on Fox Sports Network, Pittsburgh, telephone communication, May 24, 2004.

22 "NHL Enacts Rule Changes, Creates Competition Committee," July 22, 2005, NHL website <www.nhl.com/nhlhq/cba/rules_changes>.

23 "OLN and NHL Partner in Multifaceted National Media Agreement."

24 Robert W. McChesney, *The Problem of the Media: U.S. Communication Politics in the Twenty-First Century* (Madison, WI: Monthly Review Press, 2004).

25 Jon Fine, "Made Brands: Tony Plugs Cars, Phones," *Advertising Age,* July 5, 2004, pp. 1, 23.

26 Bellamy, "Evolving Television Sports Marketplace."

CHAPTER NINE

Expanding the Footprint? Questioning the NHL's Expansion and Relocation Strategy

■ DAN MASON

One key aspect of the problems facing the NHL is the extent to which professional hockey has failed to catch on in the United States. Despite a concerted effort to increase its exposure in US markets over the past decade, the National Hockey League remains a distant fourth among the four major professional sports leagues in the United States. At one point in the early 1990s, there was much optimism that the league would be able to close the gap between itself and the others. Even *Sports Illustrated*, notorious for its lack of coverage of hockey, had predicted in a cover story during the 1994 Stanley Cup playoffs that the NHL was poised to become pro sport's next big thing.[1] The NHL had recently hired its first commissioner, Gary Bettman, with a mandate to "grow the game," and Bettman's first years in office saw new expansion franchises and relocations of existing teams, as well as new television contracts and merchandising initiatives. All of these steps were designed to broaden the league's presence in US sporting culture, and to increase its revenues from US television.

In this chapter I review and assess the strategies employed by the NHL to expand its "footprint" in the United States.

The NHL and the Lure of US Markets

By the early 1990s the National Hockey League had been in operation for nearly seventy-five years. Although the NHL began as a purely Canadian league, by the late 1930s the majority of its franchises were in US markets. The league had a devout following on both sides of the border in the postwar decades, featuring six teams that had become institutions in Canada and in their home US cities (New York, Boston, Chicago, and Detroit) and that played consistently to near-capacity crowds. By the 1980s, though, the NHL was lagging badly behind the National Football League, Major League Baseball, and the National Basketball Association in respect to its visibility in the US media and growth of media revenues. In the United States the NHL was little more than a regional league that relied almost exclusively on gate revenues, while the other major league sports tapped much more successfully into lucrative television revenues.[2]

The stability that the NHL enjoyed for a time after the demise of the World Hockey Association in 1979—which saw relatively successful WHA operations in Edmonton, Winnipeg, Quebec, and Hartford absorbed into the NHL—was also undermined by a change in the leadership of the National Hockey League Players' Association. The NHL had benefited from a decidedly paternalistic labour relationship over the years, due in no small part to a cozy association between then-NHL president John Ziegler and NHLPA director Alan Eagleson. After one collective-bargaining agreement negotiation, for instance, Eagleson remarked, "We did as well or better than we could have done with a strike, and we miss all the fuss and bother."[3] That brand of leadership led observers to note, "The simple fact is that the National Hockey League Players' Association, as a labour organization and negotiating entity, has been largely ineffective since the day it was formed in 1967."[4]

Eagleson was eventually ousted as NHLPA leader and replaced by a former player agent, Bob Goodenow.[5] Under Goodenow's direction the players became less willing to give in to the demands of NHL owners, and in spring 1992 they staged the first strike in the league's history, delaying the start of the Stanley Cup playoffs. This led to Ziegler's ouster, with Gil Stein being named NHL president in June 1992.[6] By that time, though, the NHL was more interested in developing a new leadership structure, and Stein's tenure lasted less than a year. What the majority of owners thought they wanted was a version of the commissioner system that had worked well for the NBA, in which the commissioner had more authority and more strategic responsibilities than NHL presidents had ever enjoyed. In particular, NBA commissioner David Stern had successfully expanded the NBA's television revenues during the 1980s. Just as importantly, he had succeeded in negotiating frameworks for revenue-sharing—among owners, and between owners and players—that had brought unprecedented prosperity to all parties. Bettman had worked with Stern as the NBA's vice-president and general counsel and had extensive experience in both television and labour/management negotiations, and it was assumed that he would bring these skills to the NHL.

NHL television exposure and revenues had lagged behind the other major leagues in the United States for two interrelated reasons. The first was simply that for nearly twenty years the NHL did not have a major network television contract. The only way that fans could watch NHL games in the United States was to be a cable-TV subscriber. As a result hockey failed to get the national exposure that only network television could bring. Moreover, the NHL had arguably missed the boat in its cable-television strategy as well. In the late 1980s Ziegler had been roundly criticized for signing a cable-television deal with SportsChannel rather than with the vastly more popular ESPN. While the SportsChannel agreement had paid more (about $5 million [US] for the 1991–92 season), SCA had a much smaller base of subscribers, which meant a smaller pool of potential viewers for the NHL (see chapter 8).

The second problem facing the NHL was its lack of presence in many of the fastest-growing metropolitan areas in the United States. Although the NHL had teams in the big cities of the Northeast and in Los Angeles, the population of the United States was shifting south and west, and in 1992 the NHL had franchises in only eleven of the twenty-five largest US metropolitan markets. As a result, significant areas of the country did not have NHL hockey teams, making the sport less attractive to national television networks and national advertisers. With the concentration of US-based franchises only in the Northeastern states, the major national networks just weren't very interested in NHL hockey. One of Bettman's mandates was to expand the footprint of the NHL by moving into important Sunbelt markets, either through expansion franchises or the relocation of existing teams. The end result of this process, ideally, would be to create a new base of fans who would attend games, buy merchandise, and provide the audience that would allow the NHL to charge broadcasting fees in line with its major league counterparts. As Bettman explained, "The broader our footprint, the more desirable we become as a network product."[7]

Expanding the Footprint: Television

As Bettman took over the leadership of the NHL, the league continued to explore the possibility of a US network television contract. Fortunately, the US media industry was home to a new player for whom NHL hockey was a strategically desirable product. News Corp.'s Rupert Murdoch wanted to expand his media holdings in the United States, and in 1985 he bought TCF Holdings (the parent of Twentieth Century-Fox). He then spent $2 billion (all figures US) to buy seven US television stations from Metromedia to form Fox Television, and he set out to make Fox Television into a fourth major US network: a real competitor for CBS, ABC, and NBC. In order to do this, Fox needed programming that would give the fledgling network the clout to compete with the existing networks. Having enjoyed some successes in the 1980s with original programs such as *The Simpsons* and *Married … With Children*, Fox made a major move in 1993 by acquiring the rights to broadcast National Football Conference games for $1.6 billion. At the time many observers saw this as too high a price; however, according to Murdoch biographer William Shawcross, "Murdoch was certain that sports would drive his television empire. Sports were, quite simply, by far the best way, perhaps the only way, of persuading millions of men to watch television."[8] Once it began its NFL broadcasts, "Fox immediately gained in ratings and advertising revenue. A whole slew of [US affiliate] stations defected to Fox, most of them CBS affiliates."[9] And, even though the NHL did not have the same profile as football in the United States, Bettman was able to take advantage of Fox's new sports-driven strategy to negotiate a five-year $155-million contract with Fox television, starting with the 1994–95 season.

Thus, following the lockout of 1994–95, the NHL started its abridged season with US network television coverage. However, unfortunately for the league, Fox enjoyed mixed ratings success with its hockey broadcasts, and the network chose to let this contract lapse when it came up for renewal in 1998. Despite this setback, Bettman was able to negotiate an even more lucrative contract with ABC/ESPN. ESPN saw NHL broadcast rights as an investment in its own future and agreed to pay the NHL $600 million over five years for both cable and over-the-air national rights, starting in the 1999–2000 season. The $70 million per season allotted for cable rights nearly equalled what ESPN had paid over the life of its previous cable contract with the NHL, signed in 1994. Thus, while the increase in the network fee was marginal (a 38 per cent increase was not considered large by the standards of the industry at that time), the NHL was able to quadruple its cable-television agreement by leveraging the fact that ESPN2, ESPN's sister station, had grown from ten million to sixty million subscribers in five years and desperately needed more sports programming.[10]

Expanding the Footprint: Expansion and Relocation

The other issue facing the NHL in its footprint strategy was to move into larger, lucrative US markets that did not feature NHL teams. In doing so, the league hoped to achieve two goals: 1) to gain access to the untapped metropolitan statistical areas (MSAs) that these cities provided; and 2) to make the NHL a more desirable TV product by having league franchises more geographically widespread in the country. As Bettman was joining the NHL, the league had been actively courting two powerhouses in the US entertainment business, Disney's Michael Eisner and Blockbuster's Wayne Huizenga. The NHL coveted these two prospective owners, hoping that the drawing power of the Disney and Blockbuster names, as well as their marketing and business acumen, could be appropriated by the league, with positive impacts for all of its franchises. This aspiration was not lost on Disney; indeed, initially Eisner contended that the NHL should pay Disney to enter the league. Eisner had met twice during the fall of 1992 with then-president Gil Stein and the new chair of the NHL Board of Governors, Bruce McNall, and had balked at paying a $50-million expansion fee to join the league. According to Stein, "When I [raised] the prospect of bringing Disney into the NHL to the league's Advisory Committee, the first words out of [New York Rangers' governor] Stanley Jaffe's mouth were 'We should pay *them!*'"[11] However, this sentiment was not shared by other NHL owners, and the league held to its $50-million price.

Another issue for Disney lay in the proximity of Anaheim—where the team hoped to operate—to Los Angeles. In previous cases where teams had relocated or the NHL had expanded into territories already occupied by NHL teams, an indemnification fee was paid to the existing franchise. For example, when the New York Islanders entered the NHL in 1972, in addition to a $6-million expansion fee, the Islanders' owners also paid the New York Rangers a $4-million indemnification fee for moving into the Rangers' territory. By 1992 this amount had grown considerably; a precedent had been set for McNall and the Los Angeles Kings when another NHL owner, in an attempt to relocate, had offered the Kings $25 million should the team relocate to Anaheim. Thus Disney, which also sought a franchise for Anaheim, would be expected to pay a significant indemnification fee to the Kings for moving a franchise into their desig-nated market territory. However, Eisner refused to pay both a $50-million expansion fee *and* an additional $25-million indemnification fee, and when it appeared that Disney would walk away, McNall was able to persuade the other NHL owners into granting the Kings a $25-million indemnification fee out of the expansion fee itself. This resulted in the remaining NHL clubs splitting an expansion fee of only $25 million for the new Anaheim franchise.

After getting Eisner and Disney on board in the fall of 1992, Eisner urged that the NHL also get in touch with Huizenga, who was allegedly interested in acquiring a fran-chise to be based in the Miami area. The NHL had already expanded into Tampa, and another team in Florida would complement both the Tampa franchise and the NHL's broader footprint strategy. Having the CEO of Blockbuster, one of the success stories of the entertainment industry during the 1990s, join the NHL was something that the league believed it could not afford to pass up. As a result, McNall and Stein shifted their efforts to courting Huizenga in November of 1992. After getting initially favourable responses, the NHL fast-tracked the negotiations and an agreement was reached in a matter of weeks. As a result, what amounted to exploratory conversations between the NHL and Disney early in 1992 led to the announcement in December 1992 that the Anaheim Mighty Ducks and Florida Panthers would commence operations less than twelve months later, playing the 1993–94 season. This was viewed by many as a coup for the NHL—adding on two experienced entertainment organizations that would cer-tainly raise the profile of hockey in their new markets and beyond.

In the meantime two existing Canadian NHL franchises continued to struggle, due in part to poorly performing teams, but also because both of them had old arenas that lacked the amenities (especially luxury boxes) necessary to generate enough revenues to remain competitive in the NHL of the 1990s. In Quebec City the Nordiques had an abysmal record for several years. However, they had been able to take advantage of their draft position to select a number of talented young players who would provide the basis for success in the future. The team had selected Eric Lindros first overall in 1991 and were forced to trade him after his refusal to play in Quebec. A bidding war between two large-market franchises, the New York Rangers and Philadelphia, led to the Nordiques gaining several high draft picks, top players, and $15 million in cash for Lindros.[12] But the team still played in the antiquated Colisée, built in 1949 and with a seating capacity of only 15,359. Therefore, it was uncertain as to whether the Nordiques would be able to cash in on their new player resources. In addition, in the new business model of the NHL (which emphasized corporate seating, merchandising, and media revenues) Quebec City was a small market, with limited opportunities for developing these new revenue streams. Thus, after pushing unsuccessfully for public funding, owner Marcel Aubut sold the team for $75 million, and it was moved to Colorado for the 1995–96 season.

Colorado had previously been granted an expansion franchise (the Rockies) in 1976, but this franchise had struggled before relocating to New Jersey in 1982. However, the relocated Nordiques, now renamed the Avalanche, enjoyed immediate competitive and economic success. They won the Stanley Cup in their very first season in Colorado and again in 2001. The team played its first four seasons in the 16,000-seat McNichols Arena, moving into the $160-million, 18,000-plus seat Pepsi Center in 1999. The new arena featured sixty-eight luxury suites, and the team has continued to be highly successful at the gate, with over four-hundred consecutive sold-out games entering the 2003–04 season. Moving into the Colorado market again fit very well into the NHL's footprint strategy, establishing a team in a city that, while not showing success with the previous franchise, certainly possessed the market size and climate to sustain a fan base for the league. In addition, the move geographically linked the West-Coast teams to the other established franchises on the East Coast.

While Colorado was enjoying its early success in 1995–96, the Winnipeg Jets continued to struggle with financing a new home to replace the Winnipeg Arena, built in 1955. The Jets had been able to negotiate an agreement with the city of Winnipeg and the province of Manitoba that had the two governments covering the financial losses of the team from 1991 through 1997, an amount that would eventually exceed $40 million (Canadian).[13] However, even these subsidies could not guarantee the long-term viability of the franchise in Winnipeg. With player salaries rising across the NHL, the absence of a new arena with revenue-generating features like luxury suites, club seating, and more concessions was a huge liability. When it became apparent that a publicly funded arena was not to be, the Jets were sold by owner Barry Shenkarow and relocated to Phoenix for the 1996–97 season. Phoenix seemed like an ideal site for the NHL. The city had seen unprecedented growth in the 1990s and represented a growing sports-entertainment market. It also featured a significant population of Canadian "snowbirds" who might augment the local fan base.

The Phoenix team struggled on the ice, however, reaching the playoffs five times in its first eight seasons but failing to advance beyond the first round. In addition the team was not the primary tenant in its facility, America West Arena, a venue that had not been designed specifically to host hockey games. The result was that the team did not get priority in scheduling, and many of the seats had obstructed views for hockey games. After several futile years of seeking public funding for a more suitable arena, the team's future in Phoenix appeared uncertain. However, on June 22, 2000, Wayne Gretzky became the team's managing partner in charge of hockey operations, lending both "star quality" and legitimacy to the franchise. More concretely, the Phoenix suburb of Glendale agreed to finance a $180-million arena, which opened in December 2003. These changes should ensure that the team remains in Phoenix for the immediate future, a qualified success for an NHL Sunbelt strategy that has had mixed success in other Southern metropolitan areas.

Despite the efforts of the NHL to move into new US markets, at least one existing US-based franchise was struggling to remain financially viable. The Hartford Whalers had joined the NHL from the World Hockey Association in 1979, but, despite operating in a market with an established hockey tradition, the franchise had achieved few competitive or financial successes. After years of playing in the 15,365-seat Hartford Civic Center, the team had sought public funding for a new arena. When it didn't get that support, the team relocated to North Carolina for the 1997–98 season. Although it is not in the best interests of any league to acknowledge failure in any of its franchises' operations, this move did fit nicely into the footprint strategy. The Raleigh-Durham corridor represented another Sunbelt territory that was booming (due to the success of the "Research Triangle" in the emerging knowledge industries). To move the team, though, Whalers' owner Peter Karmanos was forced to pay the city of Hartford $20 million to get out of the final year of the team's arena lease in that city. Moreover, the team remained in a difficult position in that it did not have an arena in which it could play in Raleigh. In lieu of playing a lame duck season in Hartford, the team elected to temporarily relocate to Greensboro, NC, for two seasons while the RBC Center was built in Raleigh. This resulted in ninety-minute commutes each way for fans in Raleigh to see the team play, and made for an awkward transition into the new market. The Hurricanes enjoyed a remarkable playoff run in 2002, reaching the Stanley Cup finals and drawing good crowds. Success has not continued, though. In 2003–04 the team played to crowds of 12,086 in the 18,763-seat RBC Center in Raleigh, down 23 per cent from the previous season. The long-term future of this franchise remains uncertain. Attendance has waned, and hockey competes against other local sporting traditions such as collegiate basketball and NASCAR.

The addition and relocation of several franchises in the mid-1990s did not slow the NHL's footprint strategy. In June 1997 the league announced a three-phase expansion plan—Nashville, Tennessee, in 1998, Atlanta, Georgia, in 1999, and St. Paul, Minnesota and Columbus, Ohio, for the 2000–01 season. In the case of Nashville, the city had embarked on an aggressive strategy to make Nashville a "big league city." The city hoped to shed its "honky tonk" image, while also developing a facility that would allow it to host major entertainment events in the country music industry.[14] As a result, the city agreed to fund the construction of the 17,500-seat, $144-million Gaylord Entertainment Center, without even having a major league tenant to occupy the building. In 1994 and 1995 the city sent a term sheet to all NBA and NHL teams, offering a favourable lease should a team agree to relocate to Music City. After initial interest from the NBA's Minnesota Timberwolves, Nashville also commenced negotiations in 1995 with the NHL's New Jersey Devils, who were interested in relocating. However, the Devils went on to enjoy a run of success in the 1995 Stanley Cup playoffs, culminating in a Cup victory, and they were able to leverage this success—along with Nashville's interest—into a better deal from the state of New Jersey.[15] Nashville, of course, ultimately got an NHL expansion franchise, paying the $80-million expansion fee and joining the league for the 1998 season. The team has enjoyed modest success, making the playoffs for the first time in 2004. However, attendance has been modest and the long-term success of the franchise in Nashville remains uncertain.

In 1999 another major US city reacquired an NHL franchise. The city of Atlanta, Georgia, had hosted the NHL Flames from 1972 through 1980, when the team relocated to Calgary. However, in the quarter-century that the city was without a team, Atlanta had grown substantially, becoming one of the fastest-growing and most attractive markets in the United States. When it became apparent that cable-television mogul Ted Turner was interested in adding a hockey team to his stable of Atlanta-based sports franchises, the NHL granted him an expansion franchise, for the same $80-million fee charged Nashville, and the team started operations in 1999. The team has yet to make the playoffs, but has enjoyed some success in the state-of-the-art Phillips Arena.

Adding to its rapid growth in US markets, the NHL approved two more franchises for the 2000 season, the Columbus Blue Jackets and Minnesota Wild. A return to the hockey-mad state of Minnesota seemed inevitable, ever since owner Norm Green had relocated the North Stars from Minneapolis to Dallas in 1993 after failing to secure a publicly funded arena. However, the city of St. Paul was now willing to fund a $130-million arena, the Xcel Energy Center, which would provide the revenue-generating capacities that were lacking when the North Stars had left. Columbus represented an attractive market to the NHL because it was centred in a Midwestern region that did not have another major league sports franchise, and it offered an excellent new facility.

These expansions and relocations have dramatically changed the landscape of the NHL. In less than ten years the league went from fifteen US-based teams to twenty-four, and had placed teams in large markets (see Table 9.1). More importantly for the NHL, teams were no longer exclusively clustered in the Northeastern United States with a few other franchises in California and the Midwest. Obviously, the footprint of the NHL in the United States has expanded considerably. (See Figure 9.1.)

Table 9.1

Presence of NHL teams in Major US Metropolitan Areas, 1992 and 2004

1992			
Rank	Metropolitan Area Name	Population (1990 Census)	NHL Teams
1	New York-Northern New Jersey	19,549,649	3
2	Los Angeles-Riverside-Orange County	14,531,529	1
3	Chicago-Gary-Kenosha	8,239,820	1
4	Washington-Baltimore	6,727,050	1
5	San Francisco-Oakland-San Jose	6,253,311	1
6	Philadelphia	5,892,937	1
7	Boston	5,455,403	1
8	Detroit-Ann Arbor-Flint	5,187,171	1
9	Dallas-Fort Worth	4,037,282	0
10	Houston-Galveston	3,731,131	0
11	Miami-Fort Lauderdale	3,192,582	0
12	Seattle-Tacoma-Bremerton	2,970,328	0
13	Atlanta	2,959,950	0
14	Cleveland-Akron	2,859,644	0
15	Minneapolis-St.Paul	2,538,834	1
16	San Diego	2,498,016	0
17	St. Louis	2,492,525	1
18	Pittsburgh	2,394,811	1
19	San Juan-Caguas-Arecibo	2,270,808	0
20	Phoenix-Mesa	2,238,480	0
21	Tampa-St. Petersburg	2,067,959	0
22	Denver-Boulder-Greeley	1,980,140	0
23	Cincinnati-Hamilton	1,817,571	0
24	Portland-Salem	1,793,476	0
25	Milwaukee-Racine	1,607,183	0
OTHERS			
34	Buffalo-Niagara Falls	1,189,288	1
36	Hartford	1,157,585	1

Table 9.1

Presence of NHL teams in Major US Metropolitan Areas, 1992 and 2004, continued

2004			
Rank	Metropolitan Area Name	Population (2000 Census)	NHL Teams
1	New York-Northern New Jersey	21,199,865	3
2	Los Angeles-Riverside-Orange County	16,373,645	2
3	Chicago-Gary-Kenosha	9,157,540	1
4	Washington-Baltimore	7,608,070	1
5	San Francisco-Oakland-San Jose	7,039,362	1
6	Philadelphia	6,188,463	1
7	Boston	5,819,100	1
8	Detroit-Ann Arbor-Flint	5,456,428	1
9	Dallas-Fort Worth	5,221,801	1
10	Houston-Galveston	4,669,571	0
11	Atlanta	4,112,198	1
12	Miami-Fort Lauderdale	3,876,380	1
13	Seattle-Tacoma-Bremerton	3,554,760	0
14	Phoenix-Mesa	3,251,876	1
15	Minneapolis-St.Paul	2,968,806	1
16	Cleveland-Akron	2,945,831	0
17	San Diego	2,813,833	0
18	St. Louis	2,603,607	1
19	Denver-Boulder-Greeley	2,581,506	1
20	San Juan-Caguas-Arecibo	2,450,292	0
21	Tampa-St. Petersburg	2,395,997	1
22	Pittsburgh	2,358,695	1
23	Portland-Salem	2,265,223	0
24	Cincinnati-Hamilton	1,979,202	0
25	Sacramento	1,796,857	0
OTHERS			
33	Columbus	1,540,157	1
39	Nashville	1,231,311	1
41	Raleigh-Durham-Chapel Hill	1,187,941	1
43	Buffalo-Niagara Falls	1,170,111	1

Figure 9.1
Location of US-Based NHL Franchises

1992 (15 teams)

2004 (24 teams)

The Aftermath

In addition to geographic expansion, the NHL has become a much bigger business. Expansion franchise fees that were $45 million for the Ottawa Senators and Tampa Bay Lightning in 1991 are now $80 million. Ticket prices have grown from an average of $33.49 in 1994–95 to $43.47 in 2003–04. However, it is not through the average ticket-buying fan that the NHL has realized the most gains in revenues. Instead, money is derived from premium seating, luxury suites, and other arena amenities. For example, when the Florida Panthers began operating for the 1993–94 season, they played out of the Miami Arena, built in 1988. The arena could seat 14,703 for hockey games and featured sixteen luxury suites. In 1998 the team moved into the $212-million Office Depot Center. In only ten years the Miami Arena had become obsolete. The new arena can seat 19,452 for hockey, with 2,300 club seats and 70 luxury suites. These changes follow a general pattern throughout professional sport, where there has been an increasing focus on targeting lucrative corporate suite buyers as well as affluent individuals. Thus those attending games are coming from a much more upscale demographic group. This audience is arguably even more critical for a league like the NHL, which relies more heavily than the other major leagues on gate receipts as a percentage of total revenues. Indeed, between 1994 and 2004, league-wide revenues quadrupled to around $2 billion. This increase was almost entirely due to the NHL's ability to raise its arena-related revenues and revenues from licensed merchandise.[16]

Nonetheless, the NHL also began to argue that its viability as a league was not sustainable without a new collective agreement linking player salaries to revenues produced directly from individual teams. You would expect that any business that had seen its revenues grow by 400 per cent over a ten-year period could expect an increase in profitability; but this was not the case for the NHL. In the short term the $80-million expansion fees provided by the new teams proved to be lifelines for some of the existing NHL clubs that were struggling to stay afloat. But this infusion of cash only masked a set of underlying problems in the league, three of them especially notable: the escalation of operating costs, particularly players' salaries; uncertainty over the future growth of revenue sources such as television and franchise fees; and the ways in which the NHL targeted new audiences while moving its product increasingly out of reach of its traditional bases of support, blue-collar and Canadian fans. The NHL's growth strategy may well have jeopardized its relationship with existing fans, especially those in Canadian provincial cities, even before the 2004 lockout and the cancellation of the 2004–05 season.

Average player salaries in the NHL grew from $465,000 in the early 1990s, when Bettman became commissioner, to roughly $1.8 million in 2004. While growth in revenues appeared to have roughly kept pace with salary increases, the *future* growth potential of the NHL's main revenue sources became far from ensured. When owners and general managers were bidding for players and increasing salaries dramatically during the 1990s, they could rely on the expansion fees paid to all established teams; in that decade a total of $510 million in expansion fees was shared amongst the established NHL teams. Team owners also worked on the assumption that television revenues would continue to escalate, as they were doing in the other major professional sports. Furthermore, a number of NHL teams benefited from a substantial infusion of public investment that helped to subsidize the construction of new arenas in the 1990s.

None of these conditions is likely to be repeated in the immediate future. The explosion of new arena construction that characterized the 1990s is largely over, and the NHL appears to have reached the limits of US expansion. More important, the prospect of increasing revenues from television now appears to be a mirage. Poor ratings[17] and labour uncertainty have undermined the value of the NHL as a television product, so that recent agreements have been both smaller and more risky. For the ill-fated 2004–05 season, and beyond, only ESPN offered guaranteed money (as opposed to a revenue-sharing arrangement) to show games. Moreover, rights fees with ESPN were to average $65 million per season through 2006, just over half the value of the previous contract. However, after the lockout was settled ESPN chose not to exercise its option to televise games in the 2005–06 season, leaving the NHL to search for a new cable television partner (ultimately the Outdoor Life Network). The NHL has had even less success in obtaining a broadcasting contract with a major network willing to pay guaranteed money. The NHL and NBC have agreed to a new agreement with no up-front rights fee (similar to the agreement that NBC has with the minor-league Arena Football League). In an agreement that runs through 2007, the league and network will split revenues fifty-fifty once NBC has recovered its production costs.[18]

By agreeing to the revenue-sharing plan with NBC, the NHL was banking on improved audience ratings to generate revenues. But the ratings declines that NHL games have shown in recent years (for both network and cable coverage) make this plan seem optimistic. The uncertainty and anger that have surrounded the cancellation of the 2004–05 season raise even greater questions about the likelihood of strong ratings for NHL hockey in the foreseeable future. In any case it certainly appears that the NHL's attempt to expand into new US markets has not resulted in hockey becoming a national television habit in the United States, which has put the NHL in a weak bargaining position when negotiating TV contracts. For example, assuming that the contract with NBC is not renegotiated, it is far from clear how much owners will receive from their revenue-sharing agreement with the network. This will create further financial uncertainty for team owners, who can no longer rely on guaranteed network television revenues (or expansion fees) to support rising player operating costs (see also chapter 8).

In short, the excitement and promise that came with the arrival of Blockbuster and Disney in the NHL in 1992 are now a thing of the past. Today these companies have divested themselves of their hockey holdings. In June 2001 Wayne Huizenga sold his interest in the Florida Panthers. By that time, though, the Panthers were part of a publicly traded company and had been for sale for about eighteen months. Initially Huizenga had asked $175 million, but the price gradually dropped in the absence of interested buyers. Eventually, a group led by Andrx Corp. chairman Alan Cohen agreed to buy the team for $83.5 million in cash, a $7.5-million promissory note, and the assumption of debt and $10 million in construction obligations. The price amounted to only double what Huizenga had paid eight years earlier, even though the team had moved into a new arena and had control over the operating revenues from the new facility.[19]

Similarly, in July 2003 Disney retained the services of a Wall Street firm to assist it in finding a buyer for its Anaheim franchise. It had been rumoured that Disney had wanted to get rid of the team for some time, but had held off due to the team's surprising success during the 2003 Stanley Cup playoffs. In addition, Disney chief Michael Eisner was still was a fan of the team and the NHL, and it was considered a bad time to be selling a team with the uncertainty of upcoming collective bargaining talks.[20] However, despite the team's success and the poor market for NHL franchises, Disney appeared determined to pursue the sale of the club, and in summer 2005 the Mighty Ducks were purchased by Henry Samueli, whose company owns the Arrowhead Pond, for a sum reported to be in the vicinity of $70 million. The rosy business model promoted to prospective new owners in the 1990s was no longer credible. That is why Bettman risked so much in his dogged pursuit of "cost certainty" for the league by linking player salaries to revenues in the new collective agreement with the players' association.

Another important implication of the NHL's footprint strategy concerns the ability of "average" fans to attend games. Nearly 80 per cent of all revenues in the NHL are now derived from gate and venue-related revenues. By comparison, the NBA and MLB receive less than 60 per cent of their total revenues from those attending games, and the NFL less than 40 per cent. However, any decline in revenues from sources such as television and expansion fees places pressure on NHL teams to increase revenues from game attendance. So far the NHL has been able to increase gate revenues by targeting upscale fans and corporations—a strategy that has provided a blueprint for recent expansion clubs, which target corporations as buyers of luxury suites, club seats, and season's tickets. For example, in Nashville's first season in 1998, the team sold sixty-two of seventy-two luxury suites; but corporate sales were lower than anticipated. The Predators' ratio of individual fan-to-corporate season-ticket holders was about sixty-forty, and by 2000 the team was working hard to move this ratio to what it considered a more desirable fifty-fifty split.[21] But to ensure the long-term success of the team the Predators need to cultivate a base of "ordinary" fans in Nashville.

Fans, or Flaneurs?

The key flaw in the NHL's strategy in the United States may, then, be that sports franchises must consider the impact that the new focus on corporations and upscale consumers will have on the depth of their community support over the longer term. One way of understanding this problem is to see the upscale or corporate fans in new markets as *flaneurs*, rather than fans. Flaneurs are affluent consumers whose consumption patterns are driven more by social fashions than by a genuine interest in a sport, let alone a passionate identification with a team.[22] These are the types of attendees who are given corporate tickets (rather than paying their own money for tickets), and who go to a new arena or support a new team if that happens to be the new "thing to do" in a community. Many new franchises benefit briefly from this sort of "novelty effect," and the point holds for corporate and individual ticket buyers alike; indeed, it may be worth distinguishing here between the tenants of corporate boxes in cities like Toronto, Montreal, and Detroit—cities where supporting hockey is part of corporate as well as civic culture—and those in Nashville or Atlanta, where entertaining clients at hockey is a novelty that may be short-lived.

When teams are successful competitively on the ice they are also likely to get bandwagon supporters. Toronto journalist Rosie Dimanno made that point when she covered the Tampa Bay Lightning during the 2004 playoffs. The team was enjoying unprecedented success; yet Dimanno believed that, despite the Lightning's presence in the area since 1992, "the hockey imprint in this alien market has been clearly imprinted on beach sand, washed away with the tide of season after season of ineptitude and shoulder-shrugging detachment from the public."[23] With the team's success in 2004, games were sold out during the playoffs. Local celebrities such as wrestler Hulk Hogan were conspicuously present, and Hogan's daughter even emerged as the arena's anthem singer. It remains to be seen, though, if these fans will continue to support the Lightning if the team cannot maintain the same level of success. The Carolina experience of the last couple of years suggests otherwise.

According to sport sociologist Richard Giulianotti, "Traditional spectators will have a longer, more local ... identification with the [team], whereas consumer fans will have a more market-centered relationship with the club, as reflected in ... consuming club products."[24] The NHL has relied heavily on consumer fans to generate increasing revenues in the 1990s; but when the novelty of hockey wears off for such fans, it is unlikely that some of the newer Sunbelt franchises will fare very well. This is because long-term fans of the sport (any sport) are more likely to support their teams in the absence of competitive success. Put differently, *fans* support teams because they love the game or feel some civic obligation to support a local institution. *Flaneurs*, in contrast, "are liable not only to switch a connection with teams or players, but also to forsake [the sport] for other forms of entertainment."[25] If this theory is correct, the success of teams in new US markets will depend upon the development of hockey fans rather than on market size or the potential value of regional television audiences.

Thus, while the NHL actively promoted hockey in new US markets based on those markets' size and affluence (which made them desirable for network TV contracts), it may have underestimated the importance of committed hockey fans, as opposed to uncommitted consumers, in determining the long-term viability of a franchise. For example, according to *Sport Business Journal*'s Andy Bernstein, evidence from TV ratings of hockey indicates that ratings are not necessarily determined by market size.[26] For example, during the 2001 Stanley Cup playoffs, teams from smaller metropolitan areas often generated larger television audiences than did teams from major markets:

> Of the seven U.S. teams that made it to the second round of the Stanley Cup playoffs, the team with the largest average television audience was Mario Lemieux's Pittsburgh Penguins. Playing in the 21st-largest media market, the Penguins reached an average of 154,421 households on eight games on Fox Sports Net Pittsburgh, registering a 13.7 rating. With the help of Lemieux's return and an exciting seven-game series with the Buffalo Sabres, the local ratings were up 17 per cent from a year ago. The Sabres [the 43rd largest market] actually had the highest local rating of any team, an 18.0.[27]

A Work in Progress

In many respects the NHL's footprint strategy is at best a work in progress. The league has been successful in penetrating new markets in the United States, but it must now work to ensure that teams will remain successful there. Otherwise the league will have only created the potential to be successful in these new markets, simply by having a presence there. To this point, though, the NHL may have relied too heavily on corporate partners to promote the game, depending on media networks and corporate sponsors to incorporate the NHL into their own advertising and promotions.[28] This approach places too much of the NHL's future in the hands of outside parties, and it becomes especially problematic when the interests of the different organizations become incongruent, and when hockey loses money (as it did for Fox Television) or simply is no longer seen by corporate sponsors as attracting the audiences or carrying the associations that sponsors had hoped for.

The NHL arguably miscalculated when it sought to reach Sunbelt markets in the United States. It relied on the assumption that the key to success was to promote interest in new US markets in order to match the truly national footprint of the other three major professional sports. It is clear that in the Sunbelt states the NHL will never have the profile—or the place in popular culture—enjoyed by the NBA, NFL, and MLB. Perhaps the NHL's biggest error in its footprint strategy was to target new markets at the expense of its existing core of fans. As one journalist proclaimed, "It is hard to imagine any business growing by alienating or insulting its existing customers. Rather than taking their loyalty for granted or, worse, abusing and perverting it [by pandering to new audiences], it would make more sense for the NHL to discover why its fans are so loyal, [and] nurture it."[29] According to former NHL president Gil Stein, "I ... learned that the only way to get people to watch NHL hockey on television is to first make them fans, and the best way to make them fans is to put an NHL team in their city, and then, provided the club does a good job of promoting and finds a way to get people to come to games, hockey will do the rest."[30] This sentiment is shared by those within the hockey community, but it points to a fundamental flaw in the NHL's footprint strategy: how many consumers in a new NHL market will fork out the average $253.65 it costs to take a family to an NHL game?

In Canada the effects of the NHL's footprint strategy have also been significant. While television revenues did not rise as projected, operating costs increased substantially. In the 1990s and first couple of years of the new century the cushion provided by expansion fees, and the value of new revenue streams in some large markets (particularly Toronto), encouraged some Canadian owners to substantially increase their player payrolls, and pushed others to follow suit in an effort to remain competitive. Thus, the NHL's strategy of moving the game upmarket placed a burden on teams in Canadian cities, especially those in cities where the size of the corporate market was limited. Cities such as Winnipeg and Quebec City, which once hosted NHL teams comfortably (even profitably) during the 1980s, were no longer viable in this new economic scenario, and other small-market Canadian franchises (in Edmonton and Ottawa) have struggled to survive. Owners in these cities have regularly invoked the theme of civic obligation in campaigns to get both local businesses and individual fans to purchase season tickets. However, unless underwritten by owners willing to sustain ongoing operating losses, most of the existing Canadian teams have faced sale, and possible relocation. Recent years have seen improvements in this situation: changes in ownership (in Ottawa), improved performance by several of the Canadian teams, and a strengthening in the value of the Canadian dollar. But if the costs of attending NHL games continue to rise, it remains to be seen how long Canadian fans, especially those outside the largest metropolitan markets, will be willing and able to support NHL hockey financially.

A bright spot for the NHL, though, remains the loyalty of its core fan base across Canada and in scattered parts of the United States. That loyalty is what has allowed NHL teams to increase ticket prices while seeing average attendances hold steady or even increase. It is also what allows the NHL to continue to generate revenues from licensing ventures, when other leagues have seen declines. In Canada, then, despite fan unhappiness with the lockout and cancellation of the 2004–05 season, as long as the ultimate solution (a salary cap, lower player salaries, and other adjustments) allows Canadian teams to be competitive, it seems likely that fans will welcome back NHL hockey with enthusiasm. Similarly, in US cities with long NHL hockey traditions—Detroit, Boston, New York, and Chicago—we can expect something like the same outcomes, even though support may take longer to come back (in Chicago, for example, or in Boston, where new arenas have failed to produce sellout crowds in the last couple of years). In other US communities with well-established hockey traditions—for example, Philadelphia, Minnesota, and Colorado—the core of existing hockey fans is sufficient that NHL teams should be able to rebuild their audiences without too much difficulty.

In contrast, in non-traditional hockey markets such as Atlanta, Nashville, and Carolina, the viability of franchises is already tenuous, and fans who knew hockey only as a novelty entertainment option may not have missed it much when it was gone, and may be less eager to come back to it. For example, an owner of a Nashville ticket brokerage firm suggests that hockey remains unimportant in Nashville, compared with local enthusiasm for football and NASCAR. Other observers worry that NHL franchises in half a dozen Sunbelt cities could be on thin ice with the long suspension of play.[31] Spokespersons for both the league and the NHLPA vigorously discount the possibility of contraction, with the attendant loss of NHL jobs that this would entail; however, others maintain that major league hockey is on very shaky ground in at least half a dozen cities in the Southern United States. And this time there may no longer be any new US cities willing to host a relocated franchise—an outcome that would lower franchise values significantly and perhaps permanently alter the economics, and the geography, of the NHL.

Notes

1 See E.M. Swift, "Hot Not. While the NBA's Image Has Cooled, the NHL Has Ignited Surprising New Interest in Hockey," *Sports Illustrated*, 80, 24 (June 6, 1994), p. 20.

2 For example, in 2003 NFL teams averaged $77 million per team, per year, the NBA $26 million/team/year, and MLB $14 million team/year (all figures US). In contrast, NHL teams received an average of $5.7 million/team/year from television revenues.

3 Frank Orr, "NHL's Icy Waters Become Seas of Tranquility," *The Hockey News*, 39, 38 (Sept. 5, 1986), p. 6.

4 David Cruise and Alison Griffiths, *Net Worth: Exploding the Myths of Pro Hockey* (Toronto: Viking, 1991), p. 267.

5 See Russ Conway, *Game Misconduct: Alan Eagleson and the Corruption of Hockey* (Toronto: MacFarlane Walter & Ross, 1995).

6 See Gil Stein, *Power Plays: An Inside Look at the Big Business of the National Hockey League* (Toronto: Birch Lane Press, 1997).

7 A. Gerlin, "Sports: An Icy Sport Heads South to Make (It Hopes) Its Fortune," *Wall Street Journal*, Oct. 4, 1993, p. B1.

8 William Shawcross, *Murdoch: The Making of a Media Empire* (New York: Touchstone, 1997), p. 405.

9 Ibid., p. 406.

10 Andy Bernstein, "The ABCs of the NHL's Massive New Media Deal," *Sports Business Journal*, Aug. 31, 1998.

11 Stein, *Power Plays*, p. 39.

12 The Nordiques acquired Peter Forsberg, Mike Ricci, Ron Hextall, Chris Simon, Kerry Huffman, Steve Duchesne, two first-round draft choices, and $15 million for Lindros.

13 See Jim Silver, *Thin Ice: Money, Politics, and the Demise of an NHL Franchise* (Halifax: Fernwood, 1996).

14 See Michael T. Friedman and Daniel S. Mason, "'Horse Trading' and Consensus Building: Nashville Tennessee and the Relocation of the Houston Oilers," *Journal of Sport History*, 28 (2001), pp. 271-91.

15 Ibid.

16 Where the other three leagues had seen declines in licensing revenues, the NHL had been able to maintain its levels of revenue from this source; "Building NHL Brand—A Step at a Time," *Sports Business Journal*, Feb. 7, 2000.

17 By way of comparison, Wayne Gretzky's final game in 1999 received a 2.2 rating (Fox's highest rating for a regular-season game in three years); by comparison, the NFL draft that same year received a 2.8 rating on ESPN. For other games in US cities, the NHL received lower ratings than all other programs in its time slot, including PBS's *America's Historic Trails with Tom Bodett;* F. Quindt, "Despite Dinky Rink Ratings, Fox Protects the Puck," *San Diego Union-Tribune*, May 15, 1998, p. D2.

18 Andy Bernstein, "NHL Touts Value of NBC Promotion as Key to Partnership," *Sports Business Journal*, May 24, 2004, p. 1.

19 Andy Bernstein, "Panthers' $101M Price Tag Called 'In Line,'" *Sports Business Journal*, June 11, 2001.

20 Daniel Kaplan, "Disney Hires Lehman Bros. to Sell NHL Ducks," *Sports Business Journal*, July 7, 2003.

21 Mark Brender, "Teams in Non-Traditional Markets Learn to Educate Sponsors, Selves," *Sports Business Journal*, Oct. 2, 2000.

22 See Richard Giulianotti, "Supporters, Followers, Fans, and Flaneurs: A Taxonomy of Spectator Identities in Football," *Journal of Sport and Social Issues*, 26, (2002) pp. 25-46. As Giulianotti explains (p. 28), flaneurs could be considered "consumer supporters" who are "very likely to switch clubs or follow those that offer winning teams or which are more socially suited to advancing the spectator's social and economic mobility."

23 Rosie Dimanno, "Hockey and Hooters, Too: But the Game's Still Tough Sell in Tampa," *The Toronto Star*, May 11, 2004.

24 Giulianotti, "Supporters," p. 31.

25 Ibid., p. 40.

26 Andy Bernstein, "Small Cities Rule NHL TV Ratings," *Sports Business Journal*, May 21, 2001.

27 Ibid.

28 Andy Bernstein, "Growing a TV Audience the NHL Way," *Sports Business Journal*, July 15, 2002.

29 Stu Hackel, "Backtalk: Cool Fads Causing Meltdown in NHL," *The New York Times*, June 14, 1998, pp. 8-11.

30 Stein, *Power Plays*, p. 182.

31 "Non-Traditional Markets on Very Thin Ice," *Edmonton Journal*, Sept. 14, 2004.

CHAPTER TEN

From Maple Leaf Gardens to the Air Canada Centre: The Downtown Entertainment Economy in "World Class" Toronto

■ JOHN HANNIGAN

On February 13, 1999, the Toronto Maple Leafs hockey team played its final game at Maple Leaf Gardens (MLG). As anticipated, it was an evening of carefully orchestrated nostalgia. The visiting team, the Chicago Black Hawks, had opposed the Leafs on November 12, 1931, the night the arena opened its doors. At this last game Red Horner and Howard March, participants in that inaugural match (March scored the first goal) dropped the puck at the faceoff. Later, during the post-game ceremonies, Canadian folk hero Stompin' Tom Connors led the crowd in a rendition of "The Hockey Song" and Anne Murray sang "The Maple Leaf Forever." Horner, the oldest remaining Leaf captain, presented the current captain, Mats Sundin, with a corporate "Memories and Dreams" flag. "Mats, take this flag to our new home," Horner said, "but always remember us."

The move from Maple Leaf Gardens to the Air Canada Centre marks a shift in professional hockey. In the past, urban communities hosted teams owned by local entrepreneurs that played in arenas situated in distinctive downtown settings. Now, in a new era, teams are typically corporate-owned and arenas have been transformed into sites for branded, consumption-related activities bound up in tourism, entertainment, and corporate-centred revitalization strategies. This transformation is part of a larger project of economic growth "in which corporate and civic elites struggle to establish and maintain their cities' status in a transnational economic and cultural hierarchy of cities."[1] As such, it is characteristic of "fantasy city" development, which is aggressively themed and branded; deals in the marketing of images; and isolates sports and entertainment complexes from their surrounding neighbourhoods.[2]

In today's entertainment economy, it has become *de rigueur* for professional sports teams to move into new, state-of-the art arenas and stadiums or to upgrade existing ones to a comparable level. In the 1990s, sixty major league facilities were constructed by franchises in the Big Four sports leagues—the National Football League, the National Basketball Association, Major League Baseball, and the National Hockey League—at a cost of $18 billion (US).[3] From the owners' point of view, this makes good business sense. Older venues have poor sightlines and limited parking and concessions, and they are difficult or impossible to retrofit with the private boxes and suites that have outstripped regular seating as a money generator. Equally, if not more important, team owners are able to develop new revenue sources: from the sale of naming rights and seat licenses, from sponsorship deals and in-stadium advertising, and by playing cities off against one another in order to secure infrastructure improvements and tax breaks. In this new era of sports business, success means establishing a team brand with a global impact. In this, few can match Real Madrid, the Spanish soccer (or football) team, which expects to earn $224.5 million in 2004 from marketing, a figure that equals its total income from all sources only four years earlier.[4]

For urban planners and politicians, new sports palaces are seen as motors for economic recovery in city centres that have lost their tax bases and fallen into a funk. Initially, these projects were talked about in terms of spinoffs, multipliers, and job creation, but their rationale now rests upon the idea of public investment in sports facilities as a catalyst for the redevelopment of surrounding neighbourhoods. For example, the upgrading of Wrigley field, home of the Chicago Cubs baseball team, in conjunction with the decision to allow evening baseball games there, was intended to spearhead the development of the Wrigleyville entertainment zone, which, in turn, was meant to constitute a key element in Chicago's drive to refashion itself as a metropolis rich in arts, entertainment, and sports venues.[5] No matter that nearly two decades of research on the economic impacts of sports facilities have indicated that the successes are few and far between; most projects create only low-paying service jobs and do little, if anything, to reinvigorate local bars, restaurants, and stores.

Building for Dollars: The Air Canada Centre and the Pursuit of New Revenue Opportunities

At first glance the Air Canada Centre, a new multi-use facility in the old Canada Post buildings near Toronto's waterfront, does not appear to perfectly match this profile of sports facilities as urban redevelopment catalyst. Privately financed, it has not been built with direct public loans or subsidies; nor is it the centrepiece of a major downtown revitalization project. Yet the logic behind its construction is similar. A planning document[6] prepared several months after the official groundbreaking at the ACC justified, on several grounds, the building of a new, state-of-the-art sports and entertainment centre next to Toronto's Union Station. First, the authors suggested, the media exposure, both nationally and internationally, attached to a new venue "will likely generate increased interest in Toronto as a tourist destination as well as a place for conducting business." Second, they predicted that the new building would have a positive effect on core area development in the district south of Toronto's financial core:

> The proposed development will provide an impetus in the area south of Front Street and the existing Union Station. By bridging the rail corridor, the sports and

entertainment centre will provide the physical and visual linkage to act as a catalyst for real estate development in an area which is currently difficult to market because it lacks a tangible identity.[7]

For Maple Leaf Sports and Entertainment Ltd. (MLSE), which controlled both the hockey team and Maple Leaf Gardens, the prospect of a new building promised sharply increased profits. According to business journalist Theresa Tedesco, the initial call for a new arena came from George Engman and Robert Bertram, the two members on the MLSE board who represented its majority (58 per cent) owner, the Ontario Teachers' Pension Plan Board.[8] Engman and Bertram told Tedesco that, despite implementing cost controls, "We've fallen short of our targets and that has impacted our returns. So we began to explore other alternatives to make us whole." Leafs general manager Cliff Fletcher was sent on a fact-finding mission to new arenas around the league, and then a report recommending a new facility was made to the MLSE board. This activity quickly attracted the attention of the Toronto Raptors Basketball Club Inc. which had plans of its own to move out of the SkyDome, the domed baseball stadium with a retractable roof where the Toronto Blue Jays were playing their home games and where the Raptors had been playing since the team joined the NBA in 1995.[9] In the event, the two organizations agreed on a joint venture, and MLSE ended up buying the Raptors.

Despite its nickname, the "Cashbox on Carlton," Maple Leaf Gardens had long derived far too much of its income from traditional sources—gate receipts and concessions—and not enough from marketing and branding, which were fast becoming the new profit-drivers in professional sports. This tendency became especially evident in the late 1980s, when the Leafs fell behind the Toronto Blue Jays baseball club's willingness to market its logo aggressively on everything from T-shirts to coffee mugs and to license clothing products such as jerseys and sweat pants.[10] Harold Ballard, who effectively controlled both the team and the arena from 1972 through the early 1990s, was a notorious skinflint who made money by slashing the team payroll even as he raised prices. Fan satisfaction nosedived. By dividing the teams' winning percentage by their average ticket prices, journalist John Lorinc came up with a "sports gratification index." For the Leafs this index reached a low point in 1988 when the team's winning percentage (points/possible points) was .325 while its average ticket price (adjusted for inflation) was $18.[11] While Ballard significantly increased the number of non-hockey attractions, opening up the Gardens to conventions, circuses, boxing cards, and popular entertainment, he usually failed to see the marketing possibilities attached to these events, preferring to squeeze out revenue in other ways. According to one oft-repeated "legend," Ballard greeted the Beatles' first appearance in Canada by ordering Gardens' staff to crank up the heat (on one of the hottest days of the summer), turn off the water fountains, and put away small-size paper cups at the concession stands. Not surprisingly, soft drink sales were said to be significantly higher than usual.

In the post-Ballard era the Leafs' empire became increasingly directed by "the visible hand of management," whereby business policies favouring long-term stability and growth were privileged over the carnival-style promotion and quick profit-taking that had formerly reigned supreme.[12] This new approach was evident with the move to the ACC. Minor-league scouting was restored. Iconic Leaf veterans from the 1950s and 1960s—people such as Frank Mahovlich, Eddie Shack, and Darryl Sittler, who had been driven away by Ballard—were welcomed back. Rather than the owners, the visible face of the organization became its senior executives, notably Ken Dryden and Richard Peddie.

This strategy was vindicated in 1997 when a young man named Martin Kruze approached Toronto police alleging that he and other young men had been victims of a pedophile ring composed of lower-level Gardens' employees from the mid-1970s through the early 1980s. Dozens of other victims emerged, and several convictions were obtained. Dryden, a bestselling author and hockey legend from the 1970s (and, most recently, a federal government cabinet minister) handled this potentially explosive situation with sensitivity and aplomb, even though he had only recently assumed the job of president and general manager of the hockey club. After Kruze committed suicide in October 1997, Dryden attended the funeral, made the Gardens (and later the ACC) available for a series of public meetings and educational sessions, and assisted financially in launching a memorial fund to assist sexual abuse survivors and to promote public awareness of this problem.

At the same time, MLSE actively pursued new revenue opportunities. Anticipating his team's move from the Montreal Forum to the Molson Centre (now the Bell Centre), Aldo Giampaolo, an executive with the rival Montreal Canadiens, predicted that the new venue "will become known as a multi-functional building which adapts perfectly to the demands of the ever-evolving entertainment industry."[13] The expectations for the Air Canada Centre were similar. Replicating the Jumbotron in SkyDome, a huge Sony video board was installed in the ACC to allow advertising throughout Leaf and Raptor games. Television monitors (seven hundred of them) were installed throughout the building, including in the washrooms. The new arena contained 40 platinum lounges, 65 executive suites, 32 balcony suites, 24 loge suites, and 1,020 club seats. To increase the size and reach of its marketing program, MLSE attracted a wider range of sponsors willing to link their brand to a sports property. For example, Philishave was signed on as the official electric shaver of the Toronto Maple Leafs and Raptors, tying its communications, events, and promotions to the teams.[14] Air Canada agreed to pay $40 million over twenty years for the naming rights to the arena, a good bargain compared to the

$300 million (US) deal over thirty years recently accepted by Reliant Energy in return for naming the home of the NFL Houston Texans "Reliant Stadium."[15]

All of this spending paid off royally. By 2003 MLSE and its holdings were worth an estimated $1.05 billion. The most valuable asset is the Maple Leaf franchise ($450 million), followed by the Air Canada Centre ($300 million) and the Raptors franchise ($250 million). While ticket sales still represent the single largest revenue source ($116,731,000), broadcast revue ($81,353,000) and sponsorship revenue ($44,735,000) now account for more than half the total revenue.[16]

Passing the Torch: Constructing a Discourse of "Mediated Community"

With the move to the Air Canada Centre, MLSE had successfully plugged into the world of commodified sports as entertainment. Nevertheless, the company still needed to protect and enhance the value of its brand by reassuring fans that the past was not being forgotten but, rather, enriched. Partly, this strategy meant tapping into what John Nauright and Phil White call "mediated nostalgia"—a socially constructed discourse that conflates nationalism, recollections of a happier time, and the success of Canadian professional sporting teams.[17] The approach is also captured in Richard Gruneau and David Whitson's observation that sports owners who move a franchise into a new location in search of larger markets and greater profitability actively trade in the "discourse of community," urging the locals to get behind what is now "their" team.[18] Combining these two insights, I have coined the term "mediated community" to describe a constructed discourse wherein management, in conjunction with a compliant media, sells the notion of a "nation" of fans who are united in their collective devotion to the team as both a cultural touchstone and a lifestyle.

One crucial element in this discourse of mediated community is the notion that "the torch is passed" from the Maple Leaf Gardens era to the future at the Air Canada Centre. Months before the Leafs skated onto the ice for the first time at the ACC, an initiative was launched to emphasize the merging of tradition and progress. In the summer of 1998 Ken Dryden wrote to season ticket holders. "Now it is up to us," he said, "to build new memories and dreams." An Air Canada advertisement on the inside front cover of the 1998–99 issue of *Hockey Night in Toronto*, the official Maple Leafs magazine, featured a photograph of a smiling construction worker in an ACC hard hat accompanied by copy that read:

> Defy the traditional definition of progress. Build a place where the city's heart beats faster. At the Air Canada Centre, a sense of place is in every beam, every rivet. And, as the day approaches when the Maple Leafs step on the ice for the very first time, the

excitement is about to explode from every corner.... This is how landmarks are born, made, lived in and loved for a long time.[19]

A year later, in the same publication, Richard Peddie told the Leafs faithful that management had brought closure to the Gardens "faster than anyone imagined." Nevertheless, he observed, the new arena seamlessly combines physical amenities such as better sightlines and wider seats with "all those kinds of touchstones that make it new but familiar"—a media gondola (recalling the famous radio broadcasts by Foster Hewitt), the Esso Maple Leaf memories and Dream Room, and hundreds of photographs of past teams and players. Now it was time to move on. "We've had our memories," he proclaimed, "and now we have to get on to our dreams."[20]

To ensure that the passing of the torch was not just symbolic, in the 2001–02 season MLSE launched a seventy-fifth anniversary campaign called "Generations" that encouraged ticket holders to pass their seats down from one generation to the next, ensuring that the team had an audience well into the future. This was seen as crucial because of the high carryover rate from season to season—in 2002, more than 40 per cent of season seat-holders predated 1970, and 20 per cent went back beyond 1950. The Generations campaign encouraged long-time fans to submit photos and anecdotes; some of these hockey-related memories were then featured on printed ticket materials.[21] To encourage the loyalty of younger fans in the five to twelve age category, MLSE established a "Buds Club" whose more than seven thousand paid members received a raft of benefits including a pocket schedule, members-only newsletter, and exclusive entry to the Buds Club Private Practice Day. Establishing "clubs" such as this can be an effective means of targeting a message to young customers and collecting demographic information by appealing to a child's fundamental need for status and belonging.[22] According to its official web site (http://www.torontomapleleafs.com/budsclub.ml), the Buds Club has members in every province in Canada as well as in over twenty different countries throughout the world.

More recently, MLSE has encouraged the growth of a mediated community by organizing and promoting the growth of the "Leaf Nation," a quasi-network of Toronto Maple Leaf fans across the country. To implement this strategy, in 2004 the club launched the Leafs Nation Fan Club, which offers as a benefit of membership a subscription to *Leafs Nation: The Magazine*, published three times per season and also sold on newsstands across the Greater Toronto area. According to Tom Anselmi, executive vice-president and chief operating officer of the Toronto Maple Leafs, the publication is "an extension of the Leafs brand" and "reflects on hockey as part of our culture and as a lifestyle."[23] Topics in the inaugural issue included Maple Leafs goalie Ed Belfour's passion for cars; forward Gary Roberts's nutrition and fitness regime (Roberts has since gone to the Florida Panthers); and profiles of super-fans who express their loyalty to the team in a variety of different and colourful ways.

Destroying the Ice: From Hockey Palace to Grocery Emporium

When the Leafs skated off the ice there for the final time in 1999, the future of Maple Leaf Gardens was uncertain. In contrast to some other cases of decommissioned sports venues where patrons took away parts of the building as souvenirs,[24] the arena remained more or less intact. MLSE sold off about 11,000 of the 16,726 seats in the Gardens by mail order. Audio Visual Message, the firm engaged to carry out this task, deliberately hired new immigrants, largely from the Indian state of Gujurat, to remove the seats on the assumption that as newcomers from overseas they wouldn't recognize their nostalgic value. What the company wanted, its managing director said, were workers with "no emotional relationship with what they're doing."[25] This probably would not have been the case, he concluded, with "second-or-third generation Canadian boys … beer-drinking hockey fans."

For several years rumours of the imminent sale of the Gardens surfaced and then vanished. In 2000, superstar architect Frank Gehry toured the building with Ken Dryden (by then vice-chairman of MLSE) with a view towards redesigning it. At least three different developers had evidently expressed interest, but nothing specific materialized.[26] The Gardens continued to be used as a practice facility for the Toronto Rock lacrosse team; as a movie set; and as a rehearsal space for pop music stars such as Cher and the Rolling Stones. But mostly it sat empty, clicking up an annual carrying cost in excess of $1.5 million per year.[27]

Then, in October 2003, it was announced that Loblaws, the dominant supermarket chain in Canada, was planning to purchase the Gardens and convert it to a combined food and general merchandise emporium while preserving the building's roofline and façade. Loblaws was chosen over another retail giant, Home Depot, which aimed to open a home improvement store; Biovail Corp. (a pharmaceutical company) and its founder Eugene Melnyk, who owned both an NHL franchise (the Ottawa Senators) and the St. Michael's Majors of the Ontario Hockey League; and a third unidentified party, believed to be a condominium developer.[28] Two months later, Loblaws Cos. Ltd. stepped back from its offer, citing an internal study that cautioned against the company's proposed outlet on the grounds that "it would require greater financial resources than first anticipated."[29]

By April 2004, however, Loblaws was said to be preparing a second offer. Belatedly, opponents of the sale began to organize. The Friends of Maple Leaf Gardens, a group dedicated to protecting the interior and exterior character of MLG and headed by noted author, newspaper columnist, and former mayor of Toronto John Sewell, convened a public meeting, entitled "The Future of Maple Leaf Gardens," at the St. Lawrence Centre for the Arts. This community forum was moderated by Phyllis Lambert, a philanthropist and scion of the wealthy Bronfman family. Panelists were Jack Diamond, a Toronto architect and planner; Lisa Rochon, architecture critic for *The Globe and Mail*; Michael Hollett, co-editor of *Now Magazine*, an alternative weekly; Christopher Hume, *Toronto*

Star architecture writer; and Frank Mahovlich, former Leaf icon and now a Liberal Senator. Attendance totalled about two hundred, a figure that might have been much higher if the meeting had not been held on the same evening as a Leafs playoff game.

As might be expected, the majority of the panelists praised Maple Leaf Gardens as a temple of priceless memories. Lambert, who enjoys an international reputation as an architectural patron, described MLG as "a holy place." Hollett called it "a place of passion ... as iconic a building as there is." Rochon said it was "a significant container for collective memory." Only Hume demurred, confessing that he had never liked the Gardens architecture but that it "deserves some kind of respect." When it came to recommending an optimal future use, however, there was no consensus. Rochon outlined three possible scenarios: the status quo before closing (a hockey and concerts venue); a new institution such as a hockey skills centre to be built by a public-private partnership, or a new home for a major arts organization, for example, the Art Gallery of Ontario. Diamond thought it might serve as a headquarters for the exotic entertainment behemoth Cirque du Soleil, as a magnificent Central Library, or as a centre for amateur sport. Hollett favoured the Melnyk proposal, which would keep MLG as a hockey rink. Perhaps surprisingly, Mahovlich concluded that another rink would be out of the question and suggested that the building be converted to low-income housing. One point of unanimity was that the redevelopment of another iconic venue, the Montreal Forum, had been botched. After that building was closed in 1996 the site was converted into an entertainment and retail complex with a twenty-two-screen AMC movie theatre. The Forum, Hollett observed, had been turned into "a glorified mall." Mahovlich noted that "they might as well have torn it down."

During the question portion of the evening, a variety of potential uses for Maple Leaf Gardens were put forward. One citizen suggested a velodrome, or bicycling arena, another a combination of public market and skating rink. A low-income activist proclaimed that people were dying on the streets and demanded that MLG be used for public housing. The most cogent comments, however, came from two audience members who had grown up far from Toronto. A young woman from Newfoundland recalled listening to Leaf games on the radio and how for her the Gardens had taken on almost mythical qualities. A recent arrival from China lamented the potential destruction of a piece of the heritage of her new home. "You need to learn about the history and architecture," she ventured, "*before* you can appreciate it."

Over the next few months the Loblaws proposal crystallized and moved quickly through the planning process with minimal opposition. On May 6, 2004, a City of Toronto staff report recommending the Loblaws application came before the Toronto Preservation Board, whose role it is to advise Council on heritage issues. Equipped with a scale model, Jane Marshall of Loblaws Properties unveiled the plan to turn the Gardens into a food store. There would be two levels of retail space, with the ice rink area becoming the main food hall. There would be two levels of parking underground. Most of the retail frontage along Church Street would be taken up with an LCBO (Liquor Control Board of Ontario) outlet. In support of the presentation, Loblaws brought along Chris Andrews, a consultant employed by a structural engineering firm that had been involved with Maple Leaf Gardens since the 1930s. Loblaws, he told the Board, is to be commended for its intention to open up the large windows facing out onto Wood Street—windows that had been boarded up long ago in order to provide additional seating. Another coup for Loblaws was its hiring of David Crombie, a popular former mayor of Toronto, to assist in developing an "interpretive centre" within the building, a place where its history would be commemorated.

During the representations from deputants (John Sewell, on behalf of the Friends of Maple Leaf Gardens, plus two others) and the subsequent Board discussion, two flashpoints emerged. One pertained to the offer from Eugene Melnyk, who proposed creating a more intimate venue of ten thousand seats and adding a number of features: new glass corporate boxes at both ends of the arena; an interactive TV broadcasting facility on the corner of Carlton and Church streets; a two-storey, full-service restaurant with enlarged windows overlooking Church Street and interconnected to a restored Hot Stove Lounge; 4,000 square feet of prime retail space; and a Canadian Amateur Hockey Hall of Fame in the upper bowl of the arena.[30] In a statement to the Friends of Maple Leaf Gardens, eight days later, Melnyk reiterated that he was prepared to sign a deal that would commit to not hosting concerts or any other entertainment beyond minor league hockey games, a possibility that was said to be the main reason for the refusal of MLSE to pursue his offer.[31] At the May 6 Board meeting, Robert Hunter, vice-president of MLSE, questioned Melnyk's sincerity, describing his offer as falling significantly below the others, and constituting nothing more than a "media ploy."

A second flashpoint was a matter of fundamental differences over the meaning of the term "heritage." The majority on the Board, most notably Patrick Gossage, the chair, favoured a narrow interpretation that focused exclusively on the building's architecture. By this standard, the main emphasis fell on the exterior and the roof. The roof of the Gardens is generally acknowledged as an engineering marvel: massive corner pylons, one of which is mounted on rollers to allow for give, supporting the 750-tonne roof, which is separate from the arena structure itself. Only a single sentence in the staff report referred to the interior elements. The Board categorically rejected an alternative view that cited the cultural history of Maple Leaf Gardens as sufficient reason for preserving it. In doing so, it failed to recognize a section of the 1990 heritage designation statement that read:

> The property at 438 Church Street, known as Maple Leaf Gardens, is designated on architectural and historical grounds. Maple Leaf Gardens, since its construction in

1931, has been the home of the Toronto Maple Leafs, where radio coverage of "Hockey Night in Canada" began and was broadcast by Foster Hewitt for almost fifty years. As well, it has been the arena for a variety of events and public gatherings including the protest rallies of the Depression, skating carnivals, the circus, the opera, concerts and numerous sports events.[32]

At the end of the hearing, only one member of the Toronto Preservation Board voted against accepting the staff report favouring the Loblaws plan. The staff report also did not encounter any significant roadblocks at Toronto South Community Council on June 8, or at Toronto City Council, where it received approval, again with only a single dissenting vote. In each case the rationale presented for accepting the plan to turn the Gardens into a mega-box grocery store was that of "adaptive re-use." The municipal councillor for the area, Kyle Rae, was an especially enthusiastic proponent, arguing that the superstore would help to counter the rising level of economic upheaval that the surrounding neighbourhood had experienced in recent years. The Loblaws plan, Rae said, would save the building and provide local residents with stores and services that had been sadly missing.

Dollars and Dreams: Reconciling the Global and the Local

In recent years much has been written about how globalizing trends "remake our world capitals into the cookie-cutter shapes and sizes configured by Disney, Starbucks and Microsoft."[33] One visible manifestation of this creeping uniformity is the replacement of traditional arenas by more generic, full-service entertainment venues bearing interchangeable and placeless corporate names: Fleet Center, Staples Center, MCI Center, Delta Center. At the same time, in the context of vigorous intercity competition for tourist and investment dollars, urban communities must strive to distinguish themselves from their neighbours. Architecturally, there are two major ways of doing this: through emphasizing a city's built heritage; and through the innovative design of space, notably avant-garde designs for cultural flagships, for example, the Guggenheim Museum Bilbao. A city's built space is primarily local in orientation; a cultural flagship tends to be globally oriented. In combination these features are said to constitute new urban landscapes that are "glocalized."[34]

In a similar fashion, the business of professional sports in the fantasy city must reconcile the global and the local. Individual teams aim to emulate top European football clubs such as Real Madrid and Manchester United and market their brand (and their merchandise) across the globe (see chapter 12). Increasingly, players in North American leagues come from Europe, Latin America, and even Asia. Yet, paradoxically, forging a strong and distinctive brand identity necessarily requires establishing a sense of local identity. In the past this distinctiveness has mostly arisen serendipitously from a correspondence between a team's style of play and the character of the surrounding community. For example, in the NFL, the legendary Chicago Bears squads under coach Mike Ditka and the Pittsburgh Steelers were depicted by the media as being tough, defensive competitors in harmony with their salt-of-the earth, blue-collar fans. The same is true for the Philadelphia Flyers hockey teams of the 1970s, which were nicknamed the "Broad Street Bullies." For a time the Los Angeles Kings teams matched the glamour and savvy of Wayne Gretzky with the celebrity of LA's celebrity scene. Teams may also achieve distinctiveness as a result of a fabled history (New York Yankees in baseball; Montreal Canadiens in hockey) or a readily recognized physical landmark (the "Green Monster" in Boston's Fenway Park).

Contemporary sports teams and venues are rarely as fortunate. Expansion clubs often arrive in cities and regions with no prior history of a particular sport. Owners locate (or relocate) there primarily for demographic reasons, notably the presence of a potentially large middle-class fan base that is not being serviced. As Gruneau and Whitson have observed, a franchise in one of the major leagues of North American professional sports means the same thing, in practice, as a franchise in the travel or fast-food industries: namely, the right to offer a nationally recognized product in a certain market area.[35] Moreover, in contrast to new baseball parks where designers have sought to incorporate distinctive physical features (a waterfall in the outfield area of Kaufman Park in Kansas City, for example, or a brick building in Baltimore's "neo-classical" Camden Yards stadium), new arenas for hockey and basketball frequently appear remarkably similar, especially to television viewers.

Another difficulty is that new ballparks and arenas are often constructed in brown-fields and other empty or recycled spaces, rather than in established neighbourhoods from which they could derive a sense of identity. In contrast to the original stadium, the new Comiskey Park in Chicago was constructed on the former site of a small commercial enclave, cut off by freeways from the nearby residential areas of Bridgeport and South Armour Square. Moreover, to make a space for the new ballpark the builders demolished McCuddy's Tavern, an iconic local bar that had served as a crucial link between the White Sox and the surrounding neighbourhood. "There is little likelihood," Costas Spirou and Larry Bennett conclude, "that the new Comiskey Park will ever become a beloved neighborhood institution in the fashion of its predecessor."[36]

There are some striking parallels here with the Toronto case. Unlike Maple Leaf Gardens, the Air Canada Centre is not part of a functioning residential and commercial neighbourhood. The ACC occupies a stand-alone site south of Front Street, surrounded by parking lots, railroad tracks, and the Gardiner Expressway. There is no easy and direct pedestrian access to the nearby St. Lawrence neighbourhood. Spectators arrive by car or by public transit via Union Station, the major hub for suburban and inter-urban trains. Whereas Leaf fans formerly patronized restaurants and sports bars along College and Church streets, Air Canada Centre ticket holders are effectively restricted to themed food outlets, such as Lord Stanley's Mug, located within the ACC itself. South of Front Street, the only nearby dining establishment is the Harbour Sixty Steakhouse, a pricey restaurant that caters to an expense-account clientele.[37] This profile is congruent with one of the defining features of the fantasy city, whereby urban entertainment destinations are characteristically "solipsistic," that is, isolated from surrounding neighbourhoods physically, economically, and culturally.[38]

As the years go by since their move into the ACC, the Toronto Maple Leafs have become locked on the horns of a dilemma. North American pro hockey clubs have aggressively pursued a "global market logic" and work hard to convert their sport from a community passion to an expensive and de-localized consumer product aimed at wealthy and expense-account audiences. As a consequence, few teams firmly retain an "organic connection" to the cities they claim to represent.[39] Yet, as I have sought to demonstrate in this chapter, the pursuit of global dollars cannot be divorced from the strategic exploitation of past triumphs and the engineering of local dreams. Ironically, for the Leafs almost all of these cherished memories occurred within the confines of Maple Leaf Gardens, soon to be recycled as a big-box supermarket and liquor store. In cultivating the notion of a "Leaf nation," MLSE has sought both to expand its market and firm up fan loyalty through a discourse of mediated community that suggests a shared social bond and common lifestyle. In similar fashion, the Buds Club for youngsters encourages a shared status and identity, as rolled out to a generation of future fans across Canada and the world.

Dollars and dreams are not, however, always mutually compatible. MLSE discovered this near the end of 2003 when it stumbled into a public relations nightmare. After twenty-two years, the company announced that its traditional Easter Seals charity skate, at which disabled children have an opportunity to join their Maple Leaf heroes on the ice in the team's own arena, was to be cancelled on the grounds that the overhead was too high. This decision provoked a stiff backlash in the media, including negative stories on the front pages of all four Toronto dailies and irate callers telephoning the local all-sports radio station accusing the team of being uncaring.[40] Some two months later MLSE relented, reinstating the Easter Seals skate with the financial assistance of several new corporate sponsors, including the investment firm TD Waterhouse.

While this episode appeared to end happily all around, nevertheless it should be interpreted as a cautionary tale. In the brave new world of global marketing and branding, professional sports teams that overlook the importance of local communities and neighbourhoods do so at their peril.

Notes

1 Richard Gruneau and David Whitson. *Hockey Night in Canada: Sport, Identities, and Cultural Politics* (Toronto: Garamond Press, 1993), p. 223.

2 John Hannigan, *Fantasy City: Pleasure and Profit in the Postmodern Metropolis* (London and New York: Routledge, 1998).

3 Timothy S. Chapin, "Sports Facilities as Urban Redevelopment Catalysts," *Journal of the American Planning Association*, 70 (2004), p. 194.

4 "Real Madrid Claims Top Spot with €138M in Sports Marketing," *Financial Post* (Toronto), July 20, 2004.

5 Costas Spirou and Larry Bennett, "Revamped Stadium ... New Neighborhood," *Urban Affairs Review*, 37 (2002), p. 700.

6 "A Sports AND Entertainment Centre at Union Station: Economic Benefits Assessment," June 18, 1997.

7 Ibid., p. 6.

8 Theresa Tedesco, *Offside: The Battle for Control of Maple Leaf Gardens* (Toronto: Viking, 1996), p. 278.

9 Ibid., p. 279.

10 William Houston, *Inside Maple Leaf Gardens: The Rise and Fall of the Toronto Maple Leafs* (Toronto and Montreal: McGraw-Hill Ryerson Press, 1989), p. 243.

11 From 1980 through 1989 the team's winning percentage never once exceeded .500, dipping as low as .300 in 1985. During the same period, ticket prices effectively doubled. See John Lorinc, "Time for an Accounting, Sports Fans," *Toronto*, April 1991.

12 David Mills, "The Blue Line and the Bottom Line: Entrepreneurs and the Business of Hockey in Canada 1927-90," in Paul D. Staudohar and James A. Mangan, eds., *The Business of Professional Sports* (Urbana and Chicago: University of Illinois Press, 1991), p. 199.

13 Giampaolo is quoted in Christian Goyens (with Allan Turowetz and Jean-Luc Duguay), *The Montreal Forum: Forever Proud* (Westmount, QC: Les editions Effix, 1996), p. 214.

14 Michelle Warren, "The Sporting Life," *Marketing Magazine* (Toronto), Feb. 23, 2004, p. 13.

15 The Houston deal may not, however, be as solid as it looks; several Reliant Energy employees were indicted by a US federal grand jury in April 2004 on charges of manipulating prices during the California energy crisis. See Richard Sandomir, "At (Your *New* Name Here) Arena, Money Talks," *The New York Times*, May 30, 2004.

16 These figures are based on estimates obtained from sports industry consultants by the *Financial Post* in 2003. The US business magazine *Forbes* set the value of the Leafs slightly lower at $263 million (all figures US), with revenue estimated at $105 million and income at $18.8 million. The *Forbes* numbers are disputed by Richard Peddie, president and CEO of Maple Leaf Sports and Entertainment, as being misleading, insofar as the company is privately held (since September 1996) and *Forbes* did not have access to actual club financial information. See Robert Thompson, "In a League of Its Own," *Financial Post*, Dec. 6, 2003.

17 John Nauright and Phil White, "Mediated Nostalgia, Community and Nation: The Canadian Football League in Crisis and the Demise of the Ottawa Rough Riders, 1986–1996," *Sport History Review*, 33 (2002), pp. 121-37.

18 Gruneau and Whitson, *Hockey Night in Canada*, p. 233.

19 Both the Dryden quote and the ACC advertisement appear in *Hockey Night in Toronto*, Issue no.1, 1998–99.

20 *Hockey Night in Toronto*, Issue no.1, 1999–2000.

21 Wendy Cuthbert, "Hockey for Life? Maple Leaf Defends Its Brand with a Pass to the Next Generation," *Strategy* (Toronto), March 25, 2002, p. 20.

22 Eric Schlosser, *Fast Food Nation: The Dark Side of the All-American Meal* (New York: Perennial, 2002), p. 45.

23 Press release, March 23, 2004. See the team's official website <Mapleleafs.com>.

24 For example, the 31,822 patrons who attended the final Philadelphia Phillies baseball game at Connie Mack stadium on Oct. 1, 1970, pried up seats and carted off urinals, pieces of the bullpen, and turnstiles. Some even came equipped with saws and hammers. See Bruce Kuklick, *To Every Thing a Season: Shibe Park and Urban Philadelphia 1909–1976* (Princeton, NJ: Princeton University Press, 1991), p. 180.

25 Ted McDonald, the founder and managing director of Audio Visual Message, was quoted in Paul Wilson, "The Best Seat in the House," *Saturday Night*, March 27, 2001, p. 49.

26 Lisa Rochon, "The Future of Maple Leaf Gardens: A Public Meeting, St. Lawrence Centre for the Arts," *The Globe and Mail*, April 14, 2004.

27 Dana Flavelle, "Leafs Historic Home to Become Superstore," *The Toronto Star*, Oct. 22, 2003.

28 Peter Brieger, "Loblaws Ices Gardens Store Plan," *Financial Post*, Dec. 24, 2003.

29 "Maple Leaf Gardens to Become a Grocery Store," *The Toronto Sun*, Oct. 21, 2003.

30 At the May 6 Board meeting, MLSE said the company had not received an offer in writing from Melnyk. In response to Sewell's statement that Melnyk was willing to pay one dollar more than the highest offer received, Board chair Patrick Gossage ruled that the Board "can't deal with an application that is not before us." Melnyk subsequently wrote the Friends of Maple Leaf Gardens with a detailed outline of the proposal together with concept drawings commissioned from well-known Toronto architect Bruce Kuwabara.

31 This is reported in Friends of Maple Leaf Gardens, Bulletin no.3, May 14, 2004, p. 2.

32 Schedule B, Bylaw 44-91, passed by Toronto City Council, Dec. 12, 1990.

33 David Grazian, review of H.V. Savitch and Paul Kantor, *Cities in the International Marketplace: The Political Economy of Urban Development in North America and Western Europe* (Princeton University Press, 2002), in *Social Forces*, 82 (2004), p. 1648.

34 Elias Beriatos and Aspa Gospodini, "Glocalising Urban Landscapes: Athens and the 2004 Olympics," *Cities*, 21 (2004), p. 191.

35 Gruneau and Whitson, *Hockey Night in Canada*, p. 233.

36 Costas Spirou and Larry Bennett, *It's Hardly Sportin': Stadiums, Neighborhoods and the New Chicago* (Dekalb: Northern Illinois University Press, 2003), p. 104.

37 An advertisement for the Harbour Sixty Steakhouse in *Hockey Night in Toronto* (Issue no.1, 1999–2000) reads, "Just Steps from the Air Canada Centre. USDA Prime Steaks, Exceptional Wines, Late-Night Dining."

38 Hannigan, *Fantasy City*, p. 4.

39 Bruce Kidd, "Toronto's SkyDome: The World's Greatest Entertainment Centre," in John Bale and Olof Moen, eds., *The Stadium and the City* (Keele, Staffordshire: Keele University Press, 1995).

40 Michael Clarkson, "Joy for Children as Leafs Revive Charity Skate," *The Toronto Star*, Nov. 19, 2003.

CHAPTER ELEVEN

Have Skates, Will Travel: Canada, International Hockey, and the Changing Hockey Labour Market

■ HART CANTELON

A n understudied aspect of global sport concerns the effects of player migration to the countries in which a sport's major leagues are based and where the highest salaries are paid.[1] In soccer this tendency has meant migration from Latin America, Africa, and elsewhere (even Canada and the United States) to West European leagues (in Italy, Spain, and Britain, for example) where the game is big business. In hockey it has meant players coming to North America from the former Soviet Union and Czechoslovakia, as well as from Scandinavia, Germany, and even Switzerland to pursue careers in the National Hockey League. In the 2003–04 season, a record-setting three hundred NHL players were born and trained in Europe.

In this chapter I outline a brief history of the development of international hockey with specific emphasis on the history of Canadian international teams. I also explore the emergence of an increasingly transnational labour market. In addition to mapping the factors that led to the growing recruitment of international players to North American teams, I consider the impact of player migration on hockey in the home countries of players who have left to pursue their hockey careers in other countries.[2] Given that the National Hockey League has been the aspiration for so many players, I also want to question the criteria upon which widely shared beliefs about the superiority of North American hockey are based. Finally, given the 2004 lockout of players by the NHL owners, the eventual cancellation of the entire season, and the economic fragility of several NHL franchises, I raise questions about the feasibility of an alternative professional hockey "super league" developing in Europe.

The Early Development of International Hockey

The organizational history of international hockey begins early in the twentieth century with the formation of the International Ice Hockey Federation (Ligue Internationale de Hockey sur Glace, or LIHG).[3] Representatives from France, Belgium, Switzerland, and the United Kingdom (Great Britain) founded the organization after a meeting in Paris in May 1908—a founding that predates the NHL, although organized professional hockey was developing in Canada at about the same time.[4] Some two years later, in

January 1910, the LIHG organized what was to become the first European ice hockey championship, hosted by the municipality of Les Avants near Montreux, Switzerland. The tournament attracted four "official" participants—Great Britain, Germany, Belgium, and Switzerland—but in addition the "Oxford Canadiens," a team of Canadians studying in Oxford, competed as a non-official entry. These modest beginnings were the start of an annual European championship tournament, interrupted only by the two world wars. By 1929 the LIHG was confident enough in the popularity of ice hockey to consider an annual world championship tournament, with the top-finishing European team to be recognized simultaneously as the European champion.

The international status of the LIHG was enhanced when hockey was included in the 1920 Olympic (Summer) Games in Antwerp. In April of that year the LIHG members, along with teams from Canada and the United States, competed for Olympic medals. The European teams proved no match for their North American opponents, who captured the gold and silver medals. Following the tournament, North American amateur hockey organizations were admitted to the LIHG, extending the federation beyond its European borders. In 1930 Japan also joined the LIHG and almost immediately competed in that year's world championships, represented by a team made up of medical students studying in Europe. Japan's acceptance into the LIHG was closely followed by the admission of other nations. The three Baltic countries of Latvia (1931), Estonia (1937), and Lithuania (1938) all joined, as well as the Netherlands and Norway in 1935, Yugoslavia in 1939, and even South Africa in 1937. Ice hockey was becoming an increasingly international game, even though in most of these countries it didn't enjoy the mass popularity, or the participation levels, of association football.

For several decades Canada ruled supreme in international amateur hockey championships. In the years from 1920 until 1953 Canadian teams captured fifteen gold and three silver medals, losing only to the United States in 1933, Great Britain (whose team was mostly made up of expatriate Canadians) in 1936, and Czechoslovakia in 1949. Because of World War II and its aftermath, world championships were not contested between 1940 and 1947. Thus Canadian dominance of international hockey would not be seriously challenged until the mid-1950s, when the Soviet Union first emerged as a hockey superpower. By the late 1950s, though, Sweden, Czechoslovakia, and the United States were also competitive, and Canadians could no longer take success in international hockey for granted.

In 1954 the LIHG adopted the English name of International Ice Hockey Federation (IIHF). The IIHF remained committed to the idea of "amateur" sport, although tensions around the kinds of accommodation that the North American amateur associations were already making with professionalism had created infighting within the organization. Indeed, as far back as 1935 the Canadian Amateur Hockey Association had allowed amateur teams to make payments to players to compensate for lost work time, and it had allowed teams to employ former professional players.[5] In the United States the American

Hockey Association (AHA), with similarly relaxed rules concerning professionalism, fought for authority with the more pristine Amateur Athletic Union (AAU), with both claiming to be the representative body for US international hockey. When the LIHG voted in 1946 to recognize the AHA as its affiliate in the United States (with the support of Canada, Sweden, and Switzerland), the AAU enlisted the support of the United States Olympic Committee, and both bodies sent teams to represent the United States in the 1948 Olympic Games.[6]

The post-World War II admission of the USSR and its Eastern European satellite states into the international sports community brought with it a new notion of amateurism, the state-supported athlete, a phenomenon that was then foreign to the nations of Western Europe and North America that dominated the Olympic movement,[7] and tensions would result from this. Before this the migration of hockey players—whether amateur or professional—had been sporadic and infrequent. When it occurred at all, migration was typically driven by factors other than hockey ambitions, most often the opportunity to live in a new country, learn a new language, or take advantage of a well-established education system.[8] Teams such as the Oxford Canadiens or Japanese medical students, more often than not, were a loosely identified "team of nationals" rather than an official national team.

The entrance of the Soviet Union into international hockey changed this relaxed approach to eligibility, among other things. In 1948 the Communist Party Central Committee informed its national sports community that it was "obligated to increase the number of sports competitions in the USSR. This is necessary in order that Soviet sportsmen, in upcoming years, will surpass the world records in all major sports."[9] One consequence of the Soviet drive for sporting supremacy was that almost immediately the best hockey players available in the USSR were settled in Moscow, where they trained and played as a national team.[10] The subsequent international success enjoyed by the Soviet teams came largely at the expense of Canada. (See Table 11.1.)

Table 11.1
IIHF World Championships

1954–72	GOLD	SILVER	BRONZE	MEDALLING SUCCESS
USSR	11	5	2	18/19 CHAMPIONSHIPS
CANADA	4	3	4	11/19[11]

Canada and the Amateur/Professional Debate in International Hockey

Until 1954 Canada's representative in the IIHF world tournament was a Senior A or Senior B team. The high calibre of senior hockey in Canada reflected the organizational relationships that existed between amateur and professional hockey in Canada. Only the very best players turned professional, with one of the six NHL teams or their farm teams in minor professional leagues such as the American Hockey League (AHL). However, an expansive system of semi-professional and amateur leagues operated across Canada, and the calibre of play was often close to professional standards, even though the players were usually too old to hope for NHL careers.

The top senior players were amateur in the sense that they were not salaried professionals. Thus they complied, strictly speaking, with the criteria established by the International Olympic Committee (IOC) and IIHF. However, most were reinstated professionals or semi-professionals, receiving payments on a game-by-game basis as well as employment in the community in which they played. From the 1930s through the early 1960s the NHL was a relatively exclusive organization, with only six teams and roughly 120 jobs. However, NHL agreements with the minor professional leagues gave the league almost complete control over the hockey labour market, keeping salaries down at every level of the professional game. By contrast, senior amateur hockey, with its excellent calibre of play and the offer of employment in the community, was an attractive alternative for many Canadian players.[12]

In the early postwar years, then, senior teams like the Trail Smoke Eaters, Penticton Vees, Whitby Dunlops, Kitchener-Waterloo Dutchmen, Kimberly Dynamiters, Belleville McFarlands, and East York Lyndhursts represented Canada in international hockey championships sponsored by the IIHF. These teams had considerable pressure placed upon them because the Canadian public expected nothing less than a gold medal in world hockey competition. When the USSR defeated the East York Lyndhursts 7-2 in the 1954 world championship, Canada was shocked, and Canadian hockey fans wondered what had gone wrong. For the Canadian hockey establishment, the solution was simple: send a Senior A team rather than a Senior B one such as the Lyndhursts. And briefly, this did seem to be all that was needed, for the next year the Allan Cup (Canadian Senior A) champions, the Penticton Vees, defeated the Soviet Union in the final, and Allan Cup champions won again in 1958 and 1959.

However, hindsight tells us that sending even reinforced Senior A teams to the World Championships offered little more than a temporary reprieve from the increasing quality of European hockey. With the steady improvement of the Swedes, Finns, and Czechs, as well as the continuing excellence of the teams from the Soviet Union, within ten years Canadian amateur teams were hard-pressed to win any medals at all in world championship tournaments. As this occurred, moreover, European teams began to look east, to the USSR, as the best "teacher" of hockey skills and tactics. Swedish sports historian Tobias Stark describes the transformation in Sweden:

It did not take long before the Swedes ... began to copy the successful Russian game. The change in the Swedish game also was prompted by the weakened stature of

North American ice hockey.... The amateur-teams that Canada and the US sent to international tournaments could no longer count on placing high in the standings.[13]

In Canada, rather than looking frankly and critically at whether our "tried and true" methods were failing us, or acknowledging that the Europeans might have something to teach us, Canadian officials and the Canadian media accused the Soviet Union of cheating. The state-sponsored Soviet players, we maintained, were not amateurs; they were really thinly disguised professionals.

Bunny Ahearne, the Soviet Union, and the "Shamateurism" Debate

With the growing popularity in Europe of the IIHF world championships as a spectator event, leadership in the organization shifted from volunteers to administrators and businessmen who were interested in hockey for its economic potential. The first professional administrator in the IIHF was Walter Brown, but the most influential by far would be John Francis "Bunny" Ahearne, who through political manoeuvrings, diplomacy, and patronage, would lead the IIHF from 1951 until 1975. Born in Ireland, Ahearne volunteered for British military service in World War I and stayed on in London after the war. His business career began in 1927 when he was hired to work in a travel agency, and he opened his own travel business the following year. Ahearne saw his first ice hockey game in 1931 at the Golders Green Arena in North London, and he immediately recognized a great untapped potential for ice hockey as a spectator sport, in the United Kingdom and elsewhere in Europe. He also saw opportunities to position his own company as the primary travel agency for teams (and fans) attending national and international tournaments. However, realizing this potential (on both fronts) would require Ahearne's presence in the sport, as an administrator and deal-maker, and he set about achieving a leadership position. Ahearne's rise as a hockey administrator was both meteoric and sustained. He virtually ran British ice hockey from 1933 until 1982, and from 1951 to 1975 he was one of the top officers of the IIHF, alternating between the offices of president and vice-president.[14]

It was in his IIHF capacity that Ahearne and Canadian hockey officials were often at loggerheads. Ahearne could clearly see the steady improvement of European hockey and took every opportunity to needle Canadian hockey officials. Most annoying for the Canadians was that while Ahearne regularly opposed proposals that would have allowed Canada to use former NHL professionals in international hockey, he accepted the amateur status of the state-sponsored East European players. To Canadians, Ahearne was especially biased when he threatened to expel all IIHF-affiliated teams from Olympic competition if they played against a proposed professional roster of Canadians (reinstated NHLer Carl Brewer and selected American League players) at the World Championships scheduled to be held in Winnipeg. However, Ahearne was also a pragmatic businessman. While insisting on the presence of amateur teams at the IIHF tournaments, he also wanted the attractive spectator draw of the Canadians and Americans to ensure a sizeable profit for his travel agency (which had a virtual monopoly of travel arrangements to the IIHF tournaments). So he was vocal in his support for the idea of a competitive but "non-professional" Canadian national team, thereby setting the stage for an initiative that would be undertaken by Father David Bauer.

In the state-controlled economic system of the Soviet Union, there could be no "professional" athletes because there were no commercial sports, in the sense that there were in North America and Western Europe. Instead there were worker-athletes who represented the Army and other state enterprises (the railways, or chemical factories), and it was the best of these worker-athletes who represented the Soviet Union (and Czechoslovakia) in international hockey competition.[15] These worker-athletes trained full-time for their sport rather than performing normal military or factory duties, so they were professional in one sense. However, they did not enjoy the kinds of economic rewards afforded professional athletes in the West. They did get "perks" such as better housing and preferential access to scarce commodities; but as far as direct economic benefits were concerned, elite Soviet athletes were almost certainly less well off than good semi-professional senior players in Canada. Perhaps it was only semantics, but the Soviet Ice Hockey Federation could truthfully deny that its players were really professional. Worker-athletes were full-time athletes and did not have to work regularly at their nominal "jobs"; however, they were not paid in the same way that professional athletes were paid in North America and Western Europe.

The various IIHF-affiliated nations confronted this difference in interpretations of amateurism in different ways. In many West European countries, athletes in the Olympic sports were paid "under the table," and athletes and officials alike participated in the cynical disregard for the amateur rules that plagued international sport in the 1960s and 1970s (and enraged IOC president Avery Brundage). In Finland, for example, so-called Brown Envelope payments to athletes were widespread. According to one analyst:

> By the 1970s hockey players had become "professional amateurs." Officially they performed as amateurs; in reality many players were semi-professionals who earned extra income from hockey in addition to their day jobs. When it came to international competition, the double standards arising out of "semi-professionalism" were obvious, and especially when it came to the "state professionalism" that existed in Eastern Europe.[16]

The players on Canadian senior teams tended to be semi-professional (probably the most honest and accurate characterization)—often former professional players ("reinstated" amateurs) who were offered jobs (perhaps working for the team owner or another team supporter) that allowed them to devote their energies to hockey. In this, they were not unlike the Soviet bloc players. But they were clearly not Canada's best players, and by the 1960s it had become evident to most Canadians that teams made up in this way could no longer win in international hockey.

Father David Bauer's National Team Experiment: 1963–70

This brings us back to the national team experiment championed by Father David Bauer.[17] Father Bauer was a highly respected teacher and coach at St. Michael's College in Toronto, where he coached the St. Michael's Majors in the Junior A Ontario Hockey League. In 1960–61 the Majors, under Father Bauer's tutelage, won the Memorial Cup, emblematic of Canadian Junior A hockey supremacy. The next year Bauer was transferred to the University of British Columbia (UBC), where he set his sights on a different challenge, restoring Canada's reputation in international hockey. Like many Canadians at that time, Bauer underestimated the rapid improvement in the skill levels of the European hockey-playing nations. He still believed that if Canada's best junior and college players could be housed at a designated university location (UBC) and given full athletic scholarships so that they could train together as a team, rather than being selected only a few weeks before international play, this kind of Canadian national team could compete with the best European national teams, east and west. The validity of the contention will never be known because the NHL hockey establishment stymied Bauer's efforts to establish such a national team at almost every turn.

Father Bauer began his experiment on the UBC campus in the fall of 1963. His team was made up of idealistic young men who believed in Father Bauer and his dream. Several had previously played for Bauer at St. Mike's. Later many of the "Nats," including Ken Dryden, Brian Conacher, Fran Huck, Morris Mott, Roger Bourbonnais, and Brian Glennie, would go on to play in the NHL. But in 1963 the NHL vehemently opposed the creation of a Canadian national team. Not only did the presence of such a team constitute an attractive alternative to playing immediately in the NHL, thus undermining the NHL's monopoly over the future prospects of talented Junior A players, but Bauer's national team concept—with its promise of a university education—also offered players career choices that could put some of them, at least, in a stronger bargaining position vis-à-vis the professional clubs. The NHL actively discouraged the top Junior A players of the day—such as Bobby Orr, Serge Savard, and Yvon Cournoyer—from joining Father Bauer, so that Bauer never did get access to all of the best players in Canada. Nonetheless, the "Nats" gained a well-deserved reputation in Europe as a clean, skilful, aggressive hockey team whose players minimized penalties and, like their European counterparts, refused to fight. One observer describes what a (positive) surprise this was for many people: "The first test for the 'Nats' would be the 1964 Innsbruck Olympics.... They exhibited a high level of skill and sportsmanship rarely seen in previous Canadian entries in International events. European fans were amazed to see Canadian players who didn't fight, or scream at the officials."[18]

The national team under Father Bauer managed three bronze medals in international play in the late 1960s. Significantly, when the players returned to Canada, they echoed sentiments that were already being expressed in Europe concerning the quality of European play. The best Soviets, Czechs, Slovaks, Finns, and Swedes were now playing hockey as well as the NHL professionals were. However, such words mostly fell on deaf ears, and fed up with the hypocrisy of the IIHF and furious with Bunny Ahearne's leadership, Canada decided to withdraw from international hockey in 1970. With this decision, the national team experiment was effectively ended.

Canada, of course, would return to international play with much fanfare in 1972, when a select group of Canadian-born NHL all-stars met the Soviet Union in the famous Summit Series. There were several factors that led to this breakthrough. First, the Soviet Ice Hockey Federation wanted the opportunity to test Soviet hockey against the best that Canada could offer and was pressuring the IIHF to relax its opposition to an "amateur" team competing against the NHL professionals. Second, international hockey had lost a major spectator draw with the absence of the Canadian teams, something that was recognized by other IIHF countries and the Soviets, if not by Ahearne. Finally, in 1971, the International Olympic Committee removed the designation "amateur" from Article 26 of the IOC Charter, and one year later the IOC also recognized the concept of "broken-time payments," which allowed athletes to be reimbursed while absent from work.[19] Together these revisions opened the door for integrated amateur/professional competitions, and eventually led to the participation of professional hockey players for the first time at the 1998 Nagano Olympic Games.

Opening Up the North American Hockey Labour Market—The World Hockey Association

The Summit Series was a wakeup call for the North American hockey establishment, both in respect to the skill level of Soviet hockey players and the enormous spectator appeal that was generated from the games. However, Russian players were not "free," in the 1970s, to pursue professional careers in North America, and there remained considerable resistance in NHL circles to the idea that other Europeans—Swedes or Finns—could improve NHL teams, given the NHL's rougher style of play. But a new rival professional league in North America, the World Hockey Association, was formed in the fall of 1972, and its need for quality players would create new opportunities for European players.

Though ... lampooned by the NHL and given little chance of success, the WHA survived long enough to introduce big-league hockey to many cities the established league had eschewed, to reach further afield for European and occasionally younger players, to spread to North America something of European training regimes and, ultimately to champion and reward fast, offensive hockey. In all this, the WHA was the harbinger of the reinvigorated NHL of the 1980s.[20]

The creation of the WHA was the brainchild of two US entrepreneurs, Gary Davidson and Dennis Murphy, who had earlier founded the American Basketball Association to rival the NBA. Thus they understood what was required in taking on established sports leagues, and according to their market research the National Hockey League was ripe for a challenge. The NHL was financially profitable and had an enthusiastic fan base, but because of its monopoly on the hockey labour market its players were very much underpaid. Most importantly, its conservative expansion policy had ignored many potentially profitable new markets.[21]

When the WHA began play in 1972, there were suddenly seven more major professional hockey teams in North America, a 50 per cent increase over the fourteen teams that had made up the NHL the year before. In one year, then, employment opportunities for hockey players increased dramatically, and the challenge for the WHA was to attract quality players capable of convincing the paying public that the new league was truly as good as the NHL. The problem was that most established players were locked into NHL contracts. The WHA's response was both simple and effective: raid the NHL for established professionals from both the parent and farm clubs, offer more than NHL teams would pay to young (and therefore unsigned) Junior A stars, and bring over European stars, a virtually untapped market. All of these strategies worked, as the following examples attest:

- Eighteen-year-old Junior A players John Tonnelli, Ken Linseman, and Marc Napier, and a seventeen-year-old Wayne Gretzky all signed professional contracts.
- Bobby Hull left the Chicago Black Hawks to join the Winnipeg Jets; Gordie Howe came out of retirement to play with his sons Mark and Marty on the Houston Aeros.
- Swedish players Anders Hedberg, Ulf Nilsson, and Lars-Erik Sjoberg joined Hull on the Winnipeg Jets; Kent Nilsson was recruited to play for the Toronto Toros.
- Czechoslovak stars Vaclav Nedomansky and Richard Farda played for Toronto Toros, Jaroslav Krupicka for the Los Angeles Sharks, and later the Stastny brothers for the Quebec Nordiques.

Arguably the stimulus for the recruitment of elite European players by the NHL in the 1980s and 1990s was the success of skilled Europeans from the WHA after the leagues merged in 1979. Players like Hedberg, Nilsson, and the Stastny brothers were successes by any standard, and after 1980 the recruitment of Europeans became widespread. In some parts of the Canadian hockey establishment, though, animosity lingered towards European players. Some felt that the Europeans were taking jobs that Canadians had a right to; others were disparaging about the less physical style of play favoured by Europeans, and set out to give European players a rough welcome to North American hockey.

European Players: From Derision to Stardom

As early as 1947 the Boston Bruins had taken the then unprecedented step of placing Czechoslovakian player Jaroslav Drobny on the team's negotiation list. Perhaps it was more a publicity stunt than a serious attempt to sign the talented athlete, for Drobny was more committed to tennis than hockey (he later won at Wimbledon), and he never left his homeland to try out with the Bruins.

The first European to try to earn a position in the NHL was Sweden's Sven "Tumba" Johansson, who attended the Boston Bruins training camp in 1957. As a Canadian youngster growing up at that time, I recall listening to radio broadcasts and reading articles that ridiculed the Swedish player for his lack of fortitude (perhaps the birth of the "Chicken Swede" insult). Johansson's most visible sin was that, like most European-trained players, he wore a helmet for safety purposes. Nowadays, Canadian players, too, have grown up wearing helmets; but in 1957 Charlie Burns was one of the few NHL players to do so, and Johansson was a marked man. Despite his considerable size and talent, he was quite literally run out of the NHL.

Another Swedish player, Ulf Sterner, would be released by the New York Rangers several years later (1964–65) because the club had reservations about his ability to stand up to the physical punishment of NHL hockey. Countryman Thommie Bergman, playing for Detroit in 1972–73, began to dispel the myth about Swedish fragility, and Bergman became the first European to play a complete NHL season. By the end of the 1970s, the impact of talented European players in the WHA made them an attractive commodity for most NHL owners and—with the exception of a few notable dinosaurs—the animosity of Canadians towards European players has eased over time.[22]

With the exception of early political defectors (Vaclav Nedomansky, for example) virtually all import players initially came from Western Europe. This began to change after perestroika in 1986, and with the eventual collapse of the Soviet Union. When Vyacheslav Fetisov was given a work permit to leave the Soviet Union and join the New Jersey Devils in 1989, the floodgates opened. The migration of former East European players to North America began in the 1990s, and it now includes not only fully fledged professionals but also—significantly—junior-age players who hope to improve their chances of NHL careers by playing in Junior A hockey in Canada.[23] The NHL became the destination of choice for the world's best hockey players, and professional hockey's labour market became fully international.

The NHL as Global Market Destination

To fully understand the pull of the NHL as hockey's global destination, one must understand both the cultural and economic factors that make players from Europe want to
play in North America. The economic attractions are obvious, but it is important not to
discount the importance of the widely shared belief, both inside Canada and abroad, that
Canadian hockey is best and that players from other countries need to "prove" themselves here. Within Canada, there is a notion of confident superiority that continues to
saturate the Canadian hockey establishment, and Canadian hockey fans more generally.
Many Canadians stubbornly defend the notion that hockey is "our game," and of course
there is much evidence to support this *as a historical claim*. Organized hockey was first
played in Canada, and although the NHL moved very early (in the 1920s) to the more
populous metropolitan centres of the United States, until very recently most NHL players
continued to be Canadian, and the game has deeper roots in popular culture in Canada
than it does anywhere else. Most Canadian boys and a growing number of Canadian
girls have played the game at some time (from pickup shinny to highly organized league
competition), and we do it in greater numbers and with greater proficiency, over a wider
range of skill levels, than is the case in any other country. The latest of many examples of
Canada's prowess in the game are the double gold medals won by the women's and men's
hockey teams at the 2002 Salt Lake City Olympic Games. Moreover, many Canadians
grow up with hockey forming a prominent part of their family life, their school life, and
their public culture, and they learn to appreciate the game. When international events are
held in Canada, such as the 2002 World Junior Championship in Halifax, teams play
before large audiences of sophisticated hockey fans.

In addition, the NHL has a long history as the world's premier professional hockey
league, and it rarely selects senior employees (coaches, general managers) from outside
its own ranks: from Canadian or US university hockey, for example, let alone from
Europe. This creates an "insider" culture, in which NHL people believe absolutely in the
superiority of the NHL game and are condescending towards other leagues, or different
ways of playing the game. This closed attitude towards the value of other kinds of
hockey experience was reflected in the widespread opinion among NHL insiders (and
Canadian media people who covered the NHL) that Bobby Orr's progress as a hockey
player would have stalled had he joined the national team rather than the Boston
Bruins. And the NHL's prowess has been widely respected even by its opponents. Many
forget that in 1972 the Soviet hockey authorities had actively sought out a challenge
series with the NHL because, having dominated IIHF competition (including Canadian
amateur teams) throughout the 1960s, the Soviets saw that they had to test themselves
against the NHL's best if their own aspirations to hockey superiority were ever to be
taken seriously. Canadian hockey fans, for the most part, believed that our NHL professionals would easily thrash the Soviet national team, and although many were taken

aback by the closeness of the outcome, our ultimate victory encouraged many others to continue to trumpet the virtues of the Canadian game.[24]

Our convictions about the superiority of Canadian hockey also produces complacency about our hockey development system, despite accumulating evidence that European countries are producing more highly skilled players. More than thirty years after the 1972 Challenge Series Don Cherry was continuing to reassure Canadians, from his pulpit on CBC's "Coaches Corner," that the Canadian way of playing hockey was best, that Canadian players were still the best in the world, and that the apprenticeship system of the Junior A Canadian Hockey League (CHL) remained the best way for an aspiring young hockey player to reach the NHL. With that thinking widely accepted, it is hardly surprising that many young European players, especially from Eastern European countries that were in turmoil in the 1990s, choose to leave their home countries to pursue their NHL dreams in the Canadian Junior A system. Kristi Allain has documented how the number of European players in the CHL (limited to two imports per team) has increased from 1995 to 2000. (See Table 11.2.)

Table 11.2
Import Players in the CHL

CHL Affiliate	1995-96	1996-97	1997-98	1998-99	1999-2000
OHL	18	28	31	28	38
QMJHL	11	21	25	22	32
WHL	23	31	33	35	37
TOTAL	52	80	89	85	107

Whatever the effects of history and tradition, though, or widely shared beliefs in the supremacy of the Canadian game, it's important to understand that the NHL has enjoyed immense economic advantages over all other hockey leagues simply because it is based in North America, and particularly in the United States. The US and Canadian economies boomed after the war, partly because there was no need for the extensive rebuilding of the economic and social infrastructure that was required in Europe. Throughout the 1950s the United States solidified its position as the global economic leader, and the North American economy, including Canada, created millions of well-paying jobs. It's also germane that North American workers enjoyed unprecedented disposable income in the 1950s and 1960s, and leisure industries boomed: in film, television, music, and sports. In professional sports, the US major leagues all expanded into new markets and established a presence on television, and the NHL was able to participate in this growth (see also chapters 8 and 9). Hockey's established presence as a major league sport meant that when the NHL expanded its recruiting beyond North America to Europe, its reputation as hockey's premier league preceded it. What was more important than reputation, though, was that even though hockey had a long history in Europe, the domestic leagues in West European countries were semi-professional (and in some cases, not-for-profit) operations, playing in rinks that were very small by North American standards, charging low ticket prices, and paying commensurate (that is, very small) salaries.

For example, it was only in the late 1960s that Finland had more than two "spectator-friendly" indoor ice rinks. As late as 1975, Jani Mesikämmen informs us, the Finnish Elite League stipulated that all teams only had "to have a decent roofed home arena."[25] Similarly, the residues of hockey's older "shamateur" conditions lingered on. Under-table payments to hockey players continued well into the 1970s, and it was only the signing of Finnish players to WHA contracts that led to the acceptance of openly professional hockey. On this point, Mesikammen notes: "In the home country their professional status would not have been accepted, but on the other side of the world, among the 'real' professionals, it was appropriate." There was also the assumption in Finland that "no one can match the appeal of the NHL, but the Finnish league should be able to compete with the Swedes."[26]

Not dissimilar conditions existed in Sweden. In 1967 the NHL recognized the National Hockey League Players' Association as the legally certified bargaining unit for hockey players; but it was not until thirty years later that Sweden had its first-ever collective agreement in top-level professional sport. The sports culture of Sweden, much like that of its Finnish neighbour, tolerated Swedish professionals playing abroad, but Swedes were reluctant to fully embrace professionalism at home.

> There have been calls to convert the Elitserien (Swedish Premier Hockey League) to a league that models itself after the NHL, with no relegation and promotion and consisting of profit-oriented clubs, but there is a strong opposition against these suggestions. It seems that the only clubs that are interested in this are a few clubs in the Elitserien, and they alone are not strong enough to win a battle against all other clubs, the Swedish Hockey Association and the Swedish hockey fans.[27]

The situation of the former state socialist nations places them at an economic disadvantage that is even greater than that of the Scandinavian states. For most of Eastern Europe, financial support for economic reconstruction from the International Monetary Fund was forthcoming only on the condition that the social welfare programs of the planned economy would be severely reduced, if not eliminated. Moreover, business personnel in the former USSR and its former allies had to learn to make market capitalism work, and in the absence of the regulatory frameworks that provide some protections to investors (and consumers) in North America and Western Europe. The dismantling of the Soviet Union, and economic and political independence for Russia and its former satellites, has meant a much lower priority for sport than there was in the old USSR, and little if any funding for the high-performance sport systems of the USSR era. In this time of rapid changes (roughly, throughout the 1990s), the organization of hockey collapsed in the former Soviet Union, and there were similar adverse impacts on sport (if less severe) in the new Czech and Slovak Republics.

In Russia the shrinking of the social welfare system and the drying up of funding in former trade-union-operated sports clubs like Spartak, Kril'ya Sovetov, Khimik, and Tractor have taken their toll. In response, many highly skilled athletes from the former USSR and elsewhere in Eastern Europe have taken their considerable talent abroad. Today one sees these former worker-athletes, including large contingents of hockey and soccer players, performing in front of appreciative—and better-paying—foreign audiences. The consequence of this is that young athletes growing up in Eastern Europe now see this career path as the preferred one.[28]

What is thrown into relief here, above all, are the enormous economic resources of the NHL relative to other professional hockey leagues around the world. Even in the wealthiest countries of Western Europe (such as Sweden, Switzerland, and Germany), professional hockey has not been capitalized as commercial entertainment in the way it has been in North America, or in the way that football has been in Europe (see also chapter 12). Very few arenas in Europe seat more than twelve thousand spectators, and ticket prices are low by North American standards. European rinks do not yet have the luxury seating that is now an important revenue stream in all North American professional sports, as well as in newer European football stadiums, and television revenues for domestic European hockey are minimal or (in some countries) non-existent. Thus, although at least half a dozen European countries produce enough elite hockey players to ice competitive national teams, there has been no way for these players to make the kind of money in their own countries that has been available to them in the NHL. Professional hockey as a business remains underdeveloped in Europe, and it still remains unclear whether there are investors with the means and ambitions to develop a European elite league, with the kinds of arenas and salaries that would make it competitive with North American pro hockey.

NHL Hockey or World Hockey?

Few North Americans know much about the calibre of professional hockey abroad, or the challenges facing it if it is to grow into a serious alternative to the National Hockey League. NHL dominance has seemed "natural" to North American hockey enthusiasts for so long that, in contrast to European hockey fans' often detailed knowledge of the North American game, it is the exceptional Canadian hockey fan who knows much about the various European leagues. However, questions are beginning to appear in the European sports press about the status of the NHL as hockey's only major league, and this questioning predates the 2004–05 NHL lockout, though clearly the lockout gave such questions fresh impetus. Several themes are worth highlighting here.

The European Union as foil to North American dominance

Underlying some of Europe's unease about the dominance of the NHL is a more general unease about US power and influence. In visits to various European countries, one often hears arguments about the need to strengthen the European Union in order to create a counterweight, culturally and politically, as well as economically, to the "neighbourhood bully" approach to foreign policy that is widely attributed to the current US administration. In particular, there has been increasing dissatisfaction with American foreign policy since the invasion of Iraq in 2004. In addition, there continues to be discussion in the European press about the need to resist the "Americanization of our culture," be this McDonald's, Disney World, or the increasing penetration of Hollywood films. The migration of well-known European athletes to play in the NHL clearly has different origins than the spread of US brand names in Europe; but it fuels these more general debates about how to combat the dominance of American popular culture. And as this debate grows, the momentum builds for credible European cultural alternatives.

Concern about losing young players who do not go immediately to the NHL

Probably the most common complaint found in European hockey is epitomized by the old proverb about killing the goose that lays the golden egg. While it has been widely understood and accepted that Europe's top players will seek their fortunes in the NHL, many European hockey people are concerned that the mass migration of the 1990s—which included many young players who may not ever play at the NHL level—has hurt the domestic leagues in the countries they have left. For example, Vyacheslav Anisin, a star performer in the 1974 Soviet-WHA series, has expressed concern that young Russian players leave for North America as soon as they can, to the detriment of the Russian league.[29] And Urpo Helkovaara, managing director of the Finnish Ice Hockey Federation, voices similar frustrations: "I'm a supporter of international ice hockey leagues, but they should not sap the strengths of national leagues."[30] The problem is that it is hard for the European leagues to compete with the imagined glamour of life in North America, when this is combined with the lure of NHL salaries if an import player does reach the NHL.

The NHL's refusal to follow FIFA tradition concerning national team play

Another important issue concerns the "rights" of national teams to players who play professionally in the NHL, and indeed the status of world championships, relative to the professional club game. For decades, the top football leagues in Europe have honoured the rights and duties of players to represent their home countries in international competitions organized by the Fédération Internationale de Football Association (FIFA), the governing body that stages the World Cup. In contrast, the NHL has not allowed players whose teams remain in contention for the Stanley Cup to join their national teams for world championship play. From the perspective of NHL owners, it is they who are paying the players' stratospheric salaries, and NHL league play and the Stanley Cup playoffs should take precedence over international hockey. In 2002 the NHL, the NHLPA, and the IOC reached a compromise of sorts for the 2002 Salt Lake City Olympics, when it was agreed that NHL professionals would only join their national Olympic teams if the team reached the final round of the tournament, and the NHL took a short break for the period of this final round. However, some teams (like Slovakia) that failed to make this round had been severely weakened because of the absence of their top performers in the preliminary rounds. Thus, given the priority granted to international over club competitions in the rest of the world outside North America, and the tradition of release for international play in football, the NHL's insistence on giving priority to team owners' property rights does not sit well with many Europeans.

Future Possibilities

The acrimonious negotiations between the NHL and the NHLPA to secure a new collective bargaining agreement and the cancellation of the 2004–05 NHL hockey season only exacerbated dissatisfaction in many quarters with NHL hockey. As a result, previously speculative futures became more realistic, or at least more openly discussed. One scenario involves the creation of a European superleague—the same kind of superleague that Europe's major football clubs have discussed as a way of maximizing their share of television revenues. The precise makeup of such a league in hockey remains purely speculative, and would depend upon the presence of investors and suitable arenas as well as audience interest. However, a European League with teams based in Stockholm, Helsinki, Prague, Cologne, Zurich, Turin, and perhaps two locations in Russia is not far-fetched. These Western European nations are wealthy societies, with standards of living equal to or better than those in North America. They are thus fully capable of supporting elite professional sport, and most of them already do support major league football. What remains necessary, for this scenario to be realized, is, first of all, investors able and willing to build major league arenas (seating at least 17,000 spectators, with luxury boxes and multiple opportunities to sell advertising) and to pay the salaries necessary to attract elite players. What would also be necessary is interest from television networks, for without a television contract, the new league would not get the exposure it would need to take off. Nor would it get the revenues necessary to pay major league salaries without investors losing money.

However, question marks surround the role that Russian businessmen and franchises might play in such a league. There is no doubt that there are entrepreneurs in present-day Russia who could afford to purchase an NHL franchise or, for that matter, bankroll the creation of a professional league to rival the NHL. In May 2004 *Forbes* magazine noted that Russia had risen to number three ranking for the greatest number of billionaires (25), surpassed only by Germany (52) and the United States (279), and tycoons like Roman Abramovich have spent millions to buy success in European football. It is men like Abramovich that Slava Fetisov had in mind when, as the newly appointed chairman of the Russian State Sports Committee, he suggested that Russian entrepreneurs should consider the purchase of an NHL franchise that would be stocked with Russian players.[31] Some of these businessmen have talked about a Russian league that would rival the NHL, and indeed have already lured back Russian professionals from North America and Western Europe with salaries that equal or surpass those offered abroad.[32]

Despite the lure of high salaries, though, the conditions of Russian hockey remain different from those of Western Europe, with poorer rinks surrounded by very poor populations, especially in provincial cities, and living and travel conditions very different from those that NHL players are accustomed to. In addition, there are serious concerns about crime and law enforcement, and the safety of players and officials. There is suspicion that some of the money financing Russian sports today comes from dubious sources, with connections alleged to powerful politicians and industrialists, and to organized crime. It has also been alleged that Russian organized crime figures have extracted protection money from high-salaried Russian players in the NHL; while in Russia itself several high-profile sports officials have been assassinated.[33] Finally, I was told "off the record" by an NHL team official that his team refuses to meet Russian players or their agents in Russia, given the number of robberies that have occurred while scouts were in the country. Clearly, a safer and more stable environment would need to be established before foreign players would play in Russia in any numbers, and before Western European investors would feel comfortable with Russian partners or associates.

A more general set of questions concerns who would play in a European superleague. As far as European players are concerned, there is often an assumption that the European stars in NHL hockey would return to play at home, if the opportunity presented itself. Anecdotal comments about missing the environments of their home countries by players like Peter Forsberg or Jaromir Jagr are taken as evidence of a widespread desire among European players to return home if the salaries are anything like equal. However, the 2004 NHL lockout demonstrated that this assumption may not hold. Peter Forsberg and Henrik Zetterberg went to play in Sweden, but other Swedish NHL stars (Mats Sundin, Markus Naslund, and Daniel Alfredsson) did not, reportedly because of obligations to pay Swedish taxes should they take up permanent residence in that country again. Jaromir Jagr played for a short time in the Czech Republic, before moving on to Russia, when he was offered a higher salary. Almost all prominent European players, though, with the exception of a couple of Russians, signed contracts with NHL clubs for the 2005–06 season.

If the choices facing European players are complicated, those facing Canadian and US players are arguably even more difficult. Some NHL players have clearly thrived playing in Europe. Brendan Morrison of the Vancouver Canucks and Shawn Horcoff of the Edmonton Oilers have been among the leading scorers in Sweden, and apparently enjoyed the experience of living and playing in a different culture, despite making less than their NHL salaries.[34] However, other North American players returned home after short—and disappointing—stays with European teams. Brad Richards, for example, returned to Canada after brief stops in both Switzerland and Russia, having failed to reproduce the form expected of a Conn Smythe Trophy winner. Others simply found living in a foreign language and culture more difficult than they imagined, and they did not have to persevere, in the way that European players pursuing NHL careers have always had to do. Long-time Finnish coach Juhanni Wahlsten observed, "North American players don't seem to be interested in learning other languages.... They seem to be very isolated from other cultures, but this could be because English is so dominant in their part of the world."[35] There are clearly some exceptions to this generalization—in particular, among francophone Canadians. However, if North Americans are going to seek hockey careers in Europe in the future, as opposed to just going for a few months, they will need to work at learning new languages, and at fitting into the cultures of the nations where they are earning their living, just as their European counterparts have always had to do here in order to play in the NHL.

With the players' acceptance of the terms offered by the league in the wake of the cancellation of the 2004–05 season—acceptance in particular of a hard salary cap—the hockey world may well go back to normal. A few older European stars may decide that they have already made enough money and choose not to return to North America, while higher salaries in the Russian league may keep more Russian players at home. However, it also remains possible that new leagues—alternatives to the NHL—will take shape, either in Europe or North America. There have been rumours of plans to launch another version of the World Hockey Association in North America, with many "spectator-friendly" rules changes to entice hockey fans disillusioned with the defensive tactics so prevalent in the NHL today.[36] The NHL has now introduced rule changes intended to address these concerns, and while it remains to be seen how committed the league will be to eliminating defensive obstructions, let alone introducing international-size ice surfaces, any moves to minimize the differences between the North American and European game would make interlocking competition with a European superleague more viable. One could even fantasize about a truly global hockey league, which would include European and North American cities.

Yet the economics of hockey, on both continents, are such that the NHL salaries of the late 1990s—or even the salaries after the new arrangement—are unlikely to be matched by any alternative league. In Europe, even though hockey is very popular in countries like Sweden, Finland, Switzerland, the Czech and Slovak Republics, and Russia, with the qualified exception of the latter these are not the major European markets. In the biggest and wealthiest markets of Europe—Germany, France, Britain, and Italy—hockey has pockets of popularity but remains a minor sport in comparison with football. Thus supporting a hockey team would be a calculated risk for potential investors and advertisers, and hockey itself could not support football-style salaries (or NHL-style salaries), at least in its initial years. Almost certainly, any new European superleague would begin its life with some version of a salary cap.

Likewise in North America, a reborn World Hockey Association would be far from an investment slam dunk. It would not have access to NHL arenas, and so would have to base teams in venues that NHL teams have found wanting in the past: in Winnipeg, Quebec, and other so-called marginal cities, and perhaps in secondary arenas in cities like Toronto, Vancouver, Detroit, and New York. It would also need to try to secure some television revenue in an environment that would be highly sceptical. Again, it is hard to see such a league succeeding without some form of salary cap. Even in 2004–05, it did not go unnoticed that some of the NHL players who chose *not* to play in Europe but played instead in North American minor leagues were playing for much less than they would have made from their NHL employers, and were taking the jobs of minor-league pros in doing so. Kevin Kerr, a career minor-leaguer playing in Flint, Michigan, in the United Hockey League, may have spoken for many minor-league players when he "objected to the (locked-out NHL) players joining the UHL, a league with a strict salary cap, and taking jobs and ice time away from other players, who were just trying to scratch out a meagre, minor-league living."[37]

In this post-lockout period, even with a new agreement in place, it seems that the future of professional hockey is more "up for grabs" than it has been at any time in the recent past. Only time will tell if the NHL will be able to sustain its position as *the* dominant destination for highly skilled hockey players from around the world. It seems possible that someday new professional leagues will emerge in both Europe and North America and elite European players will return to Europe in significant numbers (whether Slovakians or Finns return "home" or to other European countries is another question, and will depend upon the placement of teams in whatever European league emerges). It will also be fascinating to see how many Canadians (and Americans) choose to pursue their careers in Europe, and how many cast their lot with the WHA or whatever other league may emerge on this side of the Atlantic. Whatever happens, Canadian fans might do well to consider the challenges of making a career in another country and culture, and be more appreciative of what "travelling players," both Europeans and Canadians, must do to succeed.

Notes

1 Much of the material here is primary and self-reflective. I listened to the radio as a boy when the Penticton Vees and Belleville McFarlands competed in the world championships. I know several former members of Father David Bauer's national team and have attended world hockey championships in Europe. I spent one year playing for the Solihull Barons of the English First Division.

2 When the 2003–04 version of the Calgary Flames defeated the San Jose Sharks in the NHL's Stanley Cup semi-final playoffs, it became the first Canadian-based team since 1994 to appear in the finals of the championship of what is commonly known as "Canada's game." It did so with a roster of seven Europeans, two Americans, one Brazilian (Robyn Regehr), and eighteen Canadians. None of the Canadians were born in Calgary.

3 Information gathered from the IIHF website <www.iihf.com>.

4 See R. Gruneau and D. Whitson, *Hockey Night in Canada: Sport, Identities, and Cultural Politics* (Toronto: Garamond Press, 1993); see also chapter 1 of this book.

5 R. Gruneau, "When Amateurism Mattered: Class, Moral Entrepreneurship, and the Winter Olympics," in L. Gerlach, ed., *The Winter Olympics: From Chamonix to Salt Lake City* (Salt Lake City: University of Utah Press, 2004).

6 Gruneau, "When Amateurism Mattered," pp. 147-48.

7 H. Cantelon, "Revisiting the Introduction of Ice Hockey into the Former Soviet Union," in C. Howell, ed., *Putting It on Ice*, vol. 2, *Internationalizing 'Canada's Game'* (Halifax: Gorsebrook Institute, 2001).

8 See O. Kivinen, J. Mesikammen, and T. Metsa-Tokila, "A Case Study in Cultural Diffusion: British Ice Hockey and American Influences in Europe," *Culture, Sport and Society*, 4,1 (2001), pp. 49-62.

9 Translated from V.A. Ivonin, ed., *Sputnik: Fizcul'tura i Sport* (Moscow: Fizcul'tura I Sport, 1972).

10 Cantelon, "Revisiting the Introduction of Ice Hockey."

11 Canada withdrew from International Hockey in 1970 in protest at not being able to play reinstated NHL professionals and those who play professionally below the NHL level.

12 Bruce Kidd and John Macfarlane, *The Death of Hockey* (Toronto: New Press, 1972).

13 Tobias Stark, "The Pioneer, the Pal, and the Poet: Masculinities and National Identities in Canadian, Swedish, and Soviet Russian Ice Hockey During the Cold War," in Howell, ed., *Putting It on Ice*, vol. 2.

14 <www.bihwa.co.uk>.

15 Hart Cantelon, "Stakhanovism and Its Influence on the Development of Soviet International Sport," *Proceedings of the Fourth Canadian Symposium on the History of Sport and Physical Education*, University of British Columbia, Vancouver, 1979.

16 J. Mesikämmen, "From Part-Time Passion to Big-Time Business: The Professionalization of Finnish Ice Hockey," in Howell, ed., *Putting It on Ice*, vol. 2, p. 25.

17 Information gleaned from <www.chidlovski.com>, as well as personal contacts with members of the national team.

18 Craig Wallace, "Father David Bauer and the Canadian National Team" <www.chidlovski.com>.

19 A. Strenk, "Amateurism: The Myth and the Reality," in S. Segrave and D. Chu, eds., *The Olympic Games in Transition* (Champaign, IL: Human Kinetics, 1998).

20 D. Hawthorne, "The Lid Never Completely Blew Off: A History of Labour and Management in the World Hockey Association, 1972-1979," In Howell, ed., *Putting It on Ice*, vol. 2., p. 65.

21 Ibid.

22 J. Hedman and T. Metsa-Tokila, "Performance, Ice-Time, and Compensation: A Comparative Analysis of Different Nationalities in the National Hockey League," in Colin Howell, ed., *Putting It on Ice*, vol. 2.

23 K. Allain, "In Other Words: An Examination into the Experiences of Non-North Americans in the Canadian Hockey League," unpublished M.A. thesis, Queen's University, Kingston, 2004.

24 See Ken Dryden, *The Game* (Toronto: Macmillan, 1983), for a critique of the complacency of the NHL hockey establishment.

25 Mesikämmen, "From Part-Time Passion to Big-Time Business."

26 Ibid.

27 Peter Westermark, "Swedish Hockey 101" <www.hockeyfuture.com>.

28 D. Neznanov, "The Next Generation" <www.hockeyzoneplus.com> See also chapter 12 here.

29 D. Neznanov, "The Disaster of the Russian Hockey System" <www.hockeyzoneplus.com>.

30 "Ice Hockey Conquering Europe" <www.publicscan.fi>.

31 Associated Press, "Sports Boss Tells Russia's Rich to Buy NHL Team," *The Edmonton Journal*, Aug. 8, 2003.

32 D. Neznanov, "Salaries in Russian Hockey Championship" <www.hockeyzoneplus.com>.

33 In October 1999, CBC's *Fifth Estate* and PBS's *Frontline* programs produced a joint documentary, "Mafia Power Play," which examined suspected links between organized crime in Russia and Russian players in the NHL.

34 Grant Kerr, "NHLers Accepting New Roles in Hockey's Global Marketplace," *The Globe and Mail*, Feb. 25, 2005, p. R9; E. Ebden, "The Year of Living Frugally," *The Globe and Mail*, Feb. 23, 2005, p. B10.

35 J. Wahlsten, "Understanding International Hockey" <www.members.tripod.com>.

36 K. Yorio, "Alternative Is spelled WHA" <www.findarticles.com>.

37 Eric Duhatschek, *The Globe and Mail*, Feb. 23, 2005, p. R5.

CHAPTER TWELVE

Globalization in Professional Sport: Comparisons and Contrasts between Hockey and European Football

■ JULIAN AMMIRANTE

F ootball (soccer) and hockey represent much more than sport for many fans. In South America, *futebol* (or *futesbol*) is said to "have the capacity to make people delirious."[1] In Europe as early as the 1920s football was considered a sort of cross-national Esperanto. A popular communal practice in many European countries, it provided languages of identity and rivalry that were widely understood. In Africa from the period of colonial rule through the political and economic struggles of the post-independence years, football remained a source of popular enthusiasm and passion, symbolically connected to aspirations for national identity and development.[2]

Hockey in Canada arguably serves comparable functions. Watching hockey is a favourite pastime for millions of Canadians, and during the National Hockey League playoffs the size of hockey audiences and (even more) the ubiquity of conversation about hockey make the game seem inextricably a part of Canada's national culture. Then too, while hockey perhaps does not provoke quite the same passions in other countries where it is played at a high level—countries such Sweden, the United States, the Czech Republic, and Russia—the game still has a considerable following there as well as in other West European nations (Switzerland, Germany, France, Italy, United Kingdom) that have well-established professional leagues.

Since the mid-1980s both professional football and professional hockey have undergone significant changes *as businesses*. Player salaries in the top leagues have risen dramatically, and these leagues—in football, in Spain, Italy, and England; and in hockey, in North America (the NHL)—have seen an influx of players from other countries where professional athletes make much less money. Also noteworthy has been the construction of new kinds of stadiums or arenas, each with seating aimed at corporations and higher-income fans, as opposed to the working-class or blue-collar fans who used to be the core audiences in each sport. Finally, sports ownership today requires vastly larger sums of capital, and attracts different kinds of entrepreneurs than the civic-minded individuals of earlier eras. Sports teams are structured as franchises (in North America), and publicly traded companies (in England), and in both cases are now more likely to be owned by absentee owners or by corporations, often corporations also involved in the television business.

Although professional sports teams have been business enterprises for decades, the very magnitude of the recent changes in how these businesses are run is striking. In Europe professional football clubs have transformed themselves from quasi-public institutions, whose purpose was the provision of a "public good" to local enthusiasts (sporting representatives of whom the community could be proud), into private corporations pursuing the logic of profit maximization. What is more, many sporting clubs have become part of integrated strategies of capital accumulation. Where a football or hockey club was once primarily an object of passion for local *maecenas*, a hobby business whose primary source of revenue was gate receipts, investment in sports is now seen as a rational strategy of capital speculation and accumulation, in which money can be made from advertising and merchandising, from media rights, and from increases in the market value of the team. Much, if not all, of this can be attributed to the advent of television, in particular, pay (cable and satellite) TV. Developments in television, both as a technology *and* as a business, have led to dramatically greater revenues for those professional sports able to sell themselves successfully as television entertainment. There is, as a result, far more money in sports than there used to be, and this has changed the nature of sports as a business. It has also altered the relations between team owners (now driven to evaluate their investments in bottom-line terms because of the amounts involved), players, and fans.

Yet why is it that these changes have taken place in the last ten to fifteen years and not before? And what are the factors that have spurred these extensive transformations? Here it's useful to make some general observations about the growth of the "culture industries," and the enormous profit potential of "soft" or experiential goods: products that may last only hours or even minutes (a sports event, a concert, a CD, or a movie), but are very highly valued because of their "sign values" (their cultural associations) and their popularity with other consumers.[3] It's further important to understand how the globalization of culture has opened up possibilities for globalization in the culture industries: the prospect of truly enormous worldwide audiences for products like sports and films. However, this brings with it the possibility, at least, of market domination by a handful of global entertainment conglomerates.

There is agreement among social scientists that since the early 1970s unprecedented changes have occurred in the international economy. Broadly, the 1970s were a period of economic restructuring in the so-called developed economies of Europe and North America. This meant, among other things, that investment capital became increasingly mobile, moving to wherever it could be invested most profitably. In addition, though, capital gained a greater flexibility—in particular the capacity to move money out of traditional industries where profitability was decreasing into new businesses where the rates of profit and the projected turnover times (the time frames within which returns on investment could be expected) were more promising.

Partly as a result of the growth and democratization of leisure in Western societies (many more people had free time and disposable income), and partly due to new communications technologies (at first broadcast television, but later other information technologies) that were capable of taking entertainment products across national boundaries and thus to audiences of unprecedented size, a whole range of cultural industries—including popular music and film, as well as spectator sports and the production of every other kind of infotainment programming—became objects of great investor interest. The cultural industries grew dramatically, and they became important features of the largest Western economies. For not only can the original products—a football game, a concert—be produced and sold far more frequently than hard goods like automobiles or refrigerators, but reproductions of cultural performances can also be sold many times over, and around the world. Indeed, one meaning of cultural globalization is that cultural practices that were once national or even regional are now, as cultural *products*, actively promoted in parts of the world in which they have no history. Although this project doesn't always work (the NHL's efforts to grow the game in the Southern United States have been a limited success, at best), for those cultural products that do succeed in attracting global audiences (successful Hollywood films, for example), the potential profits are staggering.

Thus, as investors and entrepreneurs began to see limits to the profits available in the production and turnover of hard goods, they not surprisingly turned to the provision of cultural commodities, now seemingly feeding an ever-expanding range of cultural goods and styles. This enterprise has led, in turn, to an unprecedented variety of consumer choices, and a corresponding range of consumer identities.[4] It has also placed a premium on aesthetic innovation and novelty, and the investment of enormous resources in advertising and promotion, as "capitalism produces fresh waves of ever more novel-seeming goods ... at ever greater rates of turnover."[5] Fashion has been mobilized to accelerate the pace of consumption, and not only in clothing (what "fashion" used to refer to), but also across a wide range of recreational activities and lifestyle choices, of which new sporting interests are only one example. Moreover, the choice of newly available leisure activities (ultimate Frisbee, for example, or rock-climbing), and the identities associated with them, are often linked, through lifestyle advertising, with the consumption of a wide range of other products.[6] In making these connections, global leisure brand names have made themselves, and indeed the idea of conspicuous consumption, the personification of self-expression.

The other important factor in the profitability of the culture industries, of course, is the almost unlimited commercial potential of globalization. Given a vastly increased capacity for transnational communications, and the increased normalcy of transnational corporate empires, the world has witnessed since the 1960s a steady intensification of cultural and economic integration. Facilitated by new information technologies and by increasing integration in the communications and entertainment industries (both geographic integration, and integration between producers of content and owners of distribution networks), the world has undergone an unprecedented compression of time and space.[7] This phenomenon has broadened the horizons of hundreds of millions of individuals who can now follow, via television and the Internet, sports events that are taking place in distant parts of the world (such as Champion's League Football, or the Super Bowl). However, it has also shifted the horizons of investors, so that figures like NFL owner Malcolm Glazer and the prime minister of Thailand now seek to buy leading English football clubs, while media giants like Fox and ESPN see the potential money to be made in the construction of global audiences.

Indeed, this drive to construct global audiences is probably the single most important factor in the creation of a "global entertainment culture" that has variously been described as homogenized, Americanized, Westernized, or simply based on the globalization of consumerism.[8] The global expansion of the leisure and entertainment industries undoubtedly brings new opportunities to many of us—opportunities to watch or even practise sports that were once not available in our home countries—and this development is heralded by those who want to celebrate the benefits of increased consumer choice.[9] However, critics point to the metropolitan derivation of most of the cultural products (and the lifestyles) that attain worldwide promotion and distribution, and to how the global entertainment industry is dominated by a handful of super-corporations.[10]

This is the larger economic and social context, then, in which the businessmen who run football in Europe and hockey in North America have tried to expand their audiences in recent years, and to cultivate new revenue streams. Yet although it is relatively easy to sketch out the economic logic behind these initiatives, and indeed to sketch the growing place of sport (or, at least, of entertainment) in global strategies of capital accumulation, it is also necessary to point to the fans—and the cultural traditions—that have been left behind as these sports have moved "upmarket." In both Canada and Europe, the close identifications that many local fans once had with their teams have been attenuated, some would say sundered. This has led sociologist Anthony King to propose that contemporary changes in sport cannot be adequately theorized within the confines of purely economic analysis,[11] and I would argue that the transformations occurring in football and hockey—social and cultural changes, as well as economic ones—reflect a transition from one kind of social order to another that is occurring in advanced capitalist societies.

This chapter examines recent developments in European football and North American hockey, focusing on the cultural and economic forces that are reshaping these two sports at the professional level. It compares the extent to which these two sports have effectively become integrated corporations, responding to global market logic. Broadly, I argue that whereas watching football or hockey was once a generally affordable leisure practice, part of the national popular cultures of their respective "homes," both sports have now become global products—and products that are increasingly priced out of reach of ordinary fans. Their corporate entities (leagues and international governing bodies) now behave in a manner more akin to international firms than to traditional sporting associations, in each case forcing innovations in the traditions of their respective sports in order to maximize the commercial potential of the product.

It would be difficult and perhaps pointless to identify precisely when these transformations took place, and arguably European and NHL hockey are at different stages in these processes of commodification. Nonetheless, four important movements—or aspects of the larger transformative process—can be brought into focus, with comparisons and contrasts between the two sports highlighted where appropriate.

1. the changing nature of the sports club, from civic institution to moveable asset;
2. merchandising, and the construction of consumer identities;
3. the liberalization of labour; the successful campaigns—very different in Europe and North America—to challenge the power and control of the owners;
4. the impacts of television on the business of professional sport.

By examining these developments, and the connections between them, I seek to demonstrate that the economic agendas of European football and NHL hockey today reflect the expansionist logic of global capitalism. I will argue that the social and cultural consequences of them—for fans, and indeed for the sports themselves—are profound.

The Changing Nature of the Sport Club

A full grasp of the changes in each of these sports calls for an examination of the changes occurring in the nature of the sporting club, association, or organization. The historical starting point here is the distinctive communal relationships that developed between fans and sporting clubs, wherein a type of collective consciousness was encouraged. In Europe these relationships produced unique subcultures based around particular football clubs; established supporters would encourage young men to join their particular "tribe," most of which were steeped in a male working-class ethos. The identities dividing one group of supporters from another were normally local rivalries, although neighbourhood rivalries within major cities such as London could reflect the class or ethnic differences between parts of the city (Millwall and Tottenham, for example). However, religious differences (notably the historic Protestant-Catholic divides in

Glasgow and Liverpool) or political affiliations (such as Lazio's historical associations with fascist "Ultras" in Rome) could give an added edge to communal animosities. What was common to all these scenarios, though, was groups of men bound together by their passions for football and for their team.[12] They were members of communities, and this sense of membership, and of clubs belonging to the membership, was strong.

Football clubs in Britain and other European countries quite often operated at a deficit, and were considered a philanthropic hobby. In many cases the men who were involved in building these clubs sought to have the team embody the values of the sponsoring institution, sometimes a church or private school, but more often a factory or other place of employment.[13] In other cases sponsors simply sought to encourage local or civic pride. Although the sense of communal solidarity and pride that accrued around successful football clubs was very male, it would typically cross generational lines and often class lines, too. Entry to the grounds was sufficiently cheap to be almost universally affordable, and as football clubs grew in popularity, local men (the rank-and-file supporters, who turned out regularly on the terraces) came to see themselves as being members of a communal enterprise, however inaccurate or exaggerated that understanding may have been.

The Canadian example is somewhat different, in that prior to World War I the highest levels of organized sport were, for the most part, the enterprise of more affluent sectors of society. In Montreal, sporting competition was first organized by upper-class and middle-class social clubs and by private schools and universities, organizations that had grounds and other facilities but were also deeply imbued with the hierarchies and attitudes of Victorian England.[14] Although most clubs sought out other good players (notably from the Irish and French communities in Montreal), sports teams of this era typically comprised men who worked and lived within the locality and acted as representatives of that locality in regional and then national competitions (see chapter 1). Moreover, given the new public identities that came with urbanization in early twentieth-century Canada, civic identifications did not follow in any automatic way, and sporting competition played an influential role in the creation of networks and rivalries among and between communities. As men from Montreal, Toronto, and other Canadian centres created national competitions such as the Stanley Cup, they not only created a structure for amateur sport—later to be appropriated by commercial interests—but also facilitated the development of civic and regional identities, *all within a framework that was national*. Indeed, national championships quickly became one of the traditions that brought people from different parts of Canada together around common interests, thus contributing to the building of a national popular culture, and a national identity.[15]

As both football in Europe and hockey in Canada became professionalized, the need for more capital (for player salaries, ground improvements, travel) would consolidate control of the club in the hands of those in a position to be investors: typically, the local bourgeoisies. Nonetheless, this type of ownership did not immediately divorce the rank-and-file supporter from the club. In their early beginnings, sporting clubs were not nearly as concerned with money-making as are the high-profile clubs of today. In fact, the sporting club or association was not seen as a profit-making institution so much as one of a community's public institutions. The sports club, in this sense, was not dissimilar to the public library or town square, that is, a public amenity to be enjoyed by the people.[16] In North America professional sport was always more business-like, not least in the sense that teams in the early twentieth century moved around, going to other communities (and arenas) where their owners thought they could operate more profitably. However, once in their new homes, teams actively sought to trade on representative sentiments and to build fan support by constructing identifications between the team and the community.[17]

The institution of the sporting club or association, then, initially supported a tradition wherein fans, or rank-and-file supporters, believed they had some control over the club's operating policies and its managing officers.[18] Since the 1970s this view has become increasingly illusory. As commercial pressures and opportunities have increased in each sport, leading to expansions and team relocations (in North America) and the proliferation and integration of international tournaments (in European football), proprietary interests have begun to dominate as never before.[19] Since at least the early 1980s, fans have been increasingly seen—at least in the eyes of owners and the mass media—primarily as consumers of sporting products (live games, televised games, licensed merchandise), rather than as supporters in the traditional sense. This restructuring may seem to be trivial; after all, almost since its inception, sport has had commercial interests and objectives attached to it. However, the development and integration of the culture industries since the 1970s represent a significant development, one that provided the impetus for the restructuring of professional sports in accordance with commercial logic. It is this that has altered the older type of relationship between supporters and sporting clubs and has set the stage for the construction of a new type of relationship, based on marketing and consumer choice.

Merchandising and the Construction of Consumer Identities

Once commercial imperatives entered the realm of sport with a new force, the relationship of the fan to the sporting club was increasingly reduced to a purely economic status, governed by the logic and incentives of the market. Substantive debate over the effects of this change is almost always sidestepped when the rules that govern market relations are granted the status of immutable logic. However, it is precisely the transformation of the sporting club into a straightforward capitalist enterprise that deserves examination—because it is a transformation that alters the relationships between sports and fans, as it has done in both European football and NHL hockey. Sport came to be seen as a profitable arena for investment, with money to be made in advertising and corporate hospitality, in media rights, in the rising values of sports franchises (or shares), and in merchandising. Famous clubs, in particular, have sought to maximize sales of licensed merchandise—jerseys, scarves, flags, caps, and other souvenirs bearing the emblem and colours of the team—while also promoting new products and services (such as videos, and Internet-based informational services). In essence, clubs like Real Madrid and Manchester United in football, the New York Yankees in baseball, and the Chicago Bulls in basketball have tried to market themselves as internationally recognized brands, and have gone to considerable lengths to maximize the value of those brands.

Of course, sports clubs have for years sold what were referred to as replica "kits," or team jerseys. However, with the promotional success of club merchandise as fashion statements, and as statements of "elective affinities,"[20] the revenues and profits would expand exponentially. In European football, English clubs were the first to realize this potential, and nowhere is this illustrated better than in the case of Manchester United. In 1994 the club revealed that it had earned £26 million from merchandising and spon-sorship, compared to just £1.3 million only seven years earlier. Even more significant, though, is that the club earned only £18 million in gate receipts in that same year, dis-tinctly less, in other words, than it did from merchandising. The club's staff included 123 people in merchandising, catering, and administration compared with 74 on the playing side (43 players, 31 coaching staff).[21] So successful was the brand of Manchester United that it expanded into the Middle East and Asia with retail shops, and signed a marketing agreement with the New York Yankees baseball team in 2001.

However, Manchester United was not alone in seeking to maximize revenues from this source. Barcelona Football Club (Barcelona FC), one of Spain's (and Europe's) most successful and widely followed clubs, made £18 million in 2001 from licensed products sold through a nationwide network of shops.[22] Adapting some of Manchester United's marketing strategies, Barcelona FC recently made plans to open more than one hun-dred small shops throughout Spain over a period of five years. Not to be outdone, Italian football clubs have also enthusiastically embraced the new merchandising ethos as club after club licensed their logos and opened shops across Italy.[23]

In the exploitation of hockey's commercial potential the NHL was slower off the mark than were the other big league sports in North America. The NHL expanded somewhat reluctantly in the 1960s, and it was also slower to embrace the potential of television. Although the NHL had contracts for US network broadcasts in 1968–72 (with CBS) and 1973–75 (with NBC), because of disappointing viewer ratings neither of these contracts was renewed, and NHL hockey fell further behind its major league competitors—NFL foot-ball, NBA basketball, and Major League Baseball—both in the revenues that it drew from television and in the more intangible quest for visibility in popular culture that turns team sweaters and caps into fashion items. By the early 1990s, when television revenue constituted more than half the total revenue of major league baseball and basketball, and almost two-thirds of the revenue of NFL football, NHL hockey was lagging far behind. The Toronto Maple Leafs and the Montreal Canadiens had always sold replica jerseys in sporting goods stores across Canada; but few other NHL teams sold merchandise beyond their own markets, and merchandise revenues in the United States remained very small.

It was not until the 1988 sale of Wayne Gretzky to the Los Angeles Kings that this would begin to change. Gretzky's move to Southern California ushered in a new era in the NHL, in which marketing, merchandising, and US expansion would move to the forefront of the strategic agenda. This was to some extent a product of a changing of the guard in the NHL power structure in the early 1990s, with Los Angeles Kings' owner Bruce McNall briefly becoming chairman of the NHL governors, and with the hiring of NBA executive Gary Bettman with a mandate to "grow the game" along the same lines that had succeeded in the NBA.[24] McNall's strategy of promoting hockey in the booming US Sunbelt states would also be evident in the speedy granting of expansion franchises to entertainment giants Disney (the Anaheim Mighty Ducks) and Blockbuster Video (the Florida Panthers) in 1992–93 (see chapter 9). With the hiring of Bettman and the advent of these two teams, the promotion of NHL licensed merchandise would take off in earnest. Alhough the NHL remained well behind the other major North American leagues in the early 1990s, the sale of licensed NHL apparel nonetheless grew tenfold from 1989 to 1999, from only $100 million to $1 billion.[25]

A key to this development was Wayne Gretzky's star power, which drove NHL merchandising in California and elsewhere in the United States. Gretzky became a familiar icon in US advertising; not unlike Michael Jordan, the Gretzky name and face became recognized even among people who had never seen him play. However, even though endorsement opportunities would increase the earning power of other NHL stars, no subsequent hockey players have become public figures of a similar stature, let alone brands in their own right, in the manner of a Gretzky, a Jordan, a David Beckham, or a Tiger Woods. Likewise, even though the Mighty Ducks of Anaheim sold many replica jerseys, lunch pails, and other Disney products to children, and the marketing strategies of the Mighty Ducks now represent an interesting case study in the dynamics of cross-marketing,[26] sales of Mighty Ducks merchandise have never come close to those of the larger European football clubs, or indeed to those of the most successful US clubs in other sports. Indeed, even though the Toronto Maple Leafs and Montreal Canadiens can still sell merchandise across Canada, no NHL hockey team has succeeded in becoming an international brand name in the manner of Real Madrid, Manchester United, and Barcelona—or the New York Yankees, Chicago Bulls, and Dallas Cowboys—all names that are famous well beyond devoted fans of their sports.

But what is it that has made teams like these into internationally recognized brands, and what does branding mean for the relationships between teams and their fans?

A successfully established brand is normally intended to create, in the minds of consumers, associations between the producer's name or logo and historical standards of excellence (or, at least, style) that consumers have come to expect. All of the teams mentioned above have records of competitive success over the years, even though it is in the nature of professional sports that consistent success is hard to sustain.[27] However, as the case of Manchester United suggests, the teams that have been most successful in constructing themselves as international brands have distinguished themselves from other successful teams (Arsenal, in England, or Juventus, in Italy) in the money and strategic effort they have devoted to promoting themselves, especially in parts of the world (in Asia, for example, and North America) where there is room for dramatic growth in the popularity of football-related products.[28] Thus we need to recognize the impacts of the advertising and marketing industries in promoting *new* markets for sports, for sports celebrities like Jordan and Gretzky, and for sports-related merchandise. Indisputably, it is advertising and marketing that have produced the explosion of money in sports in the last two decades, as well as the globalization of sporting consumption.[29]

Most importantly, whether it is Manchester United, Real Madrid, and the New York Yankees promoting new markets for their products in Asia, Barcelona promoting the sale of team jerseys all over Spain, or the NHL and the NBA promoting sales of their licensed merchandise in parts of North America where their respective games are not widely played, sports fans are being addressed as free-floating consumers. On the surface, this "de-localization" of sporting loyalties simply reflects a decline in the old norm of cheering for the home team, and an increased tendency—understandable in a media age—to follow the fortunes of famous and successful teams that get lots of media coverage.[30] At a deeper level, though, languages that spoke to identities rooted in place and in local rivalries are being actively undermined by a marketing discourse in which consumers in faraway places are invited to identify with "world class" teams and players, and to take pride in their consumption of "world class" sports products.[31] In an earlier era fan allegiances were normally expected to reaffirm the individual's membership in a local community, thereby also reaffirming traditional, place-bound, ways of defining "us" and "them." Now fan affinities are framed as consumer choices—choices to be made on the grounds of success, style, celebrity stars, and sheer presence in the media— and this is particularly apt to be true among the young, for whom the place-bound loyalties of their parents may have little appeal.[32]

The Liberalization of Labour

On December 15, 1995, the European Court of Justice (ECJ) came to a decision that reshaped the landscape of football in the European Community (EC). By ruling on a restraint of trade complaint against football authorities throughout the EC, in favour of a lower-division Belgian player named Jean-Marc Bosman, the ECJ conclusively transformed the financial and contractual traditions that had characterized European football for more than a century. At first glance the Bosman ruling was simply a good example of the power that the ECJ wields over the member states of the EC. However, the implications that this decision carried for football were far more expansive than onlookers might have initially imagined. The ruling effectively transformed football from an industry whose traditions and rules had extra-legal status into an industry that had to obey labour laws like any other. Where, before Bosman, football's labour costs were stabilized by rules and quotas set by the various national football authorities, now owners and players were obliged to adapt to market forces.

In particular, what was at stake in the Bosman ruling was the legitimacy of practices like transfer fees and restrictions on foreign players, as obstacles to player mobility. The practice of transfer fees was a system whereby football clubs had the right to set fees (typically negotiated) when one of their players moved to another club, even if his contract had expired. The objective was to protect smaller clubs from raiding by financially powerful ones, or at least to ensure that the small clubs received a fair return on their investment in the player's development. In addition, a three-plus-two rule meant that each club could employ a maximum of three non-nationals (from other EC countries) and two further non-EC nationals. The rationale for this restriction was that it would maintain opportunities for nationals within each country, while also offering clubs the opportunity to import a limited number of highly talented players, thereby improving the team and heightening interest among spectators. In the Bosman case, the player's contract with his club, RC Liege, had expired in 1990 and the club had offered him a new deal, but at a 60 per cent cut in salary. Not surprisingly, Bosman began looking for a new place to ply his trade, and he received a better offer from a French club, Dunkerque. However, RC Liege exercised its right to charge a transfer fee on his move, in this case a fee set at €250,000, which Dunkerque refused to pay. Bosman refused to re-sign with Liege and was suspended by the team. Since such suspensions were automatically honoured in all United European Football Association (UEFA) countries, Bosman would then claim that the Belgian Football Federation and UEFA rules constituted restraints on labour mobility that prevented him from working.

Between August 1990 and December 1995, Bosman attempted to persuade the European courts to call all transfer fees illegal, thereby permitting professional football players to move freely to other European clubs without any transfer fees. Bosman's lawyers sought a declaration that the transfer rules and nationality clauses were in violation of the rules on the free movement of workers established by the Treaty of Rome. Under Article 48, which deals with the free movement of labour within the UC, Bosman raised the question a) should football clubs be allowed to require and receive payment from another team for a player who has come to the end of this contract, and b) should national and international football federations be permitted to set regulations that restrict the access of players from other European Union countries to the competitions that they organize? The Court ruled broadly in Bosman's favour, declaring that clubs were no longer able place a limit on the number of EC nationals on their squads, and that players at the end of their contracts are free to move to any club in another EC country without the payment of any kind of transfer fee. The abolishment of these restrictions immediately led to a flood of players moving from one country to another, something that brought football into compliance with what the Treaty of Rome had intended to accomplish with respect to labour mobility in other fields of work.

Interestingly, though, this player movement quickly took on a pattern that was common to the flows of other migrants within the EC—players moved from poor clubs and from poor countries to wealthier clubs in wealthier countries. Immediately a flood of players moved from countries such as Portugal, Hungary, Poland, Croatia, and the former Soviet states to countries such as England, Italy, and Spain, where the wealthier clubs, in particular, are able to pay much higher salaries. In addition, there was a massive rush by South American football players of European origins to obtain EC passports from the countries from which their ancestors had emigrated.[33] Indeed, the extent to which talented Latin American players have flocked to take advantage of the higher salaries paid in Europe prompted Uruguayan writer Eduardo Galeano to suggest that in countries like Argentina, Brazil, and Uruguay, football was becoming an "export industry."[34]

In the aftermath of Bosman, critics predicted that the abolition of transfer fees would lead to the end of many small clubs in Europe. Traditionally, smaller clubs, in the lower divisions of their national leagues or even those who move back and forth between the first and second divisions, have relied heavily on selling promising players in order to survive financially. A football club's most liquid assets are its players, and selling good young players to clubs further up the league table has been a commonly used financial strategy. One big sale could bring in more money than a season's gate receipts, and it could help to keep a struggling club afloat. After the Bosman ruling, players whose contracts had expired were free to go as they pleased, and the clubs that had invested in their training and instruction were guaranteed nothing in the way of compensation.[35] Some of these clubs, and arguably lower-division football itself, now faced an uncertain future.

Conversely, the more powerful football clubs have freely exploited the possibilities available to them after Bosman. The wealthiest clubs in Europe—Manchester United and Chelsea in England, AC Milan, Inter Milan, and Juventus in Italy, Real Madrid and FC Barcelona in Spain, and Bayern Munich in Germany—now regularly field teams where imports outnumber nationals, in some cases by a significant margin. By limiting the transfer-fee system to players still under contract and eliminating the three-plus-two rule, the Bosman ruling effectively dismantled UEFA rules that had limited player mobility and helped to contain player salaries. Neo-liberals might argue that, in principle, removing barriers to labour supply and wage flexibility should lead to more efficient utilization of football labour.[36] But what has happened in practice is that the larger clubs in the wealthier Western European nations have been able to poach highly skilled players from smaller clubs, and from poorer parts of Europe and elsewhere in the world (not just from South America, but also increasingly from Africa and Asia).

In hockey the removal of restrictions on player mobility has followed different dynamics, and indeed NHL hockey remains far more regulated today than is European football. Ever since the NHL emerged in the 1930s as hockey's only major league (having driven its competitors in other parts of North America out of business), NHL owners have enjoyed a monopsony position as the only significant buyers of professional hockey talent. Monopsony is essentially the mirror image of monopoly, but where monopolists derive their power from being the only seller of a product in a given market (and thus can set the price they will sell at), monopsonists derive their power from being the sole buyer of a good or a service. When this service refers to labour, as it normally does, the effect in practice is that employers are in a position to set wage and salary levels, because there are no alternative employers in that field of work.

This was long the situation in professional hockey, with the brief exception of the 1970s when the WHA offered employment choices, and therefore salary competition. Until then, NHL owners had effectively controlled the hockey labour market through the reserve clause that was part of the standard player contract. The reserve clause effectively bound players to the team that held their contracts for as long as the teams considered their services necessary, and as was the case in football, players who were out of contract could not shop their services around to other teams. This placed NHL owners in an enviable position, because there were no other buyers of hockey labour, and disgruntled players had nowhere else to turn. However, unlike the situation in European football, where the national monopsonies enjoyed by the major national leagues in football were ended suddenly by a ruling of the European Court of Justice (and not until 1995), change came to hockey somewhat earlier but less completely. In the 1960s US court rulings against the validity of the reserve clause in baseball established an important legal precedent. In the other sports the brief existence of competitive leagues (the AFL and WHA), together with the threat of anti-trust suits from players when these leagues merged with their erstwhile rivals, persuaded the surviving leagues to negotiate looser controls on player mobility.

However, the major factor in the achievement of greater player mobility in North American professional sport has been collective bargaining, and the existence of stronger player unions than in Europe. In hockey, until the late 1980s, the NHL Players' Association was led by Toronto lawyer Alan Eagleson, who would ultimately be accused of failing to adequately represent players' interests on a series of financial issues. Following Eagleson's replacement as head of the NHLPA by Bob Goodenow, though, and a new initiative on the part of the NHLPA and player agents to publish player salaries publicly, NHL salaries rose dramatically, to levels akin to those of the other major sports (even though NHL revenues remained markedly lower). As well, hockey players had begun to use the services of agents, and these agents were able to collectively discuss how their clients' salaries could be systematically maximized, through arbitration and free agency.[37] Significantly, the terms and conditions for free agency (when players are eligible to move, and when a player's former club is entitled to compensation) became central issues, after 1989, in collective bargaining negotiations between the NHL and the NHLPA.

The wealthiest owners, meanwhile, sensing large rewards in marketing and merchandising (as well as competitive success) if the services of star players could be secured, began to spend unprecedented amounts for those services.[38] The sums of the early 1990s seem paltry by current standards; but for a league that was still surviving mainly on gate revenues, the multi-million-dollar salaries and long-term contracts were gambles on a different kind of future—a future that promised new revenues from expansion, from more lucrative television contracts, from luxury boxes, and from merchandising and endorsements. Star players were the first beneficiaries, clearly; but free agency became a predictable point in an established player's career when he could expect a large raise. Moreover, with a system of qualifying offers set at 110 per cent, and an arbitration system that established comparable salaries for players posting comparable statistics (whether their teams had large revenues or limited ones), the salaries of journeyman players also began to escalate rapidly, and owners found themselves negotiating from positions of weakness. This was the "business model," then, that owners determined to fix through a salary cap.

The Arrival of Pay TV

In Europe, some of the bigger and more ambitious clubs began to systematically pursue the same lucrative secondary sources of revenue as did their North American counterparts: merchandising and luxury seating, in particular. However, in contrast to the NHL, at least, European football generates massive television audiences, which has led, in the last twenty years, to a rapid revolution in football broadcasting. Perhaps the signature moment came in 1992, when the English Football Association and Rupert Murdoch's BSkyB satellite sports channel Sky Sports announced a groundbreaking TV deal that gave Sky exclusive rights to coverage of English football's newly established Premier League—a breakaway league made up of twenty-two of England's strongest and most wealthy clubs.[39] This new arrangement cost BSkyB £304 million over five years and became the model for the rest of Europe as the leading football clubs throughout Europe and their owners came to realize that large profits could be made through the televising and marketing of professional football. It was not coincidental, though, that Sky's rights to televise English football—which historically had been shown on the public BBC, that is, for free—were instrumental in selling millions of British viewers on the value of signing up for satellite TV subscriptions (and all the necessary equipment).

In other European countries the popularization of subscription television would also be tied closely to rights to view the most popular football competitions—and teams. In Italy, for example, Prime Minister Silvio Berlusconi, whose holding company owned a network of commercial TV stations including the flagship Canale 5, also owned the leading Italian club AC Milan, and all parties have benefited handsomely from the opportunities for cross-marketing that this presents. In 1996 Telepiu 2+, another company controlled by Berlusconi, began offering a digital service that broadcasted matches on a pay-per-view basis, following the lead of the French channel Canal Plus, a subscription-only channel that had monopolized live coverage of French football since 1984. The income potential generated by this new TV technology, with its digital services and computer links, has created rapid changes in European sport broadcasting. In Spain, Germany, Portugal, and Holland, old television agreements were replaced as soon as legally possible by agreements reflecting the new (pay-per-view) technological reality.[40] As in Britain, football has quickly disappeared from public, and indeed from free, television.

This development has had profound and controversial effects. Positively for fans of European football (though not perhaps for others), there is now more of the sport on TV than ever before. However, the costs for fans who still want to watch football in their homes (watching in pubs or cafés raises other issues) have risen steeply, now including hook-up costs, subscription payments, and the price of the decoder for satellite customers. Using U.K. prices in 1996, this meant an initial payment of anything between £200 to £500, plus £20 to £40 a month in subscription fees before a single pay-per-view game was accessed.[41] Fees for games were £10 to £15 pounds, so that if you watched your favourite team once a week and a selection of other games (such as a top of the table clash, or relegation and title deciders at the season's end) you could be paying a bill of £80 to £100 a month. The potential revenues from such audience expenditures soon had the biggest clubs in Europe either signing their own deals with existing television operators (as did Real Madrid), or looking at starting their own channels.[42] For the more ordinary clubs, though, such deals are impossible, with the result that the gap between the richest clubs and football's middle class has widened dramatically in only a few years.

Indeed, the spoils generated by subscription television in the 1990s enticed the leaders of Europe's wealthiest clubs to threaten to form a European superleague. Media Partners, a private business group linked to AC Milan's Berlusconi, first proposed a European superleague in 1999. However, although the breakaway bid failed, the members of the so-called G-14[43] continued to aggressively lobby UEFA, and they have obtained a large say in the running of its affairs, with the threat of a renewed superleague initiative always present. By the 1999–2000 season, UEFA's Champions' League competition had been expanded at the expense of the historic Cup-Winners Cup, a competition that had often offered European competition and exposure to less famous clubs. For the leading football nations (Spain, Italy, England, and Germany), the enlarged Champions' League format allows more clubs to participate (four each), which offers the established clubs of the G-14 (who come mostly from these countries) a greater certainty of participating in the top European competition. In addition, the new group format (the European Cup that the Champions' League replaced had been a knockout competition) guarantees each club that reaches the group stage at least six lucrative television dates. As a consequence, the gap between European football's elite clubs and others (including clubs from Eastern Europe that were once competitive) has been widened, with potentially grave ramifications.[44]

In hockey, and indeed in North American professional sport, both the history and current structure of television are different. Hockey has always been a successful television product in Canada, with the long-running *Hockey Night in Canada* program on CBC attracting large nationwide audiences and becoming over the years something of a national institution.[45] But in the United States hockey has historically been a regional sport at best, largely limited to the Northeastern and Great Lakes states in its popular appeal, and hockey has had severe difficulties in establishing itself on US television— and, arguably, in American popular culture (see chapters 8 and 9).

Subscription TV came to North America in the form of regional cable services well before it came to the more regulated communications environment of Europe. Sports specialty channels on cable (such as ESPN, and TSN) began to develop profitable niche markets from the early 1980s. However, where other sports—and not only the major league team sports, but golf—succeeded in developing national audiences in the United States, hockey remained regional in its appeal, and hence in its revenue potential. Although cable TV and satellite television now contribute significantly to the revenues of many sports in the United States, pay-per-view has not caught on to anything like the extent it has in Europe. As a result, US hockey operators who have tried to develop this medium as a new revenue stream have been disappointed in the results. Finally, where the NFL and the NBA have succeeded in centrally controlling their television exposure (and thus increasing the value of television rights), the NHL and MLB have historically left with member teams the rights to develop their own regional cable audiences. This has meant large advantages for teams in major metropolitan markets (New York Rangers, Toronto Maple Leafs), and for teams owned by cable television interests (Atlanta Braves, Colorado Avalanche), but slim pickings for teams based in smaller cities surrounded by dispersed rural populations (Edmonton, Calgary, Pittsburgh). As in Europe, the gap between rich and poor clubs is widening, and when the wealthiest clubs get so much of their revenue from *their own* media contracts (whether local cable contracts, in the case of NHL hockey, or the independent media deals made by widely followed clubs like Real Madrid, in football), it is almost impossible to get them to share these revenues, or to be very concerned with the fate of their small-market competitors.

Much if not all of what has been described here, in each of these sports, has to be seen in the context of the increased involvement in sports by global telecommunications corporations (the Murdoch and Disney/ESPN empires, and their Italian and French counterparts), and their efforts to gain control of hugely popular sporting content. In the NHL, the agenda has been to try to turn a predominantly regional sport into one that attracted nationwide (US) and potentially global audiences, and to capitalize on the full potential of subscription television. In Europe the involvement of media entrepreneurs has more to do with capitalizing further on an already massively popular phenomenon—the sport of football—by exploiting the revenue potential of pay TV. What is common to both examples are innovations in the technology of direct-to-home television, whether this is digital cable or satellite transmission. These technological developments, coupled with the forced liberalization of broadcast regulations, have presented challenges to traditional national broadcast networks, including public broadcasters. They have also produced staggering revenue opportunities for new kinds of television providers, and for professional sport leagues.

European football has been far more successful to date than has the NHL in taking advantage of these developments. Hockey, despite its roots in North America, the pre-eminent commercial zone in the world, does not seem able to expand beyond its original base in Canada and the Northeastern United States. This invites the question of why the NHL has directed its energies to the US market and not to Europe, where professional hockey has more history than it has in the Southern United States: in Scandinavia, in Russia, and the Czech Republic, as well as in Germany, Switzerland, France, and Italy.

The Logic of Money

A series of different dynamics and innovations, then, have combined to make elite-level sport in the early twenty-first century a bigger business than at any time in its history. Since the early 1990s the most widely followed professional sports (and, arguably, the Olympic Games, too) have become central to "circuits of promotion" that include sports events (and the cities that host them), sports celebrities (and the products they endorse), sports merchandise, and the sports media that give them relentless publicity, creating an unprecedented place for sport in global popular consciousness.[46] The monetary values that all of these now command reflect the "sign values" that many kinds of public and private enterprise now place on associations with sport, and in turn the enormous commercial importance of symbolic values (as opposed to older kinds of "use values") in a contemporary "economy of signs and spaces."[47] For it is precisely the burgeoning sums of money invested in promotional activities—including corporate seating and corporate sponsorships (of teams, of arenas, of athletes) and, of course, the advertising dollars that fuel media revenues—that have enriched the business of sport, creating huge salaries and endorsement opportunities for elite athletes, and even larger potential profits for owners and media concerns.

However, this practice has also meant, in many sports, that ever larger investments are necessary to stay in "the game" (or at least to stay competitive); which has led in turn to new kinds of owners, for whom sports is no longer their main business but part of larger strategies of capital accumulation. These new owners are usually more heavily capitalized than their predecessors, and also more concerned with corporate synergies (typically television/media, but also property development). They are also less likely to be concerned with the local community and more focused on investment objectives: on maximizing share prices (in Europe) or franchise values (in North America), and on developing new revenue streams. In this, of course, investments in sport are simply becoming more like investments in any other business.

The best-known corporate owners, not surprisingly, are major media conglomerates: Fox/Sky (Murdoch), Disney, Berlusconi, Time/Warner. Still, although in the 1990s many big media companies believed in the strategic merits of sports ownership, this strategy has produced mixed results. Notably, after about ten years in sports ownership, Disney Corp. put its sports holdings up for sale in 2003. Baseball's Anaheim Angels were sold to Hispanic-American businessman Arte Moreno, while the NHL's Mighty Ducks of Anaheim were sold in summer 2005 to Henry Samueli, after almost two years on the market. Meanwhile, Fox has also been reported to be seeking buyers for baseball's Los Angeles Dodgers, and some observers believe that Rogers has lost large sums during its brief ownership of the Toronto Blue Jays.

In Britain major outside investors have bought into several Premier League football clubs, sometimes in order to turn them into public companies in an attempt to make money on the stock market, sometimes to attract development to regions where their other businesses in these communities stand to prosper,[48] and sometimes (as in the case of Russian billionaire Roman Abramovich's purchase of Chelsea FC) simply to pursue a quixotic quest to win a European championship. However, the turmoil that hostile takeovers can produce is illustrated in the successful share bid made by the US financier Malcolm Glazer (owner of the NFL's Tampa Bay Buccaneers) to take over Manchester United, European football's richest club. Glazer's bid to purchase a majority of United's shares (at a premium price, financed largely through borrowed money) provoked fierce opposition among the club's supporters. Fans feared that Glazer planned to use the club's large annual profits—and even sell the club's hallowed Old Trafford stadium—in order to pay down his huge bank loans (reportedly over $300 million), rather than investing in the playing staff necessary to keep the club successful on the field. Whatever Glazer's intentions, investment by businessmen with this kind of wealth underscores the financial potential of football in Europe. It also marks the advent of a new era in football ownership, in which a few teams are bankrolled from massive pools of capital, while others must struggle against huge financial disadvantages in their efforts to remain competitive.

In the National Hockey League, the pursuit of big money drove some of the league's expansion decisions in the 1990s, the priority being how the game's prospects would be perceived by potential corporate investors and bankers.[49] When the NHL actively pursued Disney and Blockbuster Video, the hope was that their presence would attract other major entertainment industry owners, but the predicted corporate synergies never did materialize. Blockbuster sold its interest in the Florida Panthers in the late 1990s, while Disney sold the Mighty Ducks in 2005. Today the NHL has a handful of corporate owners and some other very rich individuals (such as Mike Ilitch in Detroit and Tom Hicks in Dallas) who have made fortunes in other businesses, fortunes that they are now willing to spend on hockey players. However, it is fair to say that there are no NHL owners quite like Abramovich, or indeed like the Agnelli family or Prime Minister Berlusconi in Italy. What may be more important, though, is that the wealth necessary to stay in the game has seen quite a few teams change hands, with merely rich owners being replaced by the very rich. This process has repeated itself in all of the Canadian-based clubs[50]—most recently in Ottawa, where local developer Rod Bryden had to sell and the team was purchased by Toronto pharmaceutical magnate Eugene Melnyk, as well as in several US-based franchises.

What are the effects of such changes in ownership on the sports themselves? Not all super-rich owners operate in the same ways. But where professional sports teams in both Europe and America could be run in an amateurish, even idiosyncratic fashion when only a few millions were at stake (as recently as the days of Harold Ballard in Toronto), today the sheer amounts of money involved require a much more businesslike approach. Teams are managed as financial assets, and owners are advised by professional money managers as well as the more traditional kind of managers whose expertise lies in the game itself. The focus of the former is not surprisingly on enhancing asset values and improving the bottom line, rather than on the results on the playing field, which are what matters most to fans. However, this tendency mirrors a process that has occurred in many other businesses over the last two decades, and it may be that the changes in sport in this respect simply reflect (perhaps belatedly) a larger transition from one kind of capitalism to another. For many fans, though, this transition has required a quick education in the business of sport, an education that was seldom called for in times past, when the sports news was about goals and heroism rather than contract negotiations. It has also required a stripping away of illusions: that sport was somehow exempt from the imperatives that structure other businesses, and that "our" teams belonged to us.

This returns us to where we began, with the changing nature of the sports club, and the changing relationships between fans and the teams that they support. Clearly, the recent developments in professional sport represent significant departures from the "good old days," that mythical time when owners were sports people first and entrepreneurs second, when professional sports teams were deeply anchored in their home communities, and players were happy just to play the game. We are often invited to think of the "heroes" of other eras as being somehow more sincere and genuine than today's celebrity athletes, as men who performed mythical feats on the field or on the ice but were just working folks like most of our parents.[51] However, the history of professional sport tells us that this kind of sepia-coloured portrait is misleading. In any serious history of professional sport, we find discussions not just of games and goals but of racial and class discrimination, labour strife, opportunistic team moves, and attempts to create new opportunities to make money. Professional sport has *always* been a business, and even though major league sports today have become much bigger businesses—a group of brand-name products promoted to consumers around the world—it is important that we recognize the continuities as well as the changes.

Professional football in Europe and professional hockey in Canada, then, developed out of popular enthusiasm for games rooted in regional or national cultures, and they grew from there into the transnational businesses they are today. Teams or clubs were once genuinely local institutions, local businesses sponsored by local investors and supported at the box office by the money that local fans could afford to spend on regularly attending games. It was for this reason that big-city clubs have historically dominated in most European football leagues, and for the same reason that the NHL consolidated in the big cities of North America in the 1920s. However, over time these two sports (and others) became bigger and more complicated businesses, offering opportunities for capital accumulation to large investors, opportunities to deliver huge audiences to major advertisers, and opportunities for the best players to make huge sums of money. With enormous sums at stake, these different groups have increasingly put their own interests ahead of the interests of the game, let alone those of fans. This should not be surprising, but what seems to be hard for many fans to surrender is the idealistic belief that sport is, or at least should be, different from other commodities that are produced and sold in the marketplace. Underpinning this resistance is a notion that some areas of life, like sport, should not be infected by the logic of profit and growth and the instrumental rationality that follows from this logic.

Resistance to these commodifying pressures in sport is widely framed as nostalgia, perhaps because criticism of the major league sports industry is rarely extended to encompass a broader critique of contemporary patterns of economic life (let alone couched in political terms). No matter how well this description seems to fit, though, as Harvey J. Kaye puts it, it "fails to distinguish between nostalgia as reminiscences and an honest wishful longing for times past, and the corporate exploitation of nostalgia with all of the kitsch this entails."[52] Very rarely is the possibility seriously entertained that, however selective or wistful are the ideas that people may have of the past, hopes for restoration of an "authentic pastime" express a legitimate perception that something is wrong in major league sports today, and in society's relationship to them.

What we need is a historical understanding that allows us to situate the transformations in sports within larger transformations in global capitalism, and apply this understanding to thinking about possible futures. This may enable us to make greater sense not only of events like the NHL lockout and eventual settlement, but of the economic transformations that are reshaping our society.

Notes

1 Armando Nogueira, in *The History of Football: The Beautiful Game*, Episode 5, *Brazil*, Freemantle Home Entertainment, 2002.

2 For an excellent example of the connection of football to everyday life, see National Geographic's Series *Africa: From the Sahara to the Serengeti*, Episode 7; *The Leopards of Zanzibar*, co-produced by National Geographic Television in association with Tigress Production and Magic Box Mediaworks, 2001. In this example, the football club (the Leopards) and its relationship to the community are tied into the subsistence garnered from fishing for octopus and lobster in the Indian Ocean.

3 See Scott Lash and John Urry, *Economies of Signs and Space* (London: Sage, 1994).

4 See Mike Featherstone, *Consumer Culture and Postmodernism* (London: Sage, 1990); cf. the debate on Juliet Schor's "The New Politics of Consumption," in *Boston Review*, 24 (Summer 1990).

5 Frederic Jameson, "Postmodernism, or the Cultural Logic of Late Capitalism," *New Left Review*, 146 (July-August 1984), p. 56.

6 The list of these linkages is enormous. They include the credit industry, tourism industry, fast-food, alcohol, and soft drink industries, sports and leisure-wear equipment, gambling, audio-visual technologies such as cameras, television, video recorders, CD players, VCRs, DVDs, personal home computers, cable television, cell phones, and as of late, libido enhancement drugs such as Viagra.

7 See the work of David Harvey, Roland Robertson, Anthony Giddens, and Manuel Castells.

8 See Jean Harvey and Francois Houle, "Sport, World Economy, Global Culture, and New Social Movements," *Sociology of Sport Journal*, 11 (1994).

9 See Theodore Levitt, *The Marketing Imagination* (London: Collier Macmillan, 1983). See discussion of this idea in R. Gruneau and D. Whitson, *Hockey Night in Canada: Sport, Identities, and Cultural Politics* (Garamond Press, 1993), pp. 243-44.

10 Ulf Hannerz, *Transnational Connections* (London: Routledge, 1996); Brian Fawcett, "The Trouble with Globalism," in Max Wyman, ed., *Vancouver Forum* (Vancouver: Douglas and McIntyre, 1992).

11 Anthony King, "New Directors, Customers, and Fans: The Transformation of English Football in the 1990s," *Sociology of Sport Journal*, 47 (1997), pp. 224-40.

12 The type of "consciousness" that I refer to here is derived from the work of Ian Taylor, "Soccer and Soccer Consciousness," in Stanley Cohen, ed., *Images of Deviance* (Harmondsworth, UK: Penguin, 1971), pp. 134-64; and it is taken up once again in Susan

Faludi, "From Team Booster to TV Backdrop: The Demise of the True Fan," *Utne Reader*, January/February 2000.

13 The history of club football in Europe is replete with the creation of these type of clubs. For instance, in England, Manchester United was started by workers on the Lancashire and Yorkshire Railway, and Arsenal was originally a team of workers from a North London gunnery. The traditional East European model was for football and hockey clubs to be sponsored by factories, ministries, or trade unions. For instance, clubs with the title Locomotive (such as Lokmotiv Moscow or Leipzig) or Dynamo (such as Dynamo Kiev) were clubs sponsored by railway workers or policemen respectively.

14 Alan Metcalfe, *Canada Learns to Play: The Emergence of Organized Sport, 1807–1914* (Toronto: McClelland and Stewart, 1987), p. 46.

15 Gruneau and Whitson, *Hockey Night in Canada*, ch.4.

16 See Simon Inglis, *The Football Grounds of Great Britain* (London: Collins, 1991).

17 See Gruneau and Whitson, *Hockey Night in Canada*, ch.9.

18 There are some rather significant examples of vestiges of this type of sentiment in European football. Perhaps nowhere is this type of "democratic" control more evident than with Barcelona FC. In 1998 the club boasted a membership of 103,000, and elections for the club's presidency are as keenly watched as is Barcelona's mayoral race. See Jimmy Burns, *Barca: A People's Passion* (London: Bloomsbury, 1998). One of Birmingham's top football clubs, Aston Villa, recently saw a "supporters' revolt." After years of poor league results, supporters and shareholders—particularly those who bought shares after the club floated itself on the stock exchange—joined together in asking for long-time chairman Doug Ellis to resign. The club seems to have improved as of late; however, this has not quelled calls for Ellis's resignation.

19 Once again in hockey this happened much earlier than in football. For instance, after its "donation" the Stanley Cup was to be a challenge trophy for which any team in any league was to be permitted to compete—subject to the discretion of the Cup trustees. After 1910, when the National Hockey Association took control of the trophy, the competition was increasingly subjected to proprietary interests until 1926, when competition for the sought-after trophy was limited to teams in the National Hockey League. See Brian McFarlane, *One Hundred Years of Hockey* (Toronto: Deneau, 1989). Later, in the early 1970s, with the famous Summit Series between Canada and the USSR, an evolution of professional/amateur international tournaments with commercial imperatives began to take place. For instance, there was the Canada Cup in 1976, later the Challenge Cup Series, and now the almost fully professional World Cup of Hockey. In European football the introduction of the European Cup, the now defunct European Cup-Winners' Cup, and the Inter-Cities Fairs Cup (now referred to as the UEFA Cup) were intended as a competition between centres of trade and commerce. Later they were seen primarily as offering the possibility of international competition on the home grounds for procuring greater gate receipts.

20 The idea of elective identities comes from Stuart Hall, "The Question of Cultural Identity," in S. Hall, D. Held, and A. McGrew, eds., *Modernity and Its Futures* (London: Polity Press and Open University, 1992), pp. 273-325.

21 See "Money-Spinners Are the Big Winners," *World Soccer*, May 1995, p. 11. In the spring of that same year, United signed what was then the most lucrative kit deal in British football. The four-year deal negotiated with sporting goods manufacturer Umbro guaranteed United £25 million, eclipsing the previous record with the English National team for £16 million

over four years. Six years later Manchester United then finagled one of the world's richest sports endorsement deals as Nike would pay nearly $440 million to outfit United from 2002–15.

22 Ibid.

23 See Angela Breckenridge, "Collaring the Market," *World Soccer*, May 1998, p. 8.

24 The question of the old guard is of particular interest when it comes to discussing the history of the NHL and we should be in some measure aware of this dynamic. From the 1930s till about the mid-1960s, NHL hockey was dominated by the Norris family and their associates and successors. It would not be an exaggeration to describe this lot as a feudal dynasty, as it appeared to survive a succession of threats from rebellious players, outside owners, and minor leagues. This order seemed to change in the mid-1980s with the movement of Gretzky along with a couple of NHL franchises to the Sunbelt. There are several books chronicling this situation. See David Cruise and Alison Griffith, *Net Worth: Exploding the Myths of Pro Hockey* (Toronto: Viking, 1991); William Houston and David Shoalts, *Eagleson: The Fall of a Hockey Czar* (Toronto: McGraw Hill Ryerson, 1993); and Russ Conway, *Game Misconduct: Alan Eagleson and the Corruption of Hockey* (Toronto: Macfarlane Walter and Ross, 1995).

25 Jim Silver, *Thin Ice: Money, Politics, and the Demise of an NHL Franchise* (Halifax: Fernwood, 1996), p. 31.

26 See Bruce Chadwin, *Rocking the Pond: The Mighty Ducks of Anaheim* (Vancouver: Polestar, 1994).

27 In North American professional sports, the annual "reverse drafts" of prospects, in which the weakest teams pick first and last year's champions pick last, make it harder to sustain winning dynasties. This is especially the case in the NBA and NFL, where salary caps make it hard for even wealthy teams like Chicago and Dallas to retain their star players. This contrasts with the situation in European football where—in Spain, Italy, and England—a small group of wealthy clubs are able to consistently stay near the top of their respective leagues by virtue of having the money to attract the best players from other teams.

28 Real Madrid, another team that has invested heavily in promoting its brand abroad, is accused by some of having signed the England captain, David Beckham, as much for his capacity to sell Real Madrid apparel in Asia (because of his looks, and his celebrity lifestyle), as for his declining football skills.

29 D.A. Leslie, "Global Scan: The Globalization of Advertising Agencies, Concepts and Campaigns," in *Economic Geography*, 71,4 (1995); Theodore Levitt, *The Marketing Imagination* (Boston: Beacon, 1983). See also Michael Silk and David L. Andrews, "Beyond a Boundary? Sport, Transnational Advertising and the Re-imagining of National Culture," *Journal of Sport and Social Issues*, 25,2 (2001), pp. 180-201.

30 The term "de-localization" is adapted from Chas. Euchner, *Playing the Field: Why Sports Teams Move and Cities Fight to Keep Them* (Baltimore: Johns Hopkins University Press, 1992).

31 For Levitt, *The Marketing Imagination*, one of the purposes of marketing is to create new (and bigger) markets for global products, precisely by undermining parochial loyalties to the home-grown and the local.

32 See Dave Whitson, "Hockey and Canadian Identities: From Frozen Rivers to Revenue Streams," in D. Taras and B. Rasporich, eds., *A Passion for Identity: Canadian Studies for the Twenty-First Century* (Toronto: Nelson, 2001), pp. 217-36. See also Garry Whannel, *Media Sports Stars* (London: Routledge, 2002).

33 See Keir Radnedge, "Cashing In," *World Soccer*, September 1996, pp. 24-25.

34 Eduardo Galeano, *Soccer in the Sun and Shadow* (London: Verso, 1998).

35 Concerning this matter vis-à-vis small clubs there are several notable examples. Perhaps the most compelling one is the case of the Spanish club Sporting Gijon, which has been famous for being "the university of football" in Spain. Sporting Gijon produced its players in a lush 30-acre complex near the Bay of Biscay. This complex includes seven full-sized pitches, hi-tech indoor facilities, and grand quarters for the first team and its managing and training staff. The money to run this widely admired school was always generated by selling players to richer clubs. Young players were kept on short, low-salary contracts. As soon as they got into the first team, the club management would place them on a new contract with an appropriate salary. However, under the Bosman ruling, the Sporting Gijon administration had difficulty in keeping the more promising graduates from its nursery system in its system because players have been reluctant to commit themselves to longer contracts. As result many of Gijon's players simply moved on to financially greener pastures at the end of their contracts. The promise of greater money that wealthier clubs could offer has been too much to resist for these young players, and Gijon was left without any compensation for its investment. Sporting Gijon incidentally was relegated to Spain's second division one year after the Bosman ruling and as of late has yet to return to La Liga—Spain's first division.

36 For a concise discussion on labour flexibility, see Jim Stanford, "Discipline, Insecurity and Productivity: The Economics Behind Labour Market Flexibility," in Jane Pulkingham and Gordon Ternowetsky, eds., *Remaking Canadian Social Policy: Social Security in the Late 1990s* (Halifax: Fernwood, 1996).

37 For instance, in hockey there is a Standard Player–Agent Contract between player and agent, introduced when the NHLPA began its agent certification program only as recently as 1996. See Daniel S. Mason and Trevor Slack, "Industry Factors and the Changing Dynamics of the Player-Agent Relationship in Professional Ice Hockey," *Sport Management Review*, 4 (2001), p. 169.

38 See Bruce Dowbiggin, *Money Players: How Hockey's Greatest Stars Beat the NHL at Its Own Game* (Toronto: McClelland and Stewart, 2003).

39 The establishment of the new league overturned at a stroke 104 years of fraternal Football League football, which had linked big and small clubs in a relationship of cross-subsidization. See Stephen Dobson and John Goddard, "Performance, Revenue, and Cross Subsidization in the Football League, 1927-1994," *Economic History Review*, 4 (1998), pp. 763-85.

40 The Spanish football league tore up its existing TV agreement and introduced four new major players: TVE, Atomics (regional), TV Antene 3, and Canal Plus (Spain). This prompted individual clubs to make deals with the channels themselves. For instance, Real Madrid concluded a £9-million pound deal with A3. The private German company SAT also agreed to a new five-year deal in 1992 with the Bundesliga, costing 700 million DM. For an overview of all these developments, see Peter Law, "Kings of Infinite Space," *World Soccer*, February 1997.

41 Ibid.

42 Ibid. See also Lynton Guest, "The Revolution Will Be Televised," *World Soccer*, February 1997, p. 25.

43 The full list of the G-14 members is AC Milan, Inter Milan, Juventus of Turin (Italy), Bayern Munich, Borussia Dortmund (Germany), Olympique Marseille, Paris St. Germain (France), FC Porto (Portugal), Real Madrid, Barcelona (Spain), Ajax of Amsterdam, PSV Eindhoven (the Netherlands), Manchester United, and Liverpool (England). They are all past winners of the European Champions Cup.

44 For an overview of this situation see Julian Ammirante, "The Changing Political Economy of European Football," *Italian Politics and Society: The Review of the Conference Group on Italian Politics and Society*, 51 (Spring 1999).

45 See Gruneau and Whitson, *Hockey Night In Canada.*

46 David Whitson, "Circuits of Promotion: Media, Marketing, and the Globalization of Sport," in Larry Wenner, ed., *MediaSport* (Routledge, 1998), pp. 57-72.

47 See Lash and Urry, *Economies of Signs and Space.*

48 Newcastle United and Middlesborough Football Club were key examples of this kind of strategy. The directors of both clubs, Sir John Hall and Steven Gibson, invested heavily in their clubs and then made efforts to gain stock-market flotation. Hall's development company, Cameron Hall, invested £20 million in ground renovations and an estimated £40 to £50 million on players. Middlesborough made very expensive purchases, including Brazilian superstar Junhino and Italian star Fabrizio Ravenelli. Hall and Gibson employed their respective football clubs as symbols of the resurgence of the Northeast of England, a region that in the era of the Thatcher regime had experienced significant de-industrialization. Both clubs built new stadiums in once-derelict areas to demonstrate to international capital that both cities were again cities in which capital could be invested with a good chance of return. The Newcastle example was seen as largely responsible in attracting the large Japanese/Korean electronic company Samsung to set up its European operations in Tyneside. See King, "New Directors, Customers, and Fans," pp. 229-33.

49 Stan Fischler, *Cracked Ice: An Insider's Look at the NHL in Turmoil* (Toronto: McGraw Hill, 1995).

50 In Toronto, grocery entrepreneur Steve Stavro, who held the controlling interest in the Leafs for a number of years after the Smythes and Harold Ballard had passed from the scene, sold out in the early 1990s to MLSE, a partnership that featured the Ontario Teachers' Pension Fund. In Vancouver, the locally based Griffith family was supplanted by Seattle communications magnate John McCaw. In Montreal, Molson's Breweries could no longer afford losses in hockey, and sold to Colorado ski developer George Gillett. The Edmonton Oilers and Calgary Flames are each owned by partnerships; but both partnerships have also seen changes in recent years, with investors unable or unwilling to meet repeated cash calls being bought out by wealthier partners who could.

51 See Whannel, *Media Sports Stars*, for a discussion of pre-television football "heros" like Sir Stanley Matthews, and the transition to celebrities like Paul Gascoigne and David Beckham.

52 Harvey J. Kaye, *Why Do Ruling Classes Fear History? And Other Questions* (New York: St. Martin's Press, 1996), Foreword by Daniel Singer.

Mary Louise Adams is an Associate Professor in the School of Physical and Health Education at Queen's University, Kingston, where she teaches sociology and cultural studies. She is the author of *The Trouble with Normal: Post-War Youth and the Making of Heterosexuality* (1997), as well as numerous book chapters and journal articles on subjects associated with gender, sexuality, and sports.

Julian Ammirante is completing his doctoral dissertation at York University, Toronto, on the transformation of professional sports in the context of global economic restructuring. He has taught courses in globalization and governance, the politics of North American integration, and Canadian political economy at Trent University, Peterborough, ON, and he maintains a passionate interest in Italian and South American football.

Robert Bellamy is Associate Professor of Communications and Rhetorical Studies at Duquesne University, Pittsburgh. His research interests include the political economy of the media industries, the impacts of technological diffusion and convergence in the media, and the globalization of media programming (with a particular emphasis on sports). He has published numerous articles and book chapters on these subjects, and his projects now include a book (*Sports as Media*) as well as articles on brand equity in television and the televising of baseball in the United States.

Hart Cantelon is now Chair of the Department of Physical Education at the University of Lethbridge after spending much of his career at Queen's University, where he taught sport history and sport sociology. He is co-editor of *Not Just a Game: Essays in Canadian Sport Sociology*, and author of many book chapters and articles on sport in Russia and the former Soviet Union.

John Hannigan is Professor of Sociology at the University of Toronto, where he teaches courses in urban sociology, environment and society, and mass communications. He is the author of *Environmental Sociology: A Social Constructionist Perspective* (1995) and *Fantasy City: Pleasure and Profit in Postmodern Metropolis* (1998). The latter book was nominated for the John Porter Prize, awarded annually by the Canadian Sociology and Anthropology Association.

Jean Harvey teaches politics and sociology of sport at the University of Ottawa, where he is Professor and Director of the Research Center for Sport in Canadian Society. His research interests include sport policy in Canada and Quebec, and globalization in the sport and leisure industries. He is co-editor of *Not Just a Game: Essays in Canadian Sport Sociology*, as well as being the author of many articles in French and English-language journals and anthologies.

Dan Mason is an Associate Professor in the Faculty of Physical Education and Recreation at the University of Alberta, Edmonton, where he teaches sport management and sport history. He is the author of several articles and book chapters on the business of sport and has recently returned to Canada from the University of Maryland, where he taught for three years.

Robert Pitter is an Associate Professor in the School of Recreation Management and Kinesiology at Acadia University, Wolfville, NS. His research interests include urban recreation and local and national sport and recreation policy, as well as geographic information systems, and race and Canadian sport. He is co-editor of *Sporting Dystopias: The Making and Meanings of Urban Sport Cultures* (2003).

Michael Robidoux is an Associate Professor at the University of Ottawa, where his teaching and research focus on the socio-cultural dimensions of sport. His research interests include hockey in First Nations communities and parental behaviour at youth hockey games. He is the author of the award-winning *Men at Play: A Working Understanding of Professional Hockey* (2001).

Mark Rosentraub is Professor and Dean at the Maxine Goodman Levin College of Urban Affairs, Cleveland State University. He is the author of *Major League Losers: The Real Cost of Sports and Who's Paying for It* (1999), as well as many scholarly articles on the politics and economics of professional sports, and on urban affairs.

Kelly Shultz is a graduate of the M.A. program in Corporate Communication at Duquesne University, Pittsburgh, and is Director of Ticketing Operations for the Washington Capitals. She has previous experience in the sports industry with the Pittsburgh Penguins, the Pittsburgh Pirates, and the Johnstown Chiefs.

Julie Stevens is an Associate Professor in the Department of Sport Management at Brock University, St. Catherines, ON, where her research interests include change management in the Canadian hockey system, and assessing organizational capacity in the staging of the Canada Games. She played varsity hockey at Queen's University, and coached elite girls' teams during her doctoral studies at the University of Alberta. She is a co-author (with Joanna Avery) of *Too Many Men on the Ice: Women's Hockey in North America* (1997).

Pierre Trudel is an Associate Professor at the University of Ottawa, where his area of research is sport pedagogy. He has published numerous scholarly articles on coaching research, much of which was conducted in a hockey context, and he has been active as a Course Conductor for the National Coaching Certificate Program (NCCP).

Brian Wilson is an Associate Professor in the School of Physical Education at the University of British Columbia, Vancouver. In addition to his work on sport, his interests include youth culture, media constructions of race and gender, audience studies, and social movements. He is the author of *Fight, Flight or Chill: Subcultures, Youth and Rave into the 21st Century* (2006).